STORIES OF THE
SOVIET EXPERIENCE

STORIES OF THE SOVIET EXPERIENCE

MEMOIRS, DIARIES, DREAMS

IRINA PAPERNO

CORNELL UNIVERSITY PRESS | ITHACA AND LONDON

Copyright © 2009 by Cornell University

All rights reserved. Except for brief quotations in a review, this book, or parts thereof, must not be reproduced in any form without permission in writing from the publisher. For information, address Cornell University Press, Sage House, 512 East State Street, Ithaca, New York 14850.

First published 2009 by Cornell University Press
First printing, Cornell Paperbacks, 2009

Printed in the United States of America

Library of Congress Cataloging-in-Publication Data

Paperno, Irina.
　Stories of the Soviet experience : memoirs, diaries, dreams / Irina Paperno.
　　p. cm.
　Includes bibliographical references and index.
　ISBN 978-0-8014-4839-3 (cloth : alk. paper) —
　ISBN 978-0-8014-7590-0 (pbk. : alk. paper)
　1. Russian prose literature—20th century—History and criticism.　2. Autobiography.　3. Autobiographical memory—Soviet Union.　4. Soviet Union—History.　5. Soviet Union—Intellectual life.　I. Title.

PG3091.9.A93P37　2009
891.7'0935—dc22

2009016842

Cornell University Press strives to use environmentally responsible suppliers and materials to the fullest extent possible in the publishing of its books. Such materials include vegetable-based, low-VOC inks and acid-free papers that are recycled, totally chlorine-free, or partly composed of nonwood fibers. For further information, visit our website at www.cornellpress.cornell.edu.

Cloth printing　10 9 8 7 6 5 4 3 2 1
Paperback printing　10 9 8 7 6 5 4 3 2 1

CONTENTS

Acknowledgments ix
Introduction xi

PART I
MEMOIRS AND DIARIES PUBLISHED AT THE END OF THE SOVIET EPOCH: AN OVERVIEW   1

Publishers, Authors, Texts, Reader, Corpus   1

The Background: Memoir Writing and Historical Consciousness   9

Connecting the "I" and History   15

Revealing the Intimate   17

Building a Community   24
Moving in with a New Text | Joining the Ranks of Victims | Remembering Stalin: Tears | Disagreeing | Family Memoirs | Two Memoirs and a Novel Tell the Same Story | Generalizations: Soviet Memoirs as a Communal Apartment

Writing at the End   41
The Archive and the Apocalypse | The End of the Intelligentsia

Qualification: The "I" in Quotation Marks   49

Excursus: Readers Respond in LiveJournal   51

Concluding Remarks   55

PART II
TWO TEXTS: CLOSE READINGS   57

1. Lidiia Chukovskaia's *Diary of Anna Akhmatova's Life*: "Intimacy and Terror"   59

    The Years of Terror: In "the Torture Chamber"   62

Family and Home: "The Cesspit of a Communal Apartment" — 66
Overview of Circumstances | The Apartment in Poems and Dreams | "To Have Dinner at the Same Table as Her Husband's Wife" | How Akhmatova Left Punin | Generalizations: The Soviet State, Domestic Space, and Intimacy

During the War — 77
Poverty and Squalor: New Living Forms and New Insight | The Helplessness and the Power | Gossip | Hardships and Privileges

"A New Epoch Began": After 1953 — 95
Did They Understand What Was Going On? | Akhmatova's Things and Manuscripts | An Aside: Memoirs as Historical Evidence | Historical Continuity: The 1930s and the 1960s | "Same Time, Same Facts, Different Memories"

Concluding Vignette: "She'll Tell You What 1937 Was Like" — 115

2. The Notebooks of the Peasant Evgeniia Kiseleva: "The War Separated Us Forever" — 118

Notebook 1: "The Story of My Life" — 120
The Separation and the War | The Second Marriage | After the Second Marriage | Here and Now

Notebooks 2 and 3 — 134
Memory and Narrative | Television and Emotion | Television and Apocalypsis | A Comment on Historical Continuity: The Past War and the Future War | Generalizations: The Soviet State in the Domestic Space | Citizens and Power | The End: "We Live Like Strangers"

How These Notebooks Reached the Reader: The Interpreters — 150
Defining the Status of the Text: "Naive Writing" | The Competition between Publishers: "Legislators and Interpreters" | The Disappearance of the Author | "Person without Subjecthood"

Concluding Remarks — 159

PART III
DREAMS OF TERROR: INTERPRETATIONS — 161

Comments on Dreams as Stories and as Sources — 161
Andrei Arzhilovsky: The Peasant Raped by Stalin — 166
Nikolai Bukharin Dreams of Stalin: Abraham and Isaac — 171
Writers' Dreams: Mikhail Prishvin — 172
Writers' Dreams: Veniamin Kaverin — 182
The Dreams of Anna Akhmatova — 187
A Comment on Writers' and Peasants' Theories of Dreams — 194

A Philosopher's Dreams: Yakov Druskin 197
Stalin's Dream 203
Concluding Remarks 205

CONCLUSION 209

EPILOGUE 211

Appendix: Russian Texts 213
Notes 259
Index 279

ACKNOWLEDGMENTS

This book began during my residency at the Netherlands Institute for Advanced Studies (1999). Major funding was provided by the National Endowment for the Humanities (2003–4). Financial support was also provided by the University of California, Berkeley, through a Humanities Research Fellowship (2007) and a Research Assistantship in the Humanities Grant (2007–8). Parts of this book have appeared as articles: "Personal Accounts of the Soviet Experience," *Kritika: Explorations in Russian and Eurasian History* 3, no. 4 (Fall 2002): 1–35; "Dreams of Terror: Dreams from Stalinist Russia as a Historical Source," *Kritika: Exploration in Russian and Eurasian History* 7, no. 4 (Fall 2006): 793–824. This material has since been revised and amended.

I would like to express my profound gratitude to colleagues and friends who read and criticized these essays and the book manuscript, which led to many revisions. Caryl Emerson, Laura Engelstein, Jochen Hellbeck, Hugh McLean, Anna Muza, Eric Naiman, Slava Paperno, Alexei Yurchak, and Alexander Zholkovsky are among them. I owe a special debt to Laura Engelstein for many stimulating conversations. The book has profited from my participation in the seminar "Dream Life: Conversations with Our Waking and Sleeping Dreams" at the Extension Division of the San Francisco Psychoanalytic Institute, 2006–7. I am grateful to Cornell University Press director John Ackerman for his support and critical judgment.

Over the years, research assistance was provided by Patrick Henry, Jane Shamaeva, Alyson Tapp, and Boris Wolfson. Jane Shamaeva translated the Russian texts in parts 1 and 3, and Alyson Tapp in part 2. To Alyson Tapp, I owe a large debt for innumerable editorial revisions of the whole manuscript.

A note on language: throughout the main text of the book, the Russian text and Russian proper names are given in the Library of Congress transliteration system, except for names with accepted English spelling (e.g., Dostoevsky). The bibliographic references in the notes use solely the Library of Congress transliteration. The names of the key figures, on their first prominent appearance within each chapter, contain the given name, the patronymic, and the family name (e.g., Anna Andreevna Akhmatova).

INTRODUCTION

Since the late 1980s, memoirs, diaries, and other personal accounts of life in Soviet society have been appearing in print in a steady stream. Some of them were written in recent years, others date from the "thaw" of the 1960s and before. Most were written by intellectuals, but documents from the working class, and even by barely literate authors have appeared as well (inevitably, edited by intellectuals). The impulse to publish arose with the policy of glasnost, with its politicized demands to uncover the Soviet past, especially the Stalinist terror. By the mid-1990s, these efforts had lost official support and public prominence.[1] But even as the political discourse of memory disappeared from the front pages of newspapers, stories of individual lives have continued to appear in print. (New documents appear to this day, though not as prominently as in the 1990s and early 2000s.) Scholars have already put these records to various uses.[2] The texts are many and varied, and so are the explicit goals, hidden agendas, and functions they may fulfill for the reader. Even so, I see a trend, a common quality: published at the decline of the Soviet regime, which coincided with the end of the century, these accounts make individual lives part of the history that has come to a close (even the recent past has become historicized). Life stories from the Soviet Union tend to derive their claim to significance from the catastrophic quality of personal experience, even when their authors do not place themselves in opposition to the Soviet regime. It should be noted that, though I did try, I did not find many documents that are written to celebrate Soviet power. Many of the authors focus on the Stalinist terror and on the Second World War; those who did not notice the terror locate the catastrophe and hardship in the war. Quite a few pursue their stories up to the present. The living look back at their past as survivors; the dead have their records brought to light by others. These publications are infused with a strong moral pathos. What is central is a shared impulse to make private documents public as a record of the end. In this sense, all of these personal records, regardless of when they were written, belong to the present moment, when they are assembled, framed, and put into the public domain for everybody to see. This moment is the end of an epoch.[3]

Arguably, these memoirs and diaries are a late product of the acute historical consciousness that has influenced European thought from the time of the French Revolution to the present, producing life-stories that make the day-to-day experiences of an individual historically significant and politically relevant. Throughout the years of Soviet power, historicism, which has a complex lineage in Russia, was all-pervasive and overwhelming, informing the writing of diaries and memoirs and even invading people's dreams.

Like most diaries and memoirs, personal documents from the Soviet Union focus on the personal, private, or intimate, all of which have been thoroughly historicized and politicized. It is well known that Soviet power restructured private life, reshaping intimate experience in a variety of intended and unintended ways. Historians have done much to investigate the specific social, political, ideological, economic, and bureaucratic institutions participating in this process, and they have explored topics ranging from family policies, the housing situation, and distribution of goods to procedures of the terror and war-time evacuation of major cities. In this book I focus on how Soviet diarists and memoirists convey and interpret their intimate experiences, and on what it means to bring those experiences into the public realm, where people's intimacies can be seen and heard by others.

I claim that, in the end, diaries and memoirs create a community where those who lived through the Soviet era can gain access to the intimate, inner recesses of one another's lives. It is no accident that the texts in this corpus are read, validated, and appropriated by fellow writers and readers, intent on a similar quest. (I trace, as far as possible, this afterlife of the texts.) So, while this book's declared subject is the personal documents of a varied set of authors, its implicit subject is, inevitably, the Russian intelligentsia under Soviet power, inasmuch as collecting, editing, and publishing such documents (including those written by simple people) was a task for intellectuals, literary intellectuals, first and foremost—and, as I argue, a major instrument in forging the intelligentsia identity.

I look at the recently published diaries and memoirs from the double perspective of literature and intellectual history, and, occasionally, I pursue a psychological and a quasi-anthropological approach (using these documents as a self-ethnography of sorts).[4] Accordingly, I try to pay equal attention to the authors of these texts and to the texts themselves, to their structure and message.

So far, I have spoken about "diaries and memoirs" in one phrase. In traditional understanding, memoirs, like other autobiographical texts, are retrospective narratives of individual life. What distinguishes memoirs from autobiographies (scholars maintain) is their emphasis on the negotiation between the self and community.[5] Memoirs define themselves as accounts of lives embedded in a social matrix. Diaries, in contrast, are produced through day-by-day writing, and do not necessarily have an addressee.[6] For the purposes of this book, I have come to downplay (but not ignore) the difference. Both genres create, each in its own way, a "textual illusion of temporal continuity" of the writer's self.[7] The memoir, written retrospectively, makes an explicit move to connect the "I then" and the "I now."[8] The diary allows for a continuous report on a shifting self, and for the perusal of such a report by the author or another in later reading. In this way, both diaries and memoirs help the writer and his or her reader to attain knowledge of the self and knowledge of the (culturally specific) temporality. Diary and memoir are two different templates for tracking the self in time, for mediating between the past, the present, and the future. Both allow the self to be linked to the evolving historical time.

I have also made a decision to consider the testimony of recounted dreams, as texts and as historical data. Dreams (ostensibly recorded on waking) appear in the diaries and memoirs in my corpus with remarkable frequency, especially dreams of terror. They are clearly used as a type of story fit to communicate "truths" about the self and, in the end, about the terror, such as might be inaccessible to the authors themselves.

In dealing with concrete texts, I employ two essential and complementary strategies: on the one hand, I provide a survey of a large number of texts by different authors, taken as a corpus and a trend, and, on the other, a close, page-by-page reading of two individual works. Historians have an obligation to go beyond individual stories; literary scholars have a duty to practice close reading. I will try to do both.

In recent years, scholars from a variety of disciplines have increasingly turned to personal narratives, producing ample methodological and political discussions.[9] My immediate goals do not include theorizing the uses of personal stories, classifying narratives, and defining (or undermining) the categories employed in such analysis. This is an empirical study, and the answers it may yield to epistemological and methodological problems (and I hope it does) are not concepts or formulas, but lie in my readings themselves. So, instead of a methodological comment, I will take the liberty to offer a few disclaimers about the use of categories.[10] Is it indeed prudent to speak of "personal narratives of the Soviet experience"? Certainly, the concept of experience has its perils (and scholars have been alerted to them), yet it has served reasonably well scores of phenomenological philosophers, anthropologists, psychoanalysts, literary critics, and cultural historians, so I too have decided to use it. The same is true of the age-old concept of "self." To bypass these complications, I rely on the common language usage of these words (this is why I speak of a "sense of self").

In the same vein, I treat personal narratives as a reliable form for expressing one's sense of being and living. Philosophers, psychologists, and literary scholars have long put their trust in people's ability to tell their life histories.[11] Like many, I accept my subjects' attempts to make their experiences coherent and meaningful and their desire to speak in terms of a "we" to which others may subscribe. My task is to illuminate the strategies by which the diarists and memoirists working in a specific culture make their stories mean and cohere. Of course, there are not only commonalities but also individual differences. Both commonalities and differences render themselves to generalization.[12]

While this is not my most important claim, I do believe that, as a corpus of texts, the stories that have appeared in Russia in recent years add up to a vision of a historically specific form of the human condition, which, for lack of a better word, I call "the Soviet experience." I am encouraged that memoirists themselves are acutely aware of this special quality of their shared, "Soviet," experience. They are also aware of the difficulty in pinpointing this quality. This double awareness, I think, accounts for another striking characteristic of this corpus: memoirists consistently reach for metaphors that help them organize a collective vision of their predicament. In the pages that follow, taking my lead from the texts themselves, I explicate and extend the use of such organizing metaphors (the metaphor of the communal apartment stands out among them).

Finally, I am, of course, aware that such documents—memoirs, diaries, dreams—are verbal artifacts, subject to literary interpretation, and I treat them accordingly. However, to limit oneself to this perspective would defy common sense. So, while I speak of personal accounts of the Soviet experience, I also speak of the experiences themselves, because, postmodernist skepticism notwithstanding, texts can be used even for their intended purposes. It is in this sense that I place the words of Hannah Arendt as an epigraph to this book:

> The sources talk and what they reveal is the self-understanding as well as the self-interpretation of people who act and who believe they know what they are doing. If we deny them this capacity [...] we have robbed them of the very faculty of speech, insofar as speech makes sense.[13]

Part I gives a broad overview of texts, authors, themes, strategies. It deals with a large corpus of memoirs and diaries published between the late 1980s and the early 2000s, suggesting ways of interpreting them as a cultural trend. In Part I, I point to commonalities and patterns as well as highlight details.

In Part II I give a close reading of two specific texts: the first is Lidiia Korneevna Chukovskaia's *Notes about Anna Akhmatova*—a diary in which a literary scholar documents the life of her friend, the great Russian poet Akhmatova. The second is the memoiristic notes of a semiliterate country woman, Evgeniia Grigor'evna Kiseleva, which were deciphered and published by a team of scholars. In Part II, I magnify some of the themes briefly noted in Part I.

Part III is devoted to dreams recounted in memoirs and diaries. The majority of such dreams have political content, and I read them as historical evidence and as a special form of self-expression. An integral part of these diaries and memoirs, dreams are also read as self-contained stories.

Hoping to reach different readers, I try to make even intimate texts, written for members of their authors' own tightly knit community, understandable to outsiders. The text itself is central, and I cite long passages. The appendix contains the Russian originals. While this research is not quantitative, let me add that I deal with about one hundred texts by more than seventy authors (whose names appear, in bold print, in the index); the whole corpus surveyed for this book contains over two hundred items.

STORIES OF THE
SOVIET EXPERIENCE

PART I

MEMOIRS AND DIARIES PUBLISHED AT THE END OF THE SOVIET EPOCH
An Overview

If, as I argue, the massive appearance of personal documents at the end of the Soviet epoch is indeed a trend, what does it mean? Some answers are obvious. Imbued with the historicist sense of an end and by specific circumstances of violent Soviet history, Russian memoirists are driven by a need to claim their survival, commemorate the dead, provide historical data and ethnographic material, talk through their traumatic past, repent, accuse, and denounce. There are also the writer's imperative to write about himself, the scholar's urge to make his life into an object of investigation, the public demand (or publisher's commission) to disclose the lives of celebrities—all encouraged by the new possibilities to speak, from the political ethos of openness during Gorbachev's glasnost to the availability of unrestrained publishing opportunities in post-Soviet Russia. In looking at personal documents from Soviet Russia, I have chosen to suspend, as far as possible, certain widely available explanatory categories, such as "memory" and "collective memory," inasmuch as they create an alternative to the traditional concepts of "history" and "historical consciousness"; the twin notions "trauma" and "testimony," insofar as they imply the therapeutic nature and value of recollection and revelation; and "mastering of the past," for its moral pathos.[1] Instead, I ask: What are the motives, uses, and meanings of the explosion of publication of personal writings in Russia in the last two decades?

PUBLISHERS, AUTHORS, TEXTS, READER, CORPUS

The explosion began with the sensational publication of personal accounts of the Stalinist terror written during and after the "thaw" (mainly in the 1960s) and circulated underground, such as, in 1988, the memoirs of Nadezhda

Iakovlevna Mandel'shtam and Evgeniia Semenovna Ginzburg. There was a strong reaction: what impressed the readers even more than the stories themselves was seeing them published. It became clear that, after all the years of strict control over what could be told, it was now possible, even desirable, to speak of the hardship and repression in Soviet times. Scores of personal accounts followed from a wide range of people. (Remarkably, many authors wrote multiple texts, and quite a few texts appeared in multiple editions.)

Such publications have been promptly institutionalized. In the late 1980s, most of the Soviet literary journals opened regular features: "Diaries, Reminiscences," "Reminiscences, Documents," "Memoirs, Archives, Testimonies," "Memoirs of the Twentieth Century," "Private Reminiscences of the Twentieth Century." The new historical journal *Odissei* included a section of memoirs in which historians speak about themselves, "The Historian and Time." In the 1990s, new post-Soviet book publishers, varied as they were, started special series with telling titles: My Twentieth Century, The Twentieth Century from the First Person, The Twentieth Century through the Eyes of Witnesses, The Family Archive of the Twentieth Century, From the Manuscript Collections, Diaries and Memoirs of St. Petersburg Scholars, Life Documents and Interpretations, the People's Archive Series, the People's Memoirs.[2] Some of these publishers clearly pursue commercial goals; others do not. And whether such series issued a steady stream of publications or a single book, the publishers claim to represent a trend.

For those without access to publishing, there was another option: they could deposit their life stories in an archive. For victims of government repression there were local chapters of the Memorial (a nongovernment society for the commemoration of political persecution in the Soviet Union, established in 1988). Another grassroots institution, the People's Archive (Narodnyi arkhiv) in Moscow, also established in 1988, started to accept diaries, memoirs, and other personal records from "everybody."[3]

Who is speaking? Purportedly, "everybody": members of different generations, the living and the dead, professional writers and illiterate peasants, public figures (writers, actors, politicians) and "ordinary people,"[4] dissidents and loyal citizens—all intent on making their intimate lives a matter of historical record. Of course, memoirs of celebrities appear in greater numbers than those of unknown people. There is a serious effort to publish memoirs and diaries of survivors and victims of the terror.[5] Dissident political activists and hidden dissidents figure prominently. But people in power—including Stalin's men—are also represented (mostly by their children).

Professional intellectuals, as can be expected, took charge of the project, and many write as members of "the Russian intelligentsia." But there is also an effort to allow "the people," even barely literate people, to speak—a paradoxical desire to create access to the "voices of the people on behalf of whom the intellectuals always spoke" (published under close editing). Special series are devoted to the publication of "people's memoirs."[6] Such is the remarkable story of Evgeniia Grigor'evna Kiseleva (1916–1990). Wanting to see her life made into a film, she described it in hesitant writing and sent the notebook to a Moscow film studio. Her manuscripts passed through the hands of many an intellectual and was published more than once, in various forms. When, in 1996, Kiseleva's life story was published by two scholars, who not only transcribed her idiosyncratic, quasi-oral narrative (from the notebooks deposited in the People's Archive) but also provided an extensive interpretation, or "reading," they put their own names in place of the author's on the book's cover.[7]

Professional writers are especially prominent. Of course, writers have always been prolific autobiographers. Still, since the late 1980s, the number and intensity of writers' self-revelations have exceeded readers' expectations—and most of them put on record their previously hidden distaste for Soviet power. The private life and secret thoughts of the prominent poet David Samoilovich Samoilov (born Kaufman, 1920–1990) was revealed through several sets of diaries and memoirs, issued and reissued in installments by the writer's widow beginning in the year of his death. There are daily recordings of thoughts (*Podennye zapisi*), a general chronicle of daily events (*Obshchii dnevnik*), and memoir essays (*Pamiatnye zapiski*); jointly, they cover almost the whole span of his life (1934 to 1990).[8]

The writer Iurii Markovich Nagibin (1920–1994) submitted his extremely intimate diary for publication in person. But Nagibin died before the diary (1942–86)—which testifies to his distaste for Soviet power—was published. Standing by his body at the funeral, the publisher felt that, as the first reader of Nagibin's diary, he alone knew the writer's true self.[9] Yet he commented in the book's annotation that "during one's lifetime, the diary should be kept in a desk drawer."[10] A year later (having sold 35,000 copies), the same publisher issued a second edition of Nagibin's diary, complete with reference material (commentaries, photographs, and a name index), that is, as a historical document.

The popular playwright Leonid Genrikhovich Zorin (born in 1924) published a "memoir-novel," entitled *Proscenium,* which takes him from 1934 to 1994. Claiming the stage for himself, he traces the "historical drama" of his confrontations with the "inhuman power system" (mostly, over the staging of his plays). He also published his scattered notes (*Green Notebooks,* held together, he tells us, by little more than the ready-made green binder); from the author's introduction, we learn that for most of his life he has also kept a diary, still unpublished.[11]

Lidiia Chukovskaia's famous *Notes about Anna Akhmatova* is a diary written by one person (a professional editor) on behalf of another (a great poet). For years, Lidiia Korneevna Chukovskaia (1907–1996) recorded, with ethnographic precision, her intimate conversations with Anna Andreevna Akhmatova (1889–1966) and details of her friend's daily life, cruelly deformed—as they both thought—by state repression. This diary, too, appeared in at least three different editions that grew and grew with each publication. Later editions contain extensive explanatory footnotes, endnotes, and name indexes prepared by the author, her daughter (who figures in the text as a child), and their helpers.[12]

Prominent as they are, professional writers are not the only ones who have published voluminous records of daily life. There is the diary of Elvira Grigor'evna Filipovich (born in 1934), issued by an obscure publisher in five hundred copies in 2000.[13] Suggestively entitled *From the Soviet Pioneer to the Pensioner and Black Marketeer*, it documents, step-by-step, the life of a Soviet teenager at the time of the war, a student at an agricultural academy in the 1950s, a livestock technician working difficult jobs in the 1960s, and, finally, a scientist with an advanced degree in animal husbandry. This is also the story of a daughter, wife, and mother, which carefully describes the minutiae of professional and family life in specific historical situations. In this case, we learn little about the author's politics. In October 1961, we see her rejoice in Khrushchev's announcement of the imminent coming of communism at the Twenty-second Congress of the Communist Party of the Soviet Union: "The party solemnly proclaims that the present generation of people will live under communism," said Nikita Sergeevich. [...] And in our country plans are being fulfilled, ahead of time even" (176). In August 1968, we see her in Czechoslovakia (the home of her husband) bewildered and embarrassed by the Soviet invasion. The title promises to show the diarist's old age, when, as a pensioner, she becomes a small-scale black marketeer, post-Soviet style (*chelnok*), but the publication—financed by the author—ceased after volume one (which takes the reader from 1944 to 1972).

The time span covered in this corpus of documents extends for the whole period of Soviet history, from the early 1920s to this day. Still, there is a tendency to focus on Stalin's time, presenting it as the defining Soviet experience, and on the years of the Second World War in the Soviet Union (1941–45). But there are also several memoirs about the recent past, "histories of yesterday." One of them, *The Seventies as an Object of Cultural History*, features essays, mostly by scholars, who subject their own personal memories to historical and semiotic analysis.[14] Another, Dmitrii Iakovlevich Severiukhin's *An Evening in the Summer Garden: Episodes from the History of a "Second Culture"*, makes a claim to represent those born between 1954 and 1974. Written by an amateur historiographer and bibliographer, this publication is justified as a record of an unofficial "second" culture, hidden from the Soviet public. One reviewer has defined this generation as those "conceived after Stalin," and its temporality as a "continuous yesterday." (This memoir takes the reader from the early 1970s through 1999.)[15] Finally, as reviewers have noted, there are "memoirs about today," written by politicians who relate current events in the mode of a memoir.*

There are ongoing diaries as well as memoirs that narrate the history of yesterday on a daily basis, striving to catch up with the moment of publication. Leonid Zorin's *Green Notebooks,* published in 1999, extend to the year 1998. The personal notebooks of the literary historian Marietta Omarovna Chudakova (born in 1937), published in 2000 and entitled "At the End of the Soviet Period," extend to 1996.[16] Then, in 2006, Chudakova published the diary of her husband, the literary scholar Aleksandr Pavlovich Chudakov (1938–2005), which covers the last year of his life. In 1999 the post-Soviet (postmodernist) writer, journalist, and feminist Mariia Ivanovna Arbatova (born in 1957) published an "autobiographical novel" called *I Am Forty,* describing her life through the year 1997. In 2002 she published an autobiography in two volumes, *Good-bye to the Twentieth Century,* extending her life story for another five years and another marriage (and more than five hundred pages)—this time, to the very moment of publication.[17] The scholarly notes to Lidiia Chukovskaia's *Notes about Anna Akhmatova,* growing from one edition to another, link the records made in 1938–41 and 1952–66 to the evolving present (the last notes were made shortly before the 1996–97 publication).

A comment is due on the documents' form. (A more thorough analysis of texts in this corpus for their literary form lies beyond the goals and possibilities of this book.) One is struck by how quite a few of these accounts are texts in flux— diverse fragments that can be, and have been, assembled and reassembled into different makeshift texts by either their authors or publishers. This is true of both self-conscious authors, who are aware of the implications of choosing a literary form (be it the finished or the unfinalized), and of amateur writers, who may feel a "naive" need to create a text that is true to their shifting lives, even in its form. At times, it is difficult to tell which is which. Take the case of the poet David Samoilov: there are several different posthumous arrangements of

---

* From Efim Ostrovskii, "O nesvoevremennosti memuarov v Rossii," *Russkii zhurnal,* November 17, 1997. This journalist laments that the genre of memoir is misused by politicians who relate current events, such as Aleksandr Korzhakov in his *Boris El'tsyn: Ot rassveta do zakata* (Moscow: Interbuk, 1997). Ostrovskii asks: "'Memoirs about today'—is this possible?"

the vast records of events, thoughts, memories, and "things to be remembered" (*pamiatnye zapiski*) that he made on a daily basis throughout his life, as if striving to catch it in its entirety and variety. The literary translator and poet Andrei Iakovlevich Sergeev (1933–1998) deliberately defined his unusual 1995 autobiography, *Stamp Album*, as "a collection of people, things, words, and relationships" (he threw in his birth certificate).[18] The journalist and filmmaker Aleksei Kirillovich Simonov (born in 1939) used the phrase "private collection" to define the genre of his 1999 book, consisting of short essays ("stories" and "portraits") and documents (photographs, letters, photographically reproduced certificates). He remarked on the seeming adequacy of this structure to that of "life itself": "life—it is but a collection of future reminiscences."[19]

Throughout her long writing life, the literary scholar Lidiia Iakovlevna Ginzburg (1902–1990)—one of the cultural heroes of late-Soviet and early post-Soviet times—deliberately cultivated an indeterminate genre called "notes" (*zapisi, zapiski*), comprising carefully shaped snapshots of everyday situations, recorded conversations (including overheard conversations), aphorisms, and occasional thematic "essays." She did this in full consciousness of the difficult predicament of a sophisticated twentieth-century autobiographical writer, especially in Soviet Russia. After modernism, retrospective all-knowing plotting, an unabashed autobiographical subject, and clear moral judgment were no longer an option (at least to a literary scholar trained by formalists in the early 1920s); neither was she ready to give up the Russian nineteenth-century obsession with history, her personal predilection for analytical and ethical self-reflection, and a strong desire to participate in the common life that she shared with many of her contemporaries (the obvious blemishes and perils of the Soviet community notwithstanding). The resulting compromise was not a memoir (or novel), not a diary, but an "in between" (her word) pseudo-genre: a collection of loosely dated "notes." In the original publication in 1989 the author arranged her "notes" in successive chronological clusters: "Notes from the 1920s–1930s," "Notes from the 1950s–1960s," and "Notes from the 1970s–1980s," and "Notes from the [Leningrad] Blockade."[20] Other editions, prepared by the author herself, rearranged these fragments, even blurring the distinction between "notes" and "essays."[21] One of her posthumous publishers and editors, "Zakharov" (who cultivates a distinctly postmodernist sensibility) rearranged Ginzburg's "notes" to make up a new book in 1999—a book of his own—and to connect it to the present moment with his editorial comments (discussed below).[22]

A striking case of a flexible text with a versatile temporal perspective is that of the playwright Evgenii L'vovich Shvarts (1896–1958). In his diaries for 1950–58, Shvarts related both his daily life (what happened "yesterday" and "today") and his consecutive recollections of his past, beginning with childhood. The posthumous publications recast his life story in different genres, or modes. One edition, from 1990, followed the order of writing, publishing a diary (albeit the one in which the story line jumps between the present and the past).[23] In another edition, from 1999, the diary notes were rearranged into a chronological description of Shvarts's life, that is, the diary was recast as a memoir.[24] Published separately is Shvarts's *Telephone Book,* a set of brief stories about people and institutions arranged alphabetically, as in a telephone or address book.[25] (One other author followed Shvarts's example and included "a telephone book" in his memoir.)[26]

The fusion of memoir and diary in one text is frequent, and many a writer comments on this move. Nagibin made a point to indicate that his diary "sometimes turns into a memoir"—not because he reminisced in his diary (as did Shvarts), but because he occasionally wrote a record of the day's events from memory.[27] One memoirist, the historian Boris Tartakovskii, warned his reader that at times his text "resembles a diary rather than a memoir; the present and the past are closely interwoven."[28]

I think that in the corpus of Soviet personal documents published since the late 1980s, these fragmentary and versatile texts stand out and make a special claim: such texts allow their authors to maintain flexibility and leave open possibilities for the future. Some texts may simply shun definitive retrospective knowledge and plotting, as many modernist and postmodernist autobiographies across the world tend to. Some do more: there are a number of texts— from the sophisticated and self-conscious to the amateur and "naive"—that deliberately blur the distinction between memoir and diary. In a manner similar to the attempts to extend the time span covered in both diaries and memoirs to the moment of publication, the move to combine the retrospective view of the memoir with the contemporaneous vision of the diary contributes to the effect of the coterminous past and present—a fundamental condition for a record of the "end"—and such an "end" that befits the Russian twentieth century, with all its contradictory legacy (from Hegelian to modernist).

Who is the intended and the actual reader? Quite a few texts bring up the question of readership; most are uncertain. Some Soviet diarists—as do diarists the world over—address themselves. Nagibin asks: "To whom is the diary addressed?" And answers: "To oneself. It is a conversation with oneself, tête à tête..." (In this, he sees his moral superiority over other diarists: "In keeping my diary I have not given a thought to the reader, unlike, say, Konstantin Simonov, who clearly prepared his diary to be made public after his death [*gotovil na vynos*].")[29] Memoirists explicitly address children and grandchildren as well as future historians. Aleksei Simonov (Konstantin Simonov's son) wonders for whom he writes: "For oneself? For the grandchildren? For a historian?"[30] Some memoirists also count on their characters—living people described in their memoirs—as immediate readers. Such is Dmitrii Severiukhin (born in 1954), who represents those conceived and born after Stalin.

The reviewer of his *Evening in the Summer Garden* made a point of discussing this memoir's peculiar situation: "Many characters are alive and well, in Russia or abroad; and the number of people mentioned in the book is clearly larger than the number of copies printed." It would seem that Severiukhin (an amateur bibliographer) "wrote his memoir for future scholars, as a source." But there is a special wisdom in its instant publication: "If printed several decades later, this book would only interest a small circle of researchers. [...] Today it has met with its characters, become a part of their lives, entered into a dialogue with them."[31]

I would suggest that these texts also invite a special reading: reading as a silent production of a story of one's own, in which (to use the formula from Michel de Certeau) the text is borrowed, "inhabited," "like a rented apartment." With such reading, another person's memoir or diary is mentally transformed into a story that accommodates one's own life or one's own self.[32] Some writers, publishers, and readers of memoirs and diaries explicitly suggest as much. One critic suggests that "we read memoirs keenly and with strained attention, but most likely this does not mean we are that interested in other people's lives. But rather in our own."[33] Nagibin offers his "half-diary–half-memoir" to others to aid them in their "self-cognition."[34] The publisher of the diary of an "ordinary woman," Elvira Filipovich, addresses the reader: "This book is gripping, for in the life and views of the author we recognize ourselves. It feels as if it's we ourselves who are thinking and writing..."[35] In other cases, we have access to the readers' responses. Thus, readers' letters to Lidiia Chukovskaia about her *Notes about Anna Akhmatova* have been made public. With remarkable uniformity, readers took it upon themselves to validate Chukovskaia's book as a "historical chronicle" of the "terrible time" they all lived through. Several described the effect of co-presence and co-experience. They felt admitted to Akhmatova's apartment: "you see, you hear [...] this apartment, the [neighbors] behind the wall"; "the reader doesn't read your books, but lives in them; he's tucked somewhere out of sight, right there alongside, he *sees* everything..."[36] (The first reader, Natalia Il'ina—a professional writer who knew Chukovskaia and Akhmatova—read the *Notes* in 1969, long before they were published; the second, N. Uritskaia, a librarian from the distant town of Ukhta, read the published, 1989, version.) This text has clearly been inhabited, accommodating its readers.

In the end, whether the implied or the actual reader is a contemporary or a descendant, an intimate friend or a stranger, the texts in this corpus aspire to turn intimate life under Soviet conditions into a shared open space.

To sum up: what we now have in the public domain is a motley, evolving corpus of texts, written by professional writers (traditionalist and modernist) and by various amateurs: memoirs, memoir-novels, memoir essays, diaries, diary-memoirs, notebooks, scattered notes, and at least two telephone books. They were written either in real time (diaries from the whole span of Soviet history); or soon after the end of Stalin's rule, when, with the "thaw," survivors of the terror wrote their first memoirs, which mostly remained unpublished; or in recent years, when the demand for uncovering the Soviet past reemerged under glasnost. I have chosen to treat a large number of different texts as a single corpus that belongs to the present moment, when individual stories of the Soviet experience are made public. Political circumstances and historical sensibilities—such as the current concern for openness in Russia and the age-old sense of an end—encouraged massive, institutionalized publication of personal documents. Authors and/or publishers clearly identify their editions by pointing to a personal, individual, or private perspective on a historical epoch, and they claim to represent a trend of the times. The metaphor "privatization of history" is present in recent editions. To claim superiority of the "true," private, history over the false, public, one is a standard, well-rehearsed move in the Soviet context. In the post-Soviet context, the policy of economic privatization gives this move additional symbolic energy.

But the relationship between life story and history is, of course, more complex than that. From historians' perspective, the process is twofold. Authors and publishers not only present historical events as a matter of personal experience but also use history—the catastrophic history of the Russian twentieth century—to claim personal significance and to justify authorship. In the end, the move to make history private turns private lives into public texts.

THE BACKGROUND: MEMOIR WRITING AND HISTORICAL CONSCIOUSNESS

An inherited tradition stands behind these memoir writings. Roughly between the French Revolution and the Napoleonic wars, across Europe, the rise of historical consciousness found expression in the form of memoir and diary writing that connect personal lives to the social and historical situation of time and place. Arguably, in Russia, the high point of such historical consciousness was the 1840s through 1860s.[37] As has been shown, the culture of the Russian intelligentsia was formed in these decades from the intimate forms of sociability in circles of family and friends (*kruzhki*) to the discourse of Russian personal documents (letters and diaries) and psychological prose (memoirs and novels). Historical self-consciousness—the sense of self derived from the coincidence of personal life and world history—shows in various private and public writings from these years.[38]

In difficult times of Soviet history, such as the 1920s and the 1930s, Russian intellectuals drew on this tradition. And at the end of the twentieth century, they reached for the trusted tools again—their power had been reinforced and their meaning transformed by historians of Russian intellectual culture who interpreted its founding texts. During the war, people read *War and Peace* comparing their own reactions to that of Tolstoy's heroes.[39] But who could aspire to produce a *War and Peace* of her or his own? Another text has been evoked as an immediate inspiration and a model for imitation by practically every Soviet memoirist: Alexander Herzen's memoirs, *My Past and Thoughts* (*Byloe i dumy*, 1852–68).

Many a memoirist thought of his or her autobiographical writings as *My Past and Thoughts* or has read the writings of another in this key. Thus, in the 1970s, Lidiia Chukovskaia suggested to David Samoilov that his memoir essays, read to friends, were another *Byloe i dumy*. Samoilov thought the same of Chukovskaia's own "notes." They supported each other in a sense of historical importance of their personal lives and their private writings. When Samoilov's widow published his scattered essays and diaries in the 1990s, she was inspired by this judgment.[40] When Chukovskaia's *Notes about Anna Akhmatova* appeared in print, reviewers were quick to connect the book to *My Past and Thoughts:* same genre, said one; another said "same absence of genre" (*bezzhanrovost'*).[41] Some admirers of Chukovskaia's *Notes* explained her strategy as a chronicler of her time, and her success, by her professional involvement with Herzen (Chukovskaia was a Herzen scholar and, to some, she was a Herzen of her time).[42] When the filmmaker Vasilii Abgarovich Katanian (1924–1999) decided to prepare his reminiscences for publication in the 1990s, he appealed to Herzen's authority (echoing the introduction to *My Past and Thoughts*) in a lighter vein: "Inspired by Herzen's words that anyone can write memoirs because *no one* is obliged to read them, I gathered together fragments from my reminiscences written at different times."[43] The archival scholar Sarra Vladimirovna Zhitomirskaia (1916–2002) used the same words in all earnestness as an epigraph to her moralizing memoir, *Simply Life*.[44] Nikolai Pavlovich Antsiferov (1889–1958), who was a Herzen scholar, not only entitled his own memoirs *From Thoughts about the Past* (*Iz dum o bylom*, written between 1945 and 1954, but published only in 1992), but also fit his life, from adolescence at the time of the 1905 revolution to the arrests in 1929 and 1937 and to the 1941–45 war, into the narrative pattern provided in Herzen's memoirs.[45] In her diaries from the 1940s, the poet Ol'ga Fedorovna Berggol'ts (1910–1975) described reading *My Past and Thoughts* and measured her own writings (including the story of her arrest in 1938) against Herzen's.[46] One did not have to be a literary professional: the popular comic actress Faina Georgievna Ranevskaia (1896–1984) reread *My Past and Thoughts* as she wrote her own diary in the 1940s (irregularly and on separate pieces of paper).⁴⁷ So did, in 1932, the peasant-turned-student Stepan Podlubnyi (1914–1998), who kept a systematic diary.⁴⁸

What do Herzen memoirs stand for? One of the founding texts of the intelligentsia culture, *My Past and Thoughts* helped to create its main institution: an intimate circle of intellectuals alienated from the state and society who felt bound by a sense of their social and historical mission. Indeed, Herzen's memoirs, and those that followed, show the working of this circle: the intensity of shared lives (from political action to erotic love to quotidian tasks) invested with distinct historical purpose and meaning. It has been argued that the genre labeled "memoirs of contemporaries"—the memoir focused on a shared experience of a historical period—played a major role in the construction of the identity and community of the Russian intelligentsia from its inception in the eighteenth or nineteenth century to Soviet times.⁴⁹

The form of Herzen's memoirs (which he famously called simply *zapisi*, "notes," or "notations")—a fragmented narrative that loosely follows the biographical line while indulging in multiple digressions—seems easy to imitate. It may also be enticing that Herzen's book relies on causerie, creating an illusion of conversation that involves the reader. But the key to the genre, I think, lies in the authorial position: the book is pervaded by Hegelian historicism of a Russian bent. In Hegel's terms, it is a sense of history immanent in the individual, internalized history, the meaning of which man is compelled to elaborate in his daily life. But Russians lived in an unjust and despotic society. Accordingly, Hegel's language of "progress in the consciousness of freedom" and his optimistic historical eschatology are replaced by the idiom of repression, violence, and catastrophe. Moreover, the drama of "world-historic individuals" is applied to the "accidental" existence of a single individual.⁵⁰ The result is a story of intimate life embedded in catastrophic history.

The opening pages of Herzen's book, familiar to every Russian schoolchild, feature the story of the author's birth (told by his peasant nanny). The year is 1812; the setting, Moscow in flames. Napoleon has just entered the city, and the (illegitimate) infant in his nanny's arms is caught in the great fire. It is in the cell of a Russian prison and in exile that the young Herzen, a budding revolutionary, comes of age. Then, he suffers deadly disillusionment—in his social activism, in his marriage, and in friendship—in the course of the failed 1848 revolution in Europe. This, I would claim, is a paradigmatic Russian story: the story of a man forged by history.

In their writing and in their lives, Soviet intellectuals appropriated Herzen and the tradition he represented. Let us take Lidiia Borisovna Libedinskaia (née Tolstaia, 1921–2006) as an example. In her memoirs, she described how in

1948 she and her husband (the writer Iurii Nikolaevich Libedinskii) read *My Past and Thoughts* together at their dacha, reliving the intimate life of Herzen and his circle ("their love, friendship, struggle"). In Moscow, the couple made a pilgrimage to the room where Herzen was born in the fateful year 1812, now the Institute of Russian Literature. In 1962, visiting the prominent writer Kornei Chukovskii (Lidiia Chukovskaia's father) in the writers' colony Peredelkino near Moscow, Libedinskaia relived emotions of Herzen's clan again ("We talked about their complex and difficult relationship, as one speaks of intimate friends who need help").[51] Libedinskaia also had professional connection to Herzen: she published an adapted edition of *My Past and Thoughts* and a book for children, *Herzen in Moscow*, in which she retold the first parts of Herzen's memoir in her own voice. The introduction and the afterword show Libedinskaia walking the same streets in Moscow that Herzen walked: she inhabited his world.[52] A direct descendant of Lev Tolstoy, who married an influential Soviet writer (after an illicit wartime love affair), Libedinskaia became a member of the Soviet literary establishment. But she writes her memoir as a member of "the intelligentsia at a turning point in history" (291). I suggest that, for such an author, to identify her family and friends with the Herzen circle meant to reach out for roots that would be more appropriate for memoir writing.

Another memoirist inspired by *My Past and Thoughts,* the dissident Liudmila Mikhailovna Alekseeva (born in 1927), speaking for "the thaw generation," described herself as a girl brought up to love Stalin and to think, with her parents, who "belonged to the revolutionary generation," that they were among "history's favorites." (This family did not include professional writers.) When, in 1937, the family moved from the provinces to Moscow, her father gave her a copy of Herzen's memoirs to use as a guide through the Moscow streets.[53] Clearly Herzen's book—a history of private life of the nascent Russian intelligentsia—provided more than a street guide.

Following Herzen's paradigmatic text, Soviet intellectuals received a license for authorship and a cue for choosing the genre. But, I think, the main thing they took from Herzen—as well as from other "memoirs of contemporaries"— was the authorial position: a historicist self-consciousness that gave meaning and value to their difficult and complex lives, turning diverse personal records into documents of potential historical significance. Memoir writing promised a sense of self and a membership in history's favorite class: the "intelligentsia."

Herzen's personalized historicism provides an emblematic self-image, which I present in its twentieth-century interpretations. Indeed, Herzen's story and his memoirs reached present-day readers through the mediation of literary historians. Prominent among them are Lidiia Ginzburg and Lidiia Chukovskaia. Prolific memoirists whose own "notes" (both used this designation) from the whole span of Soviet history are now read by many, both Ginzburg and

Chukovskaia are also known for their studies of Herzen published in the 1960s and 1970s.⁵⁴ Lidiia Ginzburg's study prominently features Herzen's famous definition of his book: "*My Past and Thoughts* is not a historical monograph but the reflection of history in someone who *accidentally* got in its way."⁵⁵ From Herzen's wording it follows that a man who has got in history's way is a victim of an accident, crushed by the wheel of history, and his shattered face bears an imprint of his epoch. Lidiia Chukovskaia, in her book (aimed at general readers), tries to explain: "The wheels of history rolled across the family hearth. Could one, in such a case, give the reader a true sense of the experience without speaking first of the wheels of history?"⁵⁶ Ginzburg (who aimed at a professional reader) described this mode of memoir writing as "an amalgam of historiography and autobiography."⁵⁷

Whether or not Herzen and his cohorts would have subscribed to this historical fatalism, late-Soviet intellectuals read Herzen and Hegel in this way: they felt that they had gotten into history's way. In her own memoir-essay from the late 1980s, Lidiia Ginzburg described conversations that took place in the 1930s, during the terror:

> Having seen Napoleon, the young Hegel said that he had seen an absolute spirit entering the city on a white horse. I remember conversations with Boris Mikhailovich Engel'gard.* In just the same Hegelian manner, he talked about a universal historical genius who in the 1930s crossed our lives. (He admitted that this did not make it easier.)⁵⁸

With this image, Lidiia Ginzburg must have struck a vein. In the 1990s several authors used Ginzburg's "notes" to express their own, or others', thoughts on the role Stalin played in their lives. The art historian Leonid Mikhailovich Batkin (born in 1932) used the image of the absolute spirit on a white horse who crossed their lives (borrowed from Ginzburg) in a solemn personal essay on the social meanings of Stalin's cult.⁵⁹ The linguist Rebbeka Markovna Frumkina (born in 1931), in her memoirs, used Ginzburg at least four times in order to describe "our" experience ("L. Ia. Ginzburg described this best"). Frumkina first brings Ginzburg's name up when she tells how, as a schoolgirl in the 1940s, she learned to see her life through the classic books of Russian literature, which at that tender age she read in scholarly editions, complete with commentaries: Belinsky's essays and Herzen's *My Past and Thoughts*.⁶⁰ For the late-Soviet and post-Soviet memoirists, Lidiia Ginzburg—a student

---

* The literary scholar Boris Engel'gard was arrested in 1930 and exiled to the Belomor Canal area. After his arrest, his wife Nataliia, née Garshina, threw herself from the window. Engel'gard died in Leningrad in 1942 during the blockade.

of nineteenth-century memoirs and a memoirist in her own right—serves as a mediator of this historicist tradition.[61]

Of course, Hegel, and the Russian Hegel mediated by Herzen and his cohorts, did not reach late-Soviet authors without many complications (and not only aesthetic complications of modernism). For one thing, nineteenth-century Hegelianism was reinforced and revamped in the 1920s and 1930s by triumphant Russian Marxism. In postrevolutionary Russia, the Hegelian-Marxist obsession with history seemed to have been justified by the actual course of events, and it became thoroughly politicized. Marxism assigned to history a strict itinerary with a rapidly approaching end point—the boundless realm of communism. This scenario gave a strictly defined role to human agents, denying any extra historical dimension to individual experience. According to recent historical research, for official Soviet ideology and for individual people who brought it to life, autobiographical writing could serve as an instrument for creating subjects for the new, communism-bound society: the "new men" felt encouraged to internalize "history," that is, internalize the goals of the communist revolution. In the 1920s and 1930s, aligning individual lives or selves with the "objective course of history" was a matter of both political and cultural imperative.[62] This cultural imperative (one should add), even when it was accepted, was not necessarily accepted with ease or joy. No wonder that personal writings from and about that era (especially the 1930s) articulate a sense of self violently reshaped—be it "reforged" (a Soviet term with positive connotations) or simply crushed—by history.

Indeed, for many a Soviet memoirist, history reveals itself in an imprint it leaves on an ordinary person overridden by its irresistible movement. This sense of self found expression in master metaphors, such as the crushing wheels of history and the accidental victim. The metaphors, I believe, carry the main weight of meaning. This particular metaphor goes back to the image that appears in Hegel's *Lectures on the Philosophy of History* and Marx's *Capital:* Juggernaut who draws people beneath the wheels of his chariot. The first published memoirist of the post-Stalin years, Ilya Grigor'evich Erenburg (1891–1967), evoked this image (and the name of Herzen) on the opening pages of his groundbreaking memoir, *People, Years, Life.* He first quoted his own essay from 1926: "Time has now acquired a high-speed automobile"; and then he added in the voice of the 1960s: "Many of my generation fell under the wheels of time."[63] (A new, heavily annotated edition of Erenburg's classic, first published in the 1960s, appeared in 1990.) In the 1990s, the emblematic image of a man injured on the road of history—the road crossed by a world-historical individual, Stalin—still haunts Russian intellectuals, obsessed as they have always been with a desire to leave a trace. It would seem that all it takes to write history is to transcribe the imprint of one's crushed self by writing a diary or memoir.

I would argue that in personal writings published at the end of the Soviet epoch, the name of Herzen and the idiom of Hegelian historicism signal the presence of the nineteenth-century tradition, albeit in a mediated twentieth-century form. Identifying with the authorial persona of the Herzen of *My Past and Thoughts,* Soviet diarists and memoirists import catastrophic historicism that contributes both to a strong sense of self and a sense of community to which one belongs—"the intelligentsia."

A countertext underscores these meanings: the popular actor Aleksandr Anatol'evich Shirvindt (born in 1934) called his flamboyant 2001 memoir *My Past without Thoughts.* He reflects on the issue "why I am not a member of the intelligentsia." Nevertheless, he speaks about his involvement in the war and the terror and states his desire to "fix my time, my friends, my house, that is, my life" in writing. As a child Shirvindt lived in a communal apartment with five other families and as an adult in the apartment building that also housed some of the other authors mentioned in this book (Lidiia Smirnova, Evgenii Evtushenko, and Faina Ranevskaia were among his neighbors).[64]

In the end, by reaching out to their nineteenth-century roots—via twentieth-century historians of Russian thought and literature—Soviet memoirists and diarists project an imaginary continuity of the Russian tradition, from its inception under the pressures of another authoritarian regime (imperial Russia) to the revolutionary era of the 1920s and 1930s to the present day.

CONNECTING THE "I" AND HISTORY

Many a Soviet memoirist (even those who do not indulge in heavy Hegelian metaphor) marks intersections between individual life and historical process by way of signposts placed at strategically important points in the text (usually at the beginning). The circumstances of the Stalinist terror and the Second World War usually provide such opportunities. These signposts exhibit the person's credentials as a hero and as an author.

Take actors, whose celebrity status, it would seem, presents a sufficient claim to authorship. In the opening scene of the memoir of Tatiana Kirillovna Okunevskaia (1914–2002), the reader sees the famous actress in the camp, standing silently amid a formation of prisoners under the sharp ray of a searchlight.[65] Here is Mikhail Mikhailovich Kozakov (born in 1934):

> I will start with what we all know. In 1956 a remarkable event occurred, which for some time determined many of life's processes—the Twentieth Congress of the Party where the cult of Stalin was openly discussed. [...] As for me, 1956 was the year that marked the beginning of my destiny. In the spring I was finishing up my studies at the theater school–studio MKhAT; at the same time, my first film appeared.[66]

Another movie actress, Stalin's favorite, Lidiia Nikolaevna Smirnova (1915–2007), does not bring Soviet power into her memoir, *My Love*. In the introduction to her book, the dissident writer Vladimir Voinovich (a friend) fills in the gap: "Smirnova lived through the years of Stalin's terror relatively safely; she was treated kindly by the Soviet regime and did not evade serving it. [...] And who could have thought that behind it all was the hard lot of an orphaned girl, the daughter of a fallen officer who had served under [the White general] Kolchak, which, of course, had to be concealed, and which made her, strangely enough, a semiunderground creature."[67] Revealing what has been concealed, this introduction turns the actress decorated by the Soviet state into a "semiunderground woman"—a subject of the repressive regime. Her life story is thus framed as a historical narrative.

And what about those who grew up after Stalin? They, too, seem to feel a need to root the self in the terror or the war, experienced, if not firsthand, then through parents or surrogate parents. The literary translator Viktor Leonidovich Toporov (born in 1946), who cultivates the cynical self-image of a drunkard and brawler, starts his 1999 memoir, *False Bottom: The Confessions of a Scandalmonger*, with a shocking revelation of his convoluted personal genealogy:

> My mother, Zoia Nikolaevna Toporova, died in her sleep during the night of June 16, 1997, following a serious argument with me the day before. In several days, on June 22, she would have turned 88. [...] My parents became close during the war—the Leningrad blockade—and never lived together: my father had another family. [...] [My mother] wrote the fictional patronymic Leonidovich on my birth certificate. [...] Leonid was the name [...] of the only man she truly loved, the St. Petersburg writer Leonid Radishchev, who was sent to camp before the war and came back only in 1956; in this way, my mother involved him, as it were, in the process of my birth. [...] Radishchev was, of course, a literary pseudonym; his real name was Livshits.[68]

As in Lidiia Smirnova's case (where this task was performed by the author of the introduction), Toporov's layered narrative reveals what has been concealed: in this case, the story of his illegitimate birth and of his name. In this way, the memoirist (as Herzen had done in his memoirs) involves history—the terror and war—in the story of his birth (it helps, too, that his mother's birthday fell on June 22).

The "ordinary woman" Elvira Filipovich starts her diary, at the age of ten, on September 15, 1944: with her mother and grandmother, she is fleeing the war; the train with refugees moves slowly past the ruins of Stalingrad. Her mother is in tears: in confusion, she lost a suitcase with her lifelong diaries.[69]

A film actor of the Brezhnev era, Rodion Rafailovich Nakhapetov (born in 1944), starts his book with excerpts from his mother's unpublished memoir—a stack of school notebooks. Speaking in stilted Soviet idiom, his mother, Galina Prokopenko (born in 1922), describes the remarkable story of her eight-month journey (in 1943–44) across the front line, which this twenty-one-year-old unmarried village woman made while pregnant. In this way, Nakhapetov, who wrote his memoir in Los Angeles in the 1990s, firmly links himself to Soviet history through the story of his birth.[70]

The tale of Nakhapetov's mother has a parallel in the life of another village woman whose life story appeared in print, Evgeniia Kiseleva. Unlike the actor's mother, who became a schoolteacher, Kiseleva dropped out of school after the fifth grade, and her writing is highly idiosyncratic. But the key moment in her autobiographical account is also historical: it is the birth of her son Anatolii on June 22, 1941 ("on the day of the War"). She starts her narrative with a brief family genealogy, bringing it to the first day of the war: "Me and my husband lived happily, but when the war began in 1941 it separated us forever. And my suffering began." What immediately follows is a painstakingly detailed account of the author's flight with a newborn baby "rotting in dirty diapers" through the war-torn countryside. Kiseleva clearly connects her authorship to suffering (if she "lived with a smile," she would not have anything to write), the suffering to the separation from her husband, and the separation to the war.[71] Most likely, Kiseleva did not follow Herzen's famous account of his birth, an infant in the fire of 1812, but her reader would. What this unschooled woman shares with her educated contemporaries—those who prepared her text for publication and those for whom it was published—is a keen sense of the historical significance of her personal suffering in its specific intimate details and an urge to make these details public.

As such moves and metaphors indicate, a memoirist tells a story of self forcibly embedded in history: the "I" confined to a prison barrack; the "I" in the womb of the mother wandering through occupied territory; the "I" born of an illicit wartime affair and named after a lover lost in the camps. By tracing one's origins or one's authorship to such formative moments, a memoirist makes a claim to personal selfhood and to authorial legitimacy.

REVEALING THE INTIMATE

An integral part of this historical-autobiographical project is self-revelation. Soviet memoirists seem to have a clear objective and an intense drive to reveal what happened to them in private, be it behind the porous walls of communal apartments or inside themselves, in their thoughts and in their dreams; what lies behind the facade of a public persona, known by reputation, or behind the anonymity of "an ordinary person." Some explicitly state their goals and intentions; others do not.

Several authors posited a simple, somewhat naive opposition between public and private. In his diary for the year 1937, the successful writer Mikhail Mikhailovich Prishvin (1873–1954) expounds his moral theory of the double man: "The intimate man is the good man. But there exists the public man: he is a coward. All that is good—this is the private man; all that is bad—the public."[72] Another prominent Soviet writer who was uneasy about his position, Veniamin Aleksandrovich Kaverin (born Zil'ber, 1902–1989), in his memoirs, *The Epilogue* (published in 1989), gave a direct political interpretation to this theory: he spoke of "double life"—"official" and "private"—spawned in "our country" by universal fear.[73] Making such claims, these authors hoped to use their personal documents to reveal the private, or "good," life that they ostensibly led apart from the "system."

In contrast, many others provided records intent on revealing the most intimate facts as evidence of the private life formed, that is, deformed, by the Soviet system. Rather than depoliticize the private, they explain the intimate by the political, and thus, in a large measure, deny themselves "good" life. In her monumental diary of Anna Akhmatova's life, Lidiia Chukovskaia self-consciously reveals peculiar intimate practices shaped by the Soviet regime. The two women became close in 1938, brought together by the arrest and disappearance of their kin (Chukovskaia's husband and Akhmatova's son) in the terror. The author is aware that the forms of private life and homes depicted in her diary are far from "normal." The journal shows how they meet in Akhmatova's bizarre Leningrad home: a product of the Soviet-era housing shortages and policies, this is a communal apartment that also houses Akhmatova's estranged third husband, Nikolai Nikolaevich Punin, his former wife, and their daughter. Formed in the 1920s, not without the influence of avant-garde life experimentation, this unconventional family, now locked together in space by Soviet-era housing conditions, maintains a tense but indissoluble relationship. They share the apartment with the working-class family of the Punins' former servants, the Smirnovs, whose small children become an object of Akhmatova's affection and care—despite her belief that their mother, who occasionally performs the duties of Akhmatova's housekeeper, is a secret informer for the state security. The journal then describes how, during the war, evacuated with the Writers' Union to Central Asia, Chukovskaia and Akhmatova continue their makeshift lives in writers' dormitories. This time, their day-to-day struggle for survival is a part of the national experience. After Stalin's death, they meet in tiny rooms or corners of crowded apartments of Moscow friends, in which Akhmatova, perpetually on the move, stays for months at a time, her belongings confined to what can be carried in a purse and suitcases. Wherever they are, believing themselves to be under surveillance, they speak in whispers. (For conspiratorial purposes, Chukovskaia recorded some of their conversations in code.) These practices continue after the end of the Stalinist terror. In the end, through this private surveillance project, secretly documented, we learn where in all these years Akhmatova lived, how she ate, drank, slept, dressed; how she looked; how she got ill; what she said to her friend and confidante; and what was overheard of her conversations with others. In the end, the text itself, and the story it tells, appear as products of the nexus "intimacy and terror." (Chapter 1 of part 2 of this book provides a close reading of this remarkable document.)

The two professionals who published the life story of the peasant woman Evgeniia Kiseleva make a point of offering it as a text that documents the specifically Soviet and profoundly anomalous private life: Kiseleva's story (they claim) reveals the social world ruled by disintegration of social norms, a "space of war of all against all."[74] Indeed, her notebooks describe disturbing situations (focusing on families). She tells how after the war, having gone in search of her missing husband, she found him illegally married to another woman (with whom he had a child); the two women and their husband (and this child) shared a meal and spent an uneasy night locked in one room of a cramped living barrack.[75] Her second marriage is depicted as a sequence of seventeen separations, occasioned by alcohol, domestic violence, and infidelity (each of which the author describes as a concurrent "marriage"). The publishers frame these revelations as an ethnographic and historical document about private life: "simply life that is written into the Soviet period in history."[76] (Chapter 2 of part 2 of this book analyzes this extraordinary document in detail.)

Whether or not she is aware of the social significance of her life story, Elvira Filipovich (an agronomist with an advanced degree) also portrays a deformed family created in a specific historical situation. Her diary documents how in 1957 she finds and meets her father, Grigorii Smirnov. Born illegitimate in 1934 (Filipovich is her mother's maiden name), she has never seen him. All contact was lost during the war. Only in 1966, when Filipovich meets her father for the second time, does she learn about all of her siblings (at least six by four or five women). Her mother, too, grew up without a father—he was a "victim of repressions" (the reader of this politically noncommittal diary learns this only from a caption on a family photograph).[77]

Some memoirists unveil with a vengeance. Thus, Nagibin's diary seems written with a calculated effect to shock the readers who know his public image as a successful Soviet writer and filmmaker. He was widely admired for his touching films about the difficult life in the Soviet village, such as, in the 1960s, *Chairman* (*Predsedatel'*) and *Women's World* (*Bab'e tsarstvo*), which may have inspired Evgeniia Kiseleva in her desire to see her life as a film. But in his diary, Nagibin describes his whoring, boozing, and brawling in the company of other writers; his squabbles with the Soviet authorities (over the censoring of his books and films and over permissions to make foreign trips); his passionate love for dogs; and his overlapping marriages. For the reader's guidance, the index to the second, annotated, edition contains a chronological list of Nagibin's six wives. Coerced into intimacy with the author and his several families, the reader is overwhelmed by the smells in Nagibin's crowded apartment with its stench of menstrual blood, vomit, and urine, all of it adding up to an emblem of the degraded Soviet system, which he learned to navigate to his advantage—a disgusting and malevolent environment, subject to imminent decomposition and decay.[78]

Shortly before he submitted his diary for publication, Nagibin also published, one after the other, several semiautobiographical novels that reveal the main hero's family secrets: his illegitimate birth and concealed parentage, his adulterous love affairs, and his intimate connections with people in power.[79] Written in the first person and infused with verifiable documentary details, the novels suggest historical and biographical authenticity without being explicitly autobiographical.* After Stalin's death, the first-person hero of *Darkness at the End of the Tunnel* learns that the man he called father did not father him. In love with the hero's mother, this man agreed to give his name to the child of a friend executed by the Bolsheviks in 1920. To be exact, by the time of this revelation, the hero has retained only his adoptive father's Jewish patronymic, "Markovich" (which the author, Nagibin, carries as well). To facilitate his career as a writer, Nagibin's hero (like Nagibin himself) has taken a pen name with a distinctly Russian ring. As he now learns, this pen name, chosen by his mother (supposedly at random), is actually the name of his real father. There are yet other complications to this scenario of manipulated origins. Thus, the hero's stepfather Mark, chosen by his mother as a protector largely on the strength of his Jewishness—which in the revolutionary years was closely associated with Bolshevism—eventually became a liability. In the years of Stalin's terror, the foster father, too, found himself under arrest. When the novel's hero marries into the family of Stalin's government elite, he has to hide this "father" from his new family. Visiting him in secret in the place of exile, he allows his wife to suspect him of adultery on account of his mysterious trips— this is preferable to telling the truth about his exiled father. Given the proximity of his parents-in-law to power, and personally to Stalin, the truth may even put both father and son in immediate danger. The reader may find all of these circumstances and their far-reaching social and emotional implications

---

* While the hero's name is not Nagibin but "Kalugin," some of his friends bear the names of well-known people who were Nagibin's own friends. For example, the novel *T'ma v kontse tunelia* discusses Kalugin's friendship with the pianist Sviatoslav Richter and his friend Vera Prokhorova; the diary, in its second edition, contains a photograph of Nagibin with Richter and Prokhorova (*T'ma v kontse tunelia* 95; *Dnevnik,* frontispiece).

hard to grasp. So does the hero himself. For the hero, the revelation of his true origins holds an additional emotional import: he realizes that, since his biological father was not a Jew but a Russian, the painful sense of alienation he has always felt as a Jew has no real, that is, genetic, basis. And yet he is reluctant to give up his Jewishness and the benefits it brings: in the postwar Soviet Union (after Stalin's anti-Semitic campaigns) Jewishness was associated with the antiregime intelligentsia.[80] So, who is he? The novel carefully explores the confusion, the ambiguity, and the irony of the hero's situation: the discrepancy between the name and ethnic identity, familial loyalty and aspirations for social promotion, calculated benefits and unforeseen perils. All of this has an impact on the hero's erotic choices: his irresistible attraction to the duplicity and deception of adultery. While one definitely needs the genre of novel in order to explore this dense network of emotions and their historical causation, elements of a memoir supply the essential dose of documentary authenticity. (In this case, we have evidence of readers' responses.)*

Another author (who, as he notes, read with sympathy Nagibin's "painful and wise" *Diary*), the art historian Mikhail Iur'evich German (born in 1933), does not reveal his sexual life in his memoirs, but he offers his reflections on the historical situation of sexual intimacy in the early 1950s when he was a student:

> Communal apartments, homelessness, and vagrancy lent an air of unsavoury hastiness to the course taken by serious and casual love affairs alike. From this stems many a genuine tragedy, to say nothing of fear. [...] One's intimate life was, above all, a "political fact" then.[81]

He then speaks in one breath about the scarcity of information on sexuality and poor hygiene and about public judgments of extramarital sexual

---

* Readers' responses to Nagibin's diary start with its publisher, Iurii Kuvaldin, who accepts the genealogy of the hero of Nagibin's novels as the life history of the writer; he believes that Nagibin took the material for his novels directly from the diary and laments that he did not choose to leave them in the diary instead. (Iurii Kuvaldin, "Iurii Nagibin," published in *Nevskoe vremia*, March 13, 1996, and as an afterword to Nagibin, *Dnevnik*, 672.) Viktor Toporov (himself an unabashed confessional memoirist) refused to accept Nagibin's self-revelations—in the diary and in the novels—as a portrait of the "true" Nagibin: he felt that confessing his own unsavory intimate life does not excuse Nagibin's success as a Soviet writer. And if the character revealed in the diary is not "true Nagibin," then (Toporov asks) "was it worth turning a diary into the *Diary* by submitting it for publication?" (Viktor Toporov, "Gibel' Nagibina," *Postscriptum: Literaturnyi zhurnal* 5 (1996); cited from www.vavilon.ru/metatext/ps5/toporov.html). A member of the opposite ideological camp, the right-wing nationalist critic Stanislav Kuniaev, also noted his disgust at the self-revelations of Nagibin's "memoirs" (he took both the diary and the novels to be "memoirs"). What offended him most was Nagibin's ambivalence about his ethnic identity: his toying with Jewishness and his refusal to accept his Russianness. (Stanislav Kuniaev, "Iz literaturnogo dnevnika smutnogo vremeni," *Zavtra*, no. 27 (32): 1994.)

relationships practiced at the time in the Communist youth organizations of Soviet universities.

The intimate revelations made in the memoirs of the clinical pathologist Iakov L'vovich Rapoport (1898–1996)—one of the surviving "Jewish doctors" accused of plotting to kill members of the government—are very different in tone, but not in purpose. He wrote because he feared that the "intimate mechanism" (his words) of the workings of Soviet power, specifically, the notorious doctors' case, might elude historians even if the archives were ever opened for "objective investigation."[82] In his memoir (written in 1973–75 and published in 1988) Rapoport gives an insider's view of the medical establishment and a detailed account of the interrogations. With clinical precision, he describes complex feelings he had then, in 1953: the shock, fear, and confusion of the arrest; distractions sought in the prison cell; tears of relief and bitterness at the news of his release; a strange sense of regret in leaving the prison; and quick dismissal of the arrest from memory. Rapoport also comments on the second emotional trauma, sustained in the days when he wrote his memoir, twenty years after the events.[83] This memoir provides a clinical anamnesis offered by a survivor who happens to be a medical expert. His daughter, Natalia Iakovlevna Rapoport, a child at the time of his arrest, published her side of the story, written in 1988. She describes, in detail, what happened in the family apartment after her father was led away in February 1953: she lost consciousness and fell to the floor. The publisher of the daughter's memoir asked Evgeny Evtushenko to provide an introduction. In his introduction, Evtushenko, so to speak, moved in with the Rapoports. He inserted a picture of himself as a young man in January 1953 when the doctors' plot was announced: "I remember a shaky streetcar ride on that dreadful day and stifled people silently holding open newspapers in their hands."[84] This popular poet, celebrated by the youth culture in the 1960s, revealed a shocking fact: back then, he believed the newspapers and thought that the "Jewish doctors" were guilty of treason against the motherland and Stalin. Jointly, these three authors created a document of historical experience revealing intense and diverse emotions.

There are other people who, while they too have published highly intimate and self-revealing documents, approach the task differently. Take a book of scattered notes published by the distinguished literary scholar Mikhail Leonovich Gasparov (1935–2005), previously known for extreme reticence. Arranged alphabetically as if in a playful comment on the futility of narrative autobiography, these aphoristic notes disclose mostly the author's judgments and tastes.[85] One reviewer called this move "the baring of thought" (*obnazhenie mysli*). While writers reveal "fights at the TsDL [Writers' Union Club], drunken debauchery, and sleeping around" (the reviewer seems to have Nagibin in mind), "a philologist bares himself differently." Thus, a philologist (says the reviewer) describes how he omitted lines from a poem he translated, "and the reader blushes as if reading the description of a bedroom scene."[86]

This reviewer chose not to mention that Mikhail Gasparov's "notes" have also revealed the secret of his illegitimate birth and concealed parentage; he, too, lived under a name that was not his own, and one that implied an ethnic origin that had no basis in genetics. This intimate story about the disintegration of family is told in the context of Soviet history.

Biographical fact and raw emotion have no place on the pages of Lidiia Ginzburg's disciplined notebooks, which are filled with carefully crafted situations, maxims, and reflections; but the notion of intimacy, history, and the catastrophic quality of experience that mark other memoirs are present. Whether the topic is frustrated passion, survivor's guilt, old age, or the Leningrad blockade, Ginzburg's "notes" present (to paraphrase her own formula) an analytical model of catastrophic feelings.[87] Ginzburg's post-Soviet publisher, Zakharov (who rearranged the order of the notes), placed a stamp that said "A Terrifying Book" (*Strashnaia kniga*) on the jacket of the 1999 edition (an actual graphic stamp); in his annotation, the publisher-editor framed this edition as a document about "the Soviet era," which is "still close to us," and as a book that is "sharper (*pokruche*) than any novel."[88]

At the opposite pole to the highly disciplined Lidiia Ginzburg is the full-exposure tactics of the feminist activist and writer Maria Arbatova, whose memoir-novels also strive to catch up with the end of the century. Her aim is to show that intimate self-revelation against the backdrop of history does not remain the prerogative of those who lived under Stalin. This flamboyant post-Soviet author owns up to her strategy:

> I am writing this text with a degree of sincerity and detail that is shocking to some because I belong to the first generation born without Stalin. And so far this generation has made rather few attempts to speak about itself in honest language. I hope that this book is not so much about me as about the times; this is striptease against the backdrop of the second half of the twentieth century, which, thank God, is over now.[89]

Like many other memoirists, this self-defined "stripper," who eagerly describes her overlapping sexual partnerships and unsavory Soviet child-rearing practices, defines herself in relation to a generation, and her generation in relation to Stalin. She, too, uses autobiography as something other than "literature" (she hastens to note), and writes not only against the background of history but also from the vantage point of the end.

To generalize about revealed intimacies. We have seen how Soviet memoirists and diarists reveal details of their intimate lives, believing them to be valuable historical material. In their relentless self-revelation they go far beyond their nineteenth-century predecessors with whom they share this belief. Needless to say, in our day radical disclosure of the intimate has become acceptable and hardly comes as a surprise. A further enabling factor may be that Soviet publishing institutions exerted strict control over private revelations (and they excluded the sexual); hence these authors' delight in "stripping." But what is more, within the corpus at hand such self-exposure makes an implicit claim to larger historical meaning: these authors present Soviet history as a force that shaped, and deformed, their private lives and selves. Many a document from (and about) the 1930s presents intimate lives as a product of what I call the nexus of "intimacy and terror."[90] Other writings, including those by loyal Soviet subjects, focus on the formative role of emotions (fear, want, loss, patriotism), material deprivations, and bodily suffering experienced in the war of 1941–45. In a number of texts the terror and the war, in their effect on personal lives, are described as mirror images of each other.[91] Quite a few accounts show that this sense of deformed and endangered life was sustained long after the end of the war and terror (texts from later years frequently depict the moral and material living conditions in similar terms). Many an author (such as Chukovskaia, Nagibin, and German) self-consciously blames the Soviet state for the deformation of intimacy and home. Others, albeit a minority (Filipovich and Kiseleva), do not. (Of course, Kiseleva's publishers assigned the blame in her place.)

BUILDING A COMMUNITY

As the preceding discussion makes clear, memoirs and diaries in this corpus create and consolidate communities: families, friendly circles, the intelligentsia, and more. This section describes how this works—by way of literary techniques, socializing strategies, and political negotiations.

Moving in with a New Text

Here is a new arrival: Inna Aronovna Shikheeva-Gaister's *Family Chronicle from the Times of the Cult of Personality, 1925–1953*. Composed orally from 1988 to 1990 and transcribed by the author's husband (for the sake of their grandchildren), it was published in 1998.[92] This document claims a place in a common corpus by clearly signaling connections to its key texts. Thus, the title echoes Evgeniia Ginzburg's pioneering terror memoir, which had the subtitle "Chronicle from the Times of the Cult of Personality." And there is an epigraph from Anna Akhmatova's *Poem without a Hero:* "Ask my contemporaries—convicts, hundred-and-fivers, prisoners—and we will tell you…"*

---

* «Ты спроси у моих современниц—каторжанок, стопятниц, пленниц, и тебе порасскажем мы…».
"Stopiatnitsy" (hundred-and-fivers) is a slang word: it refers to those who were forbidden to take residence within the one-hundred-and-five kilometer zone of major cities, typically, wives of the arrested.

The key word, I think, is "my female contemporaries" (in Russian, this and every other word in the line is marked by female grammatical gender). This poetic line is also featured prominently in Nadezhda Mandel'shtam's memoir and in Chukovskaia's *Notes about Anna Akhmatova*. The new author, Inna Shikheeva-Gaister, clearly strengthens her claim to belonging by reaching out to a specific, and prominent, subgroup: women under the terror.

Another move would be to connect not only to texts and symbolic topoi but also to the pillars of the group. For example, the poet David Samoilov pointedly describes conversations at the writers' summer colony Peredelkino with Lidiia Chukovskaia, with whom he discussed her *Notes about Anna Akhmatova* and Herzen's *My Past and Thoughts*.[93] Writers—the quintessential *intelligenty*—form a tight social circle; accordingly, there is no surprise that we find such moments in many a writer's memoir. But Shikheeva-Gaister is the daughter of a prominent Soviet administrator and an engineer by profession (born in 1925). Her *Family Chronicle* describes the destruction of a clan of believing Communists, and it is set mainly in the period from 1925 to 1953, when she did not know anybody in the literary circles. Nevertheless, this author, too, feels a need and finds a way to connect in a personal and intimate way with the core of the community. There is an epilogue, entitled "The KGB Continues Its Work"; the time of the action is 1977. The author is summoned to the KGB's headquarters. What is to be done? "I simply started calling everyone. I reached Svetka Ivanova. I tell her: 'Svetka, they are summoning me.' She tells me to hold on a second and goes to Koma for advice..."[94] Koma is a nickname of the prominent scholar Viacheslav Vsevolodovich Ivanov, the son of the established Soviet writer Vsevolod Viacheslavovich Ivanov. His wife "Svetka" (an intimate form of her name is used here) is the daughter and stepdaughter of the dissidents Raisa Orlova and Lev Kopelev. The names "Svetka" and "Koma" refer to members of extended intelligentsia families and authors of copious memoirs.[95] Before Stalin, few of these people knew one another; after Stalin, they came to be linked as fellow victims of the terror. At the end of the Soviet epoch, the sharing of a textual space in which they describe common experiences (and in which they reveal who knows whom) reinforces the memoirists' current connection to one another.

Joining the Ranks of Victims

And what if one had not been a terror victim? What would one do to join the community? Recall how in 1988, within one text, the daughter of one of the "Jewish doctors," Natalia Rapoport, met with Evgenii Evtushenko who had then (in 1953) believed that the doctors were guilty as charged. Now (in 1988), through his introduction, Evtushenko moves in, so to speak, with the Rapoports: he uses the memoir of a victim to retroactively write himself into the terror (which had not touched him). He also marked the difference between the "I then" and the "I now." There are other, similar, cases. For example, there is a memoir published under the title *Beria's Soldier: Reminiscences of a Camp Guard*, in which a former guard in a prison camp describes his life and work as a miserable existence, ruled by constraint, deprivation, and violence.[96] The guard, too, makes a move to join the ranks of victims (his memoir was published by a professional writer).

There are two memoirs that bear the title *Memoir Notes* (*Pamiatnye zapiski*). One is by the liberal poet David Samoilov; the other figures in book catalogues under the truncated title *Memoir Notes of a Worker*... The full title continues: *Communist-Bolshevik, Trade-Union, Party- and Soviet-Government Official.* The author is Lazar' Moiseevich Kaganovich (1893–1991), who lays claim, not only to his earlier identity as a "simple worker," but also to the status of a victim of repression (under Khrushchev). What this right-hand man of Stalin, who signed thousands of death sentences, shares with the victims of Stalin's terror is an irresistible urge to write his life story. Starting in the 1960s, when in the course of Khrushchev's de-Stalinization he was expelled from the Communist Party, Kaganovich worked on his memoirs. He wrote incessantly and died in 1991 (at the age of 97), literally, at his desk. (The manuscript and its published version are interrupted midsentence in the diary-style section that deals with the present, "My Thoughts on Perestroika.") Kaganovich's initial audience was fairly intimate: the neighbors (he found an audience in the inhabitants of his apartment building). A selection from the 14,000 hand-written pages (let us say, a "crash course," *kratkii kurs*) was prepared for publication by his loyal daughter, Maia, whose introduction focuses on the hardships of the author's life after the "repressions" of 1957.*

While most of Stalin's other men did not leave memoirs, children have spoken for Lavrentii Beria and Georgii Malenkov, as well as for Nikita Khrushchev, who did leave voluminous memoirs of his own.[97] Portraying their fathers as private individuals, they tend to present their entire families as victims of government repression. Thus, Beria's son suggests that his father was Stalin's potential victim—the next in line in March 1953. The sons of both Beria and Malenkov provide vivid details of the persecution of their families at the hands of Khrushchev. In his turn, Khrushchev's son vividly describes the harassment of his father by the KGB, when, after his fall from power in 1964, Nikita Khrushchev worked, in secret, on his memoirs (composed orally and

---

* Lazar' Kaganovich, *Pamiatnye zapiski rabochego, kommunista-bolshevika, profsoiuznogo, partiinogo i sovetsko-gosudarstvennogo rabotnika* (Moscow: Vagrius, 1996). It is notable that throughout his memoir, Kaganovich follows the discourse of official Soviet political documents. Notes of intimacy, in association with the theme of power, appear in letters to his daughter, which she included in this edition: "My dear sweet Maiusia. [...] Look after Mom, her health, use power on a small scale [*proiavi malen'kuiu vlast'*]" (531).

transcribed from tape by family members), which were eventually smuggled to the West for publication. Cast as victims of repression, all of them seem to qualify for entry into the domain of "memoirs of the contemporaries" and, thus, into the community of contemporaries.[98]

Remembering Stalin: Tears

Memoirists often evoke historical moments coexperienced with others. In Soviet memoirs, one such moment of intense collective emotion stands out: Stalin's death. There is hardly a text that does not describe March 5, 1953, and hardly a text that does not mention crying at the news of Stalin's death. Most memoirists use this moment to confirm the feelings in which they had then shared and to attempt to explain these feelings from the vantage point of another age. "Then" the shedding of tears seemed to indicate their innermost feelings and to visibly unite them with a community (Stalin's subjects). "Now" they are confronted with a need to realign their selves and their community.

Khrushchev, in the memoir stories told after his dismissal from power in 1964, pictures himself crying at the side of Stalin's body, admitting that he had sincerely grieved "for Stalin," for "Stalin's children," and for "the country."[99] In her 1963 memoir, Stalin's renegade daughter Svetlana gives a list of the government members she had then seen crying, Khrushchev among them.[100]

In his 1979 memoirs, largely devoted to the disavowal of his "love" (he uses this word) for Stalin, Konstantin Simonov (1915–1979), whose high standing in the literary establishment had frequently brought him into personal contact with Stalin, includes a report from the Hall of Columns where Stalin's body was displayed for the public—a diary entry he made on that day. Standing guard over Stalin's body, he observed the mourners, noting "the emotional shock" in every single person at the moment he or she saw Stalin's body. In the voice of 1979, Simonov adds a historicist explanation, calling Stalin's death "the event, which, regardless of how one felt about Stalin, objectively marked the end of a long historical period..." Back then, in that hall, Simonov observed, among others, Stalin's grieving daughter, Svetlana.[101] Someone else looked at Simonov. Each left a record, which has now been published. The memoirs of the writer Veniamin Kaverin describe how, with other writers, he had been taken to see Stalin's body in the Hall of Columns, and he reports that "Simonov was literally drowning in tears." He adds that "there is no doubt about his sincerity." As for himself, Kaverin claims that he looked at the body of the "executioner" without tears.[102] The writer Grigorii Iakovlevich Baklanov (born in 1923) admits to crying, but, from the position of the 1990s when he wrote his memoirs, he finds his tears difficult to explain. Back then, unemployed after the arrest of the Jewish doctors, this Jewish writer (the Russian name "Baklanov" is his pen name; he was born Fridman) had "no more illusions," but he, too, cried and sobbed.[103]

At the time of Stalin's death, Evgeniia Semenovna Ginzburg (1906–1977) had been a convict for more than fifteen years. At the time of her arrest, she was the wife of a party functionary and an ardent Communist; by March 1953, she held Stalin personally responsible for the destruction of her family (including the death of her small son in Leningrad, where he lived with relatives, during the blockade). And yet, she, too, reports how at the news of Stalin's death, heard on the radio, she collapsed, sobbing loudly. She adds: "I must confess that I was sobbing not for the monumental historical tragedy alone, but most of all for myself. What this man had done to me, to my spirit, to my children, to my mother..." Note that she takes the solemn historical perspective as the norm and the personal view as a deviation to be confessed. Like many others, Ginzburg describes Stalin's death as the death of God, at least for believing Communists ("they had completely overlooked the strange fact that the Generalissimus was made of the same imperfect flesh and blood as the rest of the sinful mortals...").[104]

Ilya Erenburg, in his pioneering memoir *People, Years, Life,* famously described standing in the Hall of Columns over the body of "the god who died from a stroke at the age of seventy-three, as if he were not a god but a mere mortal," feeling intense fear for the future. Like other memoirists, Ehrenburg feels compelled to explain his feelings for Stalin, and, like many after him, he uses the word "love" and resorts to religious metaphors: "I did not love Stalin but, for a long time, I believed in him, and feared him."[105] (I believe that the "death of God" metaphor may have originated in Erenburg's memoirs.)[106]

Others report both their tears and the change in feelings that occurred over time. The husband-and-wife team of Raisa Davydovna Orlova (1918–1989) and Lev Zinov'evich Kopelev (1912–1997), who were dissidents in the 1970s and 1980s, stands out for their explicit use of the Augustinian pattern of memoir writing: religious conversion and confession in the presence of the community. They reverse this pattern to report a loss of faith. Orlova, who speaks of herself as a "believing Stalinist" begins her *Reminiscences about the Non-Past Time* (written in the 1970s) with a confession of faith in Stalin and his deeds: "—*What did you believe in?* [...] *Until 1953, I believed in everything, including 'the doctors' plot.' I deeply mourned Stalin's death.*"[107] On March 5, 1953 (the memoirist tells us) she cried in despair: "I took Stalin's death as a disaster and as the end."[108] Her other memoir, written in the form of a dialogue with her husband, Communist-turned-dissident Lev Kopelev, *We Lived in Moscow: 1956–1980* opens with a metaphor that implies a conversion of the whole society to a new faith: "Many of our contemporaries create a new chronological system starting from March 5, 1953—the date of Stalin's death."[109] This family memoir contains Kopelev's confession. On the day of Stalin's death, he shed tears in prison, sharing his genuine grief with both other prisoners and the guards.

Another former inmate, the ethnographer Nina Ivanovna Gagen-Torn (1900–1986), who was in postprison exile at the time of Stalin's death, pointedly reports not crying amid the sobs and wails of others.[110] Her tone is dry, sober, and dispassionate, and she does not indulge in religious metaphor. Claiming exclusion, this writer relates herself to the community by reporting on the tears and shock of others. There are many other examples of both kinds: most report crying, gripped by complex and often not entirely clear, almost mystical emotions; some report *not* crying in the presence of those who cried.

When, in the years of the demise of the Soviet regime, all of these accounts (composed throughout the 1960s and 1980s) appeared in the public arena in Russia, they formed one textual space: the space of exposed past experience. Readers are invited to participate vicariously. Both writers and readers attempt to connect what they felt and did "then" (their tears), what others, whom they observed, felt and did "then," and what all of them think and feel "now." Many find it difficult to make both ends meet. Writing and publishing memoirs helps them to realign their selves in the face of the community, and it creates a community extended over space and time.

Disagreeing

Arguably, disagreements and controversies do as much to link people into a community as does mutual recognition. Soviet memoirists frequently find themselves at odds about both the facts and the meanings of their shared past.

A veritable "memoir war" erupted around the image of Osip Mandelshtam or, rather, around the well-known memoirs of his widow, Nadezhda Iakovlevna Mandelshtam (1899–1980)—an impassioned account focused on the intelligentsia's relationship to power in the years of the terror. Since the early 1970s, this pioneering document had circulated in the intelligentsia circles illegally, in typescript form and in Western editions. In 1988 its publication in Moscow marked (the editor claimed) the "return of memory."[111] By the time an annotated scholarly edition appeared in print (in 1999), Nadezhda Mandelshtam's *Reminiscences* and its second installment, *The Second Book*, had to share the territory with what one reader called "antimemoirs," published by a family friend and fellow intellectual, Emma Grigor'evna Gershtein (1903–2002), under the simple title *Memoirs*.[112] Gershtein made her recollections public only in the 1990s, clearly motivated by a desire to counteract earlier portrayals of the intelligentsia circles that surrounded the two "great Russian poets" Osip Mandelshtam and Anna Akhmatova. (One review saw these intelligentsia circles as the nation's two main families.[113]) Targeting the widow's "authoritarian style of remembering" and the trust many readers put in Nadezhda Mandelshtam, Gershtein (a historian of literature by profession) provided her own interpretation of the social situation of the two Russian poets caught in the Stalinist terror.[114] She spared the reader neither painful revelations of Mandelshtam's political indiscretions during the 1934 interrogations nor embarrassing details of sexual practices in the Mandelshtam family. In her *Memoirs* (a series of thematic essays that include carefully transcribed documents from her own correspondence), Gershtein also told a poignant story of the tense and painful relationship between Anna Akhmatova and her son Lev Gumilev, two "wounded souls." As Gershtein puts it, "Lev"—who spent much of his life in the camps and did not escape undamaged—had a tendency to transform the "political" in his "destiny" into the "banal" in his "everyday." (The "political" included being questioned, under torture, about his mother's suspected political secrets, such as the ash left by papers burned in her room.) Gershtein also described her own difficult love affair with Lev, interrupted by several arrests, the war, and many personal betrayals. She carefully guides the reader through the vicissitudes of love in catastrophic times: "sublime" moments of passion at the time of danger, "banal" sexual infidelities, and the ever-present resentment.[115] In her book, published at the age of ninety-five, Gershtein exercised the enviable privilege of speaking from the position of "the last living witness."[116] In the passionate public debates that followed, Gershtein's *Memoirs* found both embittered critics and gleeful supporters from the ranks of the younger generations.

The disagreements among contemporaries acquire a special moral intensity when it comes to the relationship between "power," on the one hand, and "the intelligentsia," "literature," or "culture," on the other, especially under Stalin. (I use the memoirists' own terms.) One of the new terror documents, Nina Gagen-Torn's uncompromising account of life in the camps, *Memoria*, published only in 1994, criticizes Evgeniia Ginzburg's memoirs for being narrowly focused on believing Communists among the repressed intellectuals.[117] Others were scornful about the repentance of the former Stalinists. Several readers publicly challenged the validity of Konstantin Simonov's rejection of his faith in, and love for, Stalin, made on his death bed in 1979 and published in 1988. Among them was Grigorii Baklanov, the editor in chief of the literary monthly *Znamia*, which published Simonov's confessions: "How unfree was his thought! Even when he wrote for his desk drawer, as one writes one's last testament."[118] (Baklanov himself reported a loss of faith in Stalin in his 1999 memoir.) Konstantin Simonov's son, Aleksei Kirillovich [*sic*!] Simonov, who also published memoirs, admits that he finds it difficult to write about the politically controversial figure of his famous father. (Since perestroika, Aleksei Simonov has been a freedom-of-speech activist.) Yet he registers his pain at reading dismissive responses to Simonov's confessions, and he puts on record his objections to the scathing remarks Nagibin, in his diary, made about Simonov (as Stalin's man in literature) and about his death-bed confession.* Another memoirist, Mikhail German (the son of the writer Iurii German) comments on Nagibin's dismissal of Simonov's penitent memoirs: he accepts Nagibin's diatribes for their historical value, refrains from making a personal judgment on Simonov, and, in the end, justifies the whole discussion as an emblem of the situation of literature under the Soviet regime: "It's not up to me or my generation to judge Simonov, but his whole career was such a precise indicator of the interrelationship of power and literature that one can't help recalling it." On the next page Mikhail German mentions that his father won the Stalin Prize in literature in 1948.[119] (His father, like Aleksei Simonov's father, abandoned his son in infancy.)

The monumental memoirs of the archivist and historian Sarra Vladimirovna Zhitomirskaia (1916–2002), *Simply Life,* published as late as 2006, challenge her contemporaries on several counts. This document presents a broad historical panorama: childhood in a Jewish family in southern Russia during the civil war, adolescence in a communal apartment in the famous Arbat neighborhood in Moscow, years of study at Moscow University in the 1930s (described in a chapter entitled "The History Department and the Terror"), evacuation during the war, and more than thirty years of a difficult professional career as an archivist (and one time director) in the Manuscript Division of the Lenin Library, marred by growing restrictions on scholars' access to documents in the 1970s and 1980s and by persecution for failure to enforce these restrictions (which resulted in her dismissal from the library and from the Communist Party). The narrative draws to a conclusion on the glorious day of the failed putsch, August 21, 1991.

Speaking about the 1930s, Zhitomirskaia passes a solemn moral judgment on the collective responsibility of both "the people" and "the intelligentsia" for the terror:

> If a Soviet man claims he knew nothing about the terror of the 1930s—don't believe him! Everyone knew, and guilt for the terror, for the millions

---

* Aleksei Simonov, *Chastnaia kollektsiia,* 51–57. Aleksei Simonov is one of several memoirists who have difficulty reporting their name and patronymic. In his memoirs, he speaks of his lifelong predicament in responding to the question: "How come you are Kirillovich if your father is Konstantin Simonov?" Aleksei Simonov, *Chastnaia kollektsiia,* 18 (Aleksei Simonov's parents were married shortly before his birth and divorced when he was one year old; at the time of Aleksei's birth, his father bore the name Kirill Simonov; he later changed his name from Kirill to Konstantin, but the son's patronymic remained unchanged.)

of people who died, lies with us all. [...] How did the people (*narod*) behave? What did their spiritual avant-garde, the intelligentsia, do? And not only do we not repent to this very day, but we don't even feel the urge to repent.[120]

Obviously, Zhitomirskaia applies her judgment to the sum total of her fellow citizens, but she also speaks about the immediate and tangible community of the memoirists, claiming that she sees the major failing in the description of the "Soviet epoch" in the memoirs of her "contemporaries" in "the conscious or unconscious attempts to distance themselves from involvement in the system" (115).

Much of the memoir tells a painstakingly detailed institutional history, solemnly entitled "The History of the Fall of the Manuscript Division." In respect to her institutional experience, Zhitomirskaia challenges the 1999 memoir of her highly successful colleague, Nataliia Ivanovna Tiulina (one of the few pro-Soviet memoirs in this corpus). Suggestively subtitled *Notes of a Librarian with a Happy Destiny*,[121] Tiulina's memoir celebrates the Lenin Library's, and her own, contribution to society. Zhitomirskaia comments:

> It's impossible to understand how everything that she recalls happened in that library where whole swathes of literature were sent to "special storage" [*spetskhran*, accessible only to the privileged], and where, consequently and knowingly, the reader was left in the dark or led to form a distorted impression as to historical events, scholarship, and culture.
>
> The country's main library, which did its important bit for culture, at the same time, precisely as a result of this central role, served as a conduit for everything that power did to culture. All of us who worked there are, to some extent or other, complicit in this, and to admit to it is painful but necessary (220–21).

For Zhitomirskaia, from the vantage point of the 1990s, library work under these institutional conditions counted as collaboration with the evil power. This author is equally uncompromising in her judgments on intimate life. Thus, describing her close association, professional and personal, with fellow historian and archival scholar Natan Eidel'man, Zhitomirskaia speaks of her dismay and disapproval on the discovery that her friend, whose wife and daughter she knew, had another home and a "parallel family" (367–68).

Moscow University's Department of History is also described in the 2005 diary-memoir of the historian Boris Grigor'evich Tartakovskii (1911–2002); he also devotes much attention to the war. Tartakovskii was among Zhitomirskaia's classmates from 1935 to 1940, and he is briefly mentioned in her memoirs. Like Zhitomirskaia, Tartakovskii lists students and faculty who had "disappeared" by the end of 1937. But while, in her memoirs, Zhitomirskaia claims that she then "knew" and "understood" (about the terror), Tartakovskii focuses on the irreducible distance between "then" and "now": "*Now* I think that *then*, we—or in any case, I—found in the official party explanation for all that happened some point of reason that allowed one not to lose faith."[122] Admitting that he is aware of the "responsibility of our generation" and about "the need to repent"—the topic (he adds) "much discussed in the present-day press and memoirs" (192)—Tartakovskii concludes that, try as he might, it would not be possible *now* to represent himself the way he was *then* (166). In this way, he shows both his superior historicist sense and his awareness that the memoir is a genre with a logic of its own. (He had hoped that his writings, before they saw the public light, would be evaluated by his younger brother, Andrei Grigor'evich Tartakovskii, an expert on the Russian nineteenth-century memoir culture, but Andrei Tartakovskii died suddenly in 1999.)[123] Whether or not Sarra Zhitomirskaia and Boris Tartakovskii read each other's memoirs before publication (this remains unclear), when their texts appeared in print, they entered into a dialogue, and reinforced a sense of community by disagreeing.

Family Memoirs

Many a memoir in this corpus is a product of a joint family effort, and many a text commits to paper a specific image of the family, usually, a tenuous, endangered, or a dangerously extended family. A remarkable example is provided by the book entitled: Iuliia Eidel'man, *Diaries of Natan Eidel'man*.[124] This book combines entries from the diary of the well-known historian Natan Iakovlevich Eidel'man (1930–1989) with a text written by his widow (his second wife), Iuliia Moiseevna Eidel'man, née Madora. Printed in italics, her interpolations provide biographical background, supply narrative connections, and inscribe her own life into her husband's diary. A section of this book (May–December 1979) is made up of a double narrative combining the diary of Eidel'man with that of Madora, who was his mistress at the time. Introducing the edition, the widow-editor presents her goals as twofold: to decipher and to supplement. For one, deciphering involves decoding the barely legible handwriting and reconstructing fragmentary notes casually jotted down for the diarist's future reference. But the editor also believes that her late husband's diaries are sadly lacking in the "intimate details of his life" (10). Many of the intimate details that she supplements, on the basis of her own diary, concern their somewhat special relationship: for thirteen years, from 1971 to 1984, Natan Eidel'man had two parallel families, one with his first wife (she has not published memoirs and will, therefore, remain unnamed in these pages) and the other with Iuliia Madora. This arrangement, which involved maintaining two separate residences in Moscow and two overlapping sets of friends and relatives, rested on an elaborate combination of deception and concealment, on the one hand, and tacit acquiescence and complicity, on the other (while some relatives and friends remained in the dark, others "knew" and participated in both families).

Apart from Madora's clarifications and amendments, Eidel'man's diary says little about his family or love life. His diary carefully documents intimacy with a circle of friends, from the small, intensely loyal group of seven high school classmates who became close in the first postwar years and stayed close for life to a widening circle of writers and scholars from the ranks of the antiregime intelligentsia, dating mostly from the 1960s. In one or the other family, and with friends, Eidel'man's daily life unfolds in the context of his highly personal involvement in his historical research, which focused on what he calls the "secret history" of the nineteenth century (the history of dissent and opposition, from the Decembrists to the Herzen circle). The diary reveals what was implicit in Eidel'man's deliberately personalized historical writings and in his passionate public lectures. Here, I will use the formulations of an American historian who analyzed his Soviet colleague's diary: Eidel'man saw himself as an "example of the archetypal artist in a tense but symbiotic relationship with power," replaying in his own experience the historical dramas of Pushkin's relationship with Nicholas I and Mikhail Bulgakov's with Stalin. Readers may see the picture of the double family life that emerges from this double document as an emblem of other dualities and discrepancies in the diarist's life: emotional engagement with the history of the nineteenth-century opposition and relatively successful adaptation to Soviet conditions, eager assimilation into the Russian intelligentsia, and acute consciousness of being Jewish, and yet others.[125] (Like other Soviet memoirists whose ethnic origin was Jewish—of which there were many—Eidel'man embraced his cultural Russianness without letting go of a strong sense of Jewishness.)

But we should remember that Eidel'man had not prepared his diary for publication: for him, the diary was only a collection of materials for another autobiographical work. As so many of his contemporaries, Eidel'man envisioned his "Main Book" (*Glavnaia kniga*) as a recapitulation of Herzen's memoir *My Past and Thoughts*. According to Madora, Eidel'man planned to start this memoir in the present and move the narrative "backward" to April 18, 1930, the day of his birth. On this day, Stalin had famously called Mikhail Bulgakov (in response to his letter) to discuss the writer's precarious position in the Soviet cultural establishment. (This conversation, known to many through oral stories and rumors, turned into an emblem of the intelligentsia's connection to power.) Since Eidel'man did not produce his "main book," what we know of it comes mostly from conversations his widow reported in their family diary.[126]

A memoir published by one of Eidel'man's childhood friends and lifelong companions, Iulii Zusmanovich Krelin (1929–2006), confirms and complements the portrait of this circle given in the Eidel'man-Madora diary. Krelin supplies vivid details of the "around-the-table communion" (*zastol'noe obshchenie*): boisterous drinking rituals, casual table manners, and, most importantly, intense conversations—ranging in topics from "history" (they talked at length about Eidel'man's investigations in nineteenth-century history and about the political developments they lived through) to friendly gossip. A physician by profession, Krelin has also provided clinical details of his friend's sudden death in 1989 (from a heart attack). (Krelin, who attended to many Moscow literary figures, organized his memoir, subtitled "Medical Testimony," as episodes from the case histories of his famous patients.)[127]

Two Memoirs and a Novel Tell the Same Story

When memoirs of different people, including people who knew each other, come into the public domain, the reader can reconstruct stories and situations on the basis of more than one account. I will trace one such collectively disclosed story, which stands out for the intensity and complexity of relationships and emotions it reveals.

The restrained memoirs of the folklorist Eleazar Moiseevich Meletinskii (1918–2005), published in 1998 (and written in 1971–75), tell of his life during the war and terror while carefully avoiding intimate details. This is what the memoirist says about his second arrest, in 1949, in the course of the so-called anticosmopolitan campaign, which touched mostly Jewish intellectuals:

> I am still nauseated when I recall how the whole of the investigation was most elaborately constructed on exploiting "romantic" motivations—on the denunciations from my wife's former husband (Moiseenko), who had sworn, out of revenge, to land me in prison again, and on the evidence provided by a certain lady, whose *poste-restante* correspondence with me got into the hands of the State Security. [...] The face-to-face confrontations [staged during the investigation] were, for psychological reasons, very unpleasant, both for the witnesses and for me (520).[128]

"Nauseated" by the memories of how the state security tried to use sexual jealousy to force his mistress and his friends to provide evidence that would present him as a politically unreliable "cosmopolitan," the memoirist acknowledges the basic facts but does not go into details. (Even so, for simplicity's sake, I omit some details in this complicated scenario.)* Meletinskii counts on his self-selected Russian readers to grasp the situation. (The memoir was published in a collection of his scholarship on myth and folklore.) The experienced reader would indeed understand that his position was precarious: by 1949, Meletinskii, who had been briefly detained on suspicion of treason during the war, managed to acquire a teaching position in the Humanities faculty at Petrozavodsk University, and both of these circumstances made him especially vulnerable to accusations of ideological and sexual indiscretions. An ethnic Jew, he fitted the profile of an antipatriotic "cosmopolitan" perfectly. The reader also gathers that the previous husband of Meletinskii's wife provided the denunciation that justified his arrest, and that a certain "lady," with whom Meletinskii exchanged love letters in secret from his wife (the general delivery correspondence intercepted by the security police), was successfully blackmailed to provide the necessary evidence for a conviction on a political charge. But we learn nothing about the memoirist's wife, her role in the whole affair, and her feelings; we do not even learn her name.

The wife's side of the story can be found in another personal document, published in 1994 by the dissident philosopher Grigorii Solomonovich Pomerants (born in 1918). His memoir (written in 1974–80), *V storonu Iry* (the Russian for *De côté de Ira* and an obvious evocation of Proust) is an emotional tribute to the author's late wife, "Ira."[129] Ira—Irina Ignat'evna Murav'eva— was earlier married to Eleazar Meletinskii. Here, in brief, is the story. In the early 1950s, confined to a prison camp in the Far North, Pomerants formed a friendship with a young intellectual (identified in the memoir only by the fictive name "Viktor," this is clearly Meletinskii). There, on the camp grounds, they conducted significant philosophical conversations (in which Pomerants worked through his no-longer-viable Hegelianism).[130] There, through the grill of the camp gate, Pomerants saw his friend's beautiful wife, Ira, who made a long and difficult trip for the sake of a brief prison visitation; and there he heard from Viktor the story of his wife's heroic behavior during the investigation. (Participants in the same Leningrad University seminar, V. M. Zhirmunskii's, all three knew each other before the arrest.) After release from the camp, reunited in Moscow, Viktor and Ira felt estranged from each other; Pomerants fell in love with his friend's wife, and in 1956 he became Ira's third husband. To prepare for the eventuality of a future arrest, they were married

---

* Meletinskii's memoir also describes how the investigator, who erroneously believed that he had yet another secret love affair, one with the wife of his colleague, tried—in vain—to force either the wife or the husband into denouncing him. This couple was deemed vulnerable to blackmail not only because of potential for sexual jealousy, but also because the husband, too, had been in prison during the war, and thus was a candidate for a second arrest (520). In his memoir, Meletinskii provides the name of the couple who refused to denounce him. (The "lady" who did denounce him has remained nameless.)

legally, though Ira, as her husband reports, "easily became intimate with men" and generally considered marriage "an immoral institution" (60, 57). They lived happily until her premature death in 1959 during lung surgery to relieve tuberculosis contracted in Siberia, where she lived in the years of Viktor's arrest. From her Pomerants learned other circumstances of the 1949 criminal investigation of Viktor's (that is, Meletinskii's) case. In contrast with Meletinskii, Pomerants describes the situation in great detail. Relating the stories she had once told him, he often speaks from the woman's point of view:

> Ira referred to the investigator as none other than Porfirii Petrovich. [...] The trump card was Viktor's letters to another woman. Ira read them, and looking at her husband's inimitable handwriting, firmly proclaimed that the letters were forged. Porfirii Petrovich decided to wait it out. He was certain that the feeling of wounded pride would do its work (the letters contained several hurtful lines).[131]

But the crafty investigator (nicknamed in honor of the one in charge of Raskolnikov's case) miscalculated. The investigator did not realize that, for this woman, stronger than jealousy and injured pride was another impulse: the sense of solidarity with those who were the objects of persecution by "them" (the agents of repression). Confronted by the evidence of her husband's personal betrayal, the scorned wife did not betray him to Stalin's security service despite intense interrogations, and despite the threats to arrest her as well. (What saved Ira from arrest, Pomerants suggests, was her Russian ethnic background: her husband's case was part of the campaign that targeted Jews.) Moreover, not knowing that the other woman did betray Viktor, Ira even befriended her sexual rival as a gesture of political solidarity (88–89).

In his memoir, Pomerants also provides relevant details of Ira's earlier life. He relates how she left her first husband (the father of her two sons) to marry Viktor, whom she met during the war in Tashkent. Moved by passion and jealousy, her husband, Sergei, an army officer and loyal Soviet citizen, wrote a political denunciation of his rival, a recently released political convict (85). Several years later, during the anticosmopolitan campaign of 1949, this carefully filed denunciation was used to arrest "Viktor." (Recall that in his memoirs Meletinskii provides the last name of his wife's former husband who denounced him; Pomerants gives his first name—they complement each other in making this name public.)

Today's reader may find it difficult to follow the convoluted moves of this real life story, and, like Meletinskii, the reader may find it "nauseating." I have related it, the nauseating quality notwithstanding, to show how the corpus of memoirs that appeared in the 1990s works to reveal the intertwining of intimacy and terror. We have seen several Soviet people who (like many others) easily violated marital loyalty and formed sexual unions without dissolving the previous ones. We have seen how the government authorities used the knowledge (and misinformation) about concealed sexual liaisons of private citizens, obtained through secret surveillance, to force them into collaboration in the process of political terror. We have seen how some people, voluntarily or under extreme pressure, compounded personal betrayal with political denunciation. And we have seen a hero: a woman who (in Pomerants's words) "married three times and tenfold broke the seventh commandment" (57) but who adhered to the strictest moral code in matters of political resistance to the authority of the Stalinist state. We have heard voices of two different participants in this multiangular relationship: one, nauseated by this whole affair, was reluctant to speak; another proved eager to express obvious pride in the woman's heroism and muted disapproval of the man's ("Viktor's") personal disloyalty. We have seen how these people's lives were intertwined during the terror in the 1940s and how their stories, written in private in the 1970s, became intertwined in the 1990s, after the end of Soviet power, when they were published for everybody to see.

There is a yet another perspective on this situation. Long before the two memoirs appeared in print, the story of "Ira" had been told in a novel, *My Favorite Street* (*Liubimaia ulitsa*), written by the prominent journalist and public activist Frida Abramovna Vigdorova (1915–1965)—a member of the same intelligentsia circle. It was published in 1965 at the end of the "thaw." One of the novel's characters, "Irina Ignat'evna" (she shares the name and patronymic with the real person, Irina Ignat'evna Murav'eva), confides her very special story to the main protagonist, an empathic female nurse (who obviously stands in for the author). This conversation takes place on the eve of the dangerous lung surgery that would kill the heroine:

> But this is what I want to tell you. When they took him [*kogda ego vziali*], I was summoned to the investigator and shown a bundle of letters—his letters to another woman. I only read one—no more were necessary. I thought I was going to die. What could I do?[132]

This laconic description would be sufficient for at least some readers in 1965 to grasp the situation (given the limits of what was permissible in the press at the time, the author did not have any other choice). The verb *"vziali"* ("[they] took him"), a colloquialism that denotes arrest, much in use since the 1930s, clearly signals a situation from the terror. The novel hints at the psychological situation of this doubly wronged woman: wronged by her husband, who betrayed her with another woman, and by her state, which arrested the husband and disclosed his marital betrayal, trying, for purposes of its own, to turn the wife against the husband. Indeed, what could she do? The novel's heroine explains to her confidante that she has forgiven, but not forgotten; as other terror wives, she has maintained her marriage by correspondence ("I write to him"), she has waited for his release, and she has decided to undergo risky surgery in anticipation of their reunion. But, as the novel makes clear, she has been deeply traumatized: the effect of those love letters and those interrogations (the "wound" she now carries within her) rendered her relationships with other people "ever more superficial" and her inner life "ever more hidden," at times evading even self-knowledge. She can now lead only a concealed life (332). The fact that the heroine dies the next day, during the surgery, implies that the double wound sustained in the terror proved to be fatal. In this novel (which appeared before either of the memoirs was written), the situation drawn from real life is drastically simplified: there is only one, not three, marriages for the heroine (and her two sons who figure in the novel must belong to *the* husband); there is no pressure on the wife to denounce her husband; the other woman does not give evidence; and neither the seventh commandment nor the institution of marriage has been questioned. Indeed, for reasons of both censorship and genre, a Soviet novel could hardly handle the situation in its manifold complexities (psychological, sexual, political). I would add that Proust, who inspired Pomerants, would have also been at a loss: Dostoevsky alone might have been capable of rising to the occasion. Pomerants seems to suggest as much: in telling this story, he evokes, not only Porfiry Petrovich, but also Mitia Karamazov and Rogozhin from *The Idiot* (53, 85).

So, what happens when a novel and two memoirs tell the same story? The resulting triangular structure is quite complex. Written by a woman (Frida Vigdorova), the 1965 novel took upon itself to provide a glimpse into the psychological situation of a woman at the time of the terror. Confined by restrictions inherent in the medium, it withheld the circumstances of the case, muted the woman's conflict with the state, and erased her sexuality, but, exercising poetic license, the novel created a direct link between the betrayal and the damage to the woman's soul and body. Sounding her confession, the novel purportedly allowed the dead woman to speak for herself. When, years later, the memoirs of the two men appeared in the uncensored post-Soviet press, they supplied, as befits memoirs, the missing factual details. At odds emotionally, the two men complement each other in stating the facts of the case. They also confirm the facticity of the situation described in the novel from the 1960s.

What is more, the juxtaposition of different texts reveals to the reader a secondary story: the story of telling this story. Some readers may compare the two memoirs and the novel. Indeed, in her novel, Vigdorova used the woman's real name and patronymic, making the situation identifiable. Moreover, in 1997–98, the author's daughter disclosed in a memoir (now available on the Internet) that the novel's heroine was based on Irina Murav'eva.[133] Today, readers may notice the relationship of the two memoirists, Meletinskii and Pomerants, to each other, and they may contrast the relationship of each to Irina Murav'eva, and to the act of telling the story. When two consecutive husbands of the same woman described one intimate morally and politically charged situation, they did not refer to each other's memoirs (or to the novel) and did not acknowledge reading each other. (Theoretically, Meletinskii had the opportunity to read Pomerants's memoir, which appeared in 1994, before he published his own, in 1998, at the age of eighty.) But both knew that they could not count on preserving the privacy of their lives. In their society, tangled intimacies were doubly lost: to the political surveillance and to the networking community with a marked proclivity for memoir writing. In a manner of speaking, those general delivery love letters were claimed by more than Stalin's security service: when, with the demise of the Soviet regime, memoirs and documents from Stalin's times appeared in print, these perused love letters, and more, were claimed by the reading public.

Finally, this case allows us to reflect on the relationship between the memoir and the novel. For this purpose, I will use a vignette derived from Pomerants's memoir. He speaks of his wife's remarkable ability to recall and enjoy dreams as if they were real events. For such people, he says, a "geography of dreams" comes into being, which mixes fictive dream images with memories of real places: in a dream, one sees, say, a road that turns toward the river, and feels that the place is familiar—it has been already encountered in another dream. Then, one runs across another place, say, a gate, and realizes that this is a real place and that it comes from real memories (74). The notion of a "geography of dreams" may help to compare the reading of novels and the reading of memoirs. Reading a novel is like dreaming: one encounters places or people that are not real, and thus, they should not be familiar or repeatable. Not so with memoirs: the "geography of memoirs," that is, places, people, and events described in memoirs, are factive, or real; consequently, they can appear in more than one memoir. Vigdorova's *My Favorite Street* is a novel that—in its desire to tell the hidden truth about the terror—has violated the dreamlike fiction of literature. Indeed, reading "Irina Ignatievna's" story of how she saw her husband's love letters in the criminal investigator's office, a reader may feel like a dreamer who has come across a real place in a dream. Of course, only a few readers—members of the immediate circle surrounding Irina Murav'eva who had known this story from confidences, gossip, or rumor—may have actually had this eerie feeling when they read *My Favorite Street* in 1965. But now, in the 1990s, after the memoirs of her two husbands, one after another, appeared in print, every reader can potentially find himself or herself in this situation.

Generalizations: Soviet Memoirs as a Communal Apartment

Scholars have long known that memoir writing is an instrument of both self-creation and community building. For post-Stalin and post-Soviet writers, who produced and published their memoirs under the threat of social crisis and historical rupture, aligning and realigning communities was a most important part of their mission. Soviet memoirs help to align selves, in the presence of the community, across the historical and political divide of Stalinism. By writing memoirs, Soviet people consolidate on paper the tenuous networks of dangerously extended families, intimate circles of like-minded friends, and the visionary community of the "Russian intelligentsia," which seems more important to their identity and authorship than the family. Memoirists negotiate relationships with both their intimate friends and their numberless unknown contemporaries, their potential readers. Massive publication of personal documents creates a larger network, open to all who write and read—the community of "contemporaries." The authors echo one another, disagree, collaborate, and compete in telling the same story. The texts are intertwined by multiple links. Some may claim exclusion on grounds of different political persuasions or aesthetic sensibilities. As a loosely connected, open-ended corpus, diverse personal writings published since 1988 create a space where people who lived under Soviet power gain access to one another's lives. To use a metaphor derived from the texts themselves, this is a textual communal apartment. Members of the intelligentsia come as a group; "simple people" (even illiterate people) are brought in by professional intellectuals; Stalin's loyal subjects sneak in; and Stalin's henchmen make a forceful entry, aided by their children.

A Soviet institution exerting social control through forced intimacy, the communal apartment has become one of the master metaphors of Soviet society.[134] There is not a diary or memoir in which a vivid description of living in a communal apartment does not appear, frequently as a self-conscious emblem of the Soviet experience.

WRITING AT THE END

The offering of personal writings as historical documents has been clearly prompted by a sense of "the end": the end of the Soviet epoch and the end of the twentieth century, eagerly seen as the end of history itself. (This feeling may have a special poignancy for the survivors of communism, with its initial eschatological surcharge and its unfulfilled promise of a boundless future.) Many memoirists articulate this sense. For example, let us take the literary historian and archivist Marietta Chudakova. In the year 2000, she explained in a postscript to her published diary: "With the end of the Soviet epoch and of the century that was marked by it in Russia, what one wrote for oneself lost its intimacy and became a document."[135] Indeed, we have seen how, at the end of the millennium, the Russian writer stands prepared for an instant conversion of intimate writings into historical documents (suffice it to recall the publication history of Nagibin's diary). One of the public spokespersons of perestroika, Chudakova, has been long urging her compatriots to "*create* unofficial, private sources for the future investigation of our time" (her emphasis).[136] Memoir writing is both future historical evidence and—here Chudakova resorts to a popular metaphor—a testimony at the trial of history, which is currently in session: "We testify at the trial of history that has by no means been postponed into the distant, unimaginable future, but rather continues daily, uninterrupted..." This rings of the Hegelian formula of secularized eschatology, "*Weltgeschichte ist Weltgericht*," or, in my loose translation, "World history is an international tribunal." Chudakova consistently speaks in images evocative of the Russian Hegelian tradition: "[The memoirist] carries on his own self the indelible sign of his time."[137] This image seems to echo Herzen's famous metaphor (described earlier), but, judging by her rhetoric, Chudakova envisions, not a man crushed by wheels on the path of history, but a battered defendant in a courtroom: at the end of the twentieth century, the imprints of history are the markings of torture. Memoir writing will take the place of the "Russian Nuremberg" (alas, not to be expected as a judicial procedure):

> The trial of the Communist Party can occur, not during court sessions, but on printed pages in the form of personal accounts and self-analysis of all those who lived and acted during Soviet times. [...] Yes, I am sure: each person who nowadays makes a statement in print, each person who feels a social responsibility must try to write an honest autobiography, his own account of the time he lived through.[138]

Ironically, the idea of enforcing total public accounting for one's past follows, and inverts, autobiographical practices of the early Soviet regime, which encouraged self-surveillance and self-purge as means of creating the new Soviet man.[139] Here, Hegelian historicism meets early Soviet utopianism.

Post-Stalin memoirists invoke the suggestive image of the trial of history, with its apocalyptic associations, incessantly. Veniamin Kaverin called his 1989 memoir "my testimony"; so did Leonid Zorin in the introduction to his memoir-novel: "Possibly my testimony, too, if announced during the trial, will turn out to be somewhat useful..."[140] Stalin's daughter, Svetlana Iosifovna Allilueva (who is the author of a dissertation on the historical novel), evokes the "trial of history" (and the "wheel of history") on the last page of her memoir from the 1960s, *Twenty Letters to a Friend*. Sergo Lavrent'evich Beria also hopes that his father will be judged by "history" ("*sudit' istorii*").[141] The list of examples can be extended. This imagination has been shaped by diverse sources: the Hegelian notion of history as a trial, the memories of Stalinist trials, and the expectation of a higher trial, not only a Russian Nuremberg, but also the Last Judgment.

I believe that the issue is not limited to metaphors. Indeed, in late twentieth-century Russia the familiar notion of world history as a tribunal—a secularized rendition of the idea of the Last Judgment—again acquired a religious apocalyptic ring.[142] Here is the director of the People's Archive, the historian Boris Semenovich Ilizarov, sorting through the archival holdings for accounts of Stalin's death. He imagines Stalin, "mortal like all of us," facing the trial of history, a perpetual, or permanent, trial ("he will give an account [...] eternally"), and awaiting the judgment of the "God of history" (*Bog istorii*).[143] As we learn from Allilueva's later memoir, the 1991 *Book for My Granddaughters,* in more recent years she discussed her father's legacy in the light of the Last Judgment with the head of the Georgian Orthodox Church (he told Svetlana that he had contacts with Stalin's soul in his dreams).[144]

Of course, the apocalyptic forebodings have not been limited to the intellectuals: drawing from her historical experience and from the peasant religious culture, the semiliterate memoirist Evgeniia Kiseleva expresses them as well (when she thinks about the war she had lived through and expects the future nuclear war).[145]

The Archive and the Apocalypse

To demonstrate the force, and another source, of eschatological associations, I examine current meanings of the institution of the archive. A peculiar fusion of professional historiography with religious feeling (at least, with religious metaphors) found a clear and naked expression in the program of the People's Archive. (It should be noted that in daily practice, its mostly volunteer staff conducted their work with dedication and without pathos.) The introduction to the reference guide to the archive's holdings, produced in 1998, explains its ideology: the archive is an instrument of history that extends human life through memory, thus offering a "quality life," or life everlasting. Mixing mystical notions with the Soviet idiom (and with the American coinage "quality of life") and concepts from philosophical historicism with those of computer science, this introduction sets the goals of gathering documents from "ordinary people" in order to offer each and every person immediate assistance in his or her "striving for historical being," or a striving to realize an inherent human "right to immortality" (*pravo na bessmertie*). The policy of the archive follows from its ideology: "By proclaiming that each person has the right to personal immortality, we are committed to accepting everything from everyone." In the end, the People's Archive works for the "total collection of personal documents of the masses" (*total'nyi sbor massovykh lichnykh dokumentov*).[146]

Laden with symbolism (if not mysticism), these ideas have been unfolded in many publications that advocate the People's Archive in the press.[147] By depositing a personal document in such an archive, writes its director, a person "registers in history." (The formula "to register oneself in history" [*propisat' sebia v istorii*] clearly evokes the Soviet institution of mandatory registration of residence, *propiska,* formed from the root "*pisat',*" to write.) And this is a way to immortality: "to register oneself in history means to invest one's life with a larger volume of meaning than fits into the story of a single life, to extend this life beyond the limits of physical existence."[148] But history/future is a heavily populated space: "The future is more and more densely inhabited by images from the past, and this handmade world becomes fuller and fuller."[149] Accepting personal documents from the "rank-and-file" (*riadovoi*) individual, the archive admits the masses into this space: "A person from the masses has not only taken root in the present but strives to be in the future, the last refuge of a unique person."[150] Expressed in this way, the future, identified with both history and the other world, appears as a cramped and socially diverse communal apartment, subject to another form of *propiska* (and thus to another form of surveillance).

This utopian archival policy has recognizable philosophical underpinnings in the "philosophy of the common cause" of the extravagant nineteenth-century Russian thinker Nikolai Fedorov, whose ideal of "real" immortality has exercised a powerful, though not necessarily obvious, influence on Russian thought from the 1860s to the 1930s (and beyond). In brief: fusing Christian mysticism with the positivistic trust in science, Fedorov urged his fellow citizens to devote their collective energy to the "project" (his word) of resurrecting the past in its totality by means ranging from science and cosmic exploration to art and archival preservation. He actually hoped to reassemble the bodies of ancestors from material particles that bear traces of an individual. An archivist by profession, Fedorov envisioned museums and archives as primary sites of resurrection—institutions whose immediate task, as he put it, lay in "the return of life to the remains of the dead, in the restoration of the dead through their works."[151] Fedorov definitely did not mean this metaphorically, but expected actual acts of physical resurrection from personal writings, documents, photographs, and other traces found in archives, museums, and garbage dumps. It has been long known that his vision had a special appeal to the Russian modernist writers, nurtured in the apocalyptic atmosphere of the end of the nineteenth century, and that Fedorovian ideas left an imprint on the revolutionary culture of the 1920s.[152] As I am trying to show, at the end of the twentieth century, Fedorov's utopia of positive resurrection has been consciously revived in archival, publishing, and memoir-writing practices and policies.[153]

The presence of Fedorov is not limited to one institution. Take the series Faces: A Biographical Almanac (Litsa: Biograficheskii al'manakh), devoted to publication of archival documents of individual people. In the introduction to the first issue, its editor, the prominent literary historian Aleksandr Vasil'evich Lavrov, reasons: "totalitarian power" for seventy years "exterminated" the very idea of "human personality"; what is more, it practiced posthumous extermination by obliterating traces of people's lives. Hence, there is a moral imperative to publish personal documents preserved in archives.[154] In contrast to the director of the People's Archive, Lavrov does not indulge in mysticism. But the Fedorovian genealogy of this idea is obvious. For one, the title page of the almanac has a subtitle: "The Biographical Institute [Biograficheskii institut]: Studia Biographica." The Biographical Institute is a project from the revolutionary era, described in a later issue of the almanac by another cultural historian, Aleksandr Etkind. In 1919 the ministry of culture received a proposal for the funding of an institute that would collect and investigate "biographies, autobiographies, diaries, family archives, notes, memoirs, letters, obituaries, curricula vitae, etc.": "The Institute must represent a kind of graphical memory of mankind from generation to generation. [...] At the same time, the Institute must be an international information bureau (*adresnyi stol*) where anyone who has recorded his life path in one way or another will be registered."[155] As Etkind notes, this enterprise was inspired by Fedorov's project of fighting death by means of the archive. It seems that this idea (for lack of funds, it remained unrealized in 1919) has been consciously revived in the almanac launched in 1991. Its editor, Aleksandr Lavrov, is an authority on Fedorov; it was Lavrov, who, in the 1970s, restored the forgotten name of Fedorov to the annals of Russian culture.[156] Thus, like Herzen's historicism (described earlier), Fedorov's ideas have been mediated by professional historians of Russian culture. These ideas have been transformed in accordance with the times: the almanac fights not natural death and historical oblivion, as did Fedorovian projects conceived a hundred years earlier, but the deliberate extermination of people at the hands of totalitarian power.

Individual people, too, found inspiration in Fedorov. Thus, Fedorov's words figure as an epigraph to the diary of the playwright Aleksandr Gladkov, written from 1945 to 1973 and published in 2000: "'History is always resurrection, and not a trial.' N. F. Fedorov."[157] As this gesture suggests, the Fedorovian apocalypticism may be used both as a companion (as in the case of Ilizarov, who imagines Stalin facing the "trial of history") and as an alternative to the Hegelian-Marxist historical eschatology.

The conspicuous writings on the ideology of the People's Archive transform and extend Fedorovian ideas by drawing on new technological resources. In 1998 its director unveiled a plan to open a branch of the archive on the Internet, an act that would assure total preservation of personal records of the whole population: "Virtual space is practically infinite, and new forms of information conservation allow us to pose the question about long-lasting or virtually eternal storage of information." One has to admit that "the first to follow this path were U.S. citizens. Nowadays every citizen of that country can put his memoirs and wishes on the Internet for his descendents." But Americans (the director comments) have been hindered by a lack of ideology and organization. This problem would be resolved if the digital People's Archive were launched out of Moscow, bringing far-reaching results: "The next step in the resolution of the problem of resurrection and immortality might be taken even now, and it can be begun with a total collection of all human information created on the planet Earth."[158] But due to financial difficulties, the construction of this post-Soviet utopia soon came to a halt: the People's Archive lost financial and administrative support from both the city and private organizations.*

To sum up: I suggest that behind such institutions as Chudakova's memoir-writing initiative, the People's Archive, and the biographical almanac *Faces* stands the idea of the end of the epoch, which clearly evokes apocalyptic associations. Such institutions have been consciously built on the nineteenth-century heritage—not only the personal historicism of Russian Hegelianism, but also the Fedorovian utopian philosophy of resurrection, as mediated by professional historians of Russian literature and thought. New elements are clearly identifiable in the old paradigms. Thus, from the twentieth century, these hybrid paradigms inherited, not only a moral imperative of fighting against totalitarianism, but also traces of Soviet ideology; looking toward the future, they appropriate the latest technological advances of American civilization. I would argue that, their professional earnestness notwithstanding, such publishing and archival ventures can be viewed as barely secularized salvation schemes.

The End of the Intelligentsia

It has long been argued that throughout the centuries the eschatological and apocalyptic mentality, ever present in the Western mind, was especially prominent in Russia among common people and intellectuals alike. The catastrophic events of the twentieth century have only reinforced a sense of impending

---

* Between 1988 and 2004 the People's Archive was evicted at least three times. The staff performed their work of preserving the documents in conditions devoid of basic necessities. In April 2004, I found the volunteer staff guarding their holdings in an unheated apartment of a condemned building, which lacked not only a computer but, at that moment, even electricity (Kostomarovskii pereulok 15 apartment 51). The archive was closed soon after. At the time of this writing, there are plans to incorporate the holdings into the state archive, GARF.

or realized doom in the Soviet people. It should be noted that at the end of the twentieth century, it was shared by some of their contemporaries in the West, where historians and sociologists spoke about translation of the ancient apocalyptic tradition into the present age, pondering the limits of secularization.[159] But in Russia, the end was, and still is, a matter of lived experience. With the dissolution of the Soviet regime, people have been confronted with the enormity of past horrors. The promised boundless future of the communist utopia has folded down. They not only remember the dead, but are, once again, acutely concerned with survival: what is at stake is the survival of their established individual and collective identities. Memoirists often lament the end of the "intelligentsia," now threatened in other ways than under the Soviet regime. (Scholars address the topic of the end of the intelligentsia as well.)* Many a memoir written in the 1990s expresses a sense of the vacuity of the present: for many, the Russian present no longer has meaning. And the future is uncertain. Life itself is experienced as endangered, and the feeling of endangerment is projected onto the whole of humankind. I am convinced that in post-Soviet Russia the talk of the end, and the end of the intelligentsia, is imbued with apocalyptic associations that reach beyond rhetoric and beyond metaphor. The boundaries between secular and religious are permeable: prophetic visions inform, not only institutional ideology (as in the case of the optimistic apocalypticism of the People's Archive, intent on finding universal salvation on the Internet), but also personal experience.

I will give several, diverse, examples. In his dignified memoirs completed in the 1990s, the biblical scholar Igor' Mikhailovich D'iakonov (1915–1999) introduces himself as "one of the few remaining members of the old intelligentsia," and, as such, an object of "historical interest" (he defines the "intelligentsia" as "the thinking part of humankind"). The book concludes on a somber note: "By the laws of nature, a human life cannot last forever. If the life of a person can end tragically, why cannot mankind as a whole end tragically?"[160] D'iakonov's remarks are prompted by the coincidence of his individual life with the catastrophic twentieth century. As he writes, in the language of science, "the entropy and chaos keep increasing." The tragedy has a historical motivation. In the conclusion of his memoir, D'iakonov lists names

---

* A standard argument goes as follows: because traditional intelligentsia identity, from the nineteenth century to the Soviet times, rested on opposition to the state, the intelligentsia identity weakens after the end of the repressive Soviet regime. Another argument, advanced by Katerina Clark, starts by pointing out the compatibility between the traditional nineteenth-century intelligentsia and the Soviet regime: a shared faith in the value and power of literature (including its power to "manufacture subjects"), that is, a "vested interest in a text-based culture," and a mistrust of market forces; hence a crisis of the intelligentsia in this particular sense in post-Soviet Russia. Katerina Clark, "The King Is Dead, Long Live the King: Intelligentsia Ideology in Transition," paper presented at the conference "Russia at the End of the 20th Century," Stanford University, 1998, http://www.stanford.edu/group/Russia20/.

of those people (mentioned in his narrative) "who died a nonnatural death": those who "died in genocide" (victims of Stalin's and Hitler's executions and camps), "died of hunger in the [Leningrad] blockade," "died at the front," and, notably, "were subject to repressions and arrest, but survived" (the living dead, so to speak). Entitled *Sinodik* (from the Greek *synodicon;* here, memorial book), this list evokes an Orthodox ritual: the reading of names of the dead and living at a mass to entrust them to God for "eternal memory" and salvation. The memoirist left it unclear whether this somber apocalyptic vision, evoking the past horrors, is predicated solely on the professional knowledge of the apocalyptic tradition or also on personal religious belief.

My other case is the popular Soviet poet Andrei Andreevich Voznesenskii (born in 1933). He, too, styles himself as, first and foremost, a member of the intelligentsia, and he, too, ends his 1998 memoir, *In the Virtual Wind,* with apocalyptic forebodings. Postmodern in form and flamboyant in tone, his apocalypse is presented as a statement of personal belief, not a metaphor. Mixing religious discourse with popular science, Voznesenskii speaks of "acceleration" of time approaching its final point at the millennial anniversary of the birth of Christ, and of the final return to "the genetic code God put in us." By all accounts, the memoirist argues, we should expect the end of the world in the following decade. But perhaps the "mechanical apocalypse" can be averted? Voznesenskii invests his hopes in present-day science, with its ability to transform the "real" into the "virtual." But what about our personal lives, he asks, including the life of the man who wrote this memoir? For one, his own memoir shows a life subsumed by a larger entity, "the Russian intelligentsia": "I started remembering myself, writing a book about a man in time, but what turned out were drafts, sketches of the Russian and other members of the intelligentsia at a turning point." Today, concludes Voznesenskii, "we witness the birth of the universal all-pervasive consciousness, a 'noosphere,'" inhabited by the intelligentsia.[161] This memoirist's hope for universal salvation rests on the survival of the collective spirit embodied in the intelligentsia: "Nowadays many grieve for the passing of the intelligentsia. But it will not pass. It is just changing." The last words of Voznesenskii's memoir: "Yes, Russian intelligentsia, ye..."[162]

Another popular poet of the same, 1960s, generation, Evgenii Evtushenko (born in 1933), while he is not prone to mysticism, also registers a sense of the end. Evtushenko, too, associates the continuity of life with the group of which he feels a part—the group that exemplifies a *Weltgeist* of sorts, the intelligentsia. But he is less optimistic than his fellow pop poet Voznesenskii. Evtushenko ends his 1998 memoir with the text of his appeal to Yeltsin's government, urging it to take immediate measures for the preservation of the literary intelligentsia, whose very existence is threatened. At the moment, he explains, it is threatened by "commercial censorship"—a new peril that replaced the Soviet "political censorship," which had broken so many people in the past. And without "serious literature," argues Evtushenko, the whole country is "spiritually doomed." (There was no answer from the new Russian government.)[163]

Many feel that they live in a world that has come to an end. Ironically, this concerns not only loyal Communists but also those who see themselves as members of the intelligentsia, which implies that they defined themselves in opposition to the Soviet regime. For such people, the threats of the present mirror the threats of the past, reinforcing each other. To give another example, the playwright Viktor Sergeevich Rozov (born in 1913) ends his memoir (written in 1999) with the double rejection of the past and the present, the "Communist dictatorship" and the "dictatorship of democracy" (with its commercialism) as the two forms of absolute power that have threatened his very being.[164]

In everyday life, many a member of the intelligentsia experiences the memories of past horrors, the vacuity of the present, and the uncertainties of the future in an apocalyptic perspective. We have seen that, in this situation, writing or publishing a memoir might be a step toward individual and communal salvation.

QUALIFICATION: THE "I" IN QUOTATION MARKS

In the 1990s and 2000s, postmodernism reached Russia. Remarkably, quite a few authors with distinctly postmodernist sensibilities have produced memoir prose, their distrust of the "real" notwithstanding. (I focus on those of such texts that claim biographical and historical facticity.) Self-conscious and playful, postmodernist memoirs shun the apocalyptic pathos and the Hegelian solemnity of tone. While engaging the idea of personal memory, Soviet past, and collective historical experience, they carefully avoid joining the prominent trend described above. A self-identified Russian postmodernist, Dmitrii Aleksandrovich Prigov (1940–2007), introduced the notion of "the new sincerity," eagerly echoed by critics. "The new sincerity" rests on the acceptance of the fact that "the intimate and the personal," written many times over, has become common and clichéd. The only way to express the intimate or personal would be to reiterate a cliché while claiming its existential validity as a part of *my* experience.[165] The *Stamp Album* by Andrei Iakovlevich Sergeev (1933–1998) and *Past Imperfect* (and its sequels) by the artist Grisha Bruskin (born in 1945, he lives in New York) are among such texts.[166] Defined as "a collection of people, things, words, and relationships," Sergeev's *Stamp Album* is a set of carefully crafted miniatures weaving reminiscences with an occasional document (such as a birth certificate). Bruskin's *Past Imperfect* is an album of the author's family photographs and reproductions of his own pictures, accompanied by short autobiographical stories (less than a page long) arranged in a chronological sequence. I have already mentioned the book of alphabetically arranged notes by the literary scholar Mikhail Gasparov. Another literary scholar, Alexander Zholkovsky (born in 1937, he lives in Los Angeles), cultivates the genre of "vignettes," each of which pictures the author in a situation that purports to be "nonfictional." All of these texts mark their claim to biographical and historical authenticity: Sergeev reproduces family documents; Bruskin includes family photographs; Zholkovsky uses details that call on specific readers to identify the situations from their personal experience. All of these texts also mark their distrust of such staples of the memoir genre as linear life narrative and a stable authorial "I" (or "we"). A sense of irony and a carefully cultivated aesthetic sensibility may (or may not) preserve their authors from all-too-human revelations of intimacy and from violations of the privacy of others. They would not say the word "intelligentsia" without using quotation marks. Neither do they see their writings as testimony at the Hegelian tribunal of world history. As Zholkovsky explains (in an interview posted on the Internet):

> [Vignettes]—these are reminiscences based around some kind of small, inconsequential detail [...] with pretensions to refinement and a certain degree of generalization [...] they make no pretensions to be powerful documents of historical facts or even an adequate reflection of my life or professional activity. [...] Their every word is carefully wrought.[167]

In making this statement, this author shows his awareness of the predominant presence of other memoirs that do purport to "document historical facts." So do others. Prigov called his book of quasi-autobiographical prose *Live in Moscow* (*Zhivite v Moskve*),[168] possibly mocking the title of the solemn memoir by the husband and wife team of dissidents and political émigrés, Lev Kopelev and Raisa Orlova, *We Lived in Moscow* (*My zhili v Moskve*). Using "the currently popular genre of memoirs," Prigov revisited "recognizable" "other people's" topoi of the post-Stalinist memoir: "our" communal apartment (96) and, in immediate textual proximity, Stalin's death, with its requisite tears. He marks his story as unique and real (his own) by evoking a small detail of daily routine: taking a smelly garbage pail out on the day of Stalin's death, which tempered the "mourning enthusiasm" of his thirteen-year-old self (97–105). In their insistence on irony, aesthetic detachment, and play with generic clichés, authors of such maverick texts may refuse to join the specific corpus of memoirs and diaries, but not all of them shun community altogether. Prigov comically laments that he did not know the great people who had lived side-by-side with him: Pasternak, Akhmatova, Iakov Druskin, etc. (90)—thus naming the pillars of the intelligentsia community. Andrei Sergeev supplements his "stamp collection" with the so-called portraits (of people he knew), which include Chukovskii and Akhmatova. These mavericks, too, picture a life that is distinctly "Soviet"—in idiom, setting, graphical emblem. (Perusing his family album, Bruskin comments that most figures from his childhood appear in military uniform.) Most important, they, too, use specific history as a reference point. Sergeev writes:

> I was born in the year that saw Hitler come to power, the completion of the Belomor Canal and the worst famine in the Ukraine.
> In Moscow food was also scarce. My mother couldn't stand potatoes; she lived just on turnips: "You're my turnip-grown one [she used to say]..."[169]

The circumstances of the author's birth are instantly recognizable to contemporary readers, who can not only supply the date (suggested, to suit every political background, by three different markers), but also relate to the intimate part of this story—to the woman pregnant at the time of food shortages. With this self-introduction, Andrei Sergeev makes a move to ground his self in Soviet history, which many of the aesthetically unsophisticated memoirists also made (recall Rodion Nakhapetov or Evgeniia Kiseleva), and, in the same paragraph, claims singularity in a way that is self-consciously idiosyncratic, distinctly personal, and playful. So, what can we make of this carefully crafted self-image—the turnip-grown "I" born in 1933 to the mother who abhorred common potatoes? Is it or is it not an image of self embedded in history?

EXCURSUS: READERS RESPOND IN LIVEJOURNAL

In this century, we have a new forum for reading, writing, and discussing memoirs and, especially, diaries: the Internet and its weblogs, specifically, the website LiveJournal, which has been extremely popular in Russia. Unique for its prominence on the Russian-language Web is the case of Lidiia Ginzburg. LiveJournal has a "community" devoted entirely to Ginzburg and her published notebooks, inaugurated on February 26, 2004:[170]

> This thread was founded in memory of Lidiia Ginzburg (1902–1990). A person widely known in narrow circles, intelligent, mercilessly honest, who has lived through much and survived many. The contents of the site are quotations from the books and notes of Lidiia Ginzburg.
>
> http://community.livejournal.com/lidia_ginsburg

This announcement clearly identifies the significance of Lidiia Ginzburg's name: a person with a high standing in specific circles (within the intelligentsia), she is a survivor and a private chronicler who can be trusted. As we will see, her notebooks have been put to a good use. (Ginzburg herself died in 1990, before the Internet became a household presence in Russia, and in her lifetime she made no personal appearances on the Web.)

In the section that follows, I describe Ginzburg's presence on LiveJournal today, to note her impact and to demonstrate the workings of this new medium and the insights it offers into the workings of the diary. But first, a brief explanation of how LiveJournal works, which at least some of my readers may need.

LiveJournal is a network of weblogs built in the format of personal journals or diaries (the Russian language variant, in use since 2001, is called Zhivoi Zhurnal).[171] Dated entries are placed in reverse chronological order, so that a LiveJournal (its "thread") always opens with today's entry. Depending on the "privacy tools" used, one can maintain a private journal, share one's journal with select others, or keep a public personal journal for everybody to see. Rather than write under their own names, most online diarists use assumed "usernames" and graphic personal emblems ("userpics"). A LiveJournal provides links to diaries of "friends" (Russian *frendy*), so that one can see at a glance what other people chosen for one's "friends list" wrote on a particular day. There are also group journals, dubbed "communities," open to an expandable group of members, or "users" (*iuzery*); they function as social networks by allowing a group of people to comment on one another's diaries. In a word, individual people and whole communities keep online ("live") diaries, and, moreover, build tangible communities by reading, and writing into, one another's diaries.

A search of the Russian LiveJournal websites (even apart from the Community Lidia_Ginzburg) reveals that quite a few online diarists record the very fact of reading Ginzburg's notebooks:

> mama's gone. [English in the original] I've been reading Lidiia Ginzburg all day (and—strange as it is to think, a whole day of my life, as well as its future course (because now I'll be thinking about LG nonstop for some time, recommending her to my friends...) has undergone such a change all because of a quote from LG caught my eye in the ru_history community.) And part 2 of the textbook on the Middle Ages is still lying there on my left.
>
> 2004-04-06 www.livejournal.com/users/calabazza/33836.html

> I'm reading Lidiia Ginzburg's diaries.
>
> 2005-12-12 www.azebaijan.ru/usp-frm.php?usp_id=97889&id=97889

I'm at home, sick, reading Lidiia Ginzburg.

2006-03-20 impf.livejournal.com/2977.html

I read Lidiia Ginzburg at the dacha—memoirs—interesting on the topic of old age.

2006-05-15 turchin.livejournal.com/172562.html

Some such readers use a published edition of Ginzburg's notes, but others read on the Internet, having accidentally hit upon a quotation while surfing the Web. (Such is the case of the very young diarist who reads Ginzburg in her mother's absence while neglecting a history textbook.) Having posted their diaries on the Web, these people establish a connection simply by claiming: here I sit, reading Lidiia Ginzburg. Describing the circumstances in which they read, they admit others into their domestic spaces. And such shared encounters with Ginzburg may become extremely intimate:

> I wouldn't mind getting up early, shuffling barefoot to the kitchen and making some green tea with jasmine for the one who's dear to me. I wouldn't even mind sitting for two hours, holding his head on my lap, flicking through the pages of a book by Lidiia Ginzburg with one hand and, with the other, stroking his face and long hair that spills over my bed like a stream.
>
> 2004-07-19 enka-homs.livejournal.com/33684.html

Another user shows how surfing others' LiveJournals has opened a way for intimate contact with Ginzburg:

> Of all things—I spotted Lidiia Iakovlevna Ginzburg on LJ [LiveJournal]. I'm glad. But instead of being plagued by existential problems, I ended up reading that *in Lidiia Ginzburg's home, vodka, herring and eggs in mayonnaise were plentiful.*

(The image of Lidiia Ginzburg treating her guests to vodka in her tiny kitchen is a topos of memoirs about her, which appear in abundance, in print and on the Internet.)

What immediately follows is a conscious announced act of identification with Ginzburg:

> ☺ And so—I can be just like Ginzburg now.
> But on the whole, it's hard for me to discuss such things, and good that one can read about them quietly.
>
> 2004-03-13 starushka.livejournal.com/67453.html

The screen name used in this LiveJournal, "starushka" (old woman)—this is how Ginzburg was fondly called by those who had actually partaken of vodka and eggs in mayonnaise in her tiny kitchen. (This fact, too, has been disclosed in memoirs.) This diarist uses Ginzburg's nickname as her own. And rather than discuss her reactions to Ginzburg's notes, this diarist would prefer to "be like Ginzburg," that is, to read Ginzburg's notes silently producing a story of her own life. This reaction is not unique. Another user also declares: "Instead of writing, I read." And she suggests to those who read her journal a "new game," in which she will be "our Lidiia Ginzburg. That is, now I'll be an old scholarly Jewish woman..."[172] (The old game was "our Anna Akhmatova.")

A comment is due on "he/she": tracing the real identities of some live-diarists on the Internet, I discovered that there are both women and men, mostly young, among those who project a female image by using Ginzburg's photograph in her wise old age as an identifying emblem. They could have taken the cue from Ginzburg herself, who carefully cultivated a genderless self (grammatically male) in her personal writings.

The "game"—to read and write Ginzburg's notes as one's own diary—has been practiced by the Community Lidia_Ginzburg—whose members exchange excerpts from Ginzburg's notebooks, ranging in topics from the "intelligentsia" to unrequited love to the weather to gossip. Some confirm the validity of Ginzburg's aphoristic entries with an occasional comment: "That's it exactly!" "That's about us." "I Endorse Every Word" (*Ochen' tochno! Eto pro nas. PPKS—Podpisyvaius' Pod Kazhdym Slovom*), and, in awkward English, "I thought right now the same."[173] Some appropriate Ginzburg's words to express their own reactions to specific daily events. Thus, on one April day in 2005, a live-diarist posted—without quotation marks—Ginzburg's musings on April weather, borrowed from her notebooks, which starts:

April has brought me again to the same city outskirts for a few days...

2005-04-29 http://community.livejournal.com/lidia_ginsburg/55854.html

In a word, Lidia_Ginzburg is a community of online diarists (men and women) who borrow Ginzburg's identity, her words, and her photo image to help them in self-expression.

Most of those who engage in this act of appropriation do this in full awareness of what they are doing, but some fall victim to the Internet-induced illusion of immediacy and presence. Consider the following exchange. One live-diarist (who signs "lonely-seeker") has appropriated Ginzburg's words in her own personal journal, posted on June 22, 2006, at 4:20 a.m.:

> The shortest night of the year is drawing to a close...
> *One works well and happily only when the work suffuses one's consciousness. I like writing by night, because at night that dissipating sense of the passage of time is lost....* Lidia_Ginzburg.
>
> 2006-06-22 lonely-seeker.livejournal.com

The italicized text is Ginzburg's, borrowed from the Internet Community Lidia_Ginzburg. Another user of LiveJournal, who has stumbled across this entry while surfing the Web, commented in his/her journal:

> Two weeks ago Lidia_Ginzburg wrote in her journal how valued the nighttime is for untethering one from chronology—she's my favorite user; every word comes loaded with a weightiness...
>
> 2006-02-10 bars-of-cage.livejournal.com/154086.html

This Internet diarist seems to think that Lidia_Ginzburg is a living "user" who has actually posted the passage about nighttime writing on June 22, 2006. In the end, in this, as well as other, Internet communities, the sense of time and distance between people is lost.

It may not be an accident that, of all the diarists and memoirists, it is Lidiia Ginzburg whose notebooks have been freely inhabited by our contemporaries to accommodate their own selves. A renowned literary historian who interpreted such pertinent themes, names, and forms of the Russian tradition as historicism, Herzen, and "psychological prose"; a writer in her own right, who cultivated "in-between" genres, such that would make it possible to retain nineteenth-century historicism in an atmosphere permeated with the modernist and Soviet ethos; and, as it became widely known to readers only in the late 1980s when her notebooks appeared in print, a persistent private chronicler of her age (from the 1920s to the 1980s), Lidiia Ginzburg is a prime candidate to become a literary hero of our time.[174] Throughout this book, I try to maintain the presence of her shadow.

CONCLUDING REMARKS

The texts are many and varied. As I hope to have made clear, I am not arguing for sameness. Claiming that the massive appearance of human documents represents a distinct trend, I have looked for common patterns and meanings. Diverse as they are, memoirs and diaries published en masse at the end of the

Soviet epoch tend to tell stories of intimate lives shaped by catastrophic political and historical forces, with the terror and the war figuring as the defining moments and organizing metaphors.

Obviously, commonalities stem from the shared experiences of life in the Soviet Union (diverse as they may have been) and from the shared cultural and literary tradition. And, inasmuch as the texts are constructed at the time of their publication, the commonalities also stem from a shared experience of the present: a sense of the end (inspired by influences as diverse as Christian and Hegelian/Marxist eschatology and modernist and postmodernist sensibilities).

We have seen that for Soviet authors the interrelated acts of writing about one's life, reading about the life of the other, and collecting personal documents serve not only the purposes of commemorating and mastering the past. For one, this is also about filling the vacuousness of the post-Soviet present. It is also about revealing to one another what has been hidden under the Soviet conditions. In the end, it is about realigning selves and communities. Moreover, survivors of Communism started a new utopian project: to inhabit the future. Accordingly, this project pursues a supergoal: "salvation" (in a secular or a pseudoreligious key).

So, the categories of "memory," "testimony," "trauma," and "mastering the past," which have been productively applied to the Holocaust (and other cases), may be applicable to personal accounts of the Soviet experience, but, I think, they are far from sufficient for their interpretation.

A bird's-eye view, such as the one presented above, is far from sufficient for the interpretation of these texts. On the pages that follow, I supplement this overview by providing close readings of two complete texts, chosen from this vast corpus to probe both the commonalities and the differences.

PART II

TWO TEXTS
Close Readings

To supplement the survey of a large corpus of diaries and memoirs of the Soviet experience, I will now provide slow, close readings of two specific documents, selected for their exceptional quality in scope, insight, and emotional power and for their demonstrated impact on readers. The two texts come from the opposite ends of the social and literary spectrum. Both of them present lives shaped by historical and political forces. The first text, Lidiia Chukovskaia's *Notes about Anna Akhmatova* is the work of a professional editor who aspired to document the difficult life of her intimate friend, the great Russian poet; it follows two interconnected lives between the 1930s and the 1960s. The second text, the notebooks of Evgeniia Kiseleva, is the work of a barely literate author, transcribed and published by a team of scholars; it depicts the life of a former peasant between the 1940s and the 1980s. I treat both Chukovskaia's *Notes* and Kiseleva's notebooks as autobiographical narratives and as ethnographic documents, each of which reveals—in both what it describes and in how it does it—the link between intimacy and (Soviet) history. The overt differences in literary quality notwithstanding, I have chosen to take the same approach to both of these documents. Among the questions I ask are the following: What role does life-writing play in each author's life? How is each of these documents produced? What does each document tell us about the ways in which intimate ties, families, and homes are formed, maintained, and dissolved under specific historical and social circumstances? How do the Soviet state and the idea of history enter lives and life stories?

My goal is to present the documents themselves and the people who emerge from them. The texts will lead, and my explications will follow. Accordingly, I will proceed chronologically, page by page.

CHAPTER 1

Lidiia Chukovskaia's Diary of Anna Akhmatova's Life
"Intimacy and Terror"

In the years 1938–42 and 1952–65, the editor and literary scholar Lidiia Korneevna Chukovskaia (1907–1996) documented, day by day, her meetings and conversations with her intimate friend Anna Andreevna Akhmatova (1889–1966). (As she would later explain, during the years of the terror she was unable to keep a diary of her own life.) Preparing her *Notes about Anna Akhmatova* for publication between the 1960s and 1990s, she supplied extensive historical commentary on the people and events, as known from the vantage point of later times, creating a large section entitled "Behind the Scenes" (*Za stsenoi*).[1] This formidable document—which took thirty years in writing and thirty more years in editing—serves many purposes. The status of Akhmatova—a major cult poet of the twentieth century—confers special significance on this record. For her admiring readers, Anna Akhmatova—"a sort of *mater dolorosa* of Stalinism and torchbearer of the Great Russian Cultural Tradition combined"—has come to represent the destiny of which others like to count themselves a part.[2] This document's peculiar mode makes this clear: Chukovskaia is writing Akhmatova's life, and, in the process, she is writing her own life; working for the immortality of the poet, she assures her own survival. For years, Chukovskaia served as Akhmatova's confidante, chronicler, and personal helper in charge of daily chores. A professional editor, she worked with drafts, adding punctuation marks and suggesting phrasing. A sensitive listener, Chukovskaia heard Akhmatova speak about her current family drama, her past, her fleeting thoughts, and much more. One scholar described this relationship in psychoanalytic terms as that between analysand (Akhmatova) and analyst (Chukovskaia), in which the analyst comes to serve in the role of "editor," complicit in the process of constructing a life narrative.[3] What is more, Chukovskaia memorized Akhmatova's unpublishable politically compromising verse by heart, serving as a "living archive." Chukovskaia's diary documents how Akhmatova's *Requiem* for Stalin's victims (1935–62) and her lyrical history of the twentieth century, *A Poem without a Hero* (*Poema bez geroia*, 1940–62), took form over the years: as unwritten texts, literally "embodied" by the reader.[4] Chukovskaia's notes contribute to Akhmatova's standing as a cultural icon, but there is more to this document than its mythopoetic and biographical value. For me, this document is important also for its ethnographic value: Chukovskaia worked as a self-conscious participant-observer, who meticulously described situations, settings, procedures, transactions, rituals, mythologies, and conversations. (Intent on preserving their speech, Chukovskaia strove to report conversations verbatim.) In the end, Chukovskaia's diary opens up the culture of a group of which Akhmatova was held to be an emblematic example.

Those whose daily lives are described in this document share a group identity: the Russian "intelligentsia," specifically, the literary intelligentsia. This implies an unswerving and uncritical allegiance to values associated with the nineteenth-century intelligentsia tradition: alienation from the establishment; rejection of accepted living forms; valorization of poverty, suffering, and self-denial; reliance on the written word for self-expression and self-preservation; staunch belief in literature as a source of moral authority; and an overwhelming sense of the historical significance of one's personal life. Under the Soviet regime—with the state attempting to co-opt the literary intelligentsia into the official social hierarchy—belonging to this group also implies an uneasy relationship to the state power: a double bind of privilege and martyrdom.

The diary is dominated by the terror. Begun during its worst days, the writing was fueled by preoccupation with survival—survival through a literary record that would preserve traces of endangered lives day by day. Yet, the project is fraught with paradox because it exposed both Chukovskaia and Akhmatova (who did not know of its existence, or so it seemed) to considerable danger. (Diaries were habitually confiscated during searches and used as evidence of anti-Soviet persuasion.) Chukovskaia's 1966 foreword to the first, clandestine, publication of her Akhmatova journals describes the agony she had then felt: "To write down our conversations—wouldn't that mean risking her life? Not to write anything about her? This would also be criminal" (1:12; 5). Terror is present in the act of writing, and in the potential act of not writing.

The journal begins: "10 November [19]38. Yesterday I was at Anna Andreevna's on business* (1:17; 9). The asterisked footnote explains the "business": rumors were circulating that when her son, Lev Nikolaevich Gumilev, was arrested, Akhmatova had written a letter to Stalin and he had been released. Chukovskaia, whose husband Matvei Petrovich Bronshtein had been arrested in August 1937, went to find out what she had written.* In this first entry, Chukovskaia describes her entrance step-by-step: up the "tricky" back staircase, through the shabby entrance hall with its scraps of peeling wallpaper, through the kitchen strung with washing lines, past a woman with soapy hands who opened the door—"something out of Dostoevsky"—and finally into Akhmatova's room:[5]

> The general appearance of the room was one of neglect, ruin. By the stove, an armchair, missing a leg, ragged, springs protruding. The floor unswept. The beautiful things—the carved chair, the mirror in its smooth bronze frame, the lubok prints on the walls—did not adorn the room; on the contrary, they only emphasized its squalor further. (1:17; 10)

Akhmatova explained that, for more than one reason, even hanging pictures on the wall was no longer worth the trouble: "On 19 September, I left Nikolai Nikolaevich. We lived together for sixteen years. But I didn't even notice against *this* background" (1:17; 10). The background is the terror: on September 27, her son, Lev, was sentenced to ten years and deported to the Belomor Canal construction site (he was later returned for further interrogation). The account of the next meeting between Chukovskaia and Akhmatova, on February 22, 1939, starts with Akhmatova's comment: "I can't look at those eyes. Have you noticed? They seem to exist apart from the faces" (1:22; 13). It was clear to both that the comment concerned the eyes of the women who lined up in front of the prisons and prosecutor's offices waiting for news about their arrested kin. Akhmatova then complained about her neighbors in the communal apartment, the Smirnovs: "My neighbor doesn't love her boy. When she takes the strap to him, I go into the bathroom. I tried to talk to her once—she rebuffed me" (1:22; 13).

About a week later, on March 3, the two women met in Moscow: "'What's new?' asked Anna Andreevna, jumping up from the divan and bringing her face up to mine, wide-eyes" (1:22; 14). Both women traveled to Moscow (the seat of central power) to make inquiries and appeals. As always, Chukovskaia describes the setting in detail:

> This was in Khardzhiev's tiny room, somewhere in the back of beyond; it has taken me about two hours to get there. [...] It was cold at Nikolai Ivanovich's. Anna Andreevna was sitting on the divan, her coat draped

---

* These rumors conflated two different occasions: it was in 1935 that Akhamtova's letter to Stalin helped to obtain the release of both her son and her husband, Nikolai Punin. In 1938 (when Lev was arrested again) another letter of this kind had no effect.

around her shoulders. We drank tea out of mugs, and then wine from the same ones. Nikolai Ivanovich, unshaven, yellow, is listening to the footsteps on the other side of the wall—to the neighbors' footsteps. (1:22; 15)

Nikolai Ivanovich Khardzhiev, a literary critic and collector of avant-garde art, belonged to the same close-knit milieu. All three shared a sense of displacement and danger, as well as acute ethical and aesthetic sensibilities. The diarist went on to describe their conversation about Alexander Herzen and his famous memoirs. Akhmatova commented that she did not like the flagrant revelations of his intimate life made in *My Past and Thoughts*. Chukovskaia defended Herzen: he wrote for history (1:22).

These vignettes from the opening pages of Chukovskaia's diary display several organizing principles: the primacy of the terror as a context that distorts all living forms, prompting intimacy (instant understanding among members of the group and intense fear of others); the formative pressure of the living conditions (the restriction of space and the forced proximity to one another); the poverty and neglect endowed with considerable moral value and symbolic significance; and the abiding presence of literature and history.

THE YEARS OF TERROR: IN "THE TORTURE CHAMBER"

Chukovskaia's code word for the terror was "*zastenok*"—literally, "behind-the-wall-space"; the immediate meaning, "torture chamber." In the 1966 foreword, she wrote about the terror as a total condition that remained unnamed. "Torture chamber" has swallowed up whole quarters of the city as well as "all our conscious and unconscious thoughts," and yet "demanded of us that we should not take its name in vain, even within four walls, tête-à-tête" (1:12–13; 6). *Zastenok* organized the conditions of speaking, which Chukovskaia also described in minute detail:

> women stood in line in silence, or whispering, used only indefinite forms of speech: "they came," "they took"; Anna Andreevna, when visiting me, recited parts of *Requiem* also in a whisper; suddenly, in midconversation, she would fall silent and, signaling to me with her eyes at the ceiling and walls, she would get a scrap of paper and a pencil; then she would loudly say something very mundane: "Would you like some tea?" [...], then she would cover the scrap in hurried handwriting and pass it to me. I would read the poetry and, having memorized it, would hand

it back to her in silence. "How early autumn came this year," Anna Andreevna would say loudly and, striking a match, would burn the paper over an ashtray. (1:13; 6)

She commented: "It was a ritual: hands, match, ashtray—a beautiful and mournful ritual" (1:13; 6). The diary notes the instances in which Akhmatova "performed the ritual" (1:99; 1:121). As the word choice indicates, Chukovskaia felt that she served as an ethnographer of exotic rites.[6]

In the foreword, Chukovskaia, a lifelong diarist, explained how, in the years of the terror, she found herself unable to take notes on her own life and came to write a diary for another:

Day by day, month by month, my fragmentary notes became less and less a recreation of my own life, turning into episodes in the life of Anna Akhmatova.
[...] In the mental state in which I existed during those years—stunned, deadened—I seemed to myself less and less truly alive, and my nonlife unworthy of description. By 1940, I had virtually ceased making notes about myself, whereas I wrote about Anna Andreevna more and more often. [...] Before my own eyes, Akhmatova's fate—something greater even than her own person—shaped this famous and neglected, strong and helpless, woman into a statue of grief, loneliness, pride, courage. (1:13–14; 6)

As a superindividual, a cultural artifact of sorts, Akhmatova, with all her contradictory humanity, seemed particularly durable, monumental. Accordingly, a record of Akhmatova's life assured her companion and scribe survival in history. Akhmatova's life was inhabited by the diarist's deadened self.

Prominent in the journal are step-by-step accounts of the living forms peculiar to the time of the terror. One of them was made on August 28, 1939. For the sake of conspiracy, the diary does not use the words "terror," "prison," or "deportation" even once. This is how Chukovskaia starts (I paraphrase): On August 14, I had a call. Akhmatova said one word: "Come!" I came instantly. Right by the door, she announced her news. I tried to work out what was to be done. "I managed quite quickly, by phone, to arrange for a hat, a scarf, and a sweater. Everyone I called understood everything immediately, with no questions. 'A hat? No, I don't have a hat, but do you need some mittens?'" (1:42; 31).

Even in the 1960s, a Russian reader would understand instantly what was going on, but (perhaps thinking of the distant future or foreign reader) Chukovskaia adds a footnote: that day Akhmatova learned that her son was about to be deported to a camp in the Far North; they had to obtain warm clothing for the prisoner. Things were scarce, and this called for a collective effort.

The story continues to describe a long trolley ride the two women made, in silence, to a distant neighborhood, where they went "to fetch the boots." Lev's boots (a luxury) had been lent to his friend Kolya. They found the friend in a room decorated in a "petit-bourgeois style." (Chukovskaia defines the domestic space in sociological terms, "*meshchanski ubrannuiu,*" marking its alien quality.) At the end of the day, after calling on various people, Chukovskaia, accompanied by a friend, went to Akhmatova's place again, bringing warm things. The friend, Shura, was not personally acquainted with Akhmatova, but this was of no significance. In Akhmatova's room, Chukovskaia saw a woman she did not know sewing by the window; Shura also started to sew: prison-house rules required a parcel to be packed in a hand-sewn bag made according to precise specifications (1:42–43; 31). (Akhmatova did not sew.) Next morning, Akhmatova went to visit her son in prison. Accompanied by Chukovskaia and by Lev's friend Kolya, she took her place in the notorious prison line, every moment of waiting recorded by her companion, who called it "torture by standing." Chukovskaia saw her friend to the prison door, but her account stops there. One can find the second part of the story in the 1998 memoir of another member of this circle, Emma Grigor'evna Gershtein, which describes the conversation between mother and son. (Akhmatova related it to her because Gershtein was then involved in a love relationship with Lev.)[7]

As for Chukovskaia's husband, in December 1939 Chukovskaia learned that Matvei Bronshtein, ostensibly sentenced to ten years in remote camps, had been executed. The diary does not describe what she learned; it describes her sense of pain ("everything ached: my face, feet, heart, even the skin of my head" 1:63; 48) and relates a brief conversation with Akhmatova. On that day, Akhmatova was preoccupied with the story of her sixteen visits to the *upravdom* (house manager) whose signature was required for cashing her disability pension:

> I presume I kept up the conversation very badly, as after about ten minutes, she asked: "You seem to be upset about something?"
> I said it—without bursting into tears.
> "My God. My God," repeated Anna Andreevna, "and I didn't know....My God!"
> It was time for me to pick up [my daughter] Lyusha from her teacher's. I left. (1:63; 48)

Combined with a footnote (appended much later) that tells what she had learned and told Akhmatova on that day, this understatement (caused, at least in part, by the conditions of coded writing) captures the quotidian quality of the terror—its penetration into the texture of day-to-day life, which ran its course, as always, by way of domestic arrangements.

The all-penetrating quality of the terror is at its most intense in the feeling of being under surveillance, carefully conveyed in the diary. On August 17, 1940, returning in the morning from a quick shopping trip, a loaf of bread in one hand and postal stamps in the other, Chukovskaia ran into Akhmatova's friend, caretaker, and lover, Vladimir Georgievich Garshin. In tears, Garshin told Chukovskaia a story that she encoded with the single word: "*volosok*" (a hair). An appended footnote explains the situation to the reader: suspecting that her writings were secretly perused, Akhmatova placed a hair in a notebook; when she returned to the room and found the hair missing or moved, she became certain that the room was searched while she stepped out. For Garshin (a medical pathologist by profession and a relation of the nineteenth-century writer Vsevolod Garshin, who died insane), this behavior was a sign of impending mental illness. But Chukovskaia asked: "And what if our imagination stops short of grasping her situation? What if this is not a psychosis?" Yet a visit to Akhmatova convinced her that, whether or not the hair was moved, Akhmatova—visibly agitated and irritable—was not well (1:177–78).

As Chukovskaia claimed in 1966, back then, in the late 1930s, the sense of terror had been all-pervasive: "In those years, Anna Andreevna lived under the spell of the torture chamber, demanding from herself and others constant memory of it, despising those who behaved as though it didn't exist" (1:12; 5). Chukovskaia returned to this theme in the unfinished documentary book about her husband, commenting on the clear division between those who were touched by the terror and those others—a whole cityful—who remained oblivious to it:

> The city went on living its usual life: working, studying, falling in love, reading the newspapers, taking time off, listening to the radio, going to the theater, cinema, round to friends' houses. Celebrating in earnest the birthdays of friends and loved ones. Families gathering for the May and November holidays. Merrily seeing in the New Year. [...] And all this, perhaps, was most terrible of all.[8]

But, as other memoirs reveal, not everybody shared this clear-cut vision. In her retrospective essay on the 1930s (written in 1980), the literary scholar Lidiia Iakovlevna Ginzburg (a frequent visitor to the apartment, she appears on the pages of Chukovskaia's journals) offered a different analysis of life during these years:

> The terrible backdrop did not leave one's consciousness. The very same people who, in the morning, had received news of the loss of their loved ones in the terror, attended the ballet, were entertained as guests, played cards, and relaxed at the dacha. Those same people who went cold at the

sound of every nighttime ring of the doorbell, awaiting arrest. While one is still safe, one shields oneself, distracts oneself: Seize the day.

The summer vacation offered a ready means of distraction. [...] In the summer of '37 many of my Leningrad acquaintances visited splendid Zatulenie, near Luga. There we savored the delights of forest lakes and the river Oredezh with its meadows and red clay banks. We went boating, we went on walks, and even S., whose sister was under arrest and awaiting sentence, actively participated. Psychologically, this was possible because it had become a typical scenario.

In the summer of '38, the Zhirmunskys, the Gukovskys, and I stayed in the countryside in the Poltava region [of Ukraine]. The memory of the famine [1932–33] was still recent there, and we had left devastation behind us in Leningrad. We spent the time most pleasantly. We went exploring in boats and set ashore on some uninhabited island. We went to the city of Poltava for a few days and had all sorts of amusing exploits along the way. And all the while, as we so enjoyed ourselves, conscience never once intruded. Probably because we knew something might happen to any one of us at any moment. Just as in war.[9]

We see a discrepancy between the two accounts of how "we" lived produced by people from the same milieu. It may not be possible to say whether Chukovskaia's account suffers from a (perhaps retrospective) illusion about the all-encompassing quality of the terror or whether the two small, interconnected groups indeed lived differently.

FAMILY AND HOME: "THE CESSPIT OF A COMMUNAL APARTMENT"

No other theme appears in Chukovskaia's chronicle as often as that of living space and living conditions, and often interwoven with the theme of the terror. She carefully notes the difficulties encountered by Akhmatova in her day-to-day life: resources (money, material goods, food) were scarce; neglect and decay were prevalent (affecting rooms, things, and bodies); daily life was devoid of established routine (shopping and taking meals); there was also considerable moral discomfort. Shortages and restrictions imposed by the Soviet state, experimental living inspired by the revolutionary era, and bohemian habits instilled by modernism seemed to work in tandem to produce difficult and bizarre situations. Many of those who wrote about Anna Akhmatova focus on her living situation and on the apartment on the Fontanka River. Contemporaries left meticulous accounts of the squalor. Most scholars echo the memoirists. One critic shows how Akhmatova used her complicated relationship to her immediate surroundings—"a cesspit of a communal apartment" (Chukovskaia's phrase)—as a source of poetic inspiration.[10] At the end of the Soviet regime (in 1989), the apartment became a museum (Muzei-kvartira Anny Akhmatovoi), which offers a reconstruction, and carefully arranged rooms are full of household items—mostly beautiful things. In more ways than one, the apartment has turned into a notable cultural institution: described by contemporaries in their memoirs, reproduced by museum workers, and deconstructed by today's scholars, this complicated space serves not only as a monument to the life of the great poet, but also as an emblem of the human condition under the Soviet power. What marks the present case is, above all, a combination of the ordinary and extraordinary.

Overview of Circumstances

It was at the end of 1926 that Akhmatova moved to the apartment in the kitchen wing of the Sheremetev Palace on the river Fontanka (the so-called House on the Fontanka), which Nikolai Nikolaevich Punin, her companion since 1923, shared with his wife, Anna Evgen'evna Arens-Punina, their small daughter, Irina Punina, their house servant, Anna Bogdanovna Smirnova, and her young son, Evgeny (Zhenia) Smirnov.[11] (For various reasons, Akhmatova's previous home—two rooms in the service wing of the Marble Palace, shared with her long-estranged second husband, Vladimir Kazimirovich Shileiko, and a stray dog, a St. Bernard by the name of Tap—was no longer inhabitable.)[12]

In the early 1920s, in the course of postrevolutionary redistribution of living space and public roles, Nikolai Punin, then an employee of the Russian Museum of Art, was allocated an apartment in a museum space: the kitchen wing of the eighteenth-century Sheremetev Palace.* After nationalization in 1918, the palace of the counts Sheremetevs had been turned into the Museum of Gentry Culture (Muzei dvorianskogo byta), later renamed the Museum of Serfdom (Muzei krepostnogo prava), which it remained until the mid-1930s. (In the same spirit, Vladimir Shileiko, a scholar who worked for the new Russian Academy of the History of Material Culture, was allocated a small apartment in a wing of another nationalized palace, which housed the academy and its museum.)

---

* For several years after the revolution, Nikolai Punin, then a theoretician of revolutionary and futurist art, occupied positions in the newly created organs that administered art. Between 1918 and 1921, he was a deputy head of the Department of Fine Arts (IZO), created with his active participation within the Ministry of Enlightenment (Narodnyi komissariat prosveshcheniia). Among his other government assignments, Punin was appointed "komissar of the Russian Museum" and "komissar of the Hermitage." By 1922 Punin's government career was over: it ended in August 1921, when he was arrested, with a large group of others accused of participation in a counterrevolutionary "militant organization." Among them was Akhmatova's former husband, Nikolai Gumilev, who was executed. Nikolai Punin was released. See *Mir svetel*, 11–13.

From the 1920s to the 1930s, the living space in the once large apartment of the Punins kept shrinking. It the early 1920s, life still followed the old bourgeois order: rooms were known as "the study," "the dining room," "the nursery." The kitchen was inhabited by the old servant, Anna Smirnova (called in an old-world manner by the diminutive Annushka, and in the new Soviet way, "house worker," *domrabotnitsa*), who would start the day by stoking a wood stove. By 1925, at Punin's suggestion, she was joined by her young son. (Since childhood, Evgeny had been treated as a family member by Nikolai Punin's well-to-do gentry parents, especially after his father, their coachman, was killed in the First World War.)[13]

When Akhmatova moved in, she settled in Punin's study. In 1929, Akhmatova's sixteen-year old son, Lev Gumilev (who had long lived with his paternal grandmother), joined the family; he slept on a chest in the corridor's dead end, later separated by a curtain and designated "Lev's study." Throughout the 1920s and 1930s, this relatively small apartment also sheltered many of the Punins' relatives.

In the early 1930s, Evgeny Smirnov married; his mother, the Punins' old servant Annushka, was moved to a state home for the elderly, and his wife, Tat'iana, claimed a room for the family as rightful tenants. By late 1938, when Chukovskaia started her chronicle, the Smirnovs, who worked at a shipbuilding factory, had two sons, Valya, born in 1932, and Vova, born in 1938.

Years later, Irina Punina described the installment of the Smirnovs in the dining room as a decisive transformation that turned a family home into a communal space. Speaking in the 1990s, she connected these domestic developments to the political situation in Soviet Russia after 1929: "when Stalin consolidated power [...] the gradual assault began on the whole life of our country, and our apartment was not exempt."[14] A child at the time, Irina Punina remembered how, with all its doors now opening not into the suite of interconnected rooms, as earlier, but onto the corridor, the place became cold, so that Anna Andreevna would put on a fur coat when she stepped out of her room to use the telephone.[15]

The curators of the Anna Akhmatova Apartment Museum described the situation of the Punins and Akhmatova, on the one side, and the changing Smirnov family, on the other, in class terms: Tat'iana Smirnova, who moved from the countryside to the city to take up factory work, considered herself a member of the ruling class—the proletariat. Bolstered by her new status, she took it on herself to instruct the Punins and Akhmatova in how one ought to live, and would threaten to denounce the fellow inhabitants of the apartment to the state security.[16]

Indeed, the changes in this family's domestic situation marked the consolidation of the new life order: the housing shortages (which increased in the 1930s, when forced collectivization of agriculture and rapid industrialization inspired an influx of villagers into the cities) and the policy of mixing people from different social classes created a unique Soviet institution: the communal apartment. In the 1930s, communal apartments became a staple of the Soviet way of life—an institution of shortage, social engineering, and political control.

Clearly, it would be impossible for any museum to represent this space. In the Anna Akhmatova Apartment Museum, the frozen moments from different periods coexist: the common dining room from the late 1920s; the Akhmatova room in the former "nursery" from 1938 to 1941; and the Akhmatova room in the former Smirnovs' room from 1945 to 1952.

The Apartment in Poems and Dreams

The apartment figures in Akhmatova's poetry as the domestic setting of death and terror. In her diary, Chukovskaia recorded the poem Akhmatova read to her in August 1940, which pictured the lyrical "I" at the hour of her funeral, accompanied in her last journey by a female neighbor, from a communal apartment to an unadorned grave pit: "The neighbor from pity might go two blocks" (*Sosedka iz zhalosti—dva kvartala*). This poem, Chukovskaia commented, turned the "cesspit of a communal apartment" into a solemn memorial (1:180).

Irina Punina was eager to recognize her nursery in the solemn poem from Akhmatova's *Requiem*, "They led you away at dawn..." (*Uvodili tebia na rassvete*), written after the arrest of Nikolai Punin and Lev Gumilev in 1935. "In the dark room the children were crying" [*V temnoi gornitse plakali deti*]— those weren't any children crying (claims Punina), it was me and my cousin, Igor' Arens, who lived with us because his father had already been sent to the camps..."[17]

In her memoirs, Nadezhda Mandelshtam reported Akhmatova's dream, which brings her first husband, Nikolai Stepanovich Gumilev (Lev's father), executed in 1921, to the same apartment:

> The corridor of Punin's apartment, where there is a table and at the end, behind a curtain, a bed in which Lev sleeps, when he is allowed into this house. [...] "They" are in the corridor; they show a warrant for Gumilev's arrest and ask for him. She knows that Nikolai Stepanovich is hiding in her room—the last door on the left at the end of the corridor. She brings out Lev, who's been asleep behind the curtain, and pushes him toward the policemen: "Here is Gumilev."[18]

As Nadezhda Mandelshtam makes clear, the apartment—a home to mixed families living under the terror—produced a dream that expressed conflicting loyalties.

In their memoirs and diaries, Akhmatova's contemporaries reported dreams and poems as evidence of her experience. The curators of the Anna Akhmatova Apartment Museum found use for dream evidence too: they used another memoir report of this dream in their reconstruction of the apartment's topography.[19]

"To Have Dinner at the Same Table as Her Husband's Wife"

It proved far from easy to reconstruct the family relations in this household. Those who visited the Punins and Akhmatova in the 1930s approached this task by carefully describing the spatial arrangement. One of Punin's friends, in his memoirs, explains to his readers that Punin lived in the same apartment as "his first wife and their daughter"; he proceeds to describe a common meal.[20] Another friend, when he was invited to "the Punins" for dinner had to explain to his wife that "Punin's former wife and daughter from his former marriage live in the same apartment."[21] The phrase "the Punins" seem to refer to Punin and Akhmatova: the memoirists have difficulty with the terms of kinship. Lidiia Ginzburg, who visited Akhmatova often, described the situation in her notebooks, commenting on its cultural significance. For Ginzburg, this was a story about the former "Decadents":

> Strong nerves—that's the most distinguishing characteristic of the Decadents. Without even batting an eyelid, they could endure situations next to intolerable for the ordinary person. [...] For years she [Akhmatova] could sit and have dinner at the same table as her husband's wife (Anna Evgen'evna). What's more, it was by no means an even-sided triangle; they wouldn't say a word to one another while they ate.[22]

Ginzburg offers a precise, though paradoxical, definition of kinship: for Akhmatova, Anna Arens-Punina is "the wife of her husband." (Note that Ginzburg, who viewed this situation as a trademark of the modernist artistic elite, implied that it would be impossible for "ordinary people"—in the next chapter, devoted to an ordinary woman, we will see whether she was right.)

While some commentators see a deliberate quality in this extended family, most comment not on sexual or family experimentation but on the Soviet housing shortage. Nadezhda Mandelshtam, in her famous memoirs, took it upon herself to provide a definitive interpretation and judgment:

> I don't have anything against going off with other people's husbands—it happens all the time and, therefore, this is in the nature of things. Akhmatova was speaking of herself in the splendid lines: "Most faithful mate of other women's husbands and of many the mournful widow." The only

bad thing was living all together "under the roof of the House on the Fontanka." This idyllic setup was devised by Punin to spare Akhmatova the need to keep house, and himself the strain of earning enough to support two different households. Apart from this, the desperate housing shortage inevitably complicated any divorce or love affair. It is always vital to separate completely, and the idyll did not work out. Her relations with Punin would probably have been much easier and simpler if they had not all shared the same apartment. The most important thing in life for any Soviet citizen is his tiny bit of "living space." No wonder so many crimes have been committed for the sake of it.[23]

In her youth, Nadezhda Mandelshtam (as some recent memoirs suggest) was not alien to the idea of family experimentation, but writing in the 1960s, she saw "the housing question" as a defining factor in the life of a Soviet subject in the 1930s.

How Akhmatova Left Punin

Recall that Chukovskaia paid her first visit to the apartment in September 1938, in the days when Akhmatova "left" Punin. She explained the situation to Chukovskaia in spatial terms:

> And you know how it all happened? How I left? I said to Anna Evgen'evna in front of him: "Let's exchange rooms." This suited her very well, and we immediately started moving our things. Nikolai Nikolaevich said nothing; then, when we were alone for a minute, he said: "You could have stayed with me for just one more year." (1:188; 149)

Akhmatova laughed, and Chukovskaia joined her.

To make the physical setup clear, Akhmatova moved, with her few possessions, from Punin's study into Irina's former nursery. But the large study was soon taken over by the eighteen-year-old Irina, her young husband, Genrikh Kaminskii, and their newborn daughter, Anna ("Malaika"). Anna Arens-Punina and Punin must have lived in the one remaining room, using partitions.[24]

As for the legal situation, no steps seem to have been taken. From both Chukovskaia's account and other sources, it remains unclear whether or not Akhmatova was legally married to Punin. But we do know that, in accordance with the strict administrative order, her residence in the Punin apartment was properly registered.

Living in the tense situation that followed their separation, Akhmatova seemed to believe that it was the "housing question" that prompted their misery. When Chukovskaia brought up the idea of divorce, Akhmatova agreed;

she tapped the wall behind which Punin now lived, adding that "such layering of wives" (*nasloeniia zhen*) made no sense at all (1:186). (It is worth mentioning that, in practice, Akhmatova found it difficult to dissolve a marriage bond: she retained posthumous loyalty to Gumilev, whom she had divorced long before his execution, and close friendship with her second husband, Shileiko.)

Taking cues from Akhmatova, Chukovskaia describes their continuing cohabitation as a discomfort of the type experienced by other inhabitants of communal apartments, that is, the majority of the Soviet population: "'The Punins have taken my kettle,' Anna Andreevna told me, 'they went out and locked their rooms. So I didn't even have any tea. Oh well, never mind'" (1:32; 22). "'It is noisy at our place. The Punins have parties, the gramophone is on till all hours...'" (1:26; 17). That the participants of the trivial, even banal, "teakettle" and "gramophone conflict" are members of the Russian cultural elite lends these situations an uncanny air.

Akhmatova also shared with Chukovskaia other disheartening details of her living situation:

—Nikolai Nikolaevich keeps insisting that I should move.
—Exchange your room?
—No, simply move out.... You know, in the last two years I've started to think badly of men. Have you noticed there are hardly any *there*....
(1:26; 18)

This is one of the very few comments that explicitly draws on gender distinctions. "*There*" refers to the prison lines (Chukovskaia makes this clear in a footnote). For today's reader, the rest of this statement may also require historical commentary. Throughout the years of the Soviet power, living space was scarce, and it was mainly distributed by state institutions, with a long waiting period ("queue," or "line"). In this context, a peculiar procedure of exchanging a room in a family or communal apartment for one in another apartment was the only way for the partners to cease cohabiting after a divorce. The Soviet Russian language developed a loaded term for such exchanges of living space, *obmen*.

In this case, there was another possibility to obtain living space for Akhmatova: through the intervention of the Union of Soviet Writers, which acted as a mediator in the state distribution of goods and privileges. (While many writers enjoyed much more substantial benefits, a room in a communal apartment could nevertheless be seen as a privilege.) An endnote in the "Behind the Scenes" section of Chukovskaia's diaries cites an appeal made in 1939 by the head of the Union, Aleksandr Fadeev, to Andrei Vyshinskii, who served as the head of the government committee on special pensions:

The renowned poet, Anna Akhmatova, currently lives in Leningrad in conditions of exceptional material and domestic hardship. It is hardly necessary to inform you of the injustice of this predicament for one such as Akhmatova, who—though her poetic talent is ill-accommodated by our times—was, and remains, the foremost poet of the prerevolutionary period; or to convey the unfavorable impression made by this treatment on both the old literary intelligentsia and on the younger generation who were apprenticed under Akhmatova.

To this day Akhmatova possesses not a single meter of individual living space. She lives in the room of her former husband, from whom she long ago separated. It is not necessary to prove the humiliation of these circumstances. (1:326)

Though they were addressed to high levels of the government bureaucracy (in his other role, as the general prosecutor, Vyshinskii played a leading role in the terror), then, in 1939, these requests had no effect.

At one point, seeing no change in the situation, Chukovskaia offered Akhmatova the opportunity to live with her, that is, to become her communal apartment neighbor. Her housing situation allowed for such a move. After the arrest of her husband, one room in the two-room apartment occupied entirely by her family (a rare, but not impossible case) was handed over to an NKVD (People's Commissariat of Internal Affairs) officer and the apartment became communal (1:44, 216). It was a common practice to reward staff of the state security, the NKVD, or volunteer informers with living space vacated after an arrest. (This is what Nadezhda Mandelshtam meant when she wrote in her memoirs that many crimes were committed for the sake of the "living space.") But by the end of 1940, this room was occupied by "ordinary neighbors," with whom—Chukovskaia suggested—Akhmatova could legally exchange her room in the Punin apartment:

I asked whether she had decided to move in with me.
"No. Nikolai Nikolaevich reminded me in no uncertain terms of my promise not to give my room over to people he doesn't know." (1:216; 172)

Moreover, it turned out that the two women differed in their emotional reactions to the situation.

I brought up the subject of the apartment. I so want her to have a decent place to live in! Without those footsteps and records playing from behind the wall, without continual humiliations! But she, it turned out, seems to feel quite differently: she wants to remain here, wants the Smirnovs to move to a new room and give her theirs. She wants to live here, but in two rooms.

"I truly think a communal apartment you know is better than one you don't. I am used to things here. Furthermore, when Lev returns, he will have a room. For he will come back some day..." (1:66; 52)

The conversation then turned to the children of the Smirnovs. Akhmatova was especially fond of the younger one, Vova: the toddler learned to knock at her door with his tiny fist, and he invented a funny name for her: "'T'Anna.' [Kani] You understand? The direction, where to: 'To Anna' [k Ane]" (1:66; 52). The women talked, as often, over tea; on this occasion, hot water: Akhmatova explained that she had long ago run out of tea (1:66).

Akhmatova's relationships with the Smirnovs, too, appear to be quite complex. Chukovskaia's journal provides contradictory evidence. She notes Akhmatova's love and care for the children, especially little Vova (she changed his soiled underwear and tried to introduce him to books). She also notes the socially alien, low-class behavior of the mother: the way "Tan'ka" would enter Akhmatova's room without knocking (1:91); her crude descriptions of a gastrointestinal infection, which threatened Akhmatova because they shared a toilet and kitchen (1:166); the vulgarity of her speech (1:91); the way she cursed and beat her children, audible to Chukovskaia and Akhmatova from behind the wall (1:203). One day, however, Chukovskaia also noted: "Tanya, who wanted to exchange her room, decided not to; Anna Andreevna is glad that the children aren't going to be taken away" (1:216; 172).

But there was more to this neighbor (or so Akhmatova feared). One day in June 1940, Akhmatova summoned Chukovskaia for an urgent visit. On this, as on many other occasions, Chukovskaia described how Akhmatova looked, connecting her bodily misery to the situation in the apartment:

> I arrived about two. She looked very bad. Tired eyes, her face drawn and blurred, the features seem to have lost the clarity of their outlines.
> "What's the matter with you? Have you been ill these last few days?"
> "No."
> And she told me her latest Dostoevskian episode, truly both horrifying and tiresome. What an imbroglio—those children she looks after, and this Court of Miracles. (1:134–35; 106–7)

A later footnote explains what Chukovskaia recorded here in such cryptic fashion:

> A. A. suspected that Tanya Smirnova, her neighbor, Valya and Vova's mother, had been assigned to keep watch on her, to spy on her, and she even detected some signs of this surveillance. "It always turns out," she told me, "that I end up paying my own informers." A. A. called the watch

kept on her and her manuscripts, which she felt constantly, the activity of the Court of Miracles. (1:135n; 107n)*

Months later Tanya, who shopped and cooked for Akhmatova, notified her that she was about to terminate her paid services. Now what? Akhmatova was notoriously impractical. There was a slim chance, Akhmatova told Chukovskaia, that the Punins "may" permit their household help to cook for her. The situation provoked Chukovskaia to an extreme: "Let this apartment be damned!" (1:192; 153).

The sentiment was not Chukovskaia's alone: while acknowledging that Akhmatova would not do anything to improve her life, her other caretaker, Dr. Garshin, did not for a moment doubt the role of the apartment in creating the morbidly oppressive conditions: "First of all, it is vital that she move out of here, out of this apartment. She is subject to trauma from both sides, by both neighbors" (1:160–61; 127).

Note that both witnesses of Akhmatova's domestic situation use the same word, "neighbors," to define Akhmatova's relationship to the Punins and to the Smirnovs.

Generalizations: The Soviet State, Domestic Space, and Intimacy

Extreme in its complexity and exceptionally well documented, the case at hand presents a special opportunity to reflect on the issue of intimacy and the Soviet state as articulated in the organization of domestic space. The peculiar Soviet institution of the communal apartment placed socially diverse people in close physical proximity in one cramped space, regardless of kinship and family connections. As we see from this, albeit extraordinary, example, such households fostered emotional ties, bonding people across family and class lines. New bonds were formed without dissolving the previous connections. The result was profound confusion among the categories of kinship, household, and intimacy—a confusion born of specific historical and social circumstances that reached an apogee in the 1930s.

Let us summarize the situation. In 1926, a woman (let us call her "A.") entered a household of husband, wife, and child (as well as live-in servant with her child), forming an extented family of sorts. Indeed, the threesome, joined by their children, relatives, and friends, took meals together. To capture this situation, Lidiia Ginzburg used a paradoxical phrase: "to have dinner at

---

* The phrase "the Court of Miracles" probably comes from Victor Hugo's *Notre Dame de Paris,* in which the mythical *Cour des miracles* figures prominently as the dwelling of the city's monsters, a secret space where people steal, murder, and sell their bodies and souls. For this identification, I am indebted to Anna Muza.

the same table as her husband's wife." In 1938, A. terminated the partnership with the man without leaving the household. After 1938, the members of this group in the household were now linked by two defunct marriage ties. A.'s situation became ambivalent: an (estranged) family member or a behind-the-wall neighbor in a communal apartment?

There is another group: in the early 1930s, a child of the former servants in the gentry household, without entirely shedding his former status, turned into a class-alien neighbor. This transformation in status was precipitated and exacerbated by his marriage to one within his own—changing—class, which had now become the ruling class, the proletariat.

After the 1938 separation of A. from her husband, emotional ties were formed between A. and the children of her class-alien neighbors. One may speculate that A.'s separation from her son, who was under arrest, may have inspired her attachment.

To be sure, it was not the housing shortages alone that prompted A. and others to form this layered family. There were, of course, individual emotional patterns (such as A.'s inability to dissolve an old marriage bond). There were also other, historically informed, motivations.

Our main subjects were members of the modernist artistic milieu intent on experimentation with living forms, who grew up in the atmosphere of "sexual anarchy" that extended from turn-of-the-century decadence to the revolutionary 1920s.[25] The general social anarchy of the 1920s and the early Soviet family reforms, aimed at undercutting the family as an institution, contributed to the dissolution of sexual unions and normative expectations.[26] It is in this context that Nadezhda Mandelshtam's defiant declaration that "going off with other people's husbands [...] is in the nature of things" takes its meaning. In the 1930s and 1940s, the brutal collectivization of agriculture, industrialization, the terror, and the war contributed further to the fragmentation of the family by separating spouses, parents, and children. But as of the 1930s, the Stalinist state no longer supported experimental family life and free sexuality; the state now sought to strengthen the nuclear family. But it could not relieve the housing shortage. We have seen how, in the case at hand, the shortage contributed to giving form, and a semblance of permanence, to the fragmented families and entangled personal relationships, locking them into one space. In the end, the "housing question" (a Soviet idiom) moves to the fore as an explanatory factor—or this is what the participants themselves believed.

We have seen how the Soviet state used communal apartments not only as a practical necessity in times of housing shortage, but also as an instrument of social control, mixing people of different social classes and domestic habits in one space, with shared facilities, and using (or potentially using) neighbors to inform on one another. There is no evidence as to whether or not A.'s proletarian neighbor was an NKVD informer, but we do see evidence that the idea itself worked: A. believed herself to be under surveillance and under threat from her behind-the-wall neighbor, even as she formed emotional ties to her children. There were also remnants of a former, semifeudal, relationship: A. took measures to improve the lives and education of the children from the family of her former husband's former servant; their mother (no longer labeled a "servant") provided her with services earlier obtained from live-in servants. (Strange as this may seem, people like A., their constrained financial resources notwithstanding, continued to employ household help.) But, devoid of an institutional frame, this relationship was now quite arbitrary: there was little but good will or whim that made the woman serve A. dinners, and she could withdraw services without dissolving the relationship of cohabitation (something than was not possible for a house servant before the revolution).

Obviously, communal apartments deprived the individual and the family of privacy by opening up to neighbors the essential intimacies of personal and family life (sights, sounds, smells). They also created excess intimacy among both members of the family and members of the household.

In this particular case, we have seen still other unintended effects of Soviet family and housing practices. The housing conditions obscured the nature of the bond between husband and wives. Was their cohabitation a matter of choice inspired by unconventional marriage practices, or a necessity brought about by the housing shortage? For the participants themselves, this was no longer clear. The new housing regime created a situation of institutionalized ambiguity and ambivalence. Nor only was it hard to tell who was a member of the family and who a member of a larger household, it was also hard to say who was married to whom and what one felt toward intimate others.

It may be impossible to unravel all the emotional links and practical ties that kept the inhabitants together—former husband and wives, former servants and masters—in this Soviet apartment located in the service wing of an eighteenth-century palace. A question arises: How special is this case? Of course, the household in the Sheremetev Palace is not ordinary. Yet, one could speculate that other unique emotional regimes promoted by the Soviet state—whose ubiquitous presence reached into the no-longer-private domestic spaces—ruled also in other households of Soviet Russia.

DURING THE WAR

Lidiia Chukovskaia's Akhmatova journals for the war years—which the two women spent largely in evacuation in Tashkent (Central Asia)—are a somewhat different document. Describing the period in their relationship that ended with a ten-year estrangement, the wartime diaries remained unpublished during the author's lifetime. Published by her fearless daughter, Elena

Tsezarevna Chukovskaia (in the 1997 edition), excerpts from the "Tashkent notebooks" are raw diary entries, which Lidiia Chukovskaia did not edit. (The published text even refers to the hero of the diary in code, as "NN.")

When, in the 1970s and 1990s, Chukovskaia reread her Tashkent notebooks, she was hit by a double pain: horror and helplessness experienced in the war mixed with the wounding memories of disappointment in her friend. Introducing the "Tashkent notebooks" after her mother's death, Elena Chukovskaia cited the diary entries describing these emotions. In 1979, Chukovskaia read her wartime diaries as a record of defeat ("constant defeat—no money, nowhere to live") and as her failure as a diary writer ("helpless, defenseless, failed, incompetent" [1:517]). Rereading these diaries again in the 1993, she added the word "betrayal" ("what poverty and homelessness! the betrayals!" [1:519]). In 1993 Chukovskaia perceived the wartime notebooks as a record of misery far exceeding the misery recorded for the years under the terror: "I became utterly absorbed in the Tashkent notebooks. How terrible they are! How can the "the Court of Miracles" compare with them" (1:519). (Recall that "the Court of Miracles" is a code word for living under the watchful eye of the state security.)

But when we turn to the Tashkent notebooks themselves, we find that in 1941 she reported other emotions:

> I tried to explain somehow to NN how I felt some kind of strange liberation, not only from "the Court of Miracles" but from my own self, from my past. If I had found something new—then this feeling would have been explainable, but I didn't find anything new, did I?—only that the last refuge was lost. (1:352)

It seemed to Chukovskaia that her friend, too, mobilized different parts of her personality. On December 13, Chukovskaia found her, as often, in bed in a cold room of a cramped communal apartment:

> In my presence she got up, washed the dishes, got the stove going. She made me sit down throughout. She spoke words that were cruel, and, alas, to a certain extent, truthful. "You see, I'm not actually so helpless. Rather, it's just my being perverse." (1:350)

This is a rare moment when Chukovskaia offers direct insight into the complex nature of Akhmatova's misery: poverty and squalor, valorized in the moral code of the intelligentsia, were not only imposed but also chosen.

These records were made weeks after they arrived in Tashkent. Other diarists and memoirists, who also described a sense of liberation, attributed it to the change in their civil status: the suffering caused by the terror—a secret pain shared with a few trusted companions who also felt targeted by the state—was replaced by a solidarity in suffering with the whole people, legitimized as a national experience.

Moreover, both Akhmatova and Chukovskaia were resettled in areas remote from the front as a result of a government initiative. (Evacuation of the frontline cities was a matter of government policy, but select groups, including members of the Union of the Soviet Writers, were given special privileges; small as they were—special cars in overcrowded trains or access to dormitory living space and food stores—these privileges could be a matter of life and death.) A special effort was undertaken (as Akhmatova believed, by special order of the party leadership) to fly her out of the besieged Leningrad—a sign of official recognition in which she found much comfort.

They had left the starvation and bombardments in the Leningrad blockade. In the "Behind the Scenes" section Lidiia Chukovskaia includes a glimpse of Akhmatova in Leningrad from the diary of the poet Olga Berggol'ts. With the beginning of the bombardments, the Punins moved to the bomb shelter in the basement of the Hermitage, and Akhmatova found shelter in the Writers' House on the Griboedov Canal, where—believing it to be a safer location—she slept in a basement room of the building's janitor; Garshin, who visited her daily, brought food. There she learned of the first death in her circle—the editor Tatiana Gurevich (much respected for refusing to condemn her arrested colleagues) had been killed when a bomb hit a nearby building. On September 24, 1941, Berggol'ts visited Akhmatova:

> I went round to Akhmatova's; she lives in the room of a janitor (killed by an artillery shell on Zheliabov Street) in the basement in a pitch dark, reeking corner, thoroughly Dostoevskian—a mattress on boards piled up on top of one another, and there on the edge, bundled up in cloth, with sunken eyes, was Anna Akhmatova. She sits in absolute darkness; she can't even read; just sits there as if in a cell for the condemned. She was weeping over Tanya Gurevich (everyone is remembering and grieving Tanya today), and said so aptly: "It's hateful. I hate Hitler, I hate Stalin, I hate those who are throwing bombs on Leningrad and Berlin, who are conducting this shameful, terrible war..."[27]

A few months earlier, on August 25, an old friend, Pavel Luknitskii (who in the 1920s documented her life in his diary), visited Akhmatova in the Sheremetev Palace:

> I paid a visit to A. A. Akhmatova. She was ill and in bed. She greeted me most amiably; she was in a good mood and told me, with visible pleasure, that she had been invited to speak on the radio. She is a patriot,

and she is evidently much cheered by the knowledge that she is now, in her heart, at one with the people.²⁸

His (newly acquired) stilted Soviet idiom notwithstanding, Luknitskii may be right about a sense of comfort derived from the consciousness of being at one with others. In her "blockade notes," Lidiia Ginzburg (who worked for the Leningrad radio during the blockade) legitimized the feeling of "performing the common task in a people's war" by comparing it to what Tolstoy had described in *War and Peace*.²⁹ There are reasons to believe that Akhmatova and Chukovskaia shared this sentiment. But a sense of participation in the common cause also rested on the fact that Akhmatova, long ostracized by the official press, was now invited to speak and publish: her poem, "Courage" ("Muzhestvo"), appeared in *Pravda* on March 8, 1942.

In wartime Tashkent, Leningrad was ever present in the minds of the evacuees, but mostly as a loaded silence. Chukovskaia, angry at a writer who started a conversation about the hardship in Leningrad, noted in her diary: "We keep silent about Leningrad. Or we weep" (1:416). They also dreamed of Leningrad, and Chukovskaia recorded such dreams; they speak of her longing for the city and for friends who had stayed behind (1:424). She also dreamed of her husband who was killed in the terror (1:390). When the evacuees did speak about Leningrad, they shared news about people believed to be dead. At the end of March, the Punins, who finally left Leningrad with the Academy of Arts, passed through Tashkent by train on the way to another evacuation town, Samarkand. Chukovskaia, who accompanied NN to the railroad station, noted:

> The railway station; an evacuation point. [...] The Leningrad Academy of Arts came through. Punin; Anna Evgen'evna, Irochka and Malaika. [...] Those Leningraders' terrible faces. [...] The station attendants used force against me and her [NN]—wouldn't let us onto the platform. [...] Nothing is known about Garshin. NN is certain he's dead. Zhenia Smirnov's dead. Tania, Vovochka, and Valia are close to death. Vera Anikieva's dead. Kibrik died on the journey. Punin is in a very bad way. (March 24, 1942; 1:417)

A later footnote notes that the artist Kibrik, who traveled with the Punin family, was actually alive. Just as under the terror, people lived not knowing who was dead and who alive. On another day (May 7, 1942) Chukovskaia recorded a litany of (reported and imagined) deaths recited by NN: "Lev's dead, Vova's dead, Vl. G. [Garshin] is dead" (1:440).

When the news of Vova Smirnov's death did indeed reach her (nothing was known about Lev and Garshin), Akhmatova (as Chukovskaia reports) responded with a memorial poem:

Постучись кулачком—я открою.
Я тебе открывала всегда.
Я теперь за высокой горою,
За пустыней, за ветром и зноем,
И домой не вернусь никогда...

Knock with your little fist—I will open.
I always opened the door to you.
I am beyond the high mountain now,
Beyond the desert, beyond the wind and the heat,
And I will never return home...[30]

Ten days later, she changed the last line: «Но тебя не предам никогда». / "But I will never betray you." In June, Chukovskaia records that "Vovochka" was published, with the dedication "To the memory of Vovochka Smirnov, who perished during the bombing of Leningrad." (1:430; 463) ("Vovochka" is an endearing diminutive of the boy's name.) In September Chukovskaia recorded the news that Vovochka Smirnov was alive, but his brother, Valia, was dead, and Evgeny (Zhenia) Smirnov, their father, too (1:477). (In subsequent publications the poem was rededicated "to the memory of my neighbor, the Leningrad boy, Valia Smirnov.") The communal apartment and the child neighbor (implied Chukovskaia) was immortalized in Akhmatova's verse.

Let us pause to consider the future of the inhabitants of the apartment on the Fontanka. (This information is given, in separate notes, in the "Behind the Scenes" section of Chukovskaia's journals.) Akhmatova's son, Lev, did not die: in 1944, from exile in Siberia, he volunteered to join the army and saw the end of the war in Berlin. Garshin survived the blockade; his wife died, in the street, and her body was half-eaten by rats. The Punins, after they left from Leningrad in spring 1942, settled in Samarkand, where they lived as a family—notwithstanding Punin's connection to Marta Golubeva (who was also married but joined them after the death of her husband in the Leningrad blockade). Nikolai Punin, who left Leningrad in a state of advanced dystrophy, recovered and survived. In a hospital in Samarkand he wrote Akhmatova a solemn letter that spoke of his endless gratitude, guilt, and peaceful happiness on the brink of death (for years she carried this letter in her purse, showing it to many people). Punin's wife, Anna Arens-Punina, died in Samarkand in

1943, which caused Punin piercing grief. (Akhmatova wept when she learned the news.) Igor Arens, the nephew who frequently stayed with the Punins in the 1930s because his parents were under arrest, died of starvation in Leningrad in 1942. When Akhmatova, who survived typhus in Tashkent, returned to Leningrad at the end of the war, she thought that she was going to join the widowed Garshin as his wife, but when they met at the railroad station he did not bring the matter up, taking her to stay with friends instead. Eventually, Akhmatova returned to the apartment on the Fontanka, where, once again, she settled together with the survivors of the Punin family—Nikolai Punin, his daughter Irina Punina, and her small daughter Anna ("Malaika") Kaminskaia. (At that time, they thought that Irina's husband, Genrikh Kaminskii, declared missing in action, had been killed in the war in 1941; in 1990, the family learned that he had been arrested at the front in 1941 and had died in a remote camp in 1943 at the age of twenty-three.)[31] The survivors of the Smirnov family did not return to the apartment on the Fontanka. With the help of the Writers' Union, Akhmatova claimed two rooms. When Lev returned from the army in 1945, he could have, as Akhmatova had once hoped, a room of his own; but not for long: in 1949, he was arrested again. Nikolai Punin was arrested several days earlier. Punin died in the camps from a heart attack in August 1953. In 1952, the family—what remained of it—was forced to leave the Sheremetev Palace, and until Akhmatova's death in 1966 the Punins—Irina Punina and her daughter Anna Kaminskaia—remained Akhmatova's family and shared her living space. Soon after Lev was released from the camp in 1956 the tension between mother and son, which had grown over the years, led to an estrangement. After Akhmatova's death, Lev Gumilev, on one side, and Irina Punina, on the other, were involved in a legal dispute over the inheritance: the Akhmatova archive.

To conclude: through the historical events that shaped their lives from the early 1920s to the late 1960s—the terror, the war, and their aftermaths—it proved impossible to sever the bonds between former and current spouses and their children, plagued as they were with emotional tensions and domestic conflicts, and it proved impossible to separate their lives in space.

Poverty and Squalor: New Living Forms and New Insight

Let us return to Tashkent in 1942. Once again, living conditions stand at the center of Chukovskaia's account. The living space allocated to the evacuees was, of course, limited, and it was frequently devoid of basic conveniences. There was one special aspect to the circumstances: the writers—resettled under the administration of the Union of Soviet Writers—lived together as a group.[32] NN (as Akhmatova figures in the Tashkent notebooks) was allocated a tiny and moldy attic room in the *obshchezhitie pisatelei* (communal housing facility for writers) at No. 7 Karl Marx Street. Chukovskaia and her small daughter settled in a closet-type room in another *obshchezhitie.* Inhabiting rooms in a building without running water and indoor plumbing, and eating in (or bringing food from) an institutional cafeteria, writers led a particularly miserable and remarkably exposed life.

Still, there were other facilities, and given Akhmatova's official status at the time of the war (an acknowledged literary classic), she was entitled to privileges. Chukovskaia describes how NN turned down what she thought was an offer from the Academy of Sciences to settle in its "Pushkin Communal Housing Facility" (Pushkinskoe obshchezhitie Akademii nauk). (She was actually rejected, comments Chukovskaia, but, oblivious of that fact, moved to decline.) Then another opportunity presented itself: housing for government employees. With a touch of irony, Chukovskaia reports that this development threw NN (who eventually declined) into emotional turmoil:

> The SNK [Council of People's Commissars] sent somebody to move her into another room, a luxurious one and so forth. She was in a state of despair, confusion, despondency—which vividly reminded me of when she had been offered an apartment in Leningrad. [...] It struck me as rather ridiculous. There was, of course, a whole net of interrelated reasons that came to the fore here: her horror in the face of domestic everyday life, her aversion to change, the moral value of poverty, and the fear of loneliness. (1:420)

Recall that the notes from the war have been published (by Chukovskaia's daughter) in the raw. These records offer new insights, not only into Akhmatova's choices, but also into Chukovskaia's awareness of paradoxes inherent in the Soviet condition of poverty and squalor. In this case, Chukovskaia unfolds tangled motivations underlying her friend's reluctance to leave the squalid communal living quarters for the "luxury" of a room dispensed by a high government institution. In the end, NN's deplorable living situation becomes a matter of choice, prompted by an inextricable tangle of factors, which Chukovskaia calls a "net" (*set'*) and, inevitably, arranges as a list. Clearly, it would be impossible to separate clinical anxiety from moral sensibility—a fateful fusion that made autonomous existence in relative comfort emotionally intolerable.

Note that Chukovskaia mentions in passing something that is absent from her carefully edited "notes" for 1938–41: before the war, Akhmatova had been offered, and declined, her own living space in Leningrad. According to Irina Punina, who also marveled at the paradox, Akhmatova was offered an apartment in 1940, when her standing with the authorities took a brief turn for the better, "but she did not want it—and this is a mystery of her life [...]—she did not want to leave the House on the Fontanka."[33]

The mystery or paradox of the eagerly embraced (if not self-chosen) poverty and squalor calls for a comment.[34] Chukovskaia is aware of this peculiar attitude, though, on her part, she does not seem to share it. Reluctant as she is to pass judgment on her friend, the "great poet," Chukovskaia clearly shows that Akhmatova's carefully cultivated posture involved principled rejection of domesticity and comfort, precluding any practical effort at improving her situation, such as good housekeeping. Chukovskaia's notes for August 1940 show Vladimir Garshin (Akhmatova's then lover) addressing the cultural meanings of this condition: "philosophy of poverty" (*filosofiia nishchety*), antidomesticity (*bezbytnost'*), and committed inactivity (*nichego ne khochet predpriniat'*) (1:178). The word choice places domestic issues in a broader sociophilosophical context. This theme is not new: in the wake of the first Russian revolution, the renegade authors of the collection *Landmarks* (*Vekhi*, 1909) famously discussed "love for poverty" as one of those contradictory attitudes of the "intelligentsia" that would bring about the destruction of civilized life in Russia. In the 1940s, the same issue was on the agenda of an intimate circle whose members counted themselves among the "Russian intelligentsia" as they struggled for survival.

To return to wartime Tashkent. During the war, Akhmatova lived with fellow writers in conditions that brought another feature of the Soviet condition—communality—to the extreme. Living under one another's watchful eyes in dormitories, writers (friends and rivals) shared meager material resources, scarce information about the outside world, and ample knowledge about one another (gossip); they also exchanged, and counted, favors. Everything took on radical forms: destitution, density, mutual dependency, exposure.

Now taking a clue from her subject, now working independently, Chukovskaia carefully describes these forms of cohabitation and their social and emotional consequences. Once, on a rare occasion when the two women found themselves alone, NN asked, "Why do you think it is that people here are constantly dropping in on one another?" (1:431). A comment rather than a question, this opening led to further reflections on the situation. That evening (Chukovskaia noted) "we would talk about people a lot. NN was very cruel and candid" (1:431). (In other words, they gossiped.) Now and then their intimate conversation was interrupted: "Sometimes Ranevskaia, who worships NN, would come in...other times Radzinskaia" (1:431). (The original diary used initials, but Elena Chukovskaia, while retaining "NN" for Akhmatova, deciphered coded evocations of other people for publication.) The diary shows how constant visitations linked the inhabitants of the Writers' House still more tightly. A market of goods, services, and information could be staged in the space of an individual room.

Chukovskaia's notes also suggest that this life had a theatrical quality. In this theater of wartime domesticity, NN, of course, played a leading role.

Once she told Chukovskaia that on that day alone she had had fifteen visitors (1:428); on another occasion she reported that one of her guest-helpers had counted the total for the month as four hundred and twelve people (1:455). When Chukovskaia reports from her friend's room, she dutifully notes each entrance and exit:

> Enter Elder Basov-Verkhoiantsev, whose wife is considered the Chief of the anti-Akhmatovites; he offers to carry out the bucket. [...] Some girl appears, enquires after [NN's] health and brings ten eggs. Then a doctor with the flat face of a house servant appears. (1:429)

Judging by her word choice (Elder, *starets;* Chief, *vozhd'*), the diarist drew a somewhat comical analogy between the community of displaced writers and a primitive tribe. As I keep insisting, from its beginning in the 1938, Chukovskaia viewed this diary as an ethnographic project of sorts. When chance brought her to Central Asia, this image acquired an additional validity. Set against the background of an exotic and primitive land, the position of the diary writer as ethnographer became more fitting than ever (the subjects, however, were not the local tribesmen, but the displaced Soviet writers). At the same time, Chukovskaia was, of course, aware of the literary quality of her account and she used other generic frames. Describing the theatricality of these situations, some of her diary entries read like fragments from a playwright's script, complete with stage directions:

> The room begins to fill little by little: Bragantseva, Mur, Khazin, Drobotova. They drink wine. (1:444)
>
> These days I only ever see NN in company. "A clap of thunder; enter all." (1:417)

The last phrase is a twisted quote from A. N. Ostrovsky's drama *The Thunderstorm*.

The Helplessness and the Power

Akhmatova's symbolic status in the community—her historic role as the great Russian poet in distress, which she played with relish—made her an object of general attention and common care. At the beginning of the Tashkent life, Chukovskaia described—in the idiom of the common cause, used in the Soviet context to describe tasks of national importance—what a joy it was for everybody to be mobilized in the service of Akhmatova:

> Everyone is happy to provide food, supply tobacco, stoke the stove, fetch water. This is the genuine "common cause"; genuine because it is completely voluntary. (1:419)

In her daily reports from her friend's room, Chukovskaia noted whom she found scrubbing the floor, starting the stove, taking the garbage out, or bringing a food ration from the cafeteria.[35] She notes with satisfaction the paradoxical fact that now, in this unusual situation of general mobilization, NN was better fed than before the war, when "Tan'ka [Smirnova] would boil her up *something or other now and then*"; judging by her use of reported speech here, she was speaking in NN's own words (1:374). NN herself not only permitted the fellow inhabitants of the writer's community the pleasure of serving her but also kept track of their services, and reported the list to Chukovskaia; she carefully marked those favors that she did not want. On more than one occasion, Chukovskaia related such a report (in the first person) in her diary:

> O. R. washed a towel for me, Naia washed my hair and made salade Olivier, Maria Mikhailovna boiled some eggs. [...] In the morning I opened the door and [Aleksei] Tolstoy's chauffeur had brought firewood, apples, and jam. I didn't like this at all. I do not wish to be obligated to Tolstoy. (1:373)

The last comment carries a special weight. There was something threatening in the origin of the luxury goods delivered by Aleksei Tolstoy's personal chauffeur: the whole thing bore a stamp of closeness to state power. Indeed, Aleksei Tolstoy (no relation to Lev Tolstoy) not only enjoyed the status of preeminent Soviet writer but (like others in this position) also occupied government posts, including membership in the Supreme Soviet of the USSR. As Tolstoy's beneficiary, partaking of his privilege, NN felt contaminated by proxy.

There were other complications. As it soon became clear to Chukovskaia, some of the residents of House No. 7 on Karl Marx Street found NN's position at the center of a civic cult to be objectionable:

> It turns out that there's a whole gaggle of women [...] who take umbrage at the fact that NN doesn't go and get her own piroshki, but that others are glad to get them for her. [...] Oh, it sickens me to write about it all. (1:426–27)

As time went by, her friend's attitude started to trouble her assistant and chronicler.

Much later, in a retrospective glance at the wartime events, Chukovskaia would comment (in a footnote to a diary entry from 1955) that back then the writers' wives were irritated by Akhmatova's double posture—her "helplessness and her power" (*ee bespomoshchnost' i ee vlastnost'*) (2:159). In 1962, Chukovskaia tried to explain Akhmatova's ambiguous position. Thus, she suggested that Akhmatova's acceptance of poverty involved aggressive overtones of social superiority—the superiority defined apart from the official social hierarchy. Chukovskaia explained Akhmatova's ambiguous role—her helplessness and power—as a defense against the encroachment of oppressive state power:

> The knowledge that in poverty, calamity, and grief, she had poetry, she had greatness—*she* had that, and not the powers that oppressed her—this knowledge gave her the strength to bear that poverty, humiliation, and grief. (2:502)

Chukovskaia does not go so far as to say "she had power," but she essentially describes a defense mechanism in which Akhmatova adopted the power posture of the oppressor. Chukovskaia vividly recalled a wartime episode when, in Tashkent, Akhmatova had humiliated her, Chukovskaia, her eager helper, and she pointedly applied the words "power" and "powerfully" (*vlastno*) to Akhmatova while describing her attitude and mannerisms. However, it was not Chukovskaia but the literary scholar Alexander Zholkovsky who, using Chukovskaia's notes about Anna Akhmatova, described the workings of the defensive strategy that Akhmatova had clearly manifested in Tashkent, in the situation where helplessness reached an apogee: following the same patterns as the oppressive power, the helpless resorted to gestures of power aimed at others (albeit in the domestic realm).[36]

Gossip

Chukovskaia was also troubled by other aspects of her friend's morals. Once writers settled into a new form of exceptional existence in Tashkent, an atmosphere of a "feast at the time of plague" formed around NN (Chukovskaia used Pushkin's phrase). As the diary makes clear, the relative security of the evacuees amid the war, a close community, a sense of liberation after the years of the terror—all of this contributed to a new mood. There were also chance circumstances of the evacuation: in Tashkent, writers were joined by actors—who, as her readers and fans, took the opportunity to befriend NN. Eager to bring performance and comical relief to the cramped dormitory rooms, they endowed the miserable wartime life with liberating theatricality. Chukovskaia recorded many moments in which NN laughed to tears at Faina Ranevskaia's comical skits or cynical comments on their common situation. (Ranevskaia was celebrated as the major Soviet comic actress; at least one other popular comic actress, Rina Zelenaia, was also in Tashkent.) With increasing disapproval, Chukovskaia recorded every instance in which she found NN laughing and drinking; she also noted the moments in which NN looked exceptionally beautiful.[37] Judging by her diary, Chukovskaia, who now seldom saw her friend tête-à-tête, was increasingly jealous. The old intimacy between the two women—the terror bond of grief and isolation—was crumbling. A new type of intimacy established itself among the evacuees, including a special intimacy between women (most men were at the front, and women were in the majority).

In her diary, Chukovskaia recorded both her own observations on NN's playful intimacy with her new female companions (listing each observed encounter in her journal)[38] and the rampant gossip about NN in the Writers' House, whose inhabitants ate, washed, received visitors, and slept under one another's watchful eyes.[39] In her cryptic notes, Chukovskaia does not specify the nature of the "crass gossip," but it is clear from the context that NN's "reputation" was marred by her carefree closeness with women who were reputed to be lesbians. In late May, Chukovskaia decided that it was her duty to report to NN "*what is being said about her in House No. 7 and in the Union [of Writers]*" (1:457). NN promptly reported the conversation to Ranevskaia, the main protagonist of the gossip stories. Chukovskaia acknowledged in her diary that she was hurt (this was an act of betrayal) and that she "disapproved" of Akhmatova's loose and carefree behavior—yet she did not act on her feelings:

> I am hurt and I disapprove. But I am refraining from making any "organizational conclusions" [*orgvyvody*]; now that V. G. [Garshin] isn't by her side, I must carry out my mission: NN was entrusted to me by the citizens of Leningrad. (1:458)

Describing her strained relationship with NN, Chukovskaia employed both the language of administrative procedure (note the distinctly Soviet abbreviation "*orgvyvody*," which she, of course, uses ironically) and the solemn discourse of civic duty. She tried to resolve a painful emotional conflict by casting their crumbling intimacy as a sociohistorical mission.

Akhmatova, too, saw the situation—a crisis in the writers' community brought about by gossip—in historical terms. She responded with a poem addressed to her neighbors, the gossiping women. (Akhmatova and Chukovskaia referred to these women as "knitters"—after the fearsome women of the French Revolution, who knitted while heads fell.) About a month later she read the poem, "This is how I am. I wish you another" (*Kakaia est'. Zhelaiu vam druguiu*), to Chukovskaia, who admired this lyrical masterpiece inspired by communal living (1:471). The poem's "I–you" structure articulates a historically specific social relationship. The "I" claims her right to be different from the "you," including in love life, on the basis of her terror experiences:

> Пока вы мирно отдыхали в Сочи,
> Ко мне уже ползли такие ночи,
> И я такие слышала звонки...

> While you were tranquilly resting in [the resort of] Sochi,
> Such nights were crawling up to me,
> And such ringing of the doorbell I heard...

(The image of the ringing doorbell, of course, refers to the nighttime arrival of the state security.) The poem continues with the theme of violating taboos by acting against "nature":

> Мне зрительницей быть не удавалось,
> И почему-то я всегда вклинялась
> В запретнейшие зоны естества.

> I could never manage to be a spectator,
> And somehow I always wedged
> Into nature's forbidden zones.

Given the biographical background (as explicated in Chukovskaia's journal), the connotations are sexual, but the phrasing is borrowed from the Soviet lexicon: "the forbidden zone" (*zapretnaia zona*) designates spaces excluded from common use for military exercises or incarceration of prisoners. ("Sochi" is a popular Soviet seaside resort.) The poem concludes with what would become Akhmatova's trademark self-image as a lover in the times of terror and war:

> Целительница нежного недуга,
> Чужих мужей вернейшая подруга
> И многих неутешная вдова...

> The healer of the tender ailment,
> Truest friend of other women's husbands
> And the grief-stricken widow of quite a few.[40]

In this poem, the experience of the terror and war is placed at the core of Akhmatova's lyrical identity as a lover.

Years later, in her memoirs, Nadezhda Mandelstam (Osip Mandelshtam's widow), who lived next door to Akhmatova and Chukovskaia in Tashkent, appropriated this poem to relate her own experience. She describes the situation—the nights of love and terror—in detail, in prose (her own) and poetry (Akhmatova's):

> The nighttime rings at the doorbell—"While you were tranquilly resting in Sochi, / Such nights were crawling up to me, / And such ringing of the doorbell I heard..." [...] At nighttime, in hours of love, I would

catch myself thinking—will they suddenly come in now and break this off? And that's what happened, leaving behind a peculiar trace—a mix of two memories.[41]

Reflecting on this erotic-historical situation again (in one of the variants of her memoirs), Nadezhda Mandelshtam claimed it as a shared experience and a shared memory:

> Inscribed in [Akhmatova's] book of poetry: "To my friend, Nadia: that she may remember once more what we went through." Of everything we went through, one thing underlay everything and was most intense: the fear, and the effects it produced—a loathsome feeling of shame and utter helplessness. And there is no need to remember that; "that" is always with us. As we admitted to one another, "that" proved to be stronger than love and jealousy, stronger than any of the human emotions that fell to our lot. From the very first days, when we were still brave, right to the end of the 1950s, fear smothered in us everything that people usually live by; and for every glimmer of hope we paid—awake and in dreams—with the deliriums of nighttime. There was a physiological basis to the fear: well-washed hands with short fat fingers fumbling in our pockets, the good-natured faces of the nighttime visitors, their murky eyes, and their eyelids reddened from sleeplessness. The nighttime rings at the doorbell—"While you were tranquilly resting in Sochi, / Such nights were crawling up to me, / And such ringing of the doorbell I heard..."[42]

Eclipsing in memory the nights of love, the nights of fear created a bond between the two women, which was stronger than love and jealousy (or so Nadezhda Mandelshtam claimed).

In the end, the gossip had far-reaching consequences—not among the writers in wartime Tashkent, but in the larger Russian literary community. Indeed, Akhmatova's well-wrought line took its place in the annals of Soviet poetry, and came to serve as a cue by which others set their own emotional experiences. (There are specific examples of how this happened.)* This was a feminine identity defined by a peculiar erotic situation: the nights of love and terror.

---

* In his memoir of his late wife, Grigorii Pomerants describes how "Ira" (Irina Murav'eva) used Akhmatova's poem to express her own conflicting emotions at the time when she decided to leave her then husband and join Pomerants, his prison-time friend. An intimate recital of "Kakaia est'" became a decisive moment in their relationship. Grigorii Pomerants, "V storonu Iry," *Russkoe bogatstvo*, no 2. (6) 1997, 95. (The story of Irina Murav'eva is related in part 1 of this book.)

Hardships and Privileges

What became vitally important and painfully obvious during the war was the workings of privilege. Writers among the evacuees had access to special housing, food stores, and cafeterias, but there were, of course, gradations in privilege. NN's position was uncertain. As we have seen, for a combination of reasons, attempts to procure privileged housing for her failed. Access to extra food was obtained through the mediation of several people, beginning with Chukovskaia: "Under my instructions, Tolstaya gained access for her to a marvelous food store" (1:418). (Aleksei Tolstoy and his wife, Liudmilla Tolstaya, served as privilege brokers for many.) NN was generous with the fruits of this privilege, sharing them with others, and Chukovskaia carefully recorded these acts (1:485). Then, an epidemic of typhus struck the evacuees. Chukovskaia was among the first to fall ill; the diary for July 9–11, 1942, states laconically: "I lay dying" (1:476). Concerned for her friend, Chukovskaia tried to convince Tolstaya that it was imperative to obtain for Akhmatova a medical pass (*lechkartochka*) for the government clinic (1:415). *Lechkartochka* (*lech* from *lechenie,* treatment; *kartochka,* card), was an analogue of the ration cards used in food distribution. This final privilege—access to medical treatment and care—could prove crucial for survival.

Early in November, NN, too, fell ill with typhus. Chukovskaia, lamenting that responsibilities for her care had fallen into the hands of incompetent people (among them, the negligent Faina Ranevskaia and the well-meaning but sloppy Nadezhda Mandelshtam), rushed to the government clinic for medicine. In the meantime, suspecting that NN's illness was infectious, the neighbors in the Writers' House "raised their voices." Chukovskaia records the name of a literary scholar who demanded that the patient be removed to a hospital. She commented: "They'd be better off cleaning the toilet, that cesspit" (1:495); the image of a cesspit, which Chukovskaia used to describe Akhmatova's prewar communal apartment, was at the tip of her tongue. The conditions at the Writers' House were indeed unsanitary, but NN was afraid of hospitals (rumored to be infested with cockroaches). What was to be done? Chukovskaia was no longer in charge, and things (as she observed in the diary) went terribly wrong. She was also shocked by her hero's fear of death, ill humor, and lack of graciousness toward those who tried to help her (1:497).

Relentlessly, Chukovskaia made efforts to arrange for NN be treated in "some kind of privileged hospital" (1:498). The collective efforts finally brought partial success. This humiliated NN. On the way to the hospital (a special government ward of a general hospital), accompanied by Ranevskaia, she kept complaining about Chukovskaia and others: How did they dare to beg on her behalf, to ask Aleksei Tolstoy for help? But on the same day Chukovskaia heard something that she "would have preferred not to." Nadezhda

Mandelshtam had announced (and Chukovskaia recorded her words in the first person):

> "NN announced that because she was in a government ward, she considered it impossible for me to visit her. Don't you think that that kind of caution is excessive? I don't think Osip would have been capable of such a thing." (1:499)

(The point of this situation is that Osip Mandelshtam was convicted as an "enemy of the people," and his widow, too, was persona non grata in the official sphere.) Chukovskaia added her own comment, as if in a stage whisper addressed to her friend and hero: "Oh, my poor thing. Now I won't be able to 'forgive and forget'" (1:499) (with the last phrase, she is quoting, and distorting, Akhmatova's own line). When NN persisted in banishing Nadezhda Mandelshtam from the "government ward," Chukovskaia described her condition in terms of doubling: "NN takes very good care of AA. And I find that disagreeable" (1:504). (Recall the Tashkent notebooks' use of the conspiratorial "NN" to refer to Anna Andreevna Akhmatova, known to many as "AA.")

Chukovskaia also blamed NN for callous cruelty toward the man who loved her—because he stood for "Leningrad":

> Ranevskaia told me the contents of a telegram to Leningrad, to Lidiia Ginzburg: 'Sick with typhus. Prepare Garshin.' All the same, so callous. And to Leningrad, no less! (1: 501)

The next day NN dictated to Ranevskaia (who was now constantly at her side) a letter to Garshin; she then asked Chukovskaia (through Ranevskaia) to rewrite the letter in her hand (after all, Chukovskaia was known to Garshin, and Ranevskaia was a complete stranger). For the record, Chukovskaia cited NN's letter to her lover in the diary, from memory (1:502). In this moment of crisis, while their intimacy was crumbling under the double pressure of personal jealousy and moral disapproval, the degree of Chukovskaia's penetration into her friend's intimate life (albeit in the company of another mediator, Ranevskaia) reached an apogee; and, unbeknownst to NN, she continued to take notes.

In more ways than one, this situation was fraught with irresolvable conflicts. The Tashkent notebooks provide a painstaking account of Chukovskaia's personal drama, phrased with merciless directness. But the diarist does not comment on the immediate human dynamics of this complex situation (the jealousy of a friend who used the word "love" to describe her feeling for Akhmatova and Akhmatova's for her [1:450]). Instead, the social and moral factors take precedence as explanation. The circumstances of the war and evacuation bred specific social and moral tensions: Chukovskaia and Akhmatova lived (like others) in life-threatening conditions, yet, in contrast to the terror years, in peace with the Soviet authorities and under the protection of their institutions. These tensions came to a climax in the hospital episode. The situation looks especially poignant from Chukovskaia's point of view. For her, the desire to save her friend and the great Russian poet clashed with her longstanding distaste for the privilege extended to writers by the Soviet government. Expecting Akhmatova, too, to share in this distaste, Chukovskaia was caught in a situation of paradoxical desire. In a way, what she desired was not unattainable: that Akhmatova accept the practical privileges that Chukovskaia and others carefully procured for her by way of collective appeals to authorities ("singing at power in chorus" [1:513]), while rejecting the principle of privilege. Chukovskaia's diary-for-two was perfectly suited for documenting this situation. For a while, this silent moral contract seemed to work. It collapsed when Nadezhda Mandelshtam decided to visit the sick Akhmatova in the government ward of the general hospital. Refusing to recognize Mandelshtam's widow, Akhmatova interrupted the workings of a network that, not only tied together the stigmatized and dispossessed but (as in many a community described by anthropologists) also bound the living with the dead. For Chukovskaia, who had become a keeper of this special community, this was tantamount to a violation of the ultimate taboo. In this situation, the reasons for keeping her chronicle were no longer valid.

Years later (when the two women had resumed their friendship after ten years of separation), Chukovskaia had a chance to remember the painful paradox of being ill in a privileged hospital. In February 1958 (shortly before the Soviet authorities condemned the "anti-Soviet" novel *Doctor Zhivago*), the two women discussed the situation of Boris Pasternak, who was gravely ill. Chukovskaia gave a detailed report on the collective efforts to obtain for him treatment in the special government hospital. Akhmatova interrupted her story:

"When you write what Pasternak has written, it's no good having pretensions to a separate ward in the Central Committee's hospital."
    This observation, made as if it had an utterly logical and moral basis, cut me to the quick with its unkindness. I would have been glad in her place. [...]
    "He doesn't have any pretensions," I said in a quiet voice. "Pasternak has asked not to appeal to the Union [of Writers], not to mention anywhere higher. [...] He is in pain, he's screaming with pain, and that's all. But people around him, those who love him (here I hesitated slightly), it's they that really have the pretensions. They want Pasternak to be in the best hospital in Moscow." (2:276)

Chukovskaia did not remind Akhmatova about her stay in the "government ward" in Tashkent, but, having instantly recalled this episode, she committed her memory, and judgment, to the diary:

> When she fell ill with typhus in Tashkent, Anna Andreevna [...] was more than happy to be put, thanks to the efforts of friends, in the local "Kremlin Hospital," in a separate ward...
> Does she remember that? Has she forgotten?
> No, I'm glad for him now, just as I was glad for her then, that she was in humane—i.e., privileged—conditions, and not in "democratic" ones, which here, alas, equate to inhumane ones. (2:277)

The return of this painful situation made obvious for Chukovskaia the paradox of privilege in matters of life and death. The goal was to retain moral purity while preserving a person's life (and one's right to live under "humane conditions"). There was only one way to achieve this goal: a person—the poet—was expected not to ask for anything oneself, but friends stepped in to assure the privilege. This placed a special burden on the institution of friendship and on intimacy. Needless to say, for the poet, and still more for the friend, it was not easy to maintain the precarious balance between the simultaneous denial and acceptance of privilege.

To return to Tashkent. There were, of course, other feelings underlying the tension between the two women as it mounted to a climax with Akhmatova's illness. But what the diary is intent on showing is how they could no longer maintain a comfortable level of ambiguity and ambivalence in balancing between, on the one hand, the group ("intelligentsia") morality and personal loyalty, and, on the other, the vital need to use the government institutions of privilege. We, today's readers, of course, cannot possibly judge or blame either of them. But Chukovskaia did blame NN:

> My last entry about NN as a person. As a person, she no longer interests me. [Several lines crossed out—Elena Chukovskaia.] What's left, then? Beauty, intellect, genius. No small amount—but in human terms she does not interest me any longer. I can read her poems and admire her portrait. (1:514)

This note made on December 11, 1942 (much of it, has been carefully cut or crossed out) is the last in the text published after the diarist's death by her daughter. By this time, NN, who recovered from typhus, was deliberately neglecting and humiliating her devoted old friend. They parted "without clarifying their relationship, or acknowledging the reasons" (2:21). The pressures of the much-too-close living eroded their intimacy.

There is a paradox: it is Chukovskaia's Tashkent notebooks, and not the "gossip" she had feared, that revealed NN's intimate life in the war years, and not only the wild gaiety and freedom in sexual mores reminiscent of her long-gone bohemian youth, but also weakness in the face of death, capitulation to privilege, and disloyalty to old friends (as Chukovskaia saw it).

In the end, the feeling of liberation experienced at the beginning of the war, when—in contrast to the years of the terror—the fear, deprivation, and grief were shared with the whole of the nation, did not last. For Chukovskaia and for Akhmatova, this was the time when the feeling of being threatened and the feeling of being watched proved too much to bear. During the war, Stalin and Hitler in effect joined forces to threaten them with humiliating extinction. In this situation, for Akhmatova, the recording impulse of her old friend became a burden, if not a threat. Chukovskaia's Akhmatova journals came to an end in December 1942: NN rebelled against her caretaker, editor, and chronographer; and she silenced her for the next ten years.

"A NEW EPOCH BEGAN": AFTER 1953

After the two women met again, in June 1952, their new friendship played out mainly in Moscow. After the war, both were uprooted from their Leningrad homes. Chukovskaia, to her great pain, was denied a living permit on a technicality. Akhmatova led a nomadic life, traveling between Leningrad (where she resumed cohabitation with the survivors of the Punin family) and Moscow, where she obviously enjoyed staying with friends, sometimes for months. After 1946, Akhmatova once again was out of favor with the authorities. The momentous *"Postanovlenie"*—the "Central Committee's Resolution on the Journals *Zvezda* and *Leningrad"*—in August 1946 had singled her out as a primary example of the "hollow, apolitical, bourgeois-aristocratic, decadent" poetry that was absolutely foreign to Soviet literature. Akhmatova's situation started to change for the better after Stalin's death—and this included her living situation. In fall 1953, the Writers' Union promised her a room in Moscow (in an apartment she would have shared with Nadezhda Mandelshtam). But Akhmatova found it difficult to accept such a change in her life. She brought up the old problem: were she to move, a stranger would move in, and Irina Punina would end up in a communal apartment (2:75). But Chukovskaia thought that another, emotional, reason was also in play: "Anna Andreevna isn't capable of living on her own" (2:75). Chukovskaia also reported Akhmatova's own definition of her new condition: "I have become a nomad. [...] I'm not at home in Petersburg and I'm not at home here" (2:362). After everything she went through, Akhmatova felt incapable of having a home of her own.

The main topic of the new diary is time: a historical divide that opened after Stalin's death. One of the first entries, on April 19, 1953, opens with Akhmatova's words: "I woke up several times in the night from joy" (2:58). Chukovskaia reminds the reader (though, as of today, few need reminding) that something happened since her last entry (in January): Stalin died on March 5; on April 4 the newspapers announced that the victims of the last terror campaign, the "Jewish doctors," were released. This news brought the happiness that interrupted Akhmatova's sleep.

A few months later, a new theme entered the diary: memory. What now bound the two women was a joint effort to recollect and restore Akhmatova's unpublished poems. As Chukovskaia reminded her reader, "[we] were bound by *Requiem* and by other unpublished poems she had entrusted to my memory" (2:21). The resurfacing of what the author had forgotten and her confidante remembered started suddenly, over tea:

> It was hot; my throat was dry. I was glad when Anna Andreevna offered me tea. I answered with the line:
> "And I beg, as if for charity..." [...]
> "Why ask like that?" said Anna Andreevna.
> Only in that moment did it dawn on me that she had forgotten her own verse that I quoted (2:67)

A moment later, Akhmatova's face "lit up": she recognized the line from her unpublished and forgotten poem. It seems uncanny that this was itself a poem about memory: "Cellar of Memory" ("Podval pamiati"), composed in January 1940. The poem is organized around the image of going down a steep staircase, lantern in hand, into the underground chamber and repository of painful memories. The image alludes to the artists' club the Stray Dog (Brodiachaia sobaka) in Petersburg, which Akhmatova frequented in her bohemian days, shortly before the First World War. In 1941, as she told Chukovskaia, Akhmatova was once forced to seek shelter in the former quarters of the Stray Dog, which was being used as a bomb shelter (2:298, 704).

> Когда спускаюсь с фонарем в подвал,
> Мне кажется—опять глухой обвал
> За мной по узкой лестнице грохочет.
> Чадит фонарь, вернуться не могу,
> А знаю, что иду туда—к врагу.
> И я прошу как милости...Но там
> Темно и тихо. Мой окончен праздник!

> When I descend with a lamp to the cellar,
> It seems to me a landslide

Rumbles again on the narrow stairs.
The lamp smokes, I can't turn back,
And I know that I am going toward the enemy.
And I beg, as if for charity... But there
Is dark and quiet. My holiday is finished![43]

These (and other) lines have been well known to the reader since 1966, when this poem—recovered in full only in 1955—was finally published. But that day the two women could not recall more than several fragments (2:67).

This paradoxical moment of sudden recovery (recollecting the forgotten text about the peril and pain of recovering memories) prompted them to reminisce about the past, and their thoughts turned to the worst years of the terror, spent in the same city:

> It was, perhaps, precisely because of the resurrection of the "Cellar of Memory" that we reminisced a lot that evening about the times we had lived through together in Leningrad. (2:68)

What followed was a question about the *past future*—that is, the future as it had been imagined in the past:

> And she asked me the question that everybody was asking one another these days: had I hoped to outlive Stalin?
> "No," I replied. "I somehow never thought about it. I lived in the belief that he was a constant given for us. And you? Did you hope to outlive him?"
> She shook her head.
> I asked what she thought: had he expected to die someday himself?
> "No," she replied. "Probably not. Death was only for other people, and he was in charge of it." (2:68)

Many contemporaries described Stalin's death as a Nietzschean moment of the death of God, experienced as a physical shock (tears were convulsively shed both by those who loved Stalin and those who did not). Chukovskaia and Akhmatova did not report shedding tears, but they too experienced a shift in their sense of time. In this case, it was not so much their sense of the past that changed after Stalin's death as the sense of the future. Throughout the years of the terror they had carefully preserved memories for future use. But, as it now became clear, they had not really believed that this future would ever come—at least not in their lifetime. It would seem that, against reason, they did not really believe that Stalin was mortal. What they discussed was a political theology that endowed the state and the ruler with divine power.[44] Then, as if in one moment on March 5, 1953—signaled by a death that was as shocking as the death of God—the future was now. Or was it?

In some ways, as the episode with the "Cellar of Memory" indicates, a change in preconsciousness (if not consciousness) did take place. But not much changed in the day-to-day life after March 1953: the future once again moved away. Thus, when Chukovskaia came to see Akhmatova (in the home of her Moscow friends, the Ardovs), they spent their evenings, as before, whispering about the latest actions of "the Court of Miracles" (their private euphemism for the state security). "And I had imagined that was behind us!" commented Chukovskaia on May 4, 1953 (2:64). Moreover, their emotions were tinted by the past. In the fall, Akhmatova was promised the publication of a book of her poetry (the first since the 1946 Resolution). Recording the news in the diary, Chukovskaia comments on the special quality of the joy she felt (and assumes that her feelings were shared by a community of "we"): "for some reason this joy is poisoned, just as, in some strange way, all our present joys are poisoned" (October 17, 1953; 2:74). The past continued to rule over emotions.

In March 1956, after Khrushchev's secret speech, Chukovskaia again felt that special sensation of poisoned joy. She turned to Akhmatova for explanation. Akhmatova had a theory about the nature of contradictory emotions experienced at the end of the terror. It was a theory of lived time:

> Because unconsciously, without knowing it yourself, you want those years never to have existed, but they *did*. They can't be erased. Time doesn't stand still, it moves on. The prisoners may return home from the camps, but neither you nor they can return to that day when you were parted. [...] you don't just want the people to return, but the day too, and you want the life that was forcibly broken off to safely carry on from where it was interrupted. You want to patch up the places where they hacked into it with an axe. But that doesn't work. No such glue exists. The category of time is generally far more complicated than the category of space. (2:199)

Moreover, contrary to what Akhmatova said, to return the prisoners from the camps did not prove to be easy. Nikolai Punin, who anxiously awaited a promised release, died of a heart attack on August 21, 1953, in a distant camp. The family learned the details from a letter written by his fellow inmate, a Ukrainian peasant, Ivan Prokof'evich Gorbatenko (believing her to be Punin's wife, he addressed it to Marta Golubeva, Punin's female companion in the 1940s). The 2000 edition of Punin's diaries and letters published this (badly misspelled and largely ungrammatical) letter in its original form, which can be barely grasped by the English translation:

> Auntie Maria, I am writing about your husband Nikolai Nikolaevich. He died on the 21st of August at 11:45, not having been ill. On the 20th he got money and came to me to pay debt and I look at him and say where're you going. That he brought money to pay the debt he said he'd never be able to repay me and always find an answer and he left. In the morning I went to work and he stood by the dormitory. I said hello to him and say why you are up so early and he said he couldn't sleep and thinks that they promised him that he would go home and [from home] they wrote they even sent my suit out to the cleaners and wife was getting a room ready and for some reason I don't get any packages and probably they are waiting and says when I took money from you I bought 20 apples from the man who delivers packages the Ukrainian and yesterday took a litter bottle of milk need to go eat breakfast and left. Two and a half hours later they come tell me they take Nekolai Nekolaevich Punin to hospital on stretcher I dropped everything and ran to the hospital and as soon as I went in he says, do you see? this morning I was standing talking to you and now I'm in the hospital and when I ask he says come see me at 12 there'll be a doctor. I shall ask him what to buy and I left from him at 11 exactly and I had come back at 12 they tell me Nekolai Nekolaevich died a quarter to 12.[45]

This document possesses such uncanny power that any comment may seem frivolous, but I will comment. The letter presents death in the camp in the context of mundane existence (under the relaxed post-Stalin regime). It pictures life measured by expectations of food parcels and money transfers from the outside world, life defined by small monetary exchanges converted into purchases of food. From precise circumstances ("bought from the man who delivers packages the Ukrainian") to amounts ("20 apples"), these transactions are described in minute detail. The letter conveys a special intimacy between a Petersburg art historian and a Ukrainian peasant, who—were it not for the terror that brought them together in the camp—were unlikely to have known each other. This is an intimacy based on shared rubles, apples, and hopes—hopes for release, expressed by sharing with a fellow inmate news about the precise measures taken by the family back home in anticipation of the prisoner's return ("they wrote they even sent my suit out to the cleaners and wife was getting a room ready"). It is remarkable that Punin, who addressed his lovers, Anna Akhmatova and Marta Golubeva, with the refined second person plural (*Vy*), seems to address his camp companion with the familiar second person singular (*ty*). From the careful, and tactful, description of the monetary and other transactions, it seems that Ivan Gorbatenko offered Punin a helping hand. He was clearly admitted into knowing about Punin's family. In the last lines, he describes reading Golubeva's letters together with Punin:

> and we read letters that you didn't go to vacation in the country and that you were waiting for Nekolai Nekolaevich to come. Goodbye then and hello to Anya and her mother.[46]

For the Russian reader of Punin's diaries and letters published in 2000, this eyewitness account of his death gains additional power from its language—ungrammatical, randomly spelled, and devoid of punctuation. Today's readers are touched by what the writer himself perceives—the tragedy of death away from one's family on the eve of release from the camp; and by what the writer does not know—the pathos of reading an account of an intellectual's death given by an unlikely, barely literate, witness. This, after all, is a quintessential Russian scene codified in Tolstoy's *War and Peace:* the encounter of Pierre Bezhukhov with the peasant Platon Karataev, who befriended the nobleman during the French captivity in 1812. But the roles are reversed: in real life, it is the illiterate peasant who survives to tell the story.*

After the Twentieth Congress of the Communist Party, Akhmatova's long-lasting efforts to secure the release of her son, Lev, started to gain ground. On March 4, 1956, Akhmatova told Chukovskaia that the powerful leader of the Writers' Union, Alexander Fadeev, had appealed to the highest authorities on Lev's behalf (2:190). On May 15, 1956, Chukovskaia recorded:

> Lev has returned.
> Fadeev shot himself. (2:205)

During their next meeting, they discussed rumors about the cause of Fadeev's suicide: the official version was alcoholism, but many wanted to see it as an admission of guilt (his involvement in the repression of writers) and an act of redemption.

---

* The situation of Nikolai Punin and Ivan Gorbanenko is not unique. Thus, it is from the letter of a worker, Iurii Illarionovich Moiseenko, that we now know about the circumstances of Osip Mandelshtam's death in a prison camp. The Mandelshtam scholar Alexander Morozov wrote that Mandelshtam died, having found "his Platon Karataev" (foreword to Nadezhda Mandelshtam, *Vtoraia kniga,* ix; for the text of the letter, which first surfaced in 1991, see appendix to Nadezhda Mandelshtam's *Vospominaniia* [Moscow: Soglasie, 1999], 525–26).

As for Chukovskaia's husband, Matvei Bronshtein (who in 1938 had been sentenced to "ten years without the right to correspondence"), Chukovskaia took an opportunity provided by the Khrushchev regime and petitioned for his "posthumous rehabilitation." In February 1957, she was summoned to the registry office (ZAGS) to receive a certificate of his death. Date of death: February 18, 1938. The place and cause of death: blank. In her diary, Chukovskaia told the story of the certificate twice: the second time she recorded how she told the story to Akhmatova, giving more details than in her initial entry. At her friend's request, she took Akhmatova, and with her the future readers of the Akhmatova journals, through the minute details of this procedure, gruesome in their insignificance: the cozy, homelike interior of the office, which also registered marriages; the flow of trivial chit-chat that occupied the office workers; the voice of the radio broadcast (devoted to the production of glass) in the background; and the portrait of Stalin on the wall. Deeply shaken, she defined what happened in ethnographic terms: "this rite has become an integral part of the ritual of rehabilitation. It is, indeed, posthumous: thus, first of all one needs to certify the death. Everything done properly" (2:247). It was hard for Chukovskaia to describe these events in her diary. Several months later, she made a brief summary of this "most undiarylike of times," borrowing Herzen's word to express the impossibility of speaking: "as Herzen put it, 'words do not capture this'" (2:253; 255).

Did They Understand What Was Going On?

In 1956 the future began once again. Rumors about Khrushchev's revelations of Stalin's terror crimes at the Twentieth Party Congress (the famous "secret speech" delivered at the Congress's "closed meeting" on February 25, 1956) reached Chukovskaia and her friends on February 29 (2:185). (Lev was still in the camp.) A few days later, on the eve of Stalin's death, the two women met for an intimate celebration (they had not yet read the speech). "We celebrated thus: Anna Andreevna asked for a towel to be dampened with cold water, lay down and placed it on her forehead." (2:189). From this position she made her own historical speech on the end of Stalin. Sitting at her bedside, Chukovskaia memorized her speech, recording it in her diary later that day:

"What we went through," spoke Anna Andreevna from her pillow, "yes, yes, all of us, for the torture chamber threatened everyone!—has not been captured by any work of literature. Shakespeare's dramas—all those elaborate villains, passions, duels—are mere trifles, child's play compared to the lives of each of us. And as for what the execution victims and prisoners in the camps went through, I wouldn't dare to speak of that. No words can describe that." (2:189)

Chukovskaia intervened, qualifying the "we":

> I said that lots of people, especially younger ones, were confused and upset by the exposure of Stalin. [...] "That's nonsense," replied Anna Andreevna calmly. "As the doctors say, 'The anesthetic is wearing off'." (2:190)

The clinical metaphor implies that people lived in an artificially induced state of nonawareness in Stalin's time; as this state dissolved, it left painful side effects. In the next sentence, Akhmatova revised her judgment:

> "Besides, I don't believe that nothing had been understood earlier."
> I disagreed with her. I'd had occasion to meet people—good, sincere, thoughtful people—to whom it never for a moment occurred that they were being deceived.
> "That's not true!" shrieked Anna Andreevna with such vehement rage that I was afraid for her heart. [...] "They were putting it on. It was in their interests to pretend—to their friends, and to themselves. You understood everything back then; don't let yourself be deceived now." (2:190)

What was at stake in 1956, at the moment that marked the end of Stalin's epoch, was the question of commonality in historical experience. It was easy, even comforting, to think—as Akhmatova then did—of "two Russias":

> Now when the prisoners are returning, and two Russias will look each other in the eye: the one that pronounced sentences, and the one that served them. A new epoch has begun. You and I have lived to see it. (2:190)

Akhmatova longed, not only for a clear sense of historical divide, but also for a sense of a clear division in the community.

When, on March 20, Chukovskaia (accompanied by a close friend, the writer Frida Vigdorova) actually listened to the two-hour reading of Khrushchev's "secret speech" in the Moscow offices of the Writers' Union, she, too, noted the division. The women in the audience wept: "Everyone cried, except Frida and me" (2:196). Chukovskaia felt angry at those who wept: they should have known earlier, and should have wept earlier. And she wondered: What was the exact object of their tears? Vigdorova suggested that these women wept over their lost faith in Stalin. When Chukovskaia told Akhmatova about the tears, her face registered a momentary upsurge of anger. It was important for Akhmatova to affirm that, in contrast to these women, *we* had always known everything (and, consequently, we have not cried). The meticulous Chukovskaia contradicted her: from the "secret speech" (she said) she had learned one new thing—that torture was openly acknowledged as an acceptable way of interrogating prisoners. In his speech, Khrushchev had made public a telegram, signed by Stalin, that affirmed that "the application of physical means of influencing" was an acceptable part of the Soviet investigative apparatus. Akhmatova disagreed:

> "It wasn't in the least bit new to me! [...] It even seems to me that I read that telegram with my own eyes. [...] Maybe I read it in a dream. It's a pity we didn't record our dreams during these years. That would have made for the richest historical material." (2:198)

It is remarkable that, grappling for a source of intangible knowledge, Akhmatova reached for the realm of dreams. (Akhmatova did not seem to know that her friend did in fact record her dreams during the years of the terror [1:11, 5].)

The problem of who knew and understood (and how: by personal experience, sound judgment, intuition, or by way of dreams) continued to plague them. In the years that followed Stalin's death, a new dimension opened in the lives of literary intellectuals: they met foreigners (participants in carefully monitored academic exchange)—people from beyond the curtain that had firmly separated them from the rest of the world from the early 1930s through the 1950s.

In the 1960s and beyond, such contact, mostly initiated by foreign scholars and established on the basis of common interests in specific Russian authors, took place; it was fraught with uncertainty and misunderstandings. In June 1962, Martin Malia, an American historian who worked on Herzen, was a frequent guest of Chukovskaia (also a Herzen specialist), and he visited Akhmatova as well. The visitor was an enigma to Akhmatova: "'What do you think—is he so very intelligent?' she asked. 'Does he understand life here?'" (2:504). Such, indeed, was the criterion: the foreigner's "intelligence" was measured by his ability to understand "local"—Soviet—life. Chukovskaia had an astute answer to Akhmatova's question:

> Hm. It's hard for me to judge foreigners, and the extent of their intellect and intelligence. Our experience of life is too different from theirs— everything is different. Besides, how many of them have I come across in my life? I can count on the fingers of one hand. (2:504)

Still, she decided that Malia was highly intelligent and insightful in his knowledge of the Russian nineteenth century, and that he knew Herzen better than the average Russian intellectual; but she did not know whether he understood the Soviet condition. This query prompted Chukovskaia to self-searching. Her reflections on the limitations of shared knowledge are addressed not to Akhmatova but to her diary and its potential reader:

> I talk to him without hiding anything, or without being overly cautious, but what of me, do I understand? At my age, and with my experience, it's high time I understood—but, in the absence of an honest press, our life has become so atomized that each of us is shortsighted: we only clearly discern those people and circumstances that are close by us. In a country deprived of collective memory—which might unite people—in a country bereft of literature and history, the experience of every person, group, and section of society can only be its own, limited, separate experience. The country is vast, but there's no sum to the country's experience; it's not connected or collected together; worse still—it's falsified. (2:504—5)

This remarkable passage makes several important generalization. First, speaking for a "country," Chukovskaia powerfully affirms the awareness of her own and others' "shortsighted" vision: in the absence of a free press, there is no shared horizon or backdrop to society upon which all may look with clarity. (The personal reference is underscored by the fact that Chukovskaia was extremely shortsighted.) Further, Chukovskaia explains this atomized society through the lack of "common memory," such as in national history and literature. The conclusion: the country does not have, and cannot possibly have, a "common experience" and, by implication, a common understanding. It appeared that, rather than question Martin Malia's credentials for understanding Soviet life, Chukovskaia placed herself in the position of a foreigner in her own land. The modest Chukovskaia stopped short of suggesting that her diary writing may have worked for the creation of such future memory.

Akhmatova's Things and Manuscripts

On December 23, 1959, Chukovskaia—for the first time since the war and since their estrangement—visited Akhmatova in her Leningrad home. Akhmatova no longer lived in the Sheremetev Palace Museum: this was a different apartment (also shared with the Punins). Inside, the sight of once familiar domestic objects evoked intense emotion:

> I suddenly found myself among things long forgotten and in another age: that same smooth frame of the misty mirror, that same armchair with the broken leg. And that same little mahogany table that stood twenty years

ago in a room in the Fontanka House, the place I'd so loved to visit. Then, before the war, in the Leningrad that was still mine. (2:365)

Chukovskaia is careful and precise in defining the nature of her emotion: an acute sense of recovered past triggered by an act of recognition. The effect rests on a sense of familiarity and sameness combined with the realization that something that had once been a part of life became forgotten. This something was a set of domestic objects. Chukovskaia related to these objects in a historical key:

> Things are like sponges—they soak up time and then suddenly it's all wrung out over a person, drenching him from head to toe, if he happens to come across them after a long separation.
> For Anna Andreevna, the things in her room were probably full of 1913; and for me, 1937. [...] I only saw them in 1938, but they, like me, were witnesses to the composition of *Requiem,* the greatest monument to that epoch, the epoch of the 1930s, the whole of which bears the name "thirty-seven." (2:365)

Things were condensers and dispensers of historical time and historical experience.

Of course, these were no ordinary things and no ordinary room. As another scholar noted, Chukovskaia stepped into the Akhmatova "memorial museum."[47] I will offer an anthropological reading of this episode. Anthropologists have assigned different meanings to objects in the home: status symbols, projections of self or body, signs of life's continuity, symbols of family life, indexes of group identity, aesthetic objects, etc. Not so, for Chukovskaia and, if we believe her, Akhmatova. While the specific historical value of the domestic objects was relative to the person (for Chukovskaia, these things indicated "1937"; for Akhmatova, supposedly, "1913"), the main principle seemed clear: the predominantly historical meaning of domestic things. (Across two decades, if not more, the practical value of these objects was, at best, problematic: a "misty" mirror, a chair with a broken leg.)

Anthropologists and philosophers believe that household objects fulfill an essential function: they stabilize human life by rooting it in the domestic environment (people "can retrieve their sameness, that is, their identity, by being related to the same chair and the same table").[48] Obviously, under Soviet conditions, the intimate life of a person was markedly devoid of stability, be it the stability of marriage or that of the physical household. As Chukovskaia's account suggests, domestic things were comforting in their sameness, and they reaffirmed identity, not only for their owner, but also for an intimate friend. But they did this not so much by way of domesticity as by way of history.

The household objects were vessels of historical time, charged with emotion. Being related to the same (broken) chair and the same (misty) mirror offered a sense of identity, as these objects became indexes of the historical embeddedness of intimate life (complete with dates). Outside of national, and world, history, domestic life proved incapable of creating a sense of permanence in a person's intimate life—at least, in that of persons like Chukovskaia and Akhmatova.

Note an additional task charged to these domestic objects: a mirror, a chair, a table stood as monuments or, like living people, witnesses, not to lived experience itself, but to the creation of the text (to the composition of Akhmatova's *Requiem*). This was a culture of texts: it was the text that served as the ultimate monument to the year 1937.

Given the primacy of the text, it hardly comes as a surprise that in the years of peripathetic postwar existence Akhmatova invested her sense of self and home mainly in one specific "thing": a suitcase filled with her manuscripts. (The suitcase is now exhibited in the Anna Akhmatova Apartment Museum in St. Petersburg.) On June 21, 1961, Akhmatova appeared in Chukovskaia's tiny summer cottage in Peredelkino (near Moscow) with her "battered old suitcase held together by rope" (it was carried by her companion, "Natasha," who drove Akhmatova to Peredelkino from Moscow in her car): "Evidently, Anna Andreevna would not part from the suitcase: her manuscripts were in it" (2:461). As Akhmatova explained, the suitcase now contained all that she owned: the rest of her belongings had perished in a flood. She made the announcement with characteristic pomp: "'All my books, belongings, clothes—everything's been washed away,' said Anna Andreevna. 'I have nothing now. But it's all the same to me; it fits my destiny. I'm not upset'" (2:462). In a footnote, added at some later point, Chukovskaia observed that the damage caused by the burst water pipe in Akhmatova's new apartment had not, in fact, been so catastrophic (2:462). (Chukovskaia did not seem to notice that this episode played out on the eve of the twentieth anniversary of the beginning of the war.)

This dispassionate corrective notwithstanding, the symbolic value of Akhmatova's suitcase was reaffirmed. The old rope-bound suitcase filled with manuscripts signified the poet's homelessness—the condition that, regardless of specific circumstances (regardless of whether or not she was indeed homeless), marked Akhmatova's identity as an outcast.

Carrying manuscripts in a suitcase also signified another aspect of the Soviet condition: ever-present surveillance. Left out of sight, the manuscripts would not be safe. As Akhmatova's constant companion, the suitcase seemed to replace a human companion (Chukovskaia), who had memorized the poetry in the years of the terror. In Akhmatova's view, even after Stalin, a suitcase was a poor replacement for a "living archive." Once, in June 1960,

Chukovskaia inquired whether Akhmatova now recorded her poems. Akhmatova exploded:

> "Do I write my poems down? And this is *you* asking this—you!"
> She went up to the stool upon which the suitcase sat and furiously began flinging out of it and to an ottoman all her manuscripts, books, notebooks, files, writing pads.
> "How can I write anything down? How can I keep my poems safe? Books have their spines cut into with a razor! Look, here you go! Files have their ribbons ripped! I could present a whole collection of ripped ribbons and severed bindings! And *that's* what it's like here, and *that's* what it's like in Leningrad! That's what!" (2:419)

This remonstration was meant to prove that in a home the manuscripts were not safe: Akhmatova thought that she detected signs of blatant secret perusal of her papers by state security agents (the unnamed, impersonal "them"). As in the episode with the "hair" in 1940, Chukovskaia (whether rightly or wrongly) did not doubt the realism of her friend's assessment of the situation: "How could I answer her? Evidently, in these new times, too, there was only one tried and tested means for the safe-keeping of poetry..." (2:420). (That old way was the embodied preservation of texts within a human mind.) Chukovskaia does not comment on it, but clearly shows that Akhmatova steadfastly held on to the sense of continuity of terror and victimization.

In spite of the "new times," in late May 1962, *Requiem* still existed only as an orally preserved text. One day, Akhmatova tested Chukovskaia's memory ("checked the money in the till"):

> She had long been intending to go with me somewhere outside of those four walls and check whether I remembered everything. At her sudden behest I came over to see her, and we set off for the nearby gardens. At that time, on a working day, almost all the benches were empty, and we sat down some way away from two old women tending children, from a pensioner reading the newspaper, further away from the street. [...] She listened as I recited aloud the poems that I had repeated over and over to myself so many times. (2:491)

Akhmatova proclaimed that seven other people knew *Requiem* by heart. Chukovskaia did not know their names. (On another occasion, in November, Akhmatova spoke of eleven people [2:536].)

On December 9, 1962, Akhmatova summoned Chukovskaia to announce that the text of *Requiem* was now typed (in several carbon copies). Chukovskaia recorded this fact in her journal: "And so this miracle text is well fixed; *Requiem* will not vanish, even if those seven or eleven people, who, like me, were trusted with remembering by heart all die in one go" (2:560). At this time, Akhmatova and Chukovskaia hoped that it could be published in the Soviet Union. But current events confirmed Akhmatova's sense of historical continuity: the poem was not published in the Soviet Union until 1987.

An Aside: Memoirs as Historical Evidence

Chukovskaia vividly describes an episode of June 21, 1961, when she saw the suitcase of endangered manuscripts entrusted to the protection of a certain "Natasha" (2:634). The entry of this figure—Natalia Iosifovna Il'ina (1914–1994)—into the scene becomes a point around which uncertainties proliferate. Chukovskaia herself describes Il'ina, who after 1954 was a frequent companion of Akhmatova, only sympathetically; she says nothing of the suspicions that surrounded Il'ina in writers' circles. While she chose to ignore this, Chukovskaia was certainly aware that some thought it unlikely that Il'ina—an émigré who returned to Soviet Russia from Shanghai in 1947 to become an acclaimed Soviet writer—could have gained her official standing without a significant compromise with power. And this (as it appears from other memoir sources) is the view that Akhmatova shared: despite maintaining a lively friendship with the worldly, witty, and very helpful Natalia Il'ina, Akhmatova believed her to be an informer entrusted by the state security with the surveillance of her every move.

Leaving aside the question of whether or not Il'ina was an informer, I will examine several overlapping memoirs that speak about Akhmatova and Il'ina. My goal is to reflect on the status of Soviet memoirs as historical evidence. One account of Il'ina's ambiguous status in Akhmatova's circle is known to us thirdhand—from the memoirs of Mikhail Viktorovich Ardov (born in 1937), published in 2000 and 2006. (His parents, the actress Nina Antonovna Ol'shevskaia and the satirical writer Viktor Efimovich Ardov, regularly housed Akhmatova in their apartment on the Ordynka, and he knew Akhmatova from childhood. At the time of Akhmatova's relationship with Il'ina, Mikhail Ardov was a student of journalism; he was an Orthodox priest when he published his memoirs.) According to Ardov, the poet Mariia Sergeevna Petrovykh (another member of Akhmatova's circle) once told him the following story:

> Mariia Sergeevna recounted this to me: "Natasha [Il'ina] brought me her memoir about Akhmatova, but she didn't understand herself what she had written. She apparently did not suspect that Anna Akhmatova believed her to be an informer. Here is one episode from her memoirs: on the morning of the day [in 1958] the *Doctor Zhivago* scandal broke, barely having read the newspapers, Il'ina rushed over to Akhmatova's

to ask what she thought about it all. [...] To be sure, Anna Andreevna couldn't have seen this visit as anything other than the following of official orders. Nevertheless, she said: "The poet is always right." That is to say, Akhmatova was not afraid of conveying such a sentiment to the Lubyanka [KGB headquarters]..."[49]

Let us try to unravel this entangled situation. To begin with, in her memoir, Il'ina described an encounter with Akhmatova that had occurred on the day the notorious *Doctor Zhivago* scandal broke. (The Soviet newspapers published a vehement political denunciation of the novel, akin to Stalin's campaigns, which made Pasternak into a public enemy.) We are exposed not to this memoir though, but to its reading by Maria Petrovykh, to whom Il'ina showed her Akhmatova memoir, and exposed not directly but via another mediator: Petrovykh shared her interpretation with Mikhail Ardov, who subsequently described their conversation in his memoirs. Both Petrovykh and Ardov believed that they understood what went on between Akhmatova and Il'ina better than Il'ina herself understood the episode she had described in her memoir.

This is what they thought: Akhmatova, working on the assumption that her friend Natasha Il'ina was a secret informer, thought that through "Natasha" she was speaking to the all-powerful KGB. And through the KGB, she, of course, spoke to "history"; hence the solemn tone she assumes for such a heroic occasion (proclaiming her approval of the fellow poet whose novel was publicly condemned by the Soviet authorities). After all, she was potentially taking upon herself a mantle of martyrdom akin to Pasternak's.

It should be noted that Ardov does not doubt Akhmatova's intuition in rooting out informers in her circle: he, too, believes that Il'ina was a secret agent. Thus, speaking both for himself and for Petrovykh, Ardov reads this episode from Il'ina's memoir as a story of Akhmatova's courage in the face of the secret police that penetrated her home.

But what if Akhmatova's intuition betrayed her? What if Il'ina was not an informer? In that case, with her solemn proclamation, Akhmatova was not speaking the dangerous and powerful words she thought she was: she was only addressing her (somewhat naive and politically misguided) friend, Natasha, and not the KGB. Should this be true, then the full meaning and implications of what he wrote evaded Mikhail Ardov when he described this episode.

But let us pause to ask: If Akhmatova thought that Il'ina was a secret informer, why did she put up with Il'ina for so many years? In his memoirs, Ardov gives three hypothetical reasons. First, Akhmatova believed that it was convenient and even advantageous to have a decent informer by her side: someone who would not misquote her words and opinions in her reports. The second reason, mused Ardov, lay in Il'ina's charm and wit: she was a lively conversationalist who loved to share a good meal. And lastly, there was one more reason that enabled their intimacy. Il'ina had received a substantial fee for the publication of her autobiographical novel, *The Return* (*Vozvrashchenie*), and this had allowed her to buy a car. As Ardov explained, "[S]he would gladly take Akhmatova places—and Akhmatova did love to go for a drive."⁵⁰

This insinuation has far-reaching implications. In the opinion of those who disapproved of Il'ina, her novel *The Return*—with its highly critical picture of the émigré community and enthusiastic celebration of her return to the Soviet Union—was one of the compromises with Soviet power that assured her acceptance in the society. Building on this well-known fact, Ardov implies that betrayal by way of a novel bought Il'ina a privilege: a car of her own. In a word, Ardov's carefully crafted argument seems to imply that, in more ways than one, it was Il'ina's status as a former émigré that caused both Akhmatova's suspicions and her acceptance of Il'ina—a secret informer with *savoir-vivre* and a car. What Mikhail Ardov aims at doing is to provide the readers of his memoirs with a vignette revealing the morally unsavory complexities of the Soviet condition. But he, too, fails to understand the full implications of what he wrote: after all, readers may feel appalled by the unsavory nature of his insinuations.

The story Mikhail Ardov told in his Akhmatova memoir did not go unchallenged. His (secondhand) revelation about Il'ina was questioned in public, as was his very act. In an essay that appeared on the Internet, the prominent critic and editor Alla Latynina (born in 1940) reproached Ardov for accusing Il'ina of acting as an informer for the KGB without reliable evidence. Her essay is devoted to the ethical problems of witnessing, but she speaks from a personal perspective, as a member of the same divided community: "For those who knew Natalia Il'ina, this accusation appears completely absurd." Then Latynina, in her turn, passes to personal accusations:

> Mikhail Ardov doesn't bother himself with evidence; he proceeds as if witness to the fact that this opinion existed. But another extremely widespread opinion also existed—Ardov, the elder, was accused by many of association with the KGB. If a memoirist is going to offer up rumors concerning such a sensitive subject, then why doesn't he stick first and foremost to the rumors that concern his own family?

Latynina, in her turn, does not seem to notice that, like Ardov, she makes an accusation (about Ardov's father) unsubstantiated by evidence. Yet she concludes with poignant reflections on the precarious status of memoir writing as evidence. A memoirist, Latynina argues, testifies not to a fact but to an opinion—or to the fact that a certain opinion existed in the community. At the next step, such a testimony is cited by others, acquiring the status of evidence and a semblance of legitimacy. Ambiguities and assumptions pile up, and interpretations based on assumptions and opinions are reiterated in subsequent texts as facts; in the end, the memoir becomes a historical "source":

> Worst of all is the fact that the testimony of an authoritative memoirist becomes the "source" on which others then rely (I came across the reference to M. Ardov's testimony, for example, in [the newspaper] *Moskovskii komsomolets*).
> Differentiating between testimonies and false testimonies—this is a very painful problem. I see no simple way of solving it.[51]

Indeed, there is no simple way of solving this problem. But one thing is clear: these tangled texts show that Soviet memoirists face epistemological and ethical problems of exceptional gravity. In the example at hand, the words uttered by Akhmatova, as they were reproduced and interpreted by several memoirists, became surrounded by ever-thickening layers of uncertainty, and ever more loosened from their original source. This is what happens to the status of memoir evidence in a tightly knit community that has lived under the conditions of institutionalized ambiguity.

Historical Continuity: The 1930s and the 1960s

What provided a strong sense of continuity between the years of the terror and the "new epoch" was the palpable presence of fear. The political campaign against Boris Pasternak and his *Doctor Zhivago* in 1958 served as a painful reminder, not only of the continuing threat, but also of enduring fear. Paradoxically, fear does not feature as a theme in the diary for the years 1938–42. But in 1958, Akhmatova and Chukovskaia registered the return of the fear. In her diary Chukovskaia described the animal fear that overcame her as she approached Pasternak's dacha in the writers' colony of Peredelkino on October 28, 1958, the day the newspapers announced Pasternak's expulsion from the Union of Soviet Writers (2:316). (She and Pasternak were neighbors.) She then spoke of Pasternak's letter declining the Nobel Prize (published in *Pravda* on November 2) as a text "dictated by fear" ("the fear not for oneself, but for the fate of one's loved ones, that is, a worthy fear—but *fear* all the same" [2:332]).

In September 1962, Chukovskaia reported a conversation with Akhmatova, the main subject of which was remembering the old fear:

> "In 1938," recalled Anna Andreevna, "somebody said to me, you're fearless. You're not afraid of anything." I said to him: "Hardly! The only thing I do is to be afraid. But really, is it at all possible not to be afraid? They'll take you away, and before killing you, they'll make you betray others." (2:513)

This discussion was occasioned by the appearance of Alexander Solzhenitsyn's *One Day in the Life of Ivan Denisovich* in the Moscow journal *Novyi mir* (2:513), which evoked memories of the terror. The conversation then turned to Herzen. Chukovskaia related a historical anecdote about Chaadaev and Herzen: years after he was persecuted for his "Philosophical Letter," Chaadaev hastened to denounce Herzen's *Development of the Revolutionary Ideas in Russia* (published in the West), which—to his secret delight—praised his "Letter" as an event in the history of Russian thought. Akhmatova had an explanation: "Fear. Fear stays in one's blood. Chaadaev feared the repetition of repression. After his first exile, Osip [Mandelshtam] wrote verses in praise of Stalin. Later, he said to me: 'It was a sickness'" (2:515). In December 1963, Chukovskaia recorded another conversation about fear. Akhmatova again proclaimed that in the years of the terror she was "more afraid than anyone." Chukovskaia suggested: "But you got the better of your fear and wrote *Requiem* and much else besides" (3:132).

Both felt that fear denied them a survivor's sense of heroic victory. Akhmatova advanced a theory of trauma: once experienced, fear left a residue, which undercut one's ability to withstand the next challenge. Chukovskaia advanced arguments excusing fear (Akhmatova's fear). But the very fact that they repeatedly spoke about fear was indicative of their condition: long after Stalin's terror came to an end, fear remained a palpable presence in their lives.

In 1964, the "Brodsky case"—arrest, trial, and exile of the young poet Iosif Brodsky, convicted by a Leningrad court for "parasitic existence"—brought back terror in still more tangible ways. The news reached Akhmatova and Chukovskaia in the Moscow apartment of the Ardovs, where they were surrounded by Brodsky's young friends, but the feeling was familiar: "It seemed to me as if I were back in Leningrad, back in the clutches of 1937, that same feeling of humiliation and inalienable insult." The circumstances, Chukovskaia realized, were different (and the sentence, five years of exile, was mild by the standards of 1937):

> Of course, 1964 was nothing compared to 1937—this isn't the Special Session or the military tribunals, sentencing thousands and thousands of people to instant execution or slow death every day [...] but it's the same impenetrable wall. (3:179)

The *feeling* was the same. Chukovskaia was also concerned with what she saw as the enduring attitude of those in power: "And it's the same old sadistic hate for the intelligentsia, promulgated from above, just like the anti-Semitism" (3:179). It was in terms of their group that people like Chukovskaia and Akhmatova perceived what happened to Brodsky: they were humiliated, offended, and threatened in their shared identity as "the intelligentsia."

It is worth noting that the very fact that such strong opinions were expressed in Chukovskaia's diary indicates that the quality of the terror was not the same as in 1937–38. Moreover, unlike in the years of Stalin, the trial was documented, and documented by "us": the writer and journalist Frida Vigdorova, who attended the open court hearing, made a bold move to take notes and prepare a detailed account of the trial. Chukovskaia emphasized the unique genre of this document: "Frida's account is something unique. As precise as a stenograph, as expressive as a literary work. The genre? Completely new: documentary drama" (3:182).

Yes, there were differences, such as new modes and genres for documenting terror. And yet there was a feeling of sameness, a sense that oppression possessed a mundane quality extending across time, which Chukovskaia captured in an image of movement through the monotonous landscape of Russia:

> Apart from the indignation, the "Brodsky case" brought on a feeling of hateful tedium. Our relentless quotidian existence. Like going on a train across the boundless steppe. When you look out the window, it goes on and on and on. No, it's not like the twenties. And it's not like thirty-seven. It's not like "after the war." But it's all alike. (3:201)

Something else was also similar to the terror of the 1930s: the emotional reaction of the victim. In April 1964, Akhmatova reported to Chukovskaia that although the campaign in defense of Brodsky, which involved a large group of people, was going quite well, the "hero" was not behaving so well: "Just imagine, Joseph said, 'Nobody's willing to lift a finger to help me. If they were, then they could have had me free in two days.' ('Them'—that's us!)" (3:207). Akhmatova was "breathless with anger":

> People are fussing over him as nobody fussed over any one of the eighteen million victims of oppression! [...] He has typical camp psychosis—I've seen it before—Lev said that I didn't want him to come back and was purposefully keeping him in the camp... (3:207)

For Akhmatova, the psychological dynamics of the situation were painfully familiar from her own past.[52] Chukovskaia did not say anything, but she thought: "Lev spent almost twenty years in prison and in the camps, whereas Joseph's been gone all of three weeks..." (3:207). Both women were increasingly troubled by the problem of similarity and difference in historical experience.

The problem of continuity and change was central to Chukovskaia's diary of the post-Stalin years, as it was for many other personal documents from and about his time; Chukovskaia posed it as an emotional problem. As we have seen, the Pasternak case in 1958 and the Brodsky case in 1964 evoked strong feelings and brought back old patterns both in the relationship with the state power and in intimate relationships. The old fear, tinted with shame, reemerged in the days of the Pasternak affair. The Brodsky affair was more complex. In this case, there was an unsettling feeling: a sense of familiarity mingled with awareness of difference. Confronting her own emotions and observing her friend, Chukovskaia found it difficult to unravel the two strands. Her attention focused on the relationship between an event, or fact, and a feeling. The facts of the Brodsky case were different from the terror campaigns of 1937, but her reactions to it were similar: "that same feeling of humiliation and inalienable insult." So was Brodsky's reaction: a feeling of abandonment and betrayal ("typical camp psychosis"). The 1930s and the 1960s were connected by common emotions.

"Same Time, Same Facts, Different Memories"

Looking back at the past from the vantage point of the "new epoch" (after Stalin), the two women were intensely concerned with the larger problem: commonality vs. difference, or division, in historical experience and in memory.

In December 1963, they talked about this problem (as they had in 1953) in a political key: "Who, when, and to what extent understood what was going on around them?" Chukovskaia held to her opinion: "I said, as always: 'Different people understood at different times.'" As in 1953, Akhmatova disagreed in the strongest terms and with the strongest feelings: "Oh what, so they didn't understand?" she shouted. "Rubbish. Nonsense. They didn't want to understand—that's an altogether different matter" (3:103).

For Chukovskaia, this problem was far more complex: she started to doubt that experiences and memories could be truly shared. Writing her Akhmatova journal, she noted moments of discrepancy between Akhmatova's memories and her own. Once, in a conversation, Akhmatova recalled seeing the poet Aleksandr Blok for the last time, on April 25, 1921, at a reading ("evening") in the Bol'shoi Drama Theater, which turned out to be his last public appearance. Chukovskaia remembered that she, too, had been present at this momentous event. (After Blok's death, which followed shortly, coinciding with the execution of Nikolai Gumilev, the last evening with the "great Russian poet" became a literary marker of the end of the old world.) It was clear to Chukovskaia that, with all the similarities, she had experienced and remembered this event differently:

> Blok's last evening in Petrograd—it came from my cellar of memory— mine; strange how there can exist two cellars, so different, right next to one another. In 1921 I was fourteen; I was nobody, but she had already

long been Akhmatova, and he had long been Blok. He spoke his last words to her. And *at the same time* I was also somewhere there not far off. Now it's 1962. I am not that I, she is not that she, he is no longer here. How to understand this? Our existence? Same time, same facts, different memories. I am confused. (3:108)

Chukovskaia was confused about issues that have troubled generations of writers, psychologists, and philosophers. But for her and her cohorts, the issues of common memory and common understanding had inherent social and ethical dimensions. Chukovskaia's readiness to admit that different people knew and understood differently, and Akhmatova's refusal to accept this principle in relation to the experiences of the terror, was not a matter of divergence in philosophical sensibilities. This was about a fundamental sense of commonality and community. Akhmatova's stance was not only a moral judgment on their fellow compatriots; it was tantamount to excluding some of them from membership in the community of which she felt herself a part and a voice. Chukovskaia, who was uneasy with this unflinching judgment, tried to reformulate the problem of commonality and difference in broader terms, applying it, not just to the Stalinist terror, but to the notion of historical experience and human existence. It is remarkable that trying to articulate the problem she used the image of shared domestic space: the two "cellars of memory," adjoining but separate. (The image comes from Akhmatova's poem.) In this case, the problem also had an epistemological dimension: after all, Chukovskaia's journal was a diary for two; and yet, as she started to suspect, the same lived experiences could easily produce different memories and interpretations. What good, then, was her record?

CONCLUDING VIGNETTE: "SHE'LL TELL YOU WHAT 1937 WAS LIKE"

In spring 1964, Akhmatova was interviewed by her first biographer—the young British scholar Amanda Haight. Expecting her first visit, Akhmatova asked Chukovskaia to join her. In her journal, Chukovskaia described this encounter. (Another reader has already noted the remarkable power of this episode.)[53] The interview took a bizarre turn:

"I will take a nap," announced Anna Andreevna, "and you two, go over there, to the window and sit by the table. Amanda! Lidiia Korneevna will now tell you what 1937 was like..." (3:219)

In this remarkable moment, Chukovskaia found herself at a loss. "Telling" a young foreigner about "1937" seemed an impossible feat. Moreover, she was supposed to speak on behalf of Akhmatova, whose silent presence dominated the space:

> We sat down. Anna Andreevna turned to one side, with her back to us. Tell her about 1937! [...] It wasn't just that Amanda was a foreigner. That is to say, she knew one thing: there was the terror under Stalin in the Soviet Union.

In the silent soliloquy that Chukovskaia recorded in her diary, she reflected on the difficulties of telling about the terror. First, the word itself was not reliable:

> the terror, or as it is now customary to call it, "the mass breach of socialist legality," "the consequences of the Stalin personality cult."

Further, the dating did not seem satisfactory, and, rejecting the specification "under Stalin," Chukovskaia, while admitting differences in scope and direction, identified the terror with the inception of the Soviet regime:

> The terror began in 1917 and goes on to this day. But every year it takes on another degree in its mass scale, another sense of purpose.

Then, she lamented the inexperience of her particular listener:

> What does an English woman know about the nights of terror, about the days and nights of terror? Other than the word itself?

But the difficulties of telling, as she realized, did not stop there:

> And not just an English woman, or a foreigner, but any of our younger compatriots?

Moreover, the difficulty was not a matter of generation alone, but a larger problem of atomization of the Soviet society:

> Everyone has become disconnected, and most people's memory has been plundered.

She continued in social categories:

> A person from the countryside? A person from the city? From the intelligentsia? Not from the intelligentsia? Everyone knows and remembers something different. If they remember at all. (3:220)

As we have seen, in spite of such doubts—or perhaps because of them—Lidiia Chukovskaia produced an account, *Notes about Anna Akhmatova,* that stands out for its historical scope, ethnographic precision, self-consciousness, and moral pathos. This document provides a window into an intelligentsia circle, showing the ways in which Stalin's terror and its aftermath shaped intimate lives and the stories that people tell about their lives.

And what about the "other," of whom Chukovskaia was intensely aware—a person from the countryside, a person not from the intelligentsia? There is another remarkable life story that emerged in the post-Soviet years, offering a glimpse into the historical situation of a woman from the country who also wrote a story of her life. What did such a person know and remember? How did she produce her life story and how did her story reach the reader? This document is the subject of the next chapter.

CHAPTER 2

The Notebooks of the Peasant Evgeniia Kiseleva
"The War Separated Us Forever"

Evgeniia Grigor'evna Kiseleva (1916–1990), a pensioner from a small coal mining town in Ukraine, wrote her life story with the hope that it would be made into a film, and, in 1976, she sent a handwritten notebook to a Moscow studio. The notebook attracted the attention of the journalist Elena Ol'shanskaia, who tried to have it published, but succeeded only in 1991, when, under glasnost, excerpts from Kiseleva's writings appeared, in heavily edited form, in the literary journal *Novyi mir*. Deposited in the People's Archive, the notebooks (over the years Kiseleva produced two more) then fell into the hands of scholars and were published anew in 1996 by the sociologist Natalia Nikitichna Kozlova and the linguist Irina Il'inichna Sandomirskaia, who transcribed the text "as is" and supplied it with their extensive reading. The history of the publication makes a story in itself, and I will return to it. First, my reading of the text, which I cite from the edition prepared by Kozlova and Sandomirskaia.[54] I owe them a debt of gratitude for making this document accessible. (My interpretation of the text is different.)

As we eventually learn from her notebooks, Kiseleva was born and raised in a peasant family in the village of Novozvanovka in the Luhansk Province of Ukraine. She thought of herself as Russian but completed five grades of a Ukrainian school. In 1932, during the famine that killed many people in this region, she moved to a nearby town, Pervomaisk, and became a waitress in a miners' diner, where (as she notes) she was able to survive famine without hunger (227). But Kiseleva starts her first notebook, her autobiography, in 1941, with the beginning of the war. The war dominates all three notebooks. Stalin's terror is not mentioned in her story: Kiseleva does not seem to have noticed the terror.

Below, the text is cited in long passages, but its particular quality may be lost in translation. The language of Kiseleva's writings is idiosyncratic. (For this reason, Russian originals are given in the text.) Kiseleva is inconsistent in dividing her writing into sentences (sometimes into words), and she does not divide it into paragraphs. She rarely uses punctuation marks. The spelling is mostly phonetic. In phonetics and morphology her speech mixes standard oral Russian with a Southern Russian dialect and Ukrainian (which is not unusual for the area). She capitalizes irregularly, but seems to use capitalization to mark important concepts. The syntax is mostly based on elliptical constructions and on the fusion of syntactic units. There are frequent cases of shift in tense and aspect, and a high incidence of blurring the patterns of direct and indirect speech. All of this reveals a crucial thing about this text: it is a product of oral culture.[55] All her publishers note that Kiseleva writes by ear, and her manuscript approximates a transcript of oral speech, and, what is more, speech of an uneducated person. Nevertheless, as I hope to show, Kiseleva is a competent and powerful storyteller.

This remarkable document opens itself to different uses, and the encounter it offers is special: the writer and the reader belong to different social groups and they speak different languages.[56] In its first publication, in the literary monthly *Novyi mir* in 1991, Kiseleva's story was turned into literature—"memoirs" from the "depth of simple people's life."[57] (This journal is famous for publishing *One Day in the Life of Ivan Denisovich* in 1962, in which, using an elaborate narrative device of reporting speech, *erlebte Rede*, Alexander Solzhenitsyn spoke for a Russian peasant committed to a Soviet labor camp.) The second team of editors turned the text—transcribed, annotated, and analyzed—into an object of scholarship. They analyzed it from two perspectives: as a special kind of writing—"naive writing" (by analogy with so-called naive/primitive painting); and as a self-description of a specific culture—the peasant culture forcefully modernized by the Soviet regime. The editors read Kiseleva's story as a history of the transformation of the "old," traditional peasant, values and customs as they mix with the "new," modern Soviet, ones, failing to create any stable social and cultural order. Ruled by the village ethos, this is a "world where everybody knows everybody else."[58] Governed by the Soviet regime, this is a life endangered by physical deprivations, historical catastrophes, and social disintegration, where survival becomes the main goal.[59]

In my turn, I read this text—rich in descriptions of practices and procedures of everyday life—for its ethnographic value.* But I will also read it

---

* Kiseleva's notebooks contain descriptions of rites and rituals: a curse (*porcha*) that rendered the bridegroom impotent on the wedding night (164–66); a visit to the registry office for a death certificate (147); a memorial feast for sixty people featuring a pig's head and homemade brew (136–39). There are detailed descriptions of the persistent physical hardships: periods of hunger and starvation (225, 227, 228); gross physical violence of the war; petty violence in the family and among neighbors

in accordance with the author's intentions—as an autobiographical account that presents her life—fit to become a Soviet film—against a historical background. Providing a window into the world of a semiurbanized Soviet peasant, these text shows how Soviet power shaped Kiseleva's life and how it inspired her to tell her life story.

NOTEBOOK 1: "THE STORY OF MY LIFE"

The first notebook—offered as material for a film script—tells a more-or-less coherent story, from June 22, 1941, when the Second World War reached the Soviet Union, to the present, when Kiseleva finished writing on February 24, 1976, in the days of the Twenty-fifth Party Congress.[60] This is how Kiseleva begins:

> As a child I lived not so materially well off, I had a big family. Father, mother, sister Niusia, Vera and two brothers—Vania, Vitia and me. At 17 I got married. That's in 1933. I had a husband Kiselev, Gavriil Dmitrievich. I lived with him nine years, and we had two sons Vitia and Tolia, born in 1935 04.05, and Anatoly from 1941, 22 June. My husband and I lived happily, but when the war began in 1941 it separated us forever. and my suffering began.
>
> В детстве я жила невесьма матерялно хорошо, семя моя была большая. Отец, мать, систра Нюся, Вера и два брата—Ваня, Витя и я. 17 лет я вышла замуж. Это в 1933 году. Был у меня муж Киселев Гаврил Дмитриевич. Жыли мы с ним 9 лет было у нас два сына Витя и Толя, рожденые в 1935 году 5.IV, а Анатолий с 1941 г. 22 июня. Жили мы с мужом очень хорошо, но когда началася война в 1941 году она нас розлучила навсегда. и началися мои страдания. (89)

Thus, in epic tone, evocative of a Russian fairy tale (*byli u menia...zhyli my...i bylo u nas...*), punctuated somewhat incongruously by calendar-style dates, begins a story of lifelong suffering rooted in war. Throughout all three notebooks Kiseleva would repeat again and again, as if an incantation, the historical date

---

(104, 106, 109, 111, 113, 116, 119–20, 126); minor brushes with the law (106, 119–20; 181, 183, 187). There are stories of courtship, sexual experiences, love, marriages, separations, and divorces; chronicles of illnesses, doctors' visits (191–92), and folk cures (168). The author provides menus of ritual and daily meals (153, 160, 168, 169, 174, 180, 190); lists of domestic objects, specifying those received or given as gifts (126, 214–15, 231–32), inherited (141–42, 167), and contested (141–42, 167, 221). The text contains quotations from folk songs, proverbs, and poems (135, 175, 188, 211–12, 233), summaries of television programs, and at least one dream (180).

of her son's birth: "in 1941 on the 22 June Anatoly was born on the day of the War" («1941 года 22 июня Анатолий родился в день Войны») (210). And, throughout her story, she would connect her suffering to the separation from her husband that followed the outbreak of the war. It is from this coincidence of the personal and the national that Kiseleva derives her life story's claim to significance and public attention.

When her husband departed for war, Kiseleva and her children moved in with her parents. As the German army entered their village, a mortar hit the house (at just the moment the mother came up from the cellar to wind a wall clock). The story then moves through the days and weeks that followed, as if in slow motion, providing graphic pictures of death and decay. The decaying body of the mother lies unburied in the ruins of the house; the father has been wounded in the leg, his flesh eaten by worms; an older child has been (temporarily) blinded by an explosion; and the infant who was born "on the day of the war" has almost "rotted away" in unchanged diapers" (89–92). Kiseleva describes how she took her father to the German field hospital in a cart, and how he died: "I push him and he's breathing his last, we put him on the floor, and he, died" («я его везу а он кончается, положили на пол а он, скончался») (91). She describes herself flying to safety in a torn dress with a baby in her arms, a blinded child hanging to her skirt. She composes the narrative scenically and describes the action step-by-step. The following relates the battle for her home village Novozvanovka:

> We're sitting in the trench, the war's going on, you can hear the German officers going Ein, Zwein, Ein, Zwein shouting orders, I dont understand what else the German's shouting, but all of sudden the German officer opens the door into the dugout, and I got hot all over. I'm all prepared for death, got the children pressed up close and got my eyes shut. But he comes in as far as the third step, then he's shouting, shouting something or other to the troops, and he's closed the dugout and gone off and left us. and I never knew the Lordsprayer but in that trench it was aunty Efrosiniia god bless her soul, it was, who taught me, and it could be that saved us from death, we're sitting there with the war going on, not a crust of bread to eat, no water, with the littlun sucking at the tit, but there's nuthink there and there is such horror, Airoplanes dropping Shells, Tanks, morters, machine-guns, the holy fear. all day the battle goes on...
>
> сидим в окопе, идет бой, слишно, немецкие офицеры кричать айн, цвайн, айн, цвайн руководят ну а остальное непонимаю что кричит немец и в друг откривает блинтаж немецкий офицер, меня так жаром и обдало. Я уже приготовилась к смерти прижала детей к

сибе и закрыла глаза. Но он залез на третью ступенку в окопе и
кричал кричал на войска, что-то, а потом закрил окоп и побижал.
а я некогда не знала молитву "отченаш" а у окопе выучила, меня
Ефросиния тетя учила дай бог ей здоровья, может ето и спасло нас
от смерти идет бой, сидим без куска хлеба не води, а рибенок тянет
грудь, а у ние нет ничиво да еще и страсть какая, Самолети Снаряди
кидают, Танки, менометы, автоматы, страсть господняя. идет бой
целый день ... (91–92)

The minute plotting of the scene in space, the addition of speech and sounds, and the creation of mood has a distinct cinematic quality. What is more, this episode is placed against the backdrop of the end of the world. The young woman who found herself in the midst of this battle grew up with enforced Soviet atheism and (she makes a point of saying) did not know the words of the Lord's Prayer until that day, but as the battle is described by the older Kiseleva, it is repeatedly marked as apocalyptic: "Shells bursting tanks rumbling, so much shooting, like the airoplanes are bombing it's the Last Judgement" («Снаряды рвутся танки гудут, такое стрельбище что самолеты бомбят страшный суд») (94). The language blends the personal, the historical, and the apocalyptic.

The Separation and the War

The lines "when the war began in 1941 it separated us forever" may well lead the reader to believe that the author's husband, Gavriil Kiselev, was killed in the war. We are then told:

> The war ended and people came back from the front, the men crippled, but mine never came home. I set off in search of my husband Gavriil.
>
> Война окончилася, и люди приходили из фронта калеки мущины, а моего домой нету. Поехала искать моего мужа Гавриила. (96)

Kiseleva announces her quest for her missing husband with an epic gravitas, but it comes to a rather unheroic ending: when she found him, "he got himself three wives. Vera who he had a daughter by and Valia who he had a son by and two by me, three matrimonials, whats there for me to do?" («пока [...] розискала то у ниво оказалося три жены. Вера у которой родилася доч, и Валя у которой родился сын да у миня двое, три брачных что мне делать») (96). Separated from his family by the war, in "an alien land" (*u chuzhoi storone* (101), her husband, without obtaining a divorce, had married two other women. The explanation is clear to Kiseleva: his elevated social position: "its cuz he's an officer he can have three wifes" («он-же офицер ему можно и три жены иметь дураку») (99). As she specifies, Gavriil Kiselev, who was a foreman of the town's fire brigade and a party member before the war, reached the rank of officer in the army.

Kiseleva describes in vivid detail the confusion and wonder she, a peasant woman on her first journey, felt as she went in search of her husband: the first sighting of an apartment building, the first encounter with a telephone, the kind assistance of her social superiors, and, finally, the encounter with her (remarried) husband. She relates this important scene of their meeting in the historical present, complete with the date: "now its the year 1946" (100). With its spatial precision and dialogue, this scene also possesses a cinematic quality:

> The car arrived and out gets my husband, he dont come over to me where I'm standing a bit off, and we look at each other, Come over here! And I say You come over here, and up he comes and says What you doing here, I'm married, you know.
>
> Приехала машына вылез из машыны мой муж и неподходит ко мне я стою поотдали, и смотрим друг на друга, иди сюда! я говорю иди ты сюда он подошол комне говорить чиво ты приехала я-же женился. (99)

In response, the protagonist speaks of child support, but the writer lets the reader know that what she then felt was deeper than what she said, and she accounts for the onlookers, imagining what they whisper:

> And I dont see nothing through my tears the soldiers gather round the car looking at us like we are some idiots, all winking and wispering, got married again thats thats the offiser...
>
> а сама за слезамы нечиво не вижу собрались салдаты до машыны смотрят на нас как на дураков, все подмигуют да подшенчуют вотето да офицер надел пагоны да да все женится... (99)

After some hesitation, Gavriil Kiselev takes the unwelcome visitor home, to his new wife and child; they sit down to dinner, and then they all go to bed:

> We ate and sat round til evening and then went to bed so of course Gavriil goes with his young wife, and Im offered a bed by myself next to them, but how can I sleep, with my husband whose laying there with his mistress and me right next to them, keeping vigil of course allnight long, didnt get a wink of sleep, cut me to the quick, but I kept quiet...

> Покушали и так довечера а положилися спать ну конечно Гавриил лег из женой молодой, и миня придложили леч одной на кровате рядом, ну какой мне сон, когда мой муж лежить из любовницой а я рядом, мне конечно была всюношная я не сомкнула глаз, мне так было обидно но я молчала...(100).

(Note that Kiseleva hesitates whether to call the other woman "wife" or "mistress.") Early in the morning, she starts out on the journey home, and her estranged husband accompanies her to the railroad station:

> we're walking down the road and he tooks me under the arm and he says Come on lets live together theres the two kids of ours but I cant see the road for tears, and I says to him But how can we live, you'll have to work and feed them the illegitimate ones, and I'll be feeding you and my children. Your all caught up like a spider in a web, with these marriage certificates of yours why did you register the marriages, you could go swanning off without no registering, then the war ended and you could come home.

> идем по дороге он мине взял подруку говорить давай сойдемся и будим жить у нас двое детей но я не вижу дороги плачу, говорю ему как-ж мы будим жить, ты будиш работать на незаконных детей, кормить их, а я буду тибя и своих детей кормить. ты запутался как павук у павутинне с этими брачными листамы, зачем ты росписывался гулял-бе так без росписи, а война кончилася домой приехал и все. (101)

Throughout her notebooks, Kiseleva would return to this unbearably acute episode again and again, and again and again she mourns her first husband as a casualty of the war.

The Second Marriage

Next, comes the story of the second marriage, also positioned on the chronological and historical line:

> I was twenty-seven I marry [...] a War Invalid [...] Tiurichev, Dmitrii Ivanovich—after the war he worked at the Krupskaia coal mine as a Foreman, liked his bit of vodka and other men's wives—what'd make my heart ache with jealousy—he'd come home drunk every night and carry on his debauchery in the room...

> Мне было двадцать семь лет я выхожу замуж [...] за Инвалида Отечесной войны [...] Тюричев Дмитрий Иванович, работал

после войны в шахте имени Крупской Десятником водочку любил попивать и женщин чужих любил откоторых у миня волновалось серце от ревности, прыходил чут не каждий день пяный, и подымал дыбеш в комнате... (103)

Then, mixing confused legal idiom with the colloquial, the autobiographer tries to describe the precise status of her second marriage:

I was registered with him, had marriage with him but it was fictitious because I werent divorced from Kiselev, and so I got two matrimonials going on with Kiselev and Tiurichev. But because my life with Dmitrii Ivanovich wasn't normal, I hesitated to get a divorce from Kiselev, from one day to the next and so it turned out that both marriages were invalid, Twentyone years I lived with Tiurichev and seventeen times I left him and the eighteenth time I left him for good.

Я с ним была росписана был меня брачный сним но он был фективный, потому что я не розвелася из Киселевым и у меня два брачных из Киселевым и из Тюричевым ну посколько такая жизьн мне была из Дмитрием Ивановичем ненормальная, я тирялася взять розвод из Киселевым, сиводня завтра и так дотянулося что ни тово ни другого браки недействительные, Прожила я из Тюричевым двадцать один год и из них росходилася семнадцать раз а на восемнадцатый раз розошлися навсигда. (105)

Here, she mistakenly refers to her second marriage as "fictitious" (a legal term used to refer to a different situation of illegitimacy). Later, she describes Tiurichev as *"nerodnoi muzh"* (literally, a husband who is not a family relation):

My husband Tiurichev ain't proper related to me, he's like my lover. He had no pity for me because I ain't no related wife of his and my children ain't no related children of his.

У меня муж Тюричев неродной он у меня как любовник ему меня нежалко было потому, что я ему неродная жена и мои дети ему неродные. (140)

Here she extends to marriage the word used to describe relations of stepparentage, as opposed to biological connection (such as *nerodnoi otets/syn*). But while Kiseleva is confused about the legal or civil status of her second marriage, it is quite clear to her that this relationship was not "normal."

She described a long series of domestic conflicts suffused with alcohol and accompanied by violence. For their first separation, the date is given, and the division of communal property is described in precise factual detail:

> In 1947 my husband comes home from work we had two piglets and says I'm leaving you, I found myself a woman so lets be divvying things up There wont be no divvying up of course of the cow or the chickens. it was my mother's, the cow was, and the Chickens I bought myself without him, and then theres the two piglets. Well come on then, lets be divvying them up and the drunkard goes and calls me by obscenities…

> В тисячу девятсот сорок седьмом году муж приходит из работы были у нас два поросенка я буду уходить от тибя, вот я нашол сибе женщину и давай делится, конечно корову куры я небуду делить. это было моей мамы, корова, а Куры я купила сама без ниво а потом нажили поросят двоих, ну что-ж давай делится пяный нецензурными словами узивает меня…(107)

Five days later, Kiseleva reports, the husband appears, begging to be allowed to return, and in four more days she takes him back (his share of the marital property, a piglet, has been squandered on drink). A second separation, when her husband strays into another "marriage," follows the same pattern as the first:

> A while went by then he married Zinka Kuzminova […] in four months he took up with Zinka, he left again, lived with her for four days, drank away all his belongings and comes back and cries I'll never do it again, take me back darling I forgave him and tooks him back.

> Прошло немалое время он женился на Зинке Кузминовой […] через четире месяцов он скрутился из Зинкой ушол обратно пожил четире дня с ней розкидал вещи пропил и прышол плачит я больше не буду прийми меня дорогая я обратно простила и прыняла. (107)

The initial formula marking the passage of narrative time (*proshlo nemaloe vremia*), the sequence of action verbs that follows (*skrutilsia…pozhil…roskidal…propil i pryshol*), and the merging of direct and indirect speech (*plachit ia bol'she ne budu*) follow patterns that are typical of Russian folktales.

Forgiving though she may be of her husband, the storyteller displays a vindictive streak toward her rivals, and provides descriptions of revenge, detailed to the point of vivid visualization. During separation number five, she bursts into the room of her husband's mistress:

> I grab a log out of the barrow, give the door a kick, it swung open, and there was the table all laid and I send a bottle on the table flying across

the table with the log and smashed everything on the table [...] grabbed his mistress by the hair and kick her in the belly and in the ass, teared out her hair I even drags her along abit to rip out her hair [...] I know I didn't act right, but I cant control myself...

Я хватаю из тачки дрын, ударила дверь ногой она розтворилася, и там уже стол накритый, и бутылка на столе я как ударю постолу дрыном так и розбила все что было на столе [...] схватила эту любовницу за волоса и ногой б'ю в живот и в грешное место, вырвала волосы да еще тащу что-бы вырвать волосы [...] знаю что я неправильно делаю, на я сама-собой невладаю... (109)

The use of narrative time creates a visual picture with commentary: the initial verb (*khvataiu*), in the present tense and imperfective aspect, suggest a frozen image of a sudden drastic action; a sequence of action verbs in the past tense (*rozbila, skhvatila, vyrvala*) denote rapid movement; then, another sequence of imperfective verbs marks a pause for self-reflection (*tashchu...znaiu*). (Such patterns can be found in different kinds of oral narratives, from folktales to casual oral storytelling.)

In the end, Kiseleva's second marriage, to the war invalid Tiurichev, appears in her life story as a sequence of separations occasioned by infidelity, lasting from five days to two weeks, each of which she calls a "marriage" (one of them resulted in the birth of twins) (115). (All of this went on in the tightly knit community of the small town, within its several blocks.) Passing from her first marriage to the second, her life story connects the violence of the war with domestic violence, creating a cycle of betrayal, abandonment, violence, and squandering of family property. On one occasion, Kiseleva curses Tiurichev, a bad father to her children, and, in the same, breath, she curses Hitler: "Curse him such a father and that hitler what started the War against the Soviet Union" («будь он проклят такой отец тот гитлер, что затеял Войну на Советский Союз») (113). Syntactic fusion cements the connection between "such a father" and "hitler." (Kiseleva does not capitalize Hitler's name, but, as elsewhere in her notebooks, she capitalizes the word "War.") In more ways than one, her story suggests that the root cause of the whole chain of sufferings—the dissolution of the first marriage and the unhappy second marriage—is the war.

Trying to describe her marital life, Kiseleva has spontaneously created several new concepts. One of them is *"nerodnoi muzh"* (discussed above). The other, an idiosyncratic prepositional phrase, *zhenitsia ot menia* (roughly, "marries in my presence"), refers to simultaneous cohabitation with two women: in-the-presence-of-the-wife marriage («до каких пор будиш женится от меня идиот проклятый»; «он от меня женится нещетно») (109, 111). Existing categories of family relations are no longer sufficient to describe real-life situations: clarity is lost as to what is a marriage, who is the wife, which union is legitimate, and which is illegitimate. As the story of Anna Akhmatova shows as well, all of this was no longer obvious to the Soviet people, living, they felt, in the shadow of historical catastrophe, be it the terror or the war.

After the Second Marriage

The first notebook—the film script proper—ends with a description of Kiseleva's life after her final separation from her second husband in 1966. To survive, she kept lodgers in her small apartment, sometimes three at a time. She specifies that she opted for male lodgers because they could do "man's work" in the house and in the yard. (At this time, she lived in one or two rooms in a country-style house with a fenced yard.) The lodgers drank, but, as she reasons, "who don't drink nowdays its the vodka century" («нохто сичас не пет, как сичас водочный век») (122).

Throughout her notebooks, Kiseleva provides detailed descriptions of drinking in her family and in the larger world by men, women, adolescents, and whole families, and she repeats her coinages—*vodochnyi vek* (the vodka century) and *Vodochnyi mir* (the Vodka world)—again and again (122, 166; 189).

Her notebook documents the conflicts with the families of her grown sons—the daughters-in-law and grandchildren (she does not blame her sons for anything). Frustrations, recriminations, and violent physical clashes are described in minute detail; strings of elaborate verbal abuse are faithfully recorded. One day she came to her son's house asking for help with her potato patch. In anticipation of this family event, she killed a chicken and prepared soup for an after-work meal. But the daughter-in-law, involved in painting her own apartment, unceremoniously asked the insistent Kiseleva to leave the premises. (At this time, they all lived in semiurban apartments but still had vegetable gardens and still used a peasant word for house, "*khata.*") A violent physical confrontation, in front of neighbors (listed by name), ensues:

> and she said to me, you get out the hut, and I just let myself go, oh you idiot you'd drive me out the hut when it were me as got you everything for your place, stole from Tiurichev and gave it to you [...] and your going to drive me out my son's house? you swine I grabbed a broom and knocked her glasses off Oh you ungrateful swine you how low she'd sunk in her way with me, she started to belt me for my kindness what match was I her mother-in-law for a strong young woman [...] she dragged me into the yard by the hair like the shameless hussy she was with the neighbours seeing...

а она мне говорить выйди схаты меня так и сорвало ах ты идиотка, ты миня будиш выгонять их хаты, когда я тибе все в квартиру придбала крала от Тюрича, и тибе давала [...] а ты меня из сыновой хаты выганяеш? сволоч ты схватила Я щетку да по очкам ахты сволоч неблагодарная иш ты как низко опало отношение у ния до меня, а она начала бить меня за мою доброту сильная молодая, да хто я чужая женщина свекров'я [...] она мене волочила за волосы аж надвор как хотела беммтижая сволоч и суседи видели...(126)

We see that Kiseleva puts her trust in the traditional peasant family structure, with its stable roles, and in an economy that exchanges labor and gifts for attention and acceptance, but this system no longer works.

We also see how the old life habits mix with the new. Thus, the need to be independent from her sons' families in old age was Kiseleva's primary concern after she left her alcoholic husband Tiurichev, who had supported her for the twenty years of their marriage. She put her trust in the state and in the new life order, seeking employment that would entitle her to an old-age pension. And this trust was not misplaced: for more than ten years Kiseleva worked as a security guard (later, as a cleaning woman) for the mining administration, and her exemplary service was a source of great pride (122). Describing her participation in society, its workforce, and its welfare system, Kiseleva addresses words of gratitude to the institution (the security department that employed her) and to the regime ("the Soviet power," "the Great Party," and, personally, "comrade Brezhnev"). Her speech mixes common idioms that describe her personal situation (old, poor, and sick) with fragments of formulas, borrowed by ear from the official discourse, which celebrate the achievements of Soviet power:

I would kiss everyone in the security department for taking me on to work so that I dont beg I'm poor, sick who needs me I know that well enough, I don't want to meddle in my childrens lives they've got their own family and needs. i want to earn my pension, however much it is so as not to beg thanks to the Soviet power the Great Party, and to comrade Brezhnev at its head that us invalids work and dont beg. Thank you for the rispek to us elders: and so here I sit rispekted it seems whoever the person is he's rispected here's one example...

Я бы в отдел охраны всех цилувала-б что оны меня приняли наработу что я не побираюся я-же нищая, больная кому я нужна я это хорошо знаю, детям своим мешать в жизни нехочу у них свои нужди в сем'и. хочу заработать свою пенсию, хоть сколько нибуть что-бы не побырятся, спасиба Советской власти Великой Партии, и во главе товарищу Брежневу за законы, чтомы работаем инвалиди а не побираемся. Спасибо, за унимания кнам старцам: мне сичас сижу и выжается из листка кажится человек как ни будит увыжается вглазах вот один пример.... (123)

Toward the end of this passage, language betrays her, disintegrating into the incomprehensible as she tries to convey a sense of "respect" (*vyzhaetsia... uvyzhaetsia*): Kiseleva is unable to deal with this word, its spelling and usage.

Seamlessly, in the same sentence, she passes to an example, drawn from her personal life, that is called up to illustrate the respect commanded by the working elderly under Soviet power: she saved thirty rubles from her wages to buy her sixteen-year-old grandson Yura platform shoes (123). As on many other occasions, she tries to demonstrate that, rather than being a burden to her children, she has been able to provide gifts, and even modern gifts, to the grandchildren. However, Kiseleva's attempt fails miserably: the grandson does not show up for the planned shopping expedition, and, after an hour-long wait, Kiseleva returns home in tears. She understands this as a sign of "alienation" unbridgeable by money: "they use their own money to fill their house with goods and they get alienated it hurts me so" («за свои денги думаю набиваются своим добром, а оны отчуждаются мне так обидно» (123). (Kiseleva's use of the word "alienation" [*otchuzhdaiutsia*] is noteworthy: it could have been derived from the Marxist discourse of the media and transposed to the talk about familial intimacy.) The old woman has insight into the failure of the emotional-financial economy of family relationships (material goods—a currency she tries to exchange for love and care—no longer fulfill their role), but she does not notice the failure of her narrative attempt to illustrate the success of government policy in relation to the elderly with an example drawn from her family life. (The episode with the unwanted gift of platform shoes does not speak to her position in the family.) Her participation in Soviet society and its institutions seems more successful than her role in the family.

Here and Now

Kiseleva's life story, as told in the first notebook, began with the birth of her son on the first day of the war—the moment in which the personal merged with the national and historical. The first notebook concludes with another shift to the historical-political domain. As the story reaches the present ("now"), it shows the protagonist ("I") in front of a television set watching the proceedings of the Twenty-fifth Congress of the Communist Party:

it's the year one thousand nine hundred and seventy six, I hear the approval on the television at the congress on February 24th the 25th Party

Congress everybody in accordance with his own domain the approval of Leonid Ilich Brezhnev, and as I see it Brezhnev is worthy of the whole world with his care for people not only in our own multinational country but in foreign countrys, I'm proud of my leadership in our country.

идет тисяча девятсот семдесят шестой год, слишу по телевидению, одобрение на с,езде 24 февраля 25 с'езд каждый по своему отрастлю и одобрение Лионида Илича Брежнева, как я понимаю Брежнев достойный всему миру своим отношением к людям не только к нам в нашей стране многонациональной а и за рубежними странамы, я горжуся своим руководствам в нашей стране. (127)

From her room, where she writes the story of her life for a film studio, hoping that she, too, may find her way onto the screen, Kiseleva adds her own voice and her own feeling to the general approval of the country's leader expressed at the party congress, in line with her understanding of his role: to "conquer the world" and assure world peace. Again, she mixes common words and observations with fragments of the official language borrowed by ear from the media. And, as she watches Brezhnev, a man of about her age (as she comments), confidently climb the stage, a sense of personal connection prompts her to address the leader directly from the pages of her "book." What unites them is the "knowledge," that is, experience, of the war:

Dear Lionid Ilich Brezhnev I'm writing this book and I know that Hitler drunk a sea of tears and oceans of blood, I know that in the year one thousand nine hundred and forty two in the town of Pervomaisk an unknown number of our soldiers was took prisoner, herded into the Kovolenko club, locked up and had a guard placed on them, they boarded the windows and them soldiers starved to death, they urinated and defecated in there and they didnt die straight away, and the living smelled the stench of the dead and every last one of them died [...] and they made us dig pits for the dead soldiers...

Дорогой наш Лионид Илич Брежнев я пишу эту книгу, и знаю что Гитлер попил моря слез и окианы крови, знаю в тисячу девятсот сорок фтором году, в г. Первомайске в клуб имени Коволенко загнали неизвесное количество наших солдат пленних замкнули и поставили охрану, забили окна и эти солдаты померли из голода, там и оправлялися и умирали не сразу, и жывые нухали мертвых смрад и все как один погыбли [...] а нас ганяли копать ямы для дохлых солдат...(127)

The narrative slides from an evocation of Hitler's crimes made in the official language to an episode that occurred in her own town in 1942—a vivid description of the slow execution of Soviet prisoners of war by hunger, complete with sensory images (the stench of excrement and decaying human flesh). The speaker herself is placed in this scene, forced with others to dig pits for the burial of the dead. The hope for peace binds her long-suffering "I" both to the country as a whole and to the leader in whom her hopes are invested. Moreover, the common memory of war brings the leader into proximity and into a leveled field of communication with this ordinary woman.

On the last page of her first notebook, Kiseleva appeals to the younger generation, from whom she feels increasingly separated:

> Our people especially the young don't like it that our leaders go and give help abroad, like to Cuba, Vetnam, Rumunia, Hungary and many other countrys, I dont remember I often tell them off our Young comrades our policy is like what comrade Lenin said and wrote we need to share and be friends with every country so as theres peace and no War may it be cursed. Our country is rich, our Russia is the envy of all cuz of our wealth, its better to give, worse to ask, let there be peace on earth let there be sun so as the skies is clear and theres joy in the hearts of all men.
>
> Наши люди особо молодеж недоволна, что нашы правители дают за границу помогают, как Кубе, Ветнаму, Румунии, Венгрии и многим странам, не могу вспомнить я часто ругаюсь с ними тов. Молодежь у нас такая политика как говорил и писал тов Ленин нада поделятся из любой страной и дружьть, что-бы был мир и не было Войны проклятой. У нас страна богатая, наша Россия всем зависна нашими богатствами, лучше давать, да плохо просить, путь будит мир на земле да будут сонце что-бы было небо чистое и у нас на душе радость у каждого человека. (127–28)

Here, her conflict with the younger generation is cast in political terms. One cannot help but observe that this description of a state policy—trying to assure peace by giving to others rather than asking for anything—echoes the policy Kiseleva follows in her own violence-prone family. Indeed, on the preceding pages she has described the violent conflict with her daughter-in-law and attempts to improve the family relationships by making gifts, so this strategy may well have been on Kiseleva's mind as she moved on to describe the state policy. The passage concludes with a formula from the official discourse of the Soviet peace movement, "let there be peace on earth let there be sun" (which, in turn, appropriates a biblical formula, "let there be light"), used here to conjure peace on earth and joy for every person. With this, the author signs out: "Kiseleva Evgeniia Grigorovna."

To summarize. In the first notebook Kiseleva competently constructs an autobiographical narrative, offered as material for a film script. She carefully arranges the episodes of her life in time, using the epic temporality of folk narratives ("a while went by") along with precise dating, on the personal and historical axes ("I was twenty seven I marry..." "In 1947 my husband comes home from work"). Her story follows chronological order, interrupted by occasional flashbacks and afterthoughts (which are common in autobiographies of all kinds). In her notebook, Kiseleva tells the story of a life rooted in and shaped by the war—an event of national, historical, and apocalyptic significance. In several ways—by framing the life story with two historical events (the beginning of the war and the party congress), by inserting her own "I" into the televised space inhabited by the state leader, by describing the family of nations in the same terms as her own family (under the sign of the war and the ensuing struggle for peace)—the writer reasserts the connection between the personal and the national. I believe that Kiseleva, who aims at placing her story in the official domain, works as a self-conscious autobiographer, and she may be well aware of her strategies. Thus, in the second notebook, written after the first notebook was sent off to the Moscow film studio, Kiseleva comments on the story she told, addressing her readers—"People reading this manuscript" (*Chitaiushchie liudi etu rukopis'*) (142). In clear, though somewhat idiosyncratic, language she suggests that her storytelling was enabled by suffering and again reiterates the connection between her personal suffering and the war:

> if I ever smiled, I wouldnt have nothing to write thats what I think. I then smiled for 9 years when I lived with Gavriil Kiselev. and now it's just tears and illnesses if not one thing than the other since the year 1941...
>
> еслиб я когда улибнулася мне бы нечиво былоб писать я так думаю. я тогда улыбалася, когда жила из Гаврилом Киселевым 9 лет. сичас только слезы да болезнь как не то так другое из 1941 г...(142)

The date, given in the graphic form used in official documents, plots her private loss on a historical axis. The clearly drawn dichotomy of "then" and "now" articulates her view of the distance and difference within her life. All of this, and more, allows me to apply the word "historical" to Kiseleva's writing.

The text bears witness to the author's intention to make a film. She maps key episodes of her story in space, uses visual images, provides step-by-step scenarios of movement and action, and supplies speech. Kiseleva's idea to write her life (as her publishers noted) may well have been inspired by the carefully cultivated genre of Soviet film that features a mythic image of a "simple Soviet woman" pictured against the historical background of the Great Patriotic

War. Take, for instance, the popular *Bab'e tsarstvo* (The kingdom of women, 1967), directed by Aleksei Saltykov with a script by Iurii Nagibin—a moving story of a country woman who becomes a leader in her village after losing her husband, son, and home in the war. Saltykov and Nagibin's other film about "ordinary people," *Predsedatel'* (The chairman, 1964)—famous for leaving not a dry eye in the audience—focuses on the tragedy of a war invalid who returns to his native village as chairman of the collective farm to find devastation and ruin. A woman chairman—a heroic war widow with a sharp tongue and a difficult love life—is at the center of *Prostaia istoriia* (A simple story, 1960), by Iurii Egorov and Budimir Metal'nikov, another movie with calculated emotional impact. The list might be easily expanded.

As the second and third notebooks show, Kiseleva spent much of her time watching television: she watched films about the war, identifying with their characters. In this way, she could have absorbed the Soviet historical mythology as well as basic plot moves and narrative strategies. Moreover, stories that are composed and transmitted orally (such as folktales) are known to rely on visualization as a mnemonic technique, and they use visual images as a device that brings the listener to the scene of action. It could be that Kiseleva, too, used visualization to recall or form images from her past; hence the visual-spatial quality of her narrative.[61] Both the cultural prototypes (films) and the medium (oral narrative) may be responsible for the structure of this text.

In the end, the semiliterate author, Evgeniia Kiseleva, succeeded in telling the story of her life, plotted as a film scenario about a heroic survivor. Like many Soviet war films, which justify the suffering of their ordinary protagonists by relating it to the national cause, Kiseleva's story comes to a happy, redemptive ending. But life interfered with her aesthetic choice: as Kiseleva waited for her story to be made into a film, she continued to write, encouraged by the editor who had taken up her cause. Her later writings tell a somewhat different story.

NOTEBOOKS 2 AND 3

The second and third notebooks were written as Kiseleva anticipated the making of her life into a film or a book. Throughout this period—fourteen years full of hope and frustration—she corresponded with her would-be publisher, Elena Ol'shanskaia. In her later notebooks, Kiseleva writes both for her editor and for herself, and she describes her life as it went on after she left off telling it (in 1976), enlarging on some episodes and adding still others. Having gained a reader and anticipating a wider audience, Kiseleva engages in self-reflection, speaking about the writing process and about reasons for writing: "I write because it freely flows out of my soul, this manuscript about my life"

(«Я пишу потому, что свободно льется из моей души это рукопис о моей жизьни») (148). Explaining her motivations, she suggests that she "writes her sorrows" because otherwise nobody would remember how much grief she had experienced:

> I write of my sorrows becus I've suffered so much in all these years, but there ain't nobody to remember my experience after my life only a daughter, and I don't have one, would remember how much grief her mother lived through. Today is 17 April 1982. Communist subbotnik...
>
> Пишу свои горести потому что у меня наболело за сколько лет, но нехто невспомнить переживание мое после моей жизьни, только-б вспомнила доч, но уменя ее нету что ее мама столько горя пережила. Сиводня семнадцатое апреля 1982 год. Коммунестический субботник... (183)

In this case, her narrative connects the past, the present, and the future. The date she uses, with its double designation, places the writing on the historical-political axis.

While the first notebook is a memoir conveying a distinct life story, which moves chronologically from 1941 to 1976 (while engaging in digressions), the second and the third are organized as a loosely structured diary. Quite a few entries are dated:

> Nov 24 1979. we had a memorial dinner for the fortieth day after Niusia's death (137).
> Dec 19 1979. Im ill with a cough probbly flu (139).
> Jan 30 1988. My favorite Grandson Yura's come in drunk and crying (221).
>
> 24/XI 19179 г. справляли 40 дней Нюси (137).
> 19/XII 1979 г. Я заболела кашель наверно грип (139).
> 30/I 1988. Прышол мой любимый дотошнотый Внук Юра сослезами пяный (221).

While Kiseleva is not consistent as a diarist, there is a diary template underlying the organization of the later notebooks, locating each entry in the here and now—the immediate time and place of its writing. The second notebook starts with her personal history: "I will be 63 yearsold in 1979 in November on November 1" («Мне 63 года будит в 1979 г. в ноябре 1 ноября») (129). It ends with a political-historical event: "Wednesday Nov 10 1982 I heard on the radio the sad news Brezhnev Lionid I. has died" («Среда 10/XI 1982 года Слышу по радиво печальную весть умер Брежнев Лионид И.») (185). The third notebook, made up of increasingly irregular and unformed entries, covers the period from 1983 to 1989, and seems to stop shortly before Kiseleva's death in 1990.

In these late years Kiseleva describes a life dominated by illness and conflict in the family. She chronicles the almost daily clashes with her daughter-in-law Maria (wife of Victor, who died early); growing problems with two alcoholic grandsons (Viktor's sons, Yury and Vitaly); enmity with her ever-jealous sister Vera over the property inherited from the other sister Anna (a war widow); and dramatic clashes with the authorities over housing. We learn that after Anna's death, she inherited fifty installments of *roman-gazeta*—serial publications of classic and popular novels in newspaper form, but she did not approve of her sister's passion for reading, which caused insomnia and irritability, ultimately leading to family quarrels (131, 142). The third notebook also describes Kiseleva's visits to the family of her younger son, Anatoly (who married while serving in the army and settled in the town of Murom) and lists her grievances against his wife, Nina, and his son, Sergei (divorced at the age of twenty after one year of marriage). A lonely and resentful old woman, she seeks relief in writing, using her notebooks to direct harsh and scathing words against her increasingly alienated, disintegrating family. Conscious of her readers' presence, she calls on them to serve as judges of the family conflicts: "People reading this manuscript, decide who is guilty and who is right" («Читающие люди эту рукопись определять хто виноват а хто прав») (142); "he who reads this manuscrip will understand what kind of nonconscious creature she is, how much grief Ive been through" («хто будет читать эту рукопись тот поймет какая она тварь несознательная, сколько я горя пережила») (203).

There is a distinct difference between the first notebook and the two later ones—the memoir (1941 to 1976), featuring a heroic survivor of the war, and the two diaries (1979 to 1989), revealing a garrulous, venomous old woman in a broken-down family, who is increasingly anxious over domestic and world troubles. The difference in genre, in the author's age, and in the historical period account for the production of two different stories about the same person.

Memory and Narrative

In the second and third notebooks, memories of the past constantly interrupt the here and now of the diary writing, introducing long digressions into the diarist's past. Again and again, she recalls the birth of her son on the first day of the war, the battle for her home village, and the separation from her first husband; she repeatedly evokes the hunger of 1932–33, which she survived working as a waitress in a workers' diner (134, 162, 227, 229). She returns more than once to a particular event: her cow fell through the rotten floor of the barn, got trapped in the cellar, and was recovered with the help of the German prisoners of war, who took pity of her hungry children and gave them a piece of bread (105, 226, 228). (On this occasion, she met her second husband, who, as the head of the local housing committee, was in charge of this operation.) Another hunger memory proves difficult to date, but it, too, has historical reference:

> there was either revolution or War cant tell was little we were four children [...] we sat on the stove freezing there was no wood and no food we almost died of hunger there was terrible winter...
>
> толи революция толи Война немогу описать была маленькая нас у родителей было четверо [...] сидели на печки замерзали ни топить ни варить нечиво было чуть не подохли с голоду была зима суровая...(225)

On many occasions, memories intrude into the writing process, creating digressions, not at chosen points in the narrative, but at a moment when a flashback overcomes the diarist. An aggressive monologue addressed to the sister Vera, detailing the circumstances of their conflict over inherited money, slides without a transition into the memory of her son's historical birth:

> I can't sleep at night I worry and you push me around I hope you choke on this money then you sat tight on the keys, and now you [act like] a bloodthirsty snake. [But] you wouldn't pass [the inheritance] over to the state, would you? [...] devil be with her I will wait. There is not enough money there for next year's memorial dinner. In my youth I was already married to Gavriil, and was pregnant with our second child [...] I gave birth in the morning on June 22 of the year one thousand forty one at five o'clock in the morning gave birth to my son Tolia, [and] when they brought me to the ward from the birth room, I noticed that the nurses are crying [...] The war Germany attacked the Soviet Union...
>
> я ночнамы несплю нервничаю что ты ганяеш шоб ты подавилась этыми денгами, тогда ключи задерживали, а типерь ты гадюка кровожадная. не будеш же отдавать в государство. [...] ну черт сней буду ждать. Там тех денег и на помены нехватит зделать годовые помены. В молодости я уже была замужем за Гавриилом, и ходила беременая фторым [...] я родила уже утром 22 июня тысяча девятсот сорок первого года в пять часов утра родила сына Толю, когда миня привезли в палату из родильного стола положили в постель, я смотрю санитарки плачуть [...] Война Германия напала на Советский Союз...(154–55)

Another memory of the war, the image of the mother's dead body, enters the writing in the middle of an impassioned account of a current family conflict:

> you Moscow whore I say don't measure others by your own example, I make that clear to her. My eyes won't dry I remember how my mother was laying there between the walls that had fell her head smashed and how to forget it, and how many accidents shocks like that are there to my poor head.

> потаскуха московская я говорю пусть не меряет по сибе, передай ей ясно. У меня невысыхают глаза, я вспоминаю как моя мама лежала в завалиных стенках сплющеная голова и как это забыть, да и сколько таких случаев потрясений на мою больную голову. (173)

Psychologists view such intrusive, apparently immutable memories of painful experiences as a sign of clinical trauma.[62] So does Kiseleva: here, and further, she speaks of "shock" (*potriasenii*) and lasting damage, resulting in epilepsy (215).

In other cases, memories, though they also seem to overcome the writer as flashbacks, are deliberately and carefully integrated into the narrative. In the second notebook, Kiseleva recalls how, in 1978, she learned of the death of her first husband:

> in 1978 in the month of June my husband died there in Osetia Kiselev Gavriil Dmitrovich even though I haven't been living with him since 1941 [and] many years have gone by, but when my son Vitia said that our own father Gavriil had died, I was sorry [and] I remembered him and his youth and my first love and took stock of all the life I'd lived and I cried he was so handsome and not a bad man in character he loved me but the war seperated us forever if there hadn't been for the war this wouldn't of happened.

> в 1978 г. в июне месяце умер мой муж в Осетии там Киселев Гавриил Дмитрович хотя и не живу с ним с 1941 года прошло много лет, а когда сын Витя сказал, что умер наш родной отец Гавриил то мне стало жалко его вспомнила его юность и свою первою любов и взвесила прожившую жисть плачу какой он был красивый и не плохой характером он меня любил а война нас розлучила навсигда еслиб не война этого-б небыло. (145)

In the third notebook, in 1985, she returns to the separation again, looking back at a whole series of emotional events, including this 1978 episode, in the context of her writing:

> I write this manuscrip and I cries bitterly, it's 37 years since I as lived withim my husband, who I had two children by, two sons. Why couldnt

I forgiven him then. When he died in 1978 I was sorry [like] when he begged me in 1947. i remembered my youth, how we lived with him how we loved each other but the War seperated us.

Пишу эту рукопис и горько плачу, прошло 37 лет как я не живу сним с мужем от которого у меня двое деток двое сынов. Почему я немогла ему простить тогда. Когда он умер 1978 году мне стало его жалко, когда он меня просил в 1947 г. вспомнила свою молодость как мы жили сним как мы любили друг друга а нас розлучила Война...(215)

This elaborate entry connects several moments in Kiseleva's life and in her narrative: the present time in which she writes her "manuscript"; the feelings experienced earlier, when she learned of her husband's death; and the separation itself (as described earlier in her story). The author makes a point of providing dates, creating a historical chart of her emotional life. (However, the dates do not tally: earlier, she had placed the final separation in 1946 and her second marriage in 1945 [100; 105]). She specifies the immediate circumstances in which she was overcome by this memory: it was brought on by watching a film on television, *Fialka*.* Then, she describes the experience itself, in all its immediacy (which she finds noteworthy). As she writes, she is overcome with a sense of her husband's presence: "I write this manuscript and cry bitterly [...] he's standing there the whole time before my very eyes, things like this happen" («Пишу эту рукопис и горько плачу [...] вспоминаю и он у меня все время перед глазамы стоить, такое-же бывает») (215). The author concludes this episode by explicitly addressing the reader, whom she expects to connect her situation to the clinical notion of trauma: "the Reader will understand me and how would you not fall ill in them circumstances with the Epilepsy attacks. [...] my nervous system can't get much weaker" («Читатель поймет меня и кудатам незаболеет Епелепсией приступами. [...] нервная система росшаталася дальше некуда») (215). In the end, Kiseleva reflects on the significance of the key episode in her life—the wartime separation from her husband—in two different, overlapping contexts: in the context of her life and in the context of her writing.

Television and Emotion

As the late notebooks amply document, in the 1980s television occupies an increasingly important place in Kiseleva's life. For one, living alone ("sitting in the four walls and waiting for death" [151]), the old woman spends much

---

* She probably saw *La Violetera*, a popular Spanish melodrama from 1958 that featured a tragic separation between lovers who come from different social classes.

of the day watching television, which the diary describes as an intense emotional experience. Aware of the television's significance in her life, Kiseleva welcomes this technical innovation:

> Loneliness is an awful thing [...] all thanks go to the fellow who invented the Television, raydio. I turn on that raydio but this is not enough I turn on the Television and theres talking everywhere in the room, there's shouts here and there just like there was alot of people in my room whatsmore on the Television there was a concert with songs and dancing I started to sing along *"oh my light light little basket okh lyokhka lyokhka korobushka"* "the pedlars" and I started to feel lighter in my heart...

> Одиночество страшное дело [...] да спасибо человеку который выдумал Телевизор, радиво. Я включила радиво этого мало, я включила и Телевизор говорить на всю комнату кричит и там и там как бутто-бы, у меня в комнате много людей да еще по Телевидению передавали концерт песни и танци хоровые я стала подпивать, ох лехка лехка коробушка «коробейники» и мне стало весело на душа... (166–67)

A friendly presence in her room, television becomes her one and only intimate friend: "television's my best friend in the room" («телевизор лучшей друг в комнате») (188).

An attentive reader of Kiseleva's notebooks will also notice that television does not always improve her mood or serve her interests. On quite a few occasions, watching television brings painful memories and emotions, which overpower her:

> I'm watching a film. Special Detachment and I came over ill when I saw them chase people from a truck in their underclothes, and they was all shouting and people was crying in different voices, and the executioners handed them over to be murdered shot I remembered 1941 and the German War with the [Soviet] Union. It brought back all my agonies. Pavel Zibert officer Kuznitsev served in Germany and his accomplice Valia how they trembled I feel for them, but they knew German well, but my neighbors called an ambulance and I was in bed for four days my nervous system was shaken and I try to turn off the Television when they show programs like that and I dont watch them.

> Смотрю кино. Отряд (специального назначения) исильно заболела как увидила из машины гнали людей в нательном белье, и все кричать люди плачуть разнымы голосамы, а палачи гонят выдать

на убийство ростреливать, вспомнила 1941 год Войну Немецкую с Союзом. Все мои муки роскрилися, Павель Зиберт офицер Кузницев работал в Германии и его соучасница Валя как они дрожали я сочуствую им, но они знали хорошо немецкий язык, но мне соседи вызывали скорую помощь я лежала в постели четире дня, была потрясена нервная система но я стараюсь выключать Телевизор когда передают такие передачи и несмотрю их. (231)

This entry shows how, step-by-step, Kiseleva enters the space of the war film: she feels empathy with the visibly frightened film heroes as they are led to their execution. The syntactic fusion of the two pronouns and two verbs in one construction ("how they trembled I feel for them"), which is a characteristic feature of Kiseleva's oral-based writing, underscores the fusion of the emotions reproduced in the film and the viewer's own emotions. The feature film she watches, *Otriad Spetsial'nogo Naznacheniia* (A special detachment, 1987), shows how "the officer Kuznitsev" and his comrade in arms "Valia," who work undercover in the German-occupied territory, triumph over adversity, but Kiseleva, who is not as well-equipped emotionally and linguistically, falls so ill watching them on the screen that the neighbors call an ambulance. In the same diary entry, Kiseleva also describes watching a political program on the negotiations on nuclear proliferation between the Soviet Union and the United States, and she sympathizes with the aggressive stance maintained by the Soviet side. Television—an important presence in this old woman's life—both triggers memories of the past and allows the political-historical domain to enter her life.

Television and Apocalypsis

For many of Kiseleva's contemporaries, the memory of the past horror is projected into the future as the fear of another war, creating a stable existential background: the dread that war—now a nuclear war—may repeat in one's lifetime. In her second notebook, contemplating the prospect of death and dying, Kiseleva speaks of these fears, activated by exposure to the political through television, as actual physical pain:

> Days go by and before you know it you will die soon, but no one dont want to die, and there on the Television their saying that Carter is bringing his nuclear weapons closer to our shores its another accursed Hitler, my wounds open up and my heart aches…

> Проходят дни и неоглянешся а вже скоро умирать, но нет умирать нехочится, а тут по Телевизору говорят что Картер подтянул свое

ядерное оружие поближе до наших рубежей, вот другой Гитлер проклятый, розкриваются раны аж у серце колить... (159)

Moreover, she anticipates with fear that the present Soviet leader—the protector from war—will die soon, and expresses a heartfelt wish that he may enjoy personal immortality:

> I so dont want Lionid Ilich to die, he's already an old man, I want him to be immortal...
>
> Мне так нехочится что-бы Лионид Илич умирал, он уже старинкой мне хочится чтобы он был бессмертной... (156–57)

At the end of the second notebook (as at the end of the first) the writer positions herself in front of a television set. She records the discourse on the threat of war that flows from the screen, inserting in it her personal memories of the past war. Recalling once again that decisive wartime battle in her home village, she concludes on an apocalyptic note:

> how many dead and wounded there were after the battle, like sheep after pasture laying there resting [...] some still alive and the wounded call out save us the last judgement.
>
> сколько после боя набитых людей было, што овцы лежать после пасбища отдыхают [...] хто еще живой а раненые кричать спасите страшный суд. (184)

The notebook ends with a report of Leonid Brezhnev's death, announced on television on November 10, 1982, which triggered intense physical fear and apocalyptic forebodings:

> how my heart was taken ill I was gripped with fear. my heart beat like wild tears streamed what'll happen now [...] something terrible will happen I feel.
>
> как у меня заболело серце охватил меня страх. забилося серце невольно полилися слезы, что типерь будит [...] мне кажится будит страшное. (185)

But Kiseleva soon learns that life goes on. When, in the third notebook, she describes the new leader, Mikhail Gorbachev, her strong tendency to attribute responsibility for her family to the current leader—with whom she shares domestic space through television—shows itself again:

> I cried when Brezhnev died and said what will we do without a leader like Brezhnev. But there are still better people [...] what a clever one he is that M.S. Gorbachev god give him health always I pray to the blessed saint Nicholas even though I don't go to church. i've got 5 menfolk–two sons and three Grandsons deargod let there not be War how many tears I couldn't stand I'm more than certain that they'll go off to defend the motherland all five of them, both young and old, better that theres no War.
>
> Я когда умер Брежнев, плакала и говорила что мы будим делать без такого Руководителя как Брежнев. А оно еще лучшие есть люди [...] какой умница М.С. Горбачев дай ему бог здоровя всгда молюся Николай угоднику святому [...] хотя у церкву и не хожу. у меня 5 мущин два сына и три Внука недайбог Войны сколько слез, непереживу я больше чем уверена, пойдут на защиту родины все пять, и старие и малые, желательноб что-бы не было Войны. (218)

Her one reproach to the past leader Stalin (whom she mentions only once) is that, being "trusting and kind" («Сталин был доверчив и милостив»), Stalin did not believe that Hitler would attack our country, until the very day of June 22, 1941, at 4 o'clock in the morning (136). Again and again, Kiseleva described the country's current leader both as her family's personal protector and as the world's protector from a future apocalyptic nuclear war—ultimately, an agent of salvation.

The political apocalyptic intrudes with a vengeance, when, watching television, Kiseleva follows Gorbachev in his visit to the United States on December 8, 1987. (This account is featured prominently in the third notebook.) The sight of President Reagan triggers a vision of life after the future nuclear war:

> I can not look at his mug he thinks he'll survive or rather his people will stay alive no, if the War comes to us everyone will die just thesame, on the whole earth. They say that in the USSR we've got 45 nuclear stations we will fight to the last we too can fight we can we're already wise to it But he thinks he's got these underground cities in his country but I've heard that they can't live long first the earth will be barren for 10 years what will people live on they'll beg for death, them that remain living there won't be nothing no more, no life how stupid them leader of the USA they should have thought with their clever head, why War but our leader Gorbachev fights withall his strength so that there aren't no Wars...
>
> немогу смотреть на него рожу он думает что он останитца вернея его люди жывы, нет, если пойдет на нас Войной, всярамно погибнут все, увесь земной шар. Говорят что у нас в СССР, 45 атомных

станций будим дратца до последнего мы тожет умеем воювать мы уже ученые Хотя он думает что у него в стране есть подземные города а я так слухала долго они [не] прожывут, вопервых земля не будет родить 10 лет, чем люди будит питатся жить будут просить смерти которие останутся жить больше ничиво а жизни небудит какие руководитель С.Ш.А. глупие подумалиб свей умной головой, зачем Войны но наш руководитель Горбачев борится совсей силы что-бы небыло Войнов... (230)

This picture clearly operated with the biblical apocalyptic imagery ("the earth will be barren for 10 years [...] they'll beg for death, them that remain living"), and, as the author makes clear, the origin of this imagery is oral ("I've heard it such"). We see that the peasant religious culture works side by side with Soviet political culture.

This diary entry—a report on the Soviet leader's momentous meeting with the agent of evil, President Reagan—goes so far as to transcribe Reagan's speech on December 8, 1987, which passes through the diarist's own speech:

on the Television I saw when Gorbachev M.S. was at the negotiations in the USA on Dec 12 1987 and Regan he said like the Star lit up on the top of our national Christmas tree on the day of Your coming, this meeting lights up the heavens with hope and good will for all men when we part both sides must act so as this world does not perish and must fulfil their holy dutys to the extent that we will move forward making new steps with the aim of improvement between our countrys and peoples how well he speaks at the negotiations. The door has opened and it will remain open for a serious discussion of the paths to Ceasing these Wars of fire on earth They came up with the idea of vying in heaven vying the devil took them there and they do pray to god them believers, dear lord don't let them bring death to the people with arms we wont let it happen.

в Телевизоре я видила когда Горбачев М.С. был на переговорах в США 8/XII 1987 г. но Рейган Р. говорил подробно Звезде зажженой на верхушки нашей национальной рождественой Елке в день Вашего прибытия, эта встреча озорила надеждой небо для всех людей доброй воли, когда мы ростанимся обе стороны должны следить за тем что-бы этот свет не погас и должны выполнять святие на сибе обязаности по мере как мы будим продвигатся в перед совершая новые шаги в целях улучшению между нашимы странамы и народамы как он хорошо говорить на переговорах. Дверь открылася и она останится открытой для серезного обсуждения путей Прикращения этых Войн огня на земле Придумали соревнуватся в небе соревнуватся черт их туда понес, а еще богу молятся божественые господа, недопусти господи их соружием на гибель людей недопустим. (230–31)

This is a case of the spontaneous use of what narratologists call *erlebte Rede*. As Kiseleva records Reagan's speech, she speaks in one voice with him ("like the Star lit up on the top of our national Christmas tree"). (Curiously, there is an affinity between their discourses: both Reagan and Kiseleva were inclined to use religious and apocalyptic rhetoric.) At the end of this long passage, Kiseleva's voice gradually takes over: first, she adds words of approval ("how well he speaks at the negotiations"); then, she moves back to report Reagan's speech ("The door has opened and it will remain open for a serious discussion"); and, finally, with the topic of competitive space exploration ("the vying in heaven"), she starts speaking for herself. Indeed, when it comes to the heavenly battle, Kiseleva's voice breaks through, appealing to God to put an end to it ("dear lord, don't let them"); then, in the first person plural she writes "we won't let it happen" (this is a popular formula of the aggressive Soviet antiwar discourse: *ne dopustim*).

A Comment on Historical Continuity: The Past War and the Future War

Kiseleva's diary vividly demonstrates how, almost forty years after the Second World War, the war continues to exercise its spell as a source of intense fear, experienced physically. (Recall that in the lives of the two antiregime intellectuals, Lidiia Chukovskaia and Anna Akhmatova, the fear of the terror that they had lived through plays a similar role.) In the life of the "common people" in the 1970s and 1980s, it was television—an agent of the state—that served as a main conduit of this fear. We have seen how, mediated by television broadcasts—war films, patriotic memorials of the past war, and political discussions of the threat of a future nuclear war—the fear of war works as a mechanism for inculcating loyalty to the state in the citizens.

Kiseleva's reactions to these messages are not unique: fear of a future nuclear war may well have been the dominant emotion of the postwar period, especially for those who, like Kiseleva, had experienced the horror of the war directly and had lost family through death and abandonment. For political purposes, the Soviet regime encouraged memories of the war in the population; projected into the future, these memories intensified the fear of a possible nuclear war, serving as a foundation for loyalty to the state and to the leader. Indeed, as historians know, much of the Soviet regime's postwar legitimacy rested on mobilizing this fear. Reading Kiseleva's diary, we see how this policy worked on an individual person.

Generalizations: The Soviet State in the Domestic Space

Kiseleva's diary shows the specific ways in which, during the 1970s and 1980s, the political entered everyday life. Through television—which, with the increasing disintegration of Kiseleva's family, served as her sole companion, playing a major role in her emotional life—the state entered, intimately, right into her room, speaking to this woman at the moment in her life when, old, sick, and lonely, she was most vulnerable. The diary shows how television, a cultural institution, served the interests of the Soviet state. Speaking from the television screen, the state power reached and tapped into the heartfelt, painful emotions that were rooted in the experiences of the war and maintained by lasting traces of clinical trauma. Through television, the state power addressed this barely literate woman both in the language of the political (with broadcasts of party congresses and state visits) and in the language of art (with feature films and popular songs). These appeals found an echo in traditional beliefs and images, in the folk religious culture, whose apocalyptic tendency proved well fitted to express the political concerns of the day—nuclear proliferation. When the memories of the past war met the carefully fostered fears of a future war—from which, as Kiseleva felt, only the leader (and an immortal leader) could save the people—a large space opened in the everyday life of an ordinary person: the political-historical-apocalyptic.

This diary shows that the country woman Evgeniia Kiseleva entered this space consciously, eagerly, actively, and with heartfelt feeling. She appropriated the official discourse of the threat of war, combining it with the apocalyptic discourse of the peasant religious culture. (As we have seen, the religious culture did not lose its power even though, growing up under the Soviet regime, people like Kiseleva had not learned the words of the Lord's Prayer as children and did not go to church as adults.) Kiseleva used this mixed language to express palpable and intensely painful emotions: the fear of war that she felt threatened her, her menfolk, and, with them, the whole world. Sitting in her room in front of the television set, she opened a notebook to speak. Reporting political speeches in a narrative pattern that fused her own words with the words of others, she spoke through and with Brezhnev, Gorbachev, and Reagan. To resort to metaphor, she "speaks in tongues"—as if several people and multiple languages speak through Kiseleva to conjure world peace, but, as I argue, *not* to the point of making her own voice, her fears, and her will, indistinguishable.

Citizens and Power

In more ways than one, the involvement of the Soviet citizen and the state began at home: the state owned and distributed the living space, and, throughout the existence of the Soviet regime, living space was scarce, which made the state's role so crucial for the organization of domestic life. The problems with living space—cramped living quarters and complex bureaucracy, requiring the personal intervention of someone in power—emerges in Kiseleva's diary, as they did for Akhmatova, as definitive pressure points.

After the war, if not earlier, Kiseleva and her family no longer lived in peasant houses but in state-distributed apartments: first, in small semiurban apartment buildings complete with auxiliary structures (a woodshed, a barn with chickens, a cold cellar, and a potato patch in the yard), and, finally, in the 1980s, in new high-rise apartment blocks with central heating, refrigerators, and washing machines. The shortage of living space became an especially acute problem when Kiseleva's two grandsons, who lived in a three-room apartment with their parents (Kiseleva's older son Viktor and his wife Maria), reached adult age and promptly married (193). When the family tried to resolve this situation and secure living space for the households newly formed through marriage, it came into acute conflict with the local authorities. As Kiseleva wrote her diary in the late 1970s, her desire to assure living space for her grandson's family occupied her attention as much as her palpable wish to avoid a nuclear war. She was aware that, in both cases, the key to survival and success lay in the hands of the state power and its representatives.

It should be noted that the family's positioning within the local power structure is ambiguous. On the one hand, along with other people in her social milieu, she distrusted and avoided local power.[63] But, as Kiseleva makes a point to note, quite a few members of her family worked in responsible positions: before the war, Gavriil Kiselev, she repeats on several occasions, had been a person of "authority" («авторитетный командир»), a commander of the fire brigade (89); during the war he reached the rank of officer; and in his last years of his life, she also reports, he worked for the army's recruiting office (*voenkomat*). The younger son, Anatoly, after compulsory military service, joined the militia; he rose to senior lieutenant and became the head of the passport department (239). His son, the family decided, would follow his grandfather: after military service, the family sent him to a special school for firemen, so that he could become a "boss" («устроили в училеще Пожарной Команды будит Начальником») (214). Even the no-good Tiurichev, as we are told, worked as the head of the housing committee (ZhKO, or ZhKK) when Kiseleva met him. When Kiseleva joined the workforce, at the age of fifty, it was as a night watch person, employed by the security department of the mining administration.[64] Small as these positions may be or seem, this was participation in the local power and authority structure of which the author takes pride.

In 1979, Kiseleva's twenty-year-old grandson, Yura, his wife Anna, and their three-week-old child moved into the apartment that had fallen empty following the death of Kiseleva's sister, Anna (Niusia), a war widow. From the beginning, Kiseleva knew that their position was precarious because Yura was not officially "registered" (*propisan*) in the apartment, but she found his claim compelling because the family looked after their sick relative ("grandmother") and paid for her funeral. Two different systems of norms and values, commanded by the family members in equal measure, came into conflict in this situation: the official order, where housing was distributed by state organizations (in accordance with the established waiting lists, usually sponsored at the workplace), and the traditional order of things, in which the living space is passed on in the family, with succession influenced by the fulfillment of familial obligations, such as the giving of care to the elderly and settling of funeral expenses. Feeling for her grandson, who lived in the illegally occupied apartment under constant threat of eviction, Kiseleva took an active part in the long administrative and legal battle that ensued.

Well able to navigate the system, Kiseleva gained access to the assistant head of the city executive committee (*gorispolkom*), the organization then responsible for the allocation of the living space. Trying hard to achieve her practical goal, she makes use of different cultural codes. (The diary reports the dialogue between Kiseleva and the city official, mixing syntactic patterns of direct and indirect speech.) First, she appeals to the traditional family order, arguing that her grandson did not move into somebody else's apartment but remained in the apartment of his "grandmother," whom he buried. Then, she changes her tactics and switches to party-speak: appealing (somewhat clumsily) to her antagonists' "consciousness" (a Marxist concept that gained high currency in daily life), she tries to evoke in the official a sense of political solidarity with her young grandson: "You are without consciousness, you a party member and he's a komsomol if there is trouble in the country you'd be ready and off fighting together" (146). At this point, as she positions the supplicant and the official together as fellow soldiers in a future war, she feels that she might be close to a resolution, as (in her words) "consciousness enters him," but in the end she is dismissed without ceremony. («Какой вы несознательной, вы партейный а он комсомолец если чуть в стране стрясется вы-же вместе, в переди сражатся пойдете, в него пришло сознание») (146).

On her visit to the city official, Kiseleva was counting on the intervention of a higher power: early in the conflict, she had addressed two letters to the celebrated female astronaut Valentina Tereshkova, who was known as a public advocate. She copied her second letter in the notebook. Addressed to Tereshkova as the "defender of peace of women and Children," Kiseleva's letter, positioned within the community of women, is written both on behalf and in the name of her grandson's young wife (Anna F., that is, Anna Fedorovna Kiseleva). In this situation of layered agency, Kiseleva lost control of linguistic subjectivity. Her letter, as reported in the diary, mixes the "I" of the actual writer with the "I" of the young woman for whom she writes: "I'm writing this is in the name of Anna F. that I've got a little one born in 1979 on September 5" («это пишу я на имя Анны Ф что у миня маленкой рибенок родился 1979 г. 5 сентября») (144). As in her diary, in this letter to power Kiseleva intermixes (somewhat deformed) idioms from different sources: folk culture ("help us please in our sorrow" / «помогите пожалуйста нашему горю»); common conversational language ("we've got nowhere to live" / «нам негде жить»); and official Soviet discourses, both bureaucratic ("we are on the waiting list for an apartment" / «стоим на очереди на квартиру») and ideological ("in the country's times of need we will always be at the ready" / «в трудное время в стране мы всегда будим в переди»). In the end, she makes her case clear: "it's so very hard with residency purmits and we want to be registered in this apartment Krupskaia 9 apt. 6" / «с припиской очень трудно и мы хотим что-бы нас приписали в эту квартиру Крупская 9 кв.6» (144). It seems as if several people and multiple languages speak through Kiseleva, all intent on conjuring a miraculous intervention into her grandson's housing difficulties. (All in vain.)

The End: "We Live Like Strangers"

On January 12, 1980, Kiseleva's grandson and his family, confronted with a militiaman (policeman), a housing committee official, and four workmen equipped with an axe, moved out of the apartment they had illegally occupied. They settled with the wife's family, eight people (four generations) in three rooms (140, 154). In October 1981, they did receive an apartment of their own, in accordance with the waiting list, but by that time these was "nobody to live there" (179). The grandson Yura no longer lived with his wife and child, he did not go to work, and he did not even respond to military draft notices: he drank.

It took another eight years to complete the separation of the young family by making provisions for separate living quarters, and this operation required the grandmother's participation. In February 1989, Kiseleva exchanged her one-room apartment for a room in the apartment of Yura's ex-wife Anna, who then lived in the two rooms allocated to the young family in 1981 (238). After the exchange, Kiseleva shared the two-room apartment (in a modern nine-story building) with her grandson, who drank, debauched, and watched television; he broke her washing machine and went steadily through the jars of her treasured supply of homemade preserved food. She wrote in the notebook: "we live like strangers" (*zhivem kak chuzhie*) (238). The situation soon became intolerable. In August, Kiseleva's younger son Anatoly, on a visit from Murom, where he held the post in the city militia (police), helped her to exchange this apartment for two separate rooms. (Kiseleva suggested that her son use his position to commit his nephew to substance abuse treatment, but Anatoly declined.) Kiseleva commented that in her old age she changed her home three times in one year (239). She was confused: Why am I here? What am I to do? But Kiseleva continued to write, even though she no longer believed that her life story would become a film.

Unlike her first and second notebooks, the third notebook does not end on a public or historical note; the last sentence begins: "I live alone" (*zhyvu odna*) (244). Kiseleva died in September 1990, shortly before, in February 1991, her heavily edited story was finally published in a literary journal.

HOW THESE NOTEBOOKS REACHED THE READER: THE INTERPRETERS

The story of Evgeniia Kiseleva's life reached the reader through the mediation of many people. The editors of the second, scholarly, edition in 1996 have carefully described the story of Kiseleva's text in their introduction, step-by-step, and I will present this story in their words:

> E. G. Kiseleva sends her first notebook to "Mosfilm." [...] A highly educated woman, whose whole life has been given over to the service of spiritual interests and to art, devotes her time first to copying E. G. Kiseleva's manuscript and then to publishing it. [...] We are speaking about E. N. Ol'shanskaia, who published extracts from the notebooks in *Novyi mir* in 1991. This was a publication of the text in a form purged of the author's presence, that is, in an edited form, but complete with introductory commentary by a venerable litterateur. [...]
>
> Then the selfsame E. N. Ol'shanskaia handed the notebooks over to the People's Archive.
>
> G. I. Popova, the curator of personal collections, passionate in her service to the cause, saw in E. G. Kiseleva's notebooks a thing of great value—as testimony and historical source—and handed over the notebooks to a researcher, N. N. Kozlova.
>
> N. N. Kozlova, who had worked at the Russian Academy of Sciences Institute of Philosophy for twenty years—a fact which, by definition, might seem to warn her off such materials—single-handedly copied out the notebooks. She suffocated and froze in the aforementioned archive as she meticulously copied out by hand the pensioner's work. Then she typed it up on the computer, preserving the original orthography and making every effort not to disrupt in any way the flow of the original writing—keeping in check, for example, the bad habits of the intelligentsia of inserting a comma where the enigmatic author had omitted one.

Yet another woman researcher, the linguist I. I. Sandomirskaia, agreed, as if out of sheer curiosity, to analyze the language of the notorious manuscripts, bringing to bear her great skill at discovering the screw which, once undone, can reveal how the whole apparatus is put together.

And finally, one more woman, the youngest of us—the publisher, O. Nazarova.

[...] Combining her studies for the defense of her doctoral dissertation in philosophy with work in the nascent market economy [...] she encountered all of the abovementioned individuals, as well as the notebooks in question. And she conceived the desire to publish them.[65]

The editors' introduction, cited here at length, presents a whole chain of professional intellectuals involved with the peasant text (the literary editor, the archivist, the scholar-sociologist, the scholar-linguist, the publisher), all of them women (the custodians of memory), all possessed by intense emotions: "captivation by the text," "the intense desire to understand; the incomprehension," "the desire to boast of the beloved text," "jealousy and the fear that it would be snatched out of one's hands and taken away" (12). This account may seem puzzling in its pathos. Take, for instance, the way the editors' introduction to the text carefully highlights service to the common ("spiritual") cause, hardship and self-sacrifice, skill, succession, cooperation, encounter, and rivalry. Note the careful marking of the participants' institutional affiliations: a liberal journal, *Novyi mir;* a grassroots organization from the time of perestroika, the People's Archive; an official Soviet academic establishment, the Institute of Philosophy; and, finally, the nascent market economy of post-Soviet times. I believe that Kiseleva's 1996 publishers present the history of this text as part of a larger story: the intelligentsia's age-long romance with the proverbial "ordinary," "simple," or "small" person as it unfolds at the end of the Soviet epoch. In this sense, this introduction makes a significant statement, and I will comment on the editors' claims, moves, and strategies from this perspective.

Defining the Status of the Text: "Naive Writing"

Publishing Kiseleva's notebooks in 1996, under the title *Naive Writing,* the editors purport to introduce to the "cultured reader" a whole—previously unacknowledged—class of texts: "naive writing" (10). Produced by barely literate authors, such texts do not conform to the normative conventions of writing and publishing enforced in Soviet society. Kiseleva's publishers suggest that "the interest in 'naive writing' is symptomatic of the shift away from Soviet culture" (39). Striving to pry the peasant text loose from the normative power of Soviet culture, they go so far as to suggest that "naive texts remain beyond political, aesthetic, and even moral jurisdiction because they are of life itself."[66] Unpremeditated and unaware, Kiseleva's writing is "the word that speaks itself" (*chto skazalos' samo*) (61). Her publishers were, of course, aware that the peasant author had intended to create a narrative that could be both book and film, but, for her own good, they deny her entry into their world: "Our heroine attempts to play on a field that is not her own: Writing, Literature. In just the same way she plays on the field of Social Life; but she is simply Life itself."[67]

The professional naiveté of these definitions—insisting that the author and the text represent some kind of natural state—can hardly be spontaneous and unintentional. This move creates an image of "another world" (8)—a territory populated by the "other," who is fundamentally different from the language-bound and self-conscious intellectuals. And, as the publishers of *Naive Writing* imply, through "naive texts" one may be able to access this other world. Many an intellectual, including Rousseau and Tolstoy, has longed for this ideal, idealizing the speech of the common people as a window onto "Life itself" that lies outside language, will, and rationality. This desire, it appears, has not lost its poignancy even today. It may be indicative that since the 1996 publication of Kiseleva's notebooks—and directly inspired by this edition—the concept of "naive writing" has gained currency in publishing and in scholarship in post-Soviet Russia.[68]

The Competition between Publishers: "Legislators and Interpreters"

The 1996 publishers, N. N. Kozlova and I. I. Sandomirskaia, claim precedence in bringing Kiseleva's "naive writing" into the public realm.[69] But the text had already been published (in an excerpted and edited form) in 1991 in the literary journal *Novyi mir* under the editorship of Elena Ol'shanskaia. Therefore, the task called for, not only physical heroism and self-abnegation in producing the faithful transcription from a difficult copy stored in the cold basement of the People's Archive, but also purging the text of the previous editing. They have done this with skill, expertise, and considerable force. As for purging, the pathos is directed, not at a specific person or persons who handled the text, but at a composite, symbolic figure called the "Editor"—a figure that has mediated between the original text and its first public version:

> The Editor (with a capital E) is not E. N. Ol'shanskaia. E. N. Ol'shanskaia was the first reader and devotee of the text. She only initiated this endless series. The editor of *Novyi mir* then took his/her place in this line. [...] The persona of the Editor possesses a multitude of incarnations—like an Eastern deity...[70]

Clearly, much more than a rivalry between two publications of a single text is at stake here: the difference is ideological, and the stakes are high.

The editors of the 1996 edition turn the editing performed by their predecessors into a text in itself—a text that documents the intelligentsia's idea of what constitutes the "voice of the people" (14). Provided in the book's appendix, the linguistic analysis of the editorial revisions made for the *Novyi mir* publication highlights attempts to "tame" the text: to standardize punctuation, spelling, and syntax, retaining (and occasionally even adding) only those oral patterns and nonnormative features that fit the conventional image of a folk text. In a word, conclude the scholar-publishers, the literary publication transformed the text to make it conform to the age-long stereotypes of folk culture and simple people fostered by the "great literature."[71]

Reflecting on the relationship of "the Editor" to "naive writing," the scholar-publishers focus on the Editor's hostile, repressive, and unbending will to normalize:

> The "conflict" between E. G. Kiseleva and her Editor, the product of which was the *Novyi mir* publication, is the result of a clash between two mutually untranslatable idioms. One of them possesses the force of normativity, while the other does not. Thus it follows that the interpretation of the naive idiom is inevitably accompanied by the relationship of domination/subordination. The acts of correction and editing take on a repressive character. The Editor clearly intercedes as a powerful subject, fulfilling a disciplinary function. There is, however, no malicious intent here. The publisher simply cannot allow himself to publish the original text in its "natural state." His hand cannot be halted, that is to say the norm that cannot be violated is built into the Editor's body.[72]

As such reflections indicate, the 1996 publishers define their role vis-à-vis the "simple people" and "naive writing" in opposition to the role of their predecessors, the 1991 publishers. For them, the first edition is "publication-normalization" and their own, second, edition is "publication-interpretation" (15). I believe that this dichotomy has been informed and inspired by Western social science, namely by Zygmunt Bauman's formula "legislators and interpreters."

Highly skeptical, even scornful, of intellectuals, Bauman, a Polish-born sociologist and former Marxist who moved to Britain and became a theoretician of postmodernity, distinguishes between two historical modes of intellectual activity. One, which goes back to the Enlightenment, is defined by the metaphor legislator. Intellectuals who take on the position of legislator put themselves in a position of making authoritative judgments of truth and aesthetic taste, based on the claim that intellectuals enjoy special access to knowledge—the knowledge to which the nonintellectuals, or (in Bauman's words), "ordinary people, preoccupied with their daily business of survival"—remain impervious. The other mode, which has emerged in the age of postmodernism, is defined by the metaphor interpreter. Interpreter aims at "facilitating communication between autonomous (sovereign) participants"—the intellectuals and the common people. For this purpose (Bauman says), "Interpreter promotes the need to penetrate deeply the alien system of knowledge from which the translation is to be made."[73] I believe that Bauman's paradigm—the transformation of intellectuals from legislators to interpreters, marking the transition from the failed project of modernity to postmodernity—inspired the post-Soviet publishers of the *Naive Writing* edition.[74]

Indeed, the *Naive Writing* edition has a supertask: it speaks to us about the new role of the intelligentsia after the end of the Soviet regime. The *Novyi mir* editors, who handled a peasant text in 1991, are cast as legislators intent on exercising normalizing power. The 1996 publishers make it clear that after the end of the Soviet epoch, an intellectual who "edits," "corrects," or "legislates" is to be replaced by another type of intellectual, one who "reads" or "interprets"—and they cast themselves in the role of interpreters. Their position is self-conscious and unapologetically superior.

I will pause for a disclaimer of sorts: I try to follow the procedure Kozlova and Sandomirskaia established in their forceful critique of their predecessors. They speak not about concrete people but about the function dubbed the "Editor." For me, too, the object is not a real person or persons, but a function, or persona, which (as much as possible) I will call the "Interpreter." The Interpreter exemplifies post-Soviet intellectuals who take it upon themselves to bring the life stories of nonintellectuals into the public domain.

First and foremost, the position of the Interpreter involves a move to join with, after years of enforced separation, the intellectuals of the West, specifically, postmodernist philosophers and social scientists. Indeed, the names that were unmentionable (or at least unusable) in Soviet humanities and social sciences, operating as they were under the strictly enforced methodology of Soviet Marxism, figure frequently and prominently in the speech of the Interpreter: from Eco and Barthes to Deleuze and Guattari, from Geertz and Ricouer to Bourdieu and de Certeau. The introduction to Kiseleva's notebooks cites all of these, in addition to Lyotard, Baudrillard, Foucault, Bauman, and Joan Scott (together with Rozanov, Vaginov, and Platonov—the Russian writers who were out of favor in Soviet times). Like Kiseleva (when she tries to participate in society by speaking of world peace), the Interpreter uses ready-made formulas to write herself into the dominant public discourse, this time, the discourse of postmodern social science. Like Kiseleva, who with the rise of Soviet civilization made a rapid transition from peasant to new Soviet person, the Interpreter, with the collapse of the Soviet civilization, made an instant transformation from Marxist to postmodernist.* And what seems

---

* To appreciate the shift in the discourse of social science between Soviet and post-Soviet times, one may compare two works by a single author, one from 1989, another from 1996. They are published by

to attract the Interpreter most among these new ideas is the "death of the subject" and the "disappearance of the author" (discussed at length in the section of the introduction entitled "Person without Subjecthood" [52–58]).

The Disappearance of the Author

On the cover of her second notebook, Kiseleva addresses the person who is preparing her story for publication:

You clever woman, Elena Ol'shanskaia!
I don't write very grammarly, but you make it all more correct write it your way. You form it.

Умница Вы Елена Ольшанская!
Я пишу не очень грамотно а вы все делаете вернея пишите по своему. Оформляете.* (129)

The author welcomes her editor's revisions of her text. For Kiseleva herself, writing grammatically is not unauthentic or less expressive (as it seems to our educated eyes), but simply more acceptable. Hoping that her story will reach the public, she knows that it should conform to linguistic norms. Her delight in seeing her story rewritten grammatically gives her hope that this might come to be.[75]

---

the same institution: the Institute of Philosophy of the Academy of Sciences (in 1989, the "Academy of Sciences of the USSR," and in 1996, the "Russian Academy of Sciences"). Both books address the same subject—the "masses" and the "individual" under the socialist/Soviet system. The first was written by a "Marxist scholar" (as the author defines herself on p. 13), and it was inspired (the author claims) by a desire to aid in "the attainment of the goals set forth by the party" («Достижение поставленных партией целей....», p. 3). The first book abounds in quotations from Marx and Lenin. The second book (seven years later) was penned by a scholar whose inspiration clearly came from Western postmodernist social science: there are frequent references to Bourdieu and not one to Marx or Lenin. On one occasion—speaking of the rapid transformation of former peasants into new Soviet people—the author describes, in each book, the same episode from the 1920s: in the student dormitories, young people (yesterday's peasants) proudly show a foreign visitor a volume of Marx's *Capital*, as if they wrote it themselves. In the 1989 book, our author—using both clichés of Soviet social science and sentimental idiom of Soviet populism—finds that "this touching scene [...] provides evidence of the most serious and rapid shift in the consciousness of the masses..." («Трогательная картина [...] свидетельство серьезнейшего и быстрого сдвига в сознании масс...»). In the 1996 book, she notes that Marx's volume is not read but (physically) "touched" and (adding one other example) identifies such "tactile practices" as "elements of fetishism." The language (note the Western social term "practice" and the dry tone) is markedly different from the distinctly Soviet idiom of the 1989 book: «'Дотрагивание' как тактильная практика не равно чтению. По меньшей мере—это элемент фетишизма не столько текста, сколько Книги». See N. N. Kozlova, *Sotsializm i soznanie mass (Sotsial'no-filosofskie problemy)* (Moscow: Nauka: Akademiia nauk SSSR: Istitut filosofii, 1989), 89, and N. N. Kozlova, *Gorizonty povsednevnosti Sovetskoi epokhi. Golosa iz khora* (Moscow: Nauka: Rossiiskaia akademiia nauk: Istitut filosofii, 1996), 162.

* The word «оформлять», literally, to "form" or "shape," also has a specific Soviet usage: "to make official" (as in «оформить прописку», «оформить пенсию»).

Envisioning the film that, she now believes, will be made about her life, she informs her editor that she has chosen a title:

Kishmareva
Kiseleva
Tiuricheva,
This is how how I want the movie called.

Кишмарева
Киселева
Тюричева,
я так такхочу назвать кино.⁷⁶

She has chosen her three names, the maiden name and the two married names (in this order), suggesting both a continuity and a division in her self and in her life.

In her publication in *Novyi mir* in 1991 Ol'shanskaia used this title. But not the second publishers: the author's names do not appear on the title page of the 1996 edition. On several other occasions, the publishers omit or transform the author's name and her chosen title: they consistently reverse the order of her three names, misspell "Kiseleva" (as "Kisileva"), and add punctuation marks where the author had none.⁷⁷

To comment on misprints may be frivolous, especially given the immense volume of difficult textological work undertaken for this edition. What invites such a comment is the consistency with which the 1996 publishers run into difficulty with the author's name and her chosen title as well as the force with which they attack their predecessors, the 1991 publishers, for "purging" the text from the presence of the author, emphasizing the rivals' mishandling of punctuation marks and spelling (245; 250). They ask direct questions: "E. G. Kiseleva's narrative bears the subtitle 'This is how I want the film called.' The publisher deleted it. Why?" (41).

In my turn, I will say: the publishers of the 1996 *Naive Writing* edition omit and misspell the name of the author, as if the inability to write the author's name is built into the Interpreter's body. The *Naive Writing* publishers also made a conscious decision not to include a photograph of the author that she had sent to Elena Ol'shanskaia (16). Why?

I see the explanation in the methodological and philosophical stance adopted by these self-consciously post-Soviet intellectuals.

"Person without Subjecthood"

The Interpreter asks: Could one speak of "naive writers" as subjects? Indeed, the concept of "subject" and "subjectivity" has been traditionally associated with rationality, freedom of choice, unified worldview, self-awareness, and historical consciousness. Within this framework, such authors as Kiseleva may not qualify as "subjects" (54). Her publishers believe that Kiseleva's writings are devoid of historical signposts that mark the memoir writings of her educated contemporaries:

> The names of prewar leaders are practically absent. [...] June 22, 1941, is the only historical date that E. G. Kiseleva mentions. [...] For E. G. Kiseleva there is no History, writ large—with which the notes of the "cultured people" are constantly aligning themselves. (83)

They note that "means of verbal representation of the feeling of love are absent" in her story (75). What they also deem absent are markings of narrative competence:

> The manuscript is testament to the fact that E. G. Kiseleva is not capable of constructing a narrative in linear time, the kind of time in which biography is written, according to temporal continuity. (67)

In the end, her publishers reach the following conclusion: because of all this, Kiseleva does not become, contrary to her wish, a "subject" of writing (in the traditional understanding of this concept). But rather than pass judgment on such people (as they see traditional intellectuals do), Kiseleva's post-Soviet publishers shift categories:

> this person is not the historical depravity, not the monster whom he seems to be at times to the producer of norms. But he does not act in history as an autonomous subject, and it is precisely this trait of his that politicians and intellectuals so dislike. [...] Signs of active subjects, of "masters" of history, who would desire and be able to assume responsibility for the present, the past, and the future, cannot be found in these writers. [...] Naive writing corroborates and illustrates the view held by adherents of postmodern methodologies on the death of the subject, the disappearance of the author, the existence of subjectless forms of culture (54).

In a word, informed by postmodern methodologies, these post-Soviet intellectuals—rather than lamenting that a common person, even when she writes her life story, seems devoid of free will, self-reflection, and historical consciousness—embrace the "naive writer" in all her otherness: as a "person without subjecthood."

The neologism "person without subjecthood" (*bessub'ektnyi chelovek*) has been eagerly accepted by readers. One sociologist has not only taken delight in the new postmodern category but has also welcomed this phrase as a new name for that proverbial "small person" (*malen'kii chelovek*), known from the venerable nineteenth-century literary tradition. He considers it no accident that the idea of "people without subjecthood" has been advanced not by a Western but by a Russian scholar (N. N. Kozlova). The move to treat authors such as Kiseleva as people without subjecthood (this sociologist claims) continues the "democratic tradition in Russian literature and public discourse, which finds its beginnings in Pushkin, Gogol, Dostoevsky."[78]

In this section, I have tried to interpret the historical meaning of the publishing project that brought to light the life story of a semiurbanized Soviet pensioner. I claim it as an attempt to redefine the age-old relationship of the "intelligentsia" and the "people." Unlike their nineteenth-century and Soviet predecessors, post-Soviet intellectuals (claiming a new role as interpreter rather than legislator) do not pursue the goal of bringing education or "consciousness" to the people. They do not acknowledge Kiseleva's attempts to historicize her life, and they deny her narrative competence. They cannot bring themselves to grant her wish: to give her three names to the story of her life. They regret her attempts to "play" on their field (Writing, Literature, Society), wanting her to remain as "Life itself." They reject Kiseleva's explicit desire to have her grammar "corrected" and her story "formed" by a professional editor. In the end, they deny this peasant author's desire for a rapprochement with the intellectuals, offering instead another view of a "simple person"—the celebration of the "naive"—presented within an elaborate framework of interpretive social science. This, second, story shows one way in which the Russian intelligentsia is trying to make itself relevant in post-Soviet times.

Concluding Remarks

I have chosen to read, side-by-side, two texts, one written by a member of the intelligentsia; the other, by a barely literate former peasant. Both of these texts have now become part of a single extended corpus: personal accounts of the Soviet experience. The similarities between these two documents are striking, in spite of the differences. First and foremost, both writers are inspired by an irresistible desire to project their own lives into an infinite public space, in which the reader (who is addressed by the peasant author with no less urgency than by the author-intellectual) will learn, understand, and remember. Both authors write as victims and survivors, reporting, from within the domestic sphere, on endangered lives. These texts also display remarkable similarities in form, fitted to fulfill their shared goal of the historical preservation of intimate lives. Thus, both texts possess a certain enthnographic quality. Both mix the temporal perspectives of the diary ("here and now") and the memoir (retrospection)—providing for both authenticity and retrospective insight. Both authors directly represent speech, and both texts include elements of forms from the performing arts (theater in Chukovskaia's diary; film in Kiseleva's notebooks). In these ways, they bring themselves and their homes to life with particular clarity. Both have needed mediators to reach the reader, and both have relied on complex framing at the time of publication—for this reason, both, in the end, are products of intelligentsia culture. (The story of how Kiseleva's text reached the reader shows this clearly.)

I have chosen these two texts, among many others in a large corpus, for their outstanding quality and their impact. It has so happened that both texts are produced by women—which may be taken as a confirmation of the well-known thesis that women play a leading role as conservators of culture and memory, especially when the sphere of intimacy is involved. Yet, it should be noted that other texts in this larger corpus (including those written by male authors) also exhibit many of the same qualities.

There are also obvious differences. In some ways, these women seem to have lived in two different countries: for Kiseleva, the terror under Stalin—an overarching frame in the life stories of Akhmatova and Chukovskaia—played no role whatsoever. So, as Chukovskaia suspected, in the atomized Soviet society, people from different social groups knew and remembered different things. To use her metaphor, the two "cellars of memory"—Chukovskaia's and Kiseleva's—do not belong to the same house.

Or do they? After all, the war plays the same role in Kiseleva's life that the terror played in the lives of Akhmatova and Chukovskaia. With shortsightedness that equals that of Kiseleva, who did not notice the terror, Akhmatova and Chukovskaia took the Second World War to be an extension of Stalinism. Both texts describe intimate practices, lives, and families that were shaped, and deformed, by enormous political-historical pressures, and both focus on showing how domestic spaces were invaded by the Soviet state and by catastrophic twentieth-century history. Both create a sense of continuity through emotion (fear). There is historical continuity (between the 1930s and 1940s, and the 1960s through the 1980s), rooted in the persistence of Soviet power, and personal continuity (across one's life span), rooted in the emotional reaction to trauma and in memory.

I see the most striking similarity and a definitive, distinctly Soviet influence in the way both storytellers relate to the historical-political domain and, in the end, to the Soviet state as a stand-in for history. Indeed, Akhmatova and Chukovskaia, on the one hand, and Kiseleva, on the other, come to a specific vision of their respective lives and selves—the vision that enabled them to write—via an overwhelming sense of the historical significance of their lives. As I keep insisting, this was a historicism rooted in the tradition of the nineteenth-century Russian intelligentsia and reinforced in the ideologically infused Marxist atmosphere of the Soviet regime. True, there is enormous difference between the women's relations to Soviet power. We see Kiseleva thank Brezhnev and Gorbachev for the leadership that not only frees her, a pensioner, from dependence in old age on her disintegrating family but also assures the salvation of her kin, her country, and the world in the face of a future nuclear war. Kiseleva's heartfelt participation in Soviet power, if only in the form of addressing the television screen from the privacy of her room and from the page of her notebook, seems to be the polar opposite of the dissident rejection of the Soviet state encountered in Chukovskaia's notes about Akhmatova. And yet the mechanism that enabled Kiseleva to speak is similar to the entitled-poet-and-her-editor posture that enabled Akhmatova and Chukovskaia in their prominent public roles. In each case, a framework for the self is provided by the political culture that conceives of itself historically and eschatologically. And in each case, the author clings to the political framework because it assures the anguished subject's voice its honored, signifying place in history (if not a room in a communal apartment or other place to live).[79]

PART III

DREAMS OF TERROR
Interpretations

In the 1966 foreword to the first publication of her *Notes about Anna Akhmatova,* Chukovskaia makes a stunning comment. She speaks of the diary of her own life ("my diary"), which she had attempted, but ultimately failed, to keep in the years of the terror (writing instead a diary for Akhmatova):

> My entries on the terror, incidentally, were notable in that the only things which were fully reproduced were dreams. Reality was beyond my powers of description; moreover, I did not even attempt to describe it in my diary. It could not have been captured in a diary, and anyway could one even conceive of keeping a real diary in those days?[1]

According to her daughter, Chukovskaia's own diaries (with the dream records) have not survived. Recall how Akhmatova, in her turn, regretted that they had not recorded dreams in these years ("That would have made for the richest historical material."). In 1944 the literary scholar Boris Eikhenbaum wrote that "history entered a person's life (*byt*), his consciousness, penetrated his very heart, and even began to fill his dreams."[2] Remarkably, many of the diaries, as well as memoirs, about the Soviet experience contain dreams, the majority of reported dreams have political content, and most of them deal with the terror. In this final part of the book, I will discuss these dreams.

COMMENTS ON DREAMS AS STORIES AND AS SOURCES

Long viewed as legible historical data, dreams have been of particular interest to historians of terror regimes.[3] In *A History of Private Life,* Alain Corbin writes of a dramatic change in the content of reported dreams after the French

Revolution, when political themes invaded dreams (even erotic dreams were politicized).[4] Dreams of terror recounted by the subjects of Hitler's Third Reich inspired the historian Reinhart Koselleck to claim dreams as sources that "testify to a past reality in a manner which perhaps could not be surpassed by any source."[5] The same may be true about dreams from the Stalinist terror.

First, a few words about the theories of dreams that inform my interpretations. Freud, of course, has left an indelible imprint on our understanding of dreams. While many of his dictums have been abandoned, his insistence that dreams occupy an exceptional place in psychological and cultural analysis as well as his hermeneutic approach to dreaming, viewed as a symbolic language of the individual psyche, have prevailed to this day.[6] Today, psychoanalysts and psychologists deal with dreams, in their manifest content, as articulations of mostly unconscious knowledge about the dreamer's situation. Some have viewed dreams as "human subjectivity in purest culture" and as a royal road to the "organizing principles and dominant leitmotifs that unconsciously pattern and thematize a person's psychological life."[7] For my purposes—for the historical hermeneutics of dreams—I have adopted the general notion that dreams, regardless of their psychogenesis and psychological functions, provide explanatory metaphors commenting on a person's existential situation and emotional concerns.[8] The key word is "metaphor." It has been suggested, by psychoanalysts, philosophers, and cognitive psychologists alike, that dreaming may be a paradigm or even a source for such operations as the use of images to symbolize thoughts, feelings, and situations; the transformation of one image into an expression for another; the creation of sequential narrative by fusing concordance and discordance; and for probing the reality of our lives (for the idea that "life is like a dream").[9] In a word, dreaming is an analogy of fiction, or literature. As one scholar put it, dreaming is the "ur-form of all fiction." Yet (he continues) "a dream is fundamentally unlike a fiction, structurally and affectively, in that it is a lived experience as well as a narrative."[10]

For my purposes, the status of dreams as experience and as knowledge is especially important.[11] As Freud notes, a product of our own psychic activity, the "finished dream strikes us as something alien to us."[12] Jürgen Habermas (discussing Freud's dream hermeneutics) emphasizes the unique epistemological status of dreams as "texts that confront the author himself as alienated and incomprehensible": after waking, the dreamer, who in some ways is still the author of the dream, does not understand his creation.[13] Thus, dreaming may be an experience of confronting one's hidden depth: what one knows, feels, or fears without being fully aware, and what defies control. Dreaming includes the splitting of the subject and the ambivalence of knowledge and feeling. There is a disjunction and an encounter between the nonknowing and the knowing self, amplified when the dream is recounted.

Some scholars have asked: Who is the "I" of dreams?[14] It has been suggested that the subject of the dream might not be the personage who says "I" but the whole dream in the entirety of its content.[15] In this sense, too, dreaming is like fiction: we read the dream as a story, identifying not with the hero, but more with the story itself.[16] Jung called dreams "a theater in which the dreamer is the scene, the player, the prompter, the producer, the author, the public, and the critic," adding that such an interpretation "conceives all the figures in the dream as personified features of the dreamer's own personality."[17]

There is another view—the age-long belief in the prophetic nature of dreams, which is relevant for many dreamers to this day.[18] Viewed in this perspective, dreams, whether they come from within or from without, do not reveal, but predict. A modern person (who does not believe in prophetic visitations) takes a dream for a presentiment, if not prophecy, by way of the belief that the dream, while evoking things past and pinpointing present tensions, refers to a potential action of self or other, and thus to a possible reality of what could happen. As some psychologists believe, dreams try out the possibilities of self, other, and the world, thus playing a crucial part in imagining and creating the future.[19] (Fiction, as we know since Aristotle, does this as well, and in this way, too, dreams are like fictions.)

Whether dreams are viewed as products of the self (as in psychology) or as visitations from outside the self (as in prophecy), the knowledge they communicate is seen as genuine and authentic, but from Artemidorus to Freud and beyond, the meaning of the dream is a product of interpretation. This, of course, has been well known. Yet the dreamer seldom believes in the possibility of a satisfactory interpretation. Indeed, in accounts of dreams—including the accounts that I have surveyed for this book—we almost invariably find a note of surprise and bewilderment: Is this really me? Where do my dreams come from? What do they mean? Relating a dream in the diary, the writer stumbles in his or her self-knowledge and self-revelation. Many a writer in my Soviet corpus ran into such difficulties. The dream (I think) marks the gap: the disjunction between knowledge (or feeling) and unawareness; the actual self and potential self; and between the past, the present, and the future. In the end, there is a unique relationship to self that resides in watching oneself dream and in telling one's dreams: the ultimate intimacy and the lack of transparency, the disjunction between "my text" and "my meaning-intention."[20]

I would argue that, for these and other reasons, dreams, as stories and as experiences, are capable of expressing the aporias of living faced by those who lived under terror. Indeed, since repressive regimes mobilize our ability for self-alienation, self-deception, and ambivalence, dreams can be taken as a structural analogy of self-knowledge under terror. Freud famously used the metaphor "censorship," and the example of Russian censorship, to describe "the violence done to the meaning" in dreams.[21] (From Freud's letter to Wilhelm Fliess about dream messages: "Have you ever seen a foreign newspaper which has passed the Russian censorship at the frontier? Words, whole clauses and sentences are blacked out so that what is left becomes unintelligible.")[22] What is more, because the dream (as psychologists note) is a medium of fear, it can be used as a model of feeling in the subjects of terror regimes. (Suffice it to recall that the clinical characteristics of nightmares include the perception of danger, the threat of violence, and the feeling of helplessness.)[23]

Thus it is not an accident that in his methodological statement on the value of dreams for history (the strongest we have), Koselleck draws examples from dreams collected in Hitler's Germany. His argument is twofold: as "stories" told in the context of National Socialism, dreams tell us about the regime (or about people's experience of the regime). At the same time, in their effect on the dreamer, these dreams are themselves "modes of performance of the terror."[24] In speaking of dreams as "stories," Koselleck insists that dreams, when written down, can be counted as fictional texts, even something akin to literature. Indeed, it is precisely their "poetic quality" (Koselleck argues) that allows us to obtain from dreams messages of the type "that cannot be captured through factual reports" or (I would add) through realistic representations.[25] In the end, Koselleck goes so far as to suggest that dreams may lead historians into the "recesses of the apparently private realm of the everyday," penetrated by waves of terror, disclosing "levels that are not touched even by diary entries."[26] What is more, in bringing dreams to the domain of history, Koselleck—a dedicated student of the experience of historical time—followed both an impulse to methodological innovation and a moral imperative: the historian's duty to account for "the daily and nightly world of acting and suffering mankind."[27]

The material that inspired such methodology and such sentiment came from Charlotte Beradt's *Das Dritte Reich des Traumes* (*The Third Reich of Dreams*).[28] Between 1933 and 1939, Beradt, a Communist (and a Jew) who gathered information on the Nazi regime for German émigré publications, asked people she met to share their dreams. (Of several hundred recorded dreams, she would later publish about fifty.) In 1939 she emigrated to the United States. In 1966 she submitted her old collection of dreams to the Nymphenburger Verlag in Munich, which published it on Hannah Arendt's recommendation. (A friend of Arendt's, Beradt translated *The Human Condition* into German.) At that time, Beradt, who no longer believed in communism, was motivated by a desire to demonstrate the impact of totalitarianism on the human psyche.[29]

In her book, Beradt reported the dreams recorded in the 1930s from oral stories, limiting information about the dreamers to a minimum (such as profession and age.) The collection includes dreams in which one's own thoughts and limbs (such as an arm rising in the Nazi salute) became estranged; dreams about the imperative of secrecy and silence; anxiety dreams about the all-pervasive presence of surveillance; and dreams articulating the desire to conform. Strangely enough, Beradt deliberately excluded dreams of horror and violence, believing fear to be universal. She recorded dreams about real and imaginary technological innovations of the new state: loudspeakers, radio, telephone, and an electric thought-control machine. Hitler made frequent appearances in his subjects' dreams. It becomes clear that "a great number of people were plagued by very similar dreams during the Third Reich" (12). Beradt's collection highlights the dreams that seem prophetic in retrospect because they anticipate actions of the regime (deportation of the Jews and murder in concentration camps) before they actually happened. What such dreams revealed to her was their authors' subconscious attempts to both express the inexpressible and anticipate the unimaginable. Thus, with their surreal quality, dreams provided an expression, a metaphor, for all that is illusory or unreal in the totalitarian reality (79). What is more, Beradt sees a moral lesson in "all these fables that were dreamt during the Third Reich" (147). She argues that these dreams show how subjects of totalitarian rule were produced: by dreaming that they were under constant surveillance and danger, people "began to terrorize themselves, turning themselves unawares into voluntary participants in this systematic terrorization" (48). Anticipating in their dreams what could happen, Hitler's subjects, not only confronted in dreams the fact that, at least subconsciously, they recognized the principles and the final goals of the regime, but also prepared themselves to face, and to accept, the horrors yet to come (137). In this way, implies Beradt, dreams worked not only as stories about terror but also as a mode of the performance of terror, or even as instruments of terror.

The dreams of the Soviet terror that I was able to collect from diaries and memoirs (about fifty dream stories) are both similar to and different from the dreams of the Third Reich in Beradts's collection. My approach is also both similar to and different from that of my distinguished predecessors. Thus, I treat dreams as stories about historical experience, but such stories that are inextricable from the personal accounts in which they are embedded. Tempting as it may be, I do not join Koselleck in claiming that dream stories lead historians into the deepest recesses of the private realm, which even diary entries cannot access. Rather, I try to show how, by including dreams in their narratives (which frequently involves efforts to interpret or comment on their dreams), diarists, as well as memoirists, create encounters between the intended and unintended (dreamed) meaning. In this way, the authors of these personal narratives reveal the complicated ways in which they relate to the self, to the world of terror that they inhabited, to the disjunction between past, present, and future, and to the very task of representing the terror, which, as Chukovskaia put it, seemed beyond the powers of description, at least in a regular diary.

ANDREI ARZHILOVSKY: THE PEASANT RAPED BY STALIN

Andrei Stepanovich Arzhilovsky (1885–1937), a peasant in the Tiumen Province in the Urals (educated only in a primary school in his village), found it conceivable, even essential, to keep detailed records of his daily life in the years of the terror.[30] Throughout his life he was a social activist (and he dreamed of becoming a writer): during the civil war, under the White government of Kolchak, he became a member of the civil committee of inquiry; when the Reds came in 1919, he was arrested by the Cheka and sentenced to prison for these activities. Released in 1923, he joined the inspection commission of a rural soviet and edited a wall newspaper. In 1929, he was arrested again and sentenced on charges of agitating against collectivization. In the camp, Arzhilovsky contributed satirical writings to a small-print paper published, like other such camp newspapers (most famously, at the Belomor Canal), for the purposes of "reforging" (reforming) the prisoners. Released in 1936, he worked at the Tiumen woodworking factory Red October. Against his better judgment, he wrote social satire for the factory wall newspaper and sent critical essays to the printed press. He also kept a diary. In his diary, Arzhilovsky expressed his distaste for the coercion, poverty, hypocrisy, and injustice of the Soviet regime. Carefully recorded dreams (about twenty in nine months) form a noticeable part of the diary. When, in July 1937, Arzhilovsky was arrested again, the diary was used as evidence of his counterrevolutionary views. Some passages—including dreams—were underlined in red by the NKVD investigator. The last page contains a note in Arzhilovsky's hand: "This diary was confiscated during a search in my home. It contains forty (40) sheets." Signed: "Arzhilovsky." Dated: "29 August 1937." Seven days later, Andrei Arzhilovsky was executed. In the early 1990s, an employee of the NKVD's successor organization, the KGB, gave the diary to a local writer, who published it in the literary journal *Ural*.[31] What follows is one of the dreams Arzhilovsky recorded soon after his release:

> 18 December [1936] You may call it nonsense, but still, dreams too are a fact. I want to write down an interesting dream I had. Someone

told me I could see Stalin. A historical figure, it would be interesting to get to see him. And so... A small room, simple and ordinary. Stalin is drunk as a skunk, as they say. There are only men in the room, and just two of us peasants, me and one other guy with a black beard. Without a word, [Iosif] Vissarionovich knocks the guy with the black beard down, covers him with a sheet and rapes him brutally. "I am next," I think in despair, recalling how they carry on in Tiflis, and I am thinking, how can I escape, but after his session Stalin seems to come to his senses somewhat, and he starts up a conversation. "Why were you so eager to see me personally?" "Well, why wouldn't I be? Portraits are just portraits, but a living man, and a great one at that, is something else altogether," said I. Overall, things worked out fairly well for me, they even treated me to some food. [...] I've had two dreams about Stalin: once before my release and now this time. [...] I suppose there is some reason for my Stalin dream. [...] In any case, I didn't make it up, I'm recording facts, though these are delirious facts [*fiksiruiu fakty, khotia i bredovye*].[32]

Like the historian Koselleck, the peasant Arzhilovsky insists that dreams, their delirious quality notwithstanding, are "facts"—historical facts. His nightmare has the distinct markings of a historical experience. Both the "I" of the dream narrative (who sets out to see a "historical figure") and the diarist who records the dream take it as such. The setting of the dream comes from the stock imagery of the Stalin cult, in which a meeting between the great leader and a simple Soviet man or woman played a prominent role. The powerful image of the rape (probably prompted by the popular belief in Georgians' proclivity for sodomy) is a private symbol, which hardly requires interpretation. (Arzhilovsky does not comment on it.) What intrigues him most is the general reason behind his visions, and in committing the dream to paper, Arzhilovsky follows a strong and conscious historical impulse.* (The last words of his account state: "I am recording facts.") I would claim that this dream allowed the peasant Arzhilovsky to see himself as an actor in a historical drama, operating on the same stage as the ruler, Stalin. Moreover, with the cooperation of the Soviet secret service, which preserved this diary in its archives, Arzhilovsky's dreams have actually become historical evidence. (Curiously, the

---

* Arzhilovsky seems to share in the intelligentsia-style historical consciousness. Thus, in the same diary entry he calls Stalin "a comet"—a widely known emblem of Napoleon, as a quintessential figure associated with history's effect on the average man. The idea is not as far-fetched as it might seem: in his diary Arzhilovsky mentioned Napoleon and quoted Pushkin. For Napoleon's name, see *Ural*, 141; *Intimacy and Terror*, 115; for Pushkin, *Ural*, 144; *Intimacy and Terror* 122. He also comments on the arrests as "a replay of the French Revolution" (*Ural*, 160; *Intimacy and Terror*, 162).

NKVD official who inspected Arzhilovsky's diary in search of incriminating evidence did not mark this particular dream.)

Another dream draws on the conditions of the daily life Arzhilovsky shared with his wife Liza and their five children. (Genya, who figures in the diary entry, is one of them.) To give a glimpse of their life, I quote the diary entry that culminates in a dream in full:

> 28 January [1937]. I wake up at 4. Liza leaves for the dairy by five; I light the stove. I took a sledge out to get water. I made it to the gate without incident, but at the gate the high-perched sledge capsized and the tub tipped over the side. It's a good thing I was carrying an extra bucket of water in my hand; at least I had something to show for my labor. Genya went out to get in line for bread; there is some hold up with the bread supply again: huge lines, pushing and shoving. They sell the expensive varieties of bread, which is not good for the proletariat. My side is healing, it's practically back to normal; but now there is something else: I bought myself some hard felt boots that are a little tight and chafed my toe, and now it's bothering me. "When it rains, it pours." But I wanted to write down a strange dream I had last night. I just dozed off when I dreamt I was on some new construction site [*novostroika*]. For some reason I am stoking a stove and I'm all worried: what if the buildings catch fire? Suddenly I hear the sound of an airplane. An enormous, low flying ship appears; it's loaded with huge bundles of dry firewood which, I assume, will burst into flames at any moment. I think "The moment the airplane comes even with the buildings, fire will break out and everything will burn down, including the plane." But the airplane didn't crash: I woke up just as it was flying over my head, with its tail just missing the roofs. What a strange dream! I forgot some of the second one, but in general it was about some newspaper article whose last three lines detailed an insult suffered by a Russian citizen. I even heard the phrase: "You there, here you go, and now wipe up the spit! [*Vot i vytris'*]" Dream thoughts [*sonnye mysli*], arising in a man's head against his will.[33]

The diary entry relates the grisly circumstances of one day in Arzhilovsky's wretched life, starting with stoking the wood stove at five o'clock in the morning. The dream narrative also starts with the image of stoking the stove, though not in the family's cramped shack but at a construction site—a standard emblem of nascent new life, prevalent in the Soviet iconography of the day. The dream arranges icons of the new life into a plot propelled by anxiety: the giant airplane (another symbol of Soviet progress) brings "bundles of dry firewood," not for the stove in an individual home, but for the one Arzhilovsky must stoke for the socialist construction. (Arzhilovsky uses the distinctly Soviet term *novostroika.*) This creates the danger of general destruction. A catastrophe is avoided when the dreamer briefly wakes up, to be followed in the next dream by another vignette of Soviet life—a newspaper campaign directed against an individual. Such an episode once happened in the dreamer's real life: Arzhilovsky was attacked in the prison camp newspaper for which he worked as a correspondent.

This is how he told the story: "that same camp newspaper that had printed my comments [...] turned against me. [...] The newspaper campaign against me dealt a serious blow to my morale; the only conclusion I could come to was: we are cursed to the end of our days and no matter how you try to 're-forge' [*perekovat'sia*], no one will believe you, and at the first opportunity they'll peck at you and spit at you."[34] (Both this story and the record of the dream contain the word "spit.") Recalling these events elsewhere in his diary, he commented: "It is so natural: they sense the truth and can't forgive us our protest against violence."[35] In this context, it appears that Arzhilovsky's "dream thoughts" entertain the idea of reconciliation with society and reject it as fraught with danger and humiliation.

At least one other dream has a similar structure. Once again, Arzhilovsky dreams of vehicles symbolizing the new Soviet life, which has "harnessed technology" (*osedlavshaia tekhniku*).[36] His dream symbols are borrowed from the common stock:

> I dreamed that I was flying through the air with some stranger on an airsledge and I asked, "Are cars even faster than this?" "Yes, just a little," answered my companion. Let's hope Toiba won't roll me off the factory roll; she can't stand the sight of me. I read the prosecutor's indictment in the case of the Trotsky center.[37]

The dream juxtaposes the image of folk magic (a flying sledge that appears in Russian fairy tales) with the technological wonders emblematic of the Soviet vision of progress. (So does the Soviet iconography of the time: a similar dream is dreamed by a socially mobile peasant heroine in the popular film *Svetlyi put'* [The bright path, 1940], who glides over Moscow in a flying automobile after a visit to the Kremlin.) Arzhilovsky's dream seems to propel the protagonist, who is markedly unused to this environment, toward a new life. Note that in the next line (after the dream report comes to an end) Arzhilovsky wonders whether he would be "rolled off the factory roll" (the imagery of sliding, if not flying, still on his mind) by his hostile boss, Toiba, "the little Jew" (as he called her).[38] The narrative then turns to a newspaper report of a current terror campaign.

With these dreams, it is as if Arzhilovsky watches a film (a fiction) that has taken over his life, both propelling him toward the bright future promised by the regime of technological progress and social advancement and threatening him with destruction. The dream of meeting Stalin, and the airplane and airsledge dreams, play out scenarios of participation in Soviet life, which remain out of his reach. Placing the subject in key locations of the new Soviet world, these dreams send him a signal of danger. For the reader of Arzhilovsky's diary, these dreams, infused with the emotions of temptation and terror, and marked by Soviet symbols, emblematize the diarist's uneasy position in relation to the regime: the overwhelming desire for social participation and historical agency, the distaste for the Soviet government notwithstanding, combined with the awareness of his alienation from the regime and with the fear of destruction.

One dream that the investigator underlined in red as criminal evidence told the following: "19 April [1937] I had a dream about traveling; I can see mountains and a river. *On the right is a beautiful church. Could it be a prison? I am afraid of it.*"[39] In Russian folk wisdom, to dream of a church indicates a threat of a prison sentence. To be fair, the investigator had reasons apart from a shared belief in the prophetic value of dreams: Arzhilovsky acted on his dream. Thus, the next entry reads: "1 May. These dreams were starting to frighten me so much that *I hid all my literature* and held out till 1 May. Apparently this was nothing special; they were just ordinary nighttime fantasies after all."[40] Alas, Arzhilovsky would be proven to be wrong in thinking this was nothing: when he was arrested again, this dream was used as criminal evidence against him. To us, distant readers, this episode exemplifies a curious overlapping of seemingly incompatible principles: the inexplicable logic of dreams and the two different modes of interpretation (both governed by the "hermeneutics of suspicion"). On the one hand, there is folk wisdom that, reading dream images for their displaced meaning (church = prison), attributes predictive power to dreams; on the other, the Stalinist criminal system that judged suspects based on their dreams. The story is full of tragic irony: the overlapping of different "epistemologies" contributed to a situation in which dreams came true.

A dreamer from a different class of society, the scholar of myth and folklore Eliazar Moiseevich Meletinskii (1918–2005), reported a similar experience in his memoirs. In 1949, six years after his first incarceration, he was haunted by dreams of prison: "In the daytime, I was occupied with usual pursuits and was enthusiastically engaged in my research, but at night I dreamed traumatic dreams, saw myself in prison. Although I am not in the least bit superstitious, in such a state of extreme nervousness it was unpleasant to dream of a church one night, which, according to folk beliefs, predicts prison."[41] Indeed, Meletinskii was soon arrested again. (I have told the story of his arrest in Part I of this book.)

Many years later, another man recorded the following dream: "I dreamed: the terrifying Stalin ordered me to start a fire in my room. I set it up. It started to burn brightly, but I threw in some damp wood, and it went out—and now Stalin will order me to be executed."[42] This record was made on January 4, 1971, by the Jewish artist Mikhail Grobman, a member of the underground avant-garde. He, too, lived with wife and children in a drafty shack (near Moscow); and he, too, complained in his diary about the daily chore of stoking the wood stove. Unlike Arzhilovsky, Grobman (born in 1939) had not been a victim of Stalin-led terror. Socially, the two men were worlds apart; yet they shared nightmares. Moreover, while they shared some icons of anxiety (such as the fire) with most people, other images were unique to their common historical position: Stalin invaded their dreams, menacing, threatening, terrorizing them. There is something else: the politicization of fear and hardship, personalized in the image of the ruler. Stalin was dreamed to be responsible not only for the misfortunes Arzhilovsky experienced in 1937 but also for the daily misery and anxiety Grobman experienced in 1971.

NIKOLAI BUKHARIN DREAMS OF STALIN: ABRAHAM AND ISAAC

Let us return to the year 1937. There is a rare case in which we know what a prisoner dreamed in his cell. In his prison cell, awaiting trial (which would condemn him to execution), Nikolai Ivanovich Bukharin (1888–1938) had dreams or hallucinatory visions of Stalin, on whose orders he was arrested. Unlike Arzhilovsky, he knew Joseph [Iosif] Stalin, and knew him intimately. This source is different from others: Bukharin related his dreams in a letter he wrote to Stalin (preserved in the NKVD archives, the letter has recently appeared in print):

> When I was hallucinating, I saw you several times and Nadezhda Sergeevna [Stalin's wife] once. She came up to me and said, "What have they done to you, N. I.? I'll tell Iosif [Stalin] to bail you out on his responsibility." It was so real that I almost leaped up and started writing you a letter, so that [...] you would bail me out! That is how in my mind reality interlaced with delirium. I know that N. S. would have never believed that I plotted against you, so it is no accident that the subconscious of my poor "I" conjured up these delirious dreams. I talk to you for hours. [...] God, if only there existed a device that would allow you to see my entire shredded and tortured soul! If only you could see how intimately attached I am to you. [...] Well, that is "psychology"—sorry. There is no longer an angel that would ward off Abraham's sword, so ominous fates will have to be realized![43]

In the absence of the "instrument" that could reveal his soul, ripped open by torture, relating a dream—which the well-educated Bukharin, taking a cue from Freud, took to be a product of his "subconscious"—served a similar purpose. In a language that mixed psychoanalysis with Christian symbolism, Bukharin offered his dream to Stalin as irrefutable evidence of his innocence, that is, of his love for Stalin.

Why did Bukharin summon Stalin's wife as a dream witness of his innocence? The motivation may lie in his recent experience. After her suicide in 1932, Stalin asked the Bukharins to exchange apartments with him, as if he were haunted by her ghost. In 1937, Bukharin spent the tortured months preceding his imminent arrest mostly in Stalin's former bedroom, in which Nadezhda Sergeevna Alliluyeva had shot herself after quarreling with her overbearing husband.[44]

As Bukharin knew, Stalin was not likely to accept either spectral or psychological evidence. In the same letter, the Bolshevik party's leading theoretician spoke of his impending death in terms of Hegelian historicism—and in immediate relation to Stalin: "It would be petty to consider my own persona *along with the world historical tasks,* set primarily on your shoulders."[45]

In the meantime, Bukharin's wife, Anna Mikhailovna Larina (1914–1996), who was arrested as the wife of an "enemy of the people," was plagued by recurrent dreams, or hallucinations (she survived to tell her story in a memoir): "In an upper corner of my cell, just beneath the ceiling, I would see a tortured Bukharin crucified on the cross, as on Golgotha. A black crow pecked at the martyr's bloody, lifeless body."[46] Believing that "history will acquit Bukharin," she, too, was sustained by a sense of religious and historical significance of their lives.[47]

Like Arzhilovsky's dream of Stalin, Bukharin's dream, and that of his wife, show one of the marked features of the Soviet terror: the historical and mythic quality in the subjective experience of suffering. This acute sense of the universal (historical, religious, or mythic) significance of their lives and deaths was shared by those who, like Bukharin, lived in the immediate proximity to power and by ordinary people who, like Arzhilovsky, lived far from the Moscow Kremlin. People from both groups personalized their historicism in the image of intimacy with Stalin, internalized in the deepest recesses of their subjectivity—in their dreams, as represented in their intimate writings.

WRITERS' DREAMS: MIKHAIL PRISHVIN

We have learned that quite a few successful Soviet writers used diaries to document the shadowy life that—as they wanted to believe—went on alongside their public roles and their published works. Several such writers documented their dreams in the hope that they would provide evidence of the survival of their deepest, purest selves. In such narratives, dreams serve as pillars in the construction of the self. Georg Misch, in his classic study of autobiography, speaks of oneiric autobiography—a genre in which dreams (visions or simply dreams) represent the key events in the narrative of development of the self.[48] Several diaries and memoirs of Soviet writers might qualify as oneiric autobiographies.

The lifelong, voluminous diaries of Mikhail Mikhailovich Prishvin (1873–1954)—a prominent nature writer—document his highly ambiguous, rapidly changing, and carefully hidden relations with Soviet power. It might not be possible to unravel all the mingled instances of aloofness and complicity, awareness and self-deception, experienced by Prishvin in the course of his long and distinguished career. Focusing on dreams recorded in the 1930s, I will magnify several moments and themes of Prishvin's remarkable diaries.

As did many of his contemporaries, Prishvin saw the diary as history writing, and he relentlessly pursued the historical quality of life, whether or not it revealed itself: "You have to write a diary in such a way that the personal is portrayed against the background of a great historical event—that is what makes memoirs interesting. Historical events are always occurring—if they are not visible, you have to find the invisible ones."[49] With this imperative in mind, Prishvin was able to find history in the deepest recesses of his intimate life, including his dreams. Dreams usually appear in the diary at pivotal moments in his relations with power.

Prishvin's diary for the year 1930 is suffused with pain and horror at the peasants' suffering caused by forced collectivization. He writes of the "evil," the "terrible crimes," "the horror of this winter, rivers of blood and tears" inflicted in the name of the state and Stalin and performed in the service of politics.[50] He feels threatened by the intensifying campaign against members of the old literary intelligentsia led by the militant RAPP (Russian Association of Proletarian Writers). The horror of "Bolshevik socialism" (Prishvin wrote in his diary) is that there is no longer an "intimate world" or "personal life" into which a person could escape after fulfilling his duty to society; the "new worker" is entirely visible, "as if under X-ray."[51]

Attacked by RAPP critics, he was accused of fleeing the reality of class struggle into a fairy-tale world of his own creation. There were practical consequences: Prishvin felt that he was losing access to publishing. He spent most of the summer and fall in the country in the isolated nature preserve he called (after his own novel) "Cranes' Homeland" (Zhuravlinaia rodina), trying, in vain, to find relief from a "painful feeling, akin to the pull of persecution."[52] Soon after Prishvin returned from his country retreat, he recorded the following dream:

> 18 October [1930]. Yesterday in *Novyi mir* [the journal *The New World*] they announced the list of authors whose work was published over the last year, and the fact that they forgot to mention my name, or left it out on purpose—an utmost trifle!—upset me. Before I went to sleep, I read Novikov-Priboi's amazing, horrifying story "Tsushima," and, afterward, a killer chased me throughout the night in a dreadful dream. And throughout the night I kept a revolver in my pocket, ready to fire, constantly fearing that it would fire by itself in my pocket.

Prishvin offers an immediate explication. The etiology of the dream seems clear to him: magnified by the literary images of the defeat in the Russo-Japanese War, the dream manifests a well-justified persecution mania. He relates his experience to that of a whole class, the "intelligentsia." "Fearing" is a socially induced disease, which Prishvin explains in clinical terms:

> Both this disturbed state and this dream are the individual manifestations of the persecution mania currently prevalent among the intelligentsia. I have reached the point of being afraid to open up a new issue of a journal: it constantly seems to me that I will be offended or upset by something. [Manifestations of] an acute form of the common disease of fearing.
>
> Of course, there is only one solution to this—to devote myself decisively to work, for which I will need to create good working conditions.[53]

What Prishvin does not seem to notice is that the dream also expresses his awareness of the danger presented by self-defense (the fear that the revolver hidden in the pocket might fire). He is aware, however, that a cure from the epidemic persecution mania, which is to be found in writing, requires "good working conditions."

By 1934, Prishvin's situation had changed. His tormentor RAPP, together with all other literary associations, was dissolved in 1932 by a government decree and replaced by the centralized state-sponsored party-led organization, the Union of Soviet Writers. In 1933, Prishvin published, to wide acclaim, a major novel, *Jen sheng (Zhen'-shen')*.

In summer 1933 he traveled to the remote natural area in the Far North that had inspired him to write his first book—*The Land of Untamed Birds (Krai nepugannykh ptits*). It was now the site of a socialist construction project, the Belomor Canal (connecting the White and Baltic seas), much publicized in the Soviet press for its double purpose of (in the idiom of the day) "subjugating nature" and "reforging people" (the socially alien elements of the population).

I will make a brief digression to describe the notorious Belomor. Dedicated to Stalin, the project was completed, in record time in 1933–34 by convicts—common and political prisoners condemned to rehabilitation through hard labor in the extreme conditions of the Russian Far North under the administration of the GULAG. (Several of this book's protagonists were imprisoned at Belomor.) It was a concentration camp equipped with a printing press, which issued the camp newspaper called *Perekovka* (Reforging). Rooted in a New Testament metaphor, the well-known Soviet concept "reforging" captures the idea that stands behind such initiatives. In a word, convicts were expected to eagerly embrace the hard labor of building socialism, thus generating a process of self-transformation from the old bourgeois self into a "new man." (One scholar has commented that "reforging" was predicated on turning coercion into desire.)[54] Soviet writers were strongly encouraged to glorify the project in works of documentary prose, drama, and fiction.[55]

When Prishvin revisited the "land of untamed birds" (which he considered to be the "motherland" of Prishvin-the-writer) in the summer 1933, he had this goal in mind. A dedicated nature writer (an environmentalist *avant la lettre*), he did feel uneasy about the idea of changing, or "conquering," nature. But he was ready to accept the change in people. Traveling toward the canal through his beloved wild landscape, he tried to come to terms in his diary with this project:

> I place value on this cause of remaking geography for what it does to many homeless, desperate, joyless people, who become reborn in this creative process, and, having recreated the geography of this land, find a new motherland for themselves.[56]

He mused: "Motherland is a segment of my own labor for the common cause."[57] Clearly, he, too, wanted to participate. But while other writers celebrated the project in print, in 1934 Prishvin remained silent.[58]

In these years, Prishvin's strategy was to take refuge in private life. He lived in the small town of Zagorsk (Sergiev Posad) near Moscow, keeping a rural household with his wife, Efrosiniia Pavlovna Smogaleva (a peasant whom he taught to read and write). He frequently roamed the neighboring forests with a hunting rifle, lost for weeks in barely accessible areas that sheltered migrant birds (he called one of these spots, a long-time favorite, "Cranes' Homeland"). However, "fleeing from reality" (as his Communist critics put it) was not easy; for one thing, there were technical difficulties. Early in 1934, Prishvin confronted this problem in a dream:

> 20 February [1934]. I had not spent the last two summers at Cranes' Homeland because I found it difficult getting there from my place in Zagorsk, even though the distance is only forty miles! [...] That is how I ended up staying at home. Two years passed, and I started to miss the swamps, as if I really were a crane who went astray and lost his homeland. One night—in a dream, even—it occurred to me that an automobile would provide a solution in my situation. Forty miles in an automobile would only take about an hour—one hour—and I would reach Cranes' Homeland. This thought, as it sometimes happens in hunters' dreams, dissolved into a particularly acute and happy feeling of nature, where flying around me were not cranes and not ordinary titmice but some wondrous birds. In the morning, having initially retained in myself only the feeling of having a pleasant dream, little by little, shifting from one bird to another, as if going up a ladder, I recovered the idea of an automobile. It seemed possible to me: we do manufacture automobiles nowadays [*teper' ikh delaiut u nas*], and if I submit a request now [*zaiavliu*], they would add my name to the list [*menia zapishut v ochered'*], and, sooner or later, they would grant [*dadut*] me a car.[59]

In the dream, step-by-step, Prishvin climbs the ladder of compromise. The fairy-tale imagery of this dream, suggestive of a flying car, brings him—a nature writer at odds with the Soviet regime—to a doubly incongruous idea: to retreat to the wilderness by means of an automobile and to seek assistance in obtaining a car (a luxury item, distributed to the privileged) in the institutions of Soviet power. He expertly describes the necessary procedure in new Soviet terms: *delaiut u nas, zaiavliu, menia zapishut v ochered', dadut.*

Prishvin made his appeal at the ministry level (Sovnarkom), and the result exceeded all expectations:

> Three days later, I had already received a document from Sovnarkom with the order to make a vehicle available to me. In a few more days, having run around to all the publishers, I scraped together the necessary sum of money to pay for the automobile. [...] Along with receiving the letter from Sovnarkom, I—by nature far removed from machines—started to conceive of myself as a landsman or a craftsman who won a car in an automobile lottery. That could make a great plot for a story depicting the mentality of a peasant and of a new type of person for our country—the machine operator. I tried to approach this topic many times, and with this purpose went to visit large factories. But no! I could

not put myself in a situation that would enable me to embrace the machine not merely with my mind but with my entire being. [...] Now it was turning out that the automobile, like a magic force that could at any point transport me to the birds at Cranes' Homeland, was becoming a part of my artistic personality.[60]

It seems that this dream led to no less than a personality change. With remarkable insight, Prishvin observed that the moment his dream came true he experienced an empathic understanding of a position that had previously been deeply alien and emotionally incomprehensible to him: the situation of a man of the land turned into a man of the machine (a widely accepted emblem of the Soviet project). Soviet writers were called on to describe such transformations in works of literature; it was to this end that Prishvin (as was the practice of the day) toured new factories and construction sites. In his deliberate attempts to master this theme as a writer expected to work for the regime, Prishvin had failed. But a moment of personal participation in the new civilization, mediated by privilege, brought about a transformation: Prishvin wholeheartedly embraced the machine and, with it, the Soviet regime. (As in other cases, an automobile emerges as a symbol of mobility, progress, collaboration, and desire for acceptance.) As his dream came true—an automobile was ready to transport him into the sheltered homeland of migrant birds—Prishvin became conscious of a change in the self, and a change in his relations to the regime. (The idea that dreams can bring about or mark a vast change in the self has been suggested by self psychologists, and there are other remarkable examples of such dreams, including from Nazi Germany.)*

Like the peasant Arzhilovsky (who once dreamed of being on a flying sledge speeding faster than an automobile), the writer Prishvin used folk-tale imagery—something akin to the magic bird carriers of Russian fairy tales—to marvel at the magic quality of modern transportation. He also marveled at the miraculous internal transformation the Soviet regime had brought about in its unwilling subjects.

---

* See Heinz Kohut, *The Search for the Self: Selected Writings of Heinz Kohut,* ed. Paul H. Ornstein, 4 vols. (Madison, CT: International Universities Press, 1978–91), 3:138–39. Heinz Kohut discusses an example from the Hitler era. It concerns the Austrian peasant Franz Jägerstätter who, on the basis of his religious ideals, refused to serve in the German army. Describing how he came to this decision, Jägerstätter relates the dream he had in the summer of 1938 (after the Anschluss): He saw adults and children who streamed toward a beautiful railroad train that circled around a mountain; very few resisted being carried along. A voice told him: "This train is going to Hell." After the dream, step-by-step he came to the idea that death was preferable to surrender. (He was guillotined in 1943.) Mechal Sobel discussed Franz Jägerstätter's dream in her *Teach Me Dreams,* 10–11.

In the years of high terror, 1936–38, Prishvin made brief records of the public trials of the party officials accused of treason. His horror and scorn are unmistakable, but, judging from some of his comments, he may have believed that the "Trotskyites" and others in what he called "the Jewish trial" were guilty as charged (at least, that they were guilty of plotting against Stalin). On August 26, he pasted in his diary a newspaper cutting with the text of the verdict passed at the First Moscow Trial, complete with a one-line announcement of the same-day execution. He made no comment. Two days later, he recorded a nightmare:

> 28 August [1936]. I had a dream that I, along with some peasants, was riding in a cart that was carrying my mother's coffin, and just across from Khrushchev's estate [the home of the Prishvin family before the revolution] one of the cart wheels hit a pothole, and the coffin flew over to that side. "And the body, tell me, how's the body?" I kept repeating in horror, not daring to look in that direction. "The body came out," they replied. I brought myself to look and saw that my mother's legs were sticking up and were slowly lowering, as if the body were thawing, sinking. Is this hideous dream the free and random play of my dreamy imagination, or an expression of my inner discord, or possibly of my recently especially strong anxiety over the well-being of my motherland?[61]

The dream image of "motherland" as a violated woman is a stable private symbol: the image of a sexually violated woman as an emblem of political violence appears in Prishvin's diary on other occasions. Thus, in April 1939 he dreamed about a Komsomol girl who asked a doctor whether it was possible to restore lost virginity by surgical means. This record is juxtaposed with Prishvin's musings on whether it was possible to hide the traces of the recent terror campaign, or, as he put it, the "act of violence" (*akt nasiliia*—in Russian the phrase has connotations of sexual violence).[62] I would argue that the sexual meaning is overridden by the political.

It was in 1937 that Prishvin returned to the idea of writing a book about the construction of the Belomor Canal. "July 12 [1937]. St. Peter's Day. I started working on the "Canal" book, and I have to squeeze all the juice out of this idea."[63] He felt that writing such a book was an act of self-coercion emblematizing his own role in the larger Soviet project. As the diary makes clear, his "canal"—the book about the canal—itself became a private labor camp in which Prishvin worked on "reforging" his own self:

> July 21 [1937]. With this canal [book project] I, as a writer, have essentially, entered the canal [camp] myself, and I need to overcome my own will...[64]

(Here, and further, Prishvin plays with different meanings of the word "canal.")

Throughout 1937, entries that refer to Prishvin's work on the "Canal book" are interspersed with the chronicle of a different construction project: the Union of Writers was building a luxury cooperative for its members in the center of Moscow. Many writers fought fiercely for the privilege of being granted an apartment in the Writers' House. While his rural cottage in Zagorsk (without indoor plumbing or running water) was a retreat of sorts, such life placed an increasing physical burden on the aging writer. Moreover, he was reassessing the idea of a refuge:

[June 24, 1937] An apartment in Lavrushivsky Lane facing the Tretiakov Gallery begins to seem like a mad dream about a refuge in the very throat of a volcano. And yet this is a correct strategy: a refuge is now possible only in the very throat of the volcano.[65]

Throughout much of 1937, Prishvin chronicles his involvement in the two construction projects (the Canal book and the apartment in the Writers' House) in parallel entries:

August 5. The construction of my canal should, in essence, be the construction of the world.
August 11. I am working hard on the "Canal."
August 12. Going to Moscow to look over the apartment.[66]

The irony of the situation did not escape him. On both counts—his mad desire (or calculated move?) for a safe house in the volcano and his wish to write a book about self-transformation in the labor camp—he was not free of doubt, and the diary reflects these doubts.

In August 1937 Prishvin moved into an apartment in the Writers' House in Lavrushinsky Lane. (Several of those who appear on the pages of this book, Vsevolod Ivanov, Lidiia and Iurii Libedinskii, and Boris Pasternak, were now his neighbors.) His peasant wife Efrosiniia Pavlovna stayed behind in Zagorsk: their marriage came to an uneasy end. On August 6, Prishvin noted: "Here finally is the much desired apartment, and I have no one to share it with."[67]

These events unfolded against the background of the intense terror campaign, which finds only a scarce mention in his diary. Still, on October 25, 1937, Prishvin recorded that all the "active" (his word) people he knew in Zagorsk were arrested. On December 25, he recorded a rumor that he himself was under arrest.[68]

In September 1938 (after a month spent in the forest, hunting), Prishvin recorded another dream of terror:

> 22 September [1938]. Hunting is dear to me because I work with my feet and not my head, but everything that I skip over later comes back into my mind with a force that is impossible to attain in regular life.
>
> I had a nightmare that I was among a multitude of people, as if in a forest piled up with dry branches arranged in three layers. People were lying on all sides and even underneath me. I spat down and, glancing in the direction of my spit, saw two doctors cutting into someone's fat leg. I shuddered and gasped with horror. "What a sissy!" sounded a voice from below, "You're still not used to it?" Embarrassed, I came back with a clever retort: "I wasn't horrified because they're cutting a man but because I didn't see them and spit there." And then I noticed that there were big rats everywhere, running across the gray people lying on the ground. One ran across my stomach, another one came closer, and I even pushed it away with my hand. Suddenly it stopped and gave me a terrifying look. It was ready to attack, and I realized that now it had assumed its rat rights, more powerful than human rights, and that I had mortally offended it, and an offended rat may do anything that it wants with me.[69]

Unlike in other cases, Prishvin did not comment on this dream. But the diary provides clues for its reading: the key images can be found elsewhere in the diary. Thus, in the summer of 1937, Prishvin undertook an expedition to study the forest habitat—the way each animal kept to its stratum, or, as he called this arrangement, the "forest layers" (*etazhi lesa*—Prishvin wrote a story under this title). The dream pictures such a layered arrangement, though not of animals but of living human bodies. Another key image, dismemberment, appeared in the diary in the days of the Second Moscow Trial (in January 1937). Prishvin wrote, with unmistakable scorn, that from morning till night the radio broadcasted "people's wrath," and at one factory it was decided that traitors "should be quartered rather than shot." Prishvin notes that his son was "so gripped by it" that he was actually expecting that the accused would "have their body parts cut off, their fingers chopped off, etc."[70] Recorded more than a year later, the amputation dream articulates contradictory emotions of the dreaming "I" in a synthesis that does not appear elsewhere in the diary and that may not be possible in rational self-reflection: the visceral horror evoked by the terror (focused on the image of carnage), the hope that violence is a necessary or beneficial measure (the image of medical procedure), the immediacy of personal involvement (the dream makes the "I" an eyewitness), the embarrassment at his own discomfort when it is noted by an unseen observer, and the expectation that one can or should get used to the sight of violence. Finally, there is the realization that the slightest gesture of self-protection may offend the attackers. (The concluding image identifies the agents of the terror not as doctors but as rats.) This dream also testifies to the penetration of the terror into the deep recesses of the life Prishvin had hoped to preserve: not only the world of nature (in this dream, the setting of the horrible confrontation), but also into the world of his creative imagination. This dream record seems to indicate Prishvin's awareness of his vacillating status as a partially Sovietized but still threatened writer. But he does not comment on his dream: Prishvin-the-diarist stands silently outside his dream as an observer of his own, otherwise unexpressed (perhaps inexpressible?), emotions.

As for his "canal," Prishvin continued to work on the project for the rest of his life. When he resumed it after the war, he described its self-coercive quality with complete clarity, excusing it as an elemental force of "history":

> February 24 [1946]. I, as an author, have to subjugate myself, my opinion, my "I wish" to that unity of opinions which, in my "Canal," I call "One should" [*Nado*]. In a word, I do to myself what all of my heroes, the army of the canal builders, do to themselves. One has to write the "Canal" in such a way that shows that, by comparison with the canal workers, we, the free people, are only relatively free, and that all of us are illuminated by the light of this "One should," and that this "One Should" is brought to us by the wind of history.[71]

When he finally submitted his book for publication in 1948 he felt satisfied: it was "modern," and it was "good," but, mainly, it was "evidence" of "the author's personal participation in contemporary life."[72] Alas, the editor requested extensive revisions. Prishvin, who fell ill on receiving this judgment, complied. A year later, he noted that he felt "imprisoned" in his novel.[73] A few years later, the eighty-year-old writer (who was still working on his "Canal book") described his enduring project of self-transformation in the following, painfully direct, yet somewhat self-flattering terms:

> August 25. For the whole of the Soviet time, my task was to adapt to the new environment while remaining myself. This task called for a heroic feat, and I did perform a heroic feat, but, in the end, it seems that little has been done: much energy was spent on the *acquisition* of the new.[74]

Prishvin died in January 1954 (surviving Stalin by almost a year). His book about the canal was published in 1957 (under the title *The Emperor's Road*

[*Osudareva doroga*]—an evocation of Peter the Great's plan to build a canal at this location).

Oleg Volkov (1900–1992) was, like Prishvin, a hunter and a nature writer. He spent much of his life in the camps and in exile in the Far North. When he wrote memoirs (in the late 1970s), Prishvin was on his mind. One of the chapters of Volkov's memoir, set in the Solovki forced-labor camp (which Prishvin had also visited in 1934), was entitled *In the Land of Tamed Birds* (*V kraiu pugannykh ptits*) (he plays on Prishvin's formula, reversing it). Volkov had respected Prishvin, but, on behalf of all camp inmates, he passed uncompromising judgment:

> I think that not one person among those who found themselves under the millstones of the GULAG could recall the books, brochures, and essays that glorified "reforging through labor" without distaste. Even Prishvin, who published *Osudareva doroga*, destroyed his reputation of honest writer-humanist with this lackey-cooked dish![75]

WRITERS' DREAMS: VENIAMIN KAVERIN

In 1989, Veniamin Aleksandrovich Kaverin (1902–1989), another prominent writer caught between aloofness and desire for participation in society, fear and complicity, published his memoir *The Epilogue*, written in the 1970s. Beginning in the 1960s, Kaverin published several successive memoirs, disclosing his life in accordance with what was permissible at the moment of publication. This last memoir was meant as an epilogue to his life, and to his life stories. He was clearly anxious to show his readers that, his record as a widely published Soviet author notwithstanding, he did not offer to "raise my arms up and surrender" (the image he used to speak of another writer, who did). Dreams form the backbone of Kaverin's final memoir, making it into another "oneiric autobiography."

A dream concludes the chapter entitled "One Day in the Year 1937." In this chapter, Kaverin, who felt threatened by the regime for most of his (distinguished) career as a Soviet writer, created a retroactive diary of sorts: he tried to describe one day at the peak of the terror. But how to convey (he asks) "the feeling of how we lived in the years of the terror": the humiliating fear, habitual caution, all-pervading insecurity, and disturbing silence? Finding himself at a loss, Kaverin repeated what Lidiia Chukovskaia said of her diary: "My entries on the terror, incidentally, are notable in that the only things that are fully reproduced are dreams. Reality was beyond my powers of description..."[76]

Kaverin ended his description of one day in the year 1937 with the record of a dream he had made at the time:

> 19 February 1937. I don't remember how it starts. I am in hiding. People who don't know that I need to be in hiding come in, and I easily talk to them. But one of them seems to suspect something. Still, the room is dimly lit, and he can't see me very well. I think that I am alone in the apartment and go from my room (with the door leading to the street) into another one. But there I see a small man with a large face, a policeman. He asks me something as if I am on trial. I don't answer, return to my room, open the door to the street, and run. I see lots of people flocking together and dozens of cars at the corner. I run as fast as I can, now together with some poor little boy. We run up the road—we are being pursued—when we see a side path covered with snow going up into the mountains. We go there. Snow, snow is everywhere, and some man, falling into it, is herding sheep. I yell to him: "Is it far to the village?" He doesn't respond, but we run after him. The sky becomes more and more pink. I realize that it's because of the light coming from below. And then "the arranged chasm" [*ustroennaia propast'*] opens up. This is a colony of some runaway schismatics [*beguny*] who have been living here for a long time. We climb down along the ledges. We're not greeted very well, not particularly warmly. Now Yury [Tynianov] is with me. He is led away somewhere. I am talking to these people. Around me are children: happy, noisy, they're playing. This is a village built inside a fortress. They show me where my bunk is, but I first want to find Yury. I climb up a wooden staircase with thick oak handrails, look for number 42 but do not find it. [...] I walk further, along a different staircase, and ask an old woman servant where room number 42 is. She says: "But that's a foreign currency room!" [*Da ved' eto valiutnyi!*] I tell her that I don't care, and finally I am shown to the room. I enter without knocking. Sitting at a long table are about eight people; all of them have unpleasant square wooden faces. Yury is asleep. They say that he was tired and fell asleep. I wait. They sit in silence. One should say something, but it is best to be silent [*nado zagovorit', no luchshe molchat'*]—maybe then they will leave. And they do leave. Yury wakes up, and I ask him why they exchanged looks in that way when I came in. He tries to calm me down: it's nothing, it will all work out. Then I write down everything I saw in "the arranged chasm" and, for some reason, put the sheets of paper on the road. They are thick like cardboard. A boy comes running toward me (a different boy from the one I ran here with) and kicks a sheet with his foot. I run and collect the sheets.[77]

As Kaverin notes, this is a typical anxiety dream that draws its material from concrete historical circumstances. The dominant emotion of the dream is, of course, the feeling of persecution. Some images require explanatory comments, which I will supply. The image of the arranged, or manmade, abyss (it is ambiguous whether it is a refuge or a prison) derives its identity from the Russian schismatic community of *beguny* (literally, runners/escapees). Danger is shared with Kaverin's close friend, the literary scholar and writer Yury Nikolaevich Tynianov. The dream image of a foreign currency cell, as Kaverin himself comments, is an "echo" of incarcerations for the purposes of confiscating hidden property (gold or hard currency), widely practiced in the late 1920s and early 1930s. (Those who surrendered the property were released.) As Kaverin also notes, this inspired a chapter in Mikhail Bulgakov's novel *The Master and Margarita* (written mostly in the 1930s, but not published until the 1960s), in which Bulgakov represented this Soviet judicial procedure through the phantasmagoria of a character's dream. At the end of the dream, the subject sees himself as a record-keeper concerned with the survival of his records, and the dream narrative makes these meanings clear. But there is also something else (on which Kaverin does not comment)—the dream expresses a double imperative of speech and silence: "one should speak, but it's better to keep silent" (*nado zagovorit', no luchshe molchat'*).

The fear, humiliation, and misery of the 1930s is the topic of another dream story Kaverin included in his memoir. Experienced and recorded on August 8, 1964, long after the end of the terror, this dream also binds the feeling of persecution with the double imperative of action and inaction:

> I was dreaming that I have been summoned somewhere, and I have to go there, where they will talk to me and demand that I tell them everything. In a street of an old provincial town, a heavy cart, or an old-fashioned car with large wheels that reminds me of a heavy tall unwieldy wagon is moving toward me. Sitting inside are people with strange faces: pale, with flat noses and low foreheads, they are talking loudly and confidently about something relating to the affair for which I was summoned. Along the way, I climb down some slippery stairs to the dirty toilet in the basement, and when I come out, a hunchback leans out and screams after me in a rage: "You should turn off the lights!"
>
> I go down on one knee near the entrance to a building, where they invited not only me but also others—people like Tikhonov, that is, the bosses. He nods at me and goes up the stairs, seeming preoccupied and serious. He throws a joke to me, and I respond half-jokingly but think that both of us are going to have problems but that, for him, everything will work out. Finally, I enter. This is the reception area as well as a barbershop, where they're cutting hair and shaving people. On the table are

dog-eared magazines and old newspapers. They sit in silence. I sit down, too. It might be possible to walk out, but it can't be done. It might be possible to take a breath, but it can't be done. [*Mozhno uiti, no nel'zia. Mozhno vzdokhnut', no nel'zia.*] I am already in the chair, and they start to cut my hair. An elderly, calm gray-haired barber does his job carefully. At the same time, from the office where I am supposed to go after my haircut appears one of the people who rode in the wagon. He tells the barber: "I bet, Major Lykov, they picked this one up in Peredelkino." Both of them laugh. I am frightened but I say nothing. I am in the chair, and the major is holding the scissors. In a second, he will bend toward me and start poking at my eyes, but nothing can be done about this [*nichego nel'zia sdelat'*]. I sit and wait.[78]

Like the previous dream, this story articulates the dominant emotion—fear—in a sequence of bizarre images typical of dreams. But at least some of them can be read as emblems of the peculiar misery of "everyday Stalinism" (whatever else their etiology may be).[79] Thus a raging assault (or political denunciation) from those with whom one shares a dirty toilet (in a communal apartment) can be regarded as a quintessential Soviet experience. As in the previous dream, the threat is cast by a small group of menacing people. The setup suggests preparations for an act of public scrutiny, known in the 1930s as "purging," to take place in the Writers' Union (note the presence of Nikolai Semenovich Tikhonov, an official of the Union, and the mention of the writers' summer colony Peredelkino). But the public "purging" ceremony turns into an arrest by an officer of the secret police ("Major Lykov, this one was taken in Peredelkino"). Such metamorphoses of images and situations are, of course, typical of dreams, but they are also typical of the Stalinist terror: this writer's dream works as a "realistic" representation of terror, realistic in the sense that it captures the surreal quality of the experience. Of course, a writer as skilled as Kaverin, who started his career in the 1920s as a modernist, could well have been aware of the far-reaching aesthetic meanings of his dream stories.

Let us focus on the trope present in all three dreams from Kaverin's memoir (of which I discuss two): the double imperative of speech and silence, action and inaction. What stands out in Kaverin's skillfully written dream story is the paradoxical use of modal words (used to express possibility, permissibility, and necessity) and impersonal passive constructions: *mozhno uiti, no nel'zia; mozhno vzdokhnut', no nel'zia* (roughly: it might be possible to walk out, but it can't be done/it's prohibited; it might be possible to take a breath, but it can't be done/it's prohibited). And finally: *nichego nel'zia sdelat'* (nothing can be done). Drawing on the specific grammatical resources the Russian language offers for expressing modality and subjectivity, Kaverin creates phrases in which possibility/permissibility clashes with impossibility/prohibition in a syntactic construction that does not allow for an active subject. (Such impersonal passive constructions are a grammatical feature that is specific to Russian.) In the end, these dream stories capture what linguistic categories can barely grasp, but what (from many people's experience) is typical for dreams: recurrent dreams in which we discover, with horror, that no matter how much we wish or try, we cannot speak or move. In a word, dream dynamics, transcribed in Russian, can naturally accommodate frozenness in the face of everyday terror. I would suggest that, elaborating this situation, Kaverin uses his dream stories, with their emphasis on grammatical immobility and lack of agency, to emblematize the position of a subject of the terror regime.

The dreams Kaverin placed at the key points of his final memoir read as his definitive statements about the terror. Indeed, hardly any other medium could capture the peculiar experience of the Soviet terror, from the bizarre transformation of a public meeting into an arraignment before a court to the inexplicable but palpable inability to act in the face of danger—an inability created by an uncertainty about what is possible, impossible, or necessary, and by an uncertainty about personal agency. What Kaverin implies (echoing Chukovskaia) is that, while the reality of terror could not be captured by a diary, it could be captured by a dream experience and reproduced in narratives based on dreams.

There are, of course, examples of fiction that use dreams as a model for narrative. Indeed, narrated by a professional writer, Kaverin's dreams have both a distinct literary quality and a possible intertextual source. Consider the image of a small man with a large face in the next room asking questions "as if I am on trial"; or the eight people with square wooden faces silently sitting around the table; or the setting of the trial in a hotel. Consider the intense feeling of dreamlike, seemingly involuntary, submission to necessity, up to the final execution in a barber's chair. These, and other, features of Kaverin's dreams come as if from Kafka's *Trial*. Kafka, known to few people in Russia at the time (sometimes only from hearsay), intrigued Russian readers. On October 31, 1959, Lidiia Chukovskaia recorded in her diary:

> [Anna Akhmatova] recounted the whole of Kafka's novel *The Trial* for us, from beginning to end. This is how she spoke of the novel: when you are reading it, it is as if someone takes you by the hand and leads you back into your nightmares. She also told us Kafka's biography. He is immensely famous in the West, but here he is not published.[80]

Whether or not Anna Akhmatova knew this, Kafka took his bad dreams—dreams of persecution, flight from attackers, conflicts with the overbearing father figure, torture, bodily mutilation, filth, and excrement, which he meticulously recorded in his notebooks—as models for his literary writings.

It has been suggested that "a kind of sensory knowledge of dreams," based on self-observation, informs Kafka's fiction, including *The Trial* (written in 1914–15 and published in 1925): the story of a man who is tried and executed according to absurd laws and procedures everybody seems to accept as a necessity.[81] Discussing Kafka with her Russian contemporaries, Akhmatova reversed the process: to her and her contemporaries, Kafka's *Trial* reads like their bad dreams—dreams inspired by real life under the Stalinist terror. If Kafka's later readers across the world saw in *The Trial* an uncanny prediction of the real totalitarian terror that was to follow, for Soviet readers, the novel also meant something else. Having shown the power of prediction, the novel—clearly based on dream logic—endowed their real dreams with the status of recognizable representations of their experiences. Dreams could even be seen as more effective representations than documentary writings. (This is how Kaverin understood Chukovskaia's reflections on diaries and dreams of the terror.) Reading Kafka (or hearing *The Trial* retold by a better-informed friend), Russian men and women of letters felt encouraged to treat their dreams as stories about the terror. Thus, Kaverin, who used Kafkaesque images, offered his dream from 1937 as the best way to convey the "feeling of how we lived." In his memoir, the writer Kaverin demonstrated this move with complete clarity, but, as I argue, many of Stalin's contemporaries also offered their nightmares as authentic and authoritative representations of their historical experience.

THE DREAMS OF ANNA AKHMATOVA

Given the symbolic standing Anna Akhmatova enjoyed among contemporaries in her roles of "tragic prophetess Cassandra" and "the reader's intimate friend," it is no wonder that her dreams gained the status of texts and exercised far-reaching influence.[82] What is more, her image entered the dreams of her readers—and all of this under the sign of state terror and universal history. Using Akhmatova's dreams and dreams about Akhmatova as an example, in this section I show how the circulation of dreams served as an instrument of mythmaking and community building. Here, I highlight the social function of Soviet dreams.

Akhmatova herself took her dreams extremely seriously, and in the years 1958 to 1966 she recorded them in her multipurpose notebooks (first published in 1996). A visitation (in 1958) from her first husband, Nikolai Gumilev, who was executed (several years after their divorce) in 1921, was a melancholy dream.[83] A dream (in 1965) about the eviction from the apartment on the Fontanka (which she shared in the 1930s with her husband, Nikolai Punin, and his previous wife and child) "by someone I once loved" was a nightmare full of "monstrous details."[84] In a most solemn dream, Sir Isaiah Berlin appeared to take her to the top of a mountain for an important announcement. (Akhmatova believed that her conversation with this British diplomat and philosopher of history in 1946, when Soviet citizens were discouraged from meeting foreigners, held far-reaching historical significance.)* In another dream (the last she recorded in her notebook, shortly before her death) Akhmatova saw herself pursued by the terrifying, crazed Juggernaut—a symbol of history in this community.[85] Most, if not all, of Akhmatova's dreams recorded in 1965–66 draw their significance from direct or implied historical reference, and most relate to the events of the Soviet terror. (In the years of the terror, Akhmatova did not record her dreams, and she later lamented the loss of important historical material [2: 198].)

One of the recorded dreams, from August 1964, is an eschatological vision, or revelation. On that day Akhmatova traveled through the flooded city of Leningrad to her cabin in the country (she called this tiny country cottage, allotted to her by the Writers' Union in the writer's colony Komarovo, "Kennel," *budka*).

> August 30 is the day of departure for Budka. O[l'ga] A[leksandrovna] and Tolia [Naiman]. We are taking a fantastical route (through parks) through a very strange, very beautiful flood. The water (there is no wind) is exactly like liquid silver or mercury. The water heavily and slowly overflows the banks, forming unexpected islands and threatening to cause a disaster. I saw the oak planted by Peter the Great for the first time. The sky is eschatological, almost with a menacing inscription.

On the other side of this page, Akhmatova describes an eschatological dream:

> My dream last night exceeded everything that I had experienced in my whole life. I saw the planet Earth the way it was some time (how much time?) after its complete destruction. I think that I would give anything to be able to forget this dream!

---

* According to Berlin, Akhmatova believed that "we—that is, she and I—inadvertently, by the mere fact of our meeting [in 1946], had started the cold war and thereby changed the history of mankind. [...] she saw herself and me as world-historical personages chosen by destiny to begin a cosmic conflict (this is indeed directly reflected in one of her poems). I could not protest that she had perhaps [...] somewhat overestimated the effect of our meeting on the destinies of the world, since she would have felt this as an insult to her tragic image of herself as Cassandra—indeed, to the historico-metaphysical vision which informed so much of her poetry. I remained silent." Isaiah Berlin, "Meetings with Russian Writers," in his *Personal Impressions* (London: Hogarth Press, 1980), 202. For the dream, see *Zapisnye knizhki Anny Akhmatovoi,* 692. Judging by the fact that Anatoly Naiman wrote a book about this meeting, Akhmatova's belief was shared in the community: Anatolii Naiman, *Ser* [Sir] (Moscow: Eksmo-Press, 2001).

On the next page she describes the lasting impressions of that day and that dream:

> The dream on the night of August 30 continues to haunt me and grows more frightening with every day.
> On the other hand, the departure along the mysterious windless flood grows better and better. It is useless to ask my companions about it.[86]

But Akhmatova did talk about her dream with others. Years later, this dream was made public by Anatoly Naiman. (A young poet whom she patronized at the time, he accompanied her on the drive through the flood waters.) The opening scene of Naiman's *Stories about Anna Akhmatova,* published in 1989, shows the two poets sharing their dreams. First, Naiman told Akhmatova his dream:

> I had a dream: the white, tall Leningrad ceiling above me instantly swells with blood, and its scarlet stream pours down onto me. Several hours later, I saw Akhmatova; the memory of the dream wouldn't leave me, and I related it to her.
> "Not bad," she said. "Generally, the most boring things in the world are other people's dreams and other people's sexual affairs. But you deserve it. I had my dream on the night of September 30.
> After a world catastrophe, I, all alone in the world, stand on the ground, on slush, on dirt; I am slipping, I can't keep my feet on the ground because the soil is being washed away. From somewhere up above me, expanding as it approaches and threatening me more and more, a torrent comes rushing down, bringing together all the great rivers in the world: the Nile, the Ganges, the Volga, the Mississippi..."[87]

Whether or not this is what Akhmatova dreamed (either on August 30 or on September 30, as Naiman has it), related by a memoirist, along with his own apocalyptic dream, her dream became a social fact with far-reaching implications. Reinforced by the coincidence of the two dreams, these apocalyptic visions acquired a social and historical quality. The two poets seem to have taken their dreams as a reflection of the human condition and mood in their time.

It should be noted that such dreams were dreamed, across the centuries, by many, especially those who shared the knowledge of biblical apocalyptic imagery. Thus, Albrecht Dürer saw in his dream "how many big waters fell from the firmament," hitting the earth violently and with enormous noise, and drowning the whole land. Frightened, he woke before the other waters fell and drew a picture of the floods beside his account of his dream.[88] These Russian intellectuals use common emblems of loss, despair, and desolation, and they express their sense of the universal significance of their suffering in apocalyptic imagery. Yet common images are endowed with specific, historically concrete connotations, instantly identifiable by members of the group. First, apocalyptic waters hold special meaning for the inhabitants of Petersburg and readers of Pushkin. Moreover, in these dreams, the world comes to an end in the streets and apartments of Leningrad after the Stalinist terror and the Second World War. (Later, I discuss the dream of the Petersburg philosopher Yakov Druskin, who pictured himself facing the end of the world, linked to the terror and the war, amid the empty waters.) The biblical image of the apocalyptic flood is mobilized to convey personal experience with political reference and local relevance. In their notebooks and memoirs, these Russian intellectuals speak of their most intimate experiences, dreams, in imaginative language that fuses the biblical, political, and local meanings, uniting people even as they sleep—both in the larger community of suffering humanity and in the smaller group of those whose symbols are marked for particular use.

The story of Anatoly Naiman and Anna Akhmatova is not the only episode of the community of Russian writers sharing apocalyptic dreams. My other example also finds Akhmatova at its starting point. In her notebook, we find a shorthand record of another person's dream: "The letter (V Ivanov's dream—28 June 1963. Shortly before his death)."[89] This record can be unfolded by drawing on another personal document. Apparently, the deathbed dream of the prominent Soviet writer Vsevolod Viacheslavovich Ivanov (1895–1963) was related to Akhmatova by the writer's son, the scholar Viacheslav Vsevolodovich Ivanov (born in 1929), in a letter written in late August 1963. In his 1991 memoir *Conversations with Anna Akhmatova,* Viacheslav Ivanov told the whole story:

In [...] the letter, I retold Anna Andreevna the dream—or vision?—my father had before he died. This dream intertwined Greece and China, but the main heroine of the dream was Akhmatova.

On June 28, when I went to see my father at the hospital that morning, he was in a lucid state and told me the dream ...: "In the dream I saw a world congress of writers in Greece, which—imagine—was attended by Akhmatova. Right at that time, Socrates' house in Pieria was found. That's where she was housed; his table and chair were there. And I stayed on the top floor. In the morning I come downstairs: the woman is sitting at the desk and crying. I ask her: 'Anna Andreevna, what's the matter?' She says that she saw her child in this desk, only he was pink, but the desk is made from black marble. It was so strange for her to see her own child amid these slabs by the sea. I told her: 'Even Homer is not depicted on every object, why should we, ordinary people, expect that?'

And I told her: 'At some point in our country, as in China, poetry will be at every step, on every object.' She answered, 'Maybe.'"

When we met, Akhmatova told me that she saw in this dream echoes of two of her poems on ancient themes. And China, I will add, is a trace of the translation readings mentioned earlier.* Akhmatova thus immersed us—those around her—along with herself, in the behind-the-looking-glass world of her dreams and prophetic images, in comparison to which other impressions faded.[90]

Bracketing its poignant emotional content, I will comment on those images of this dream that seem to have social and political reference. Indeed, the dream is set in the milieu of Soviet writers, with its country cottages (which were allotted by the Writers' Union to its members in accordance with one's rank or standing) and congresses (which dispensed rewards and reprimands capable of changing one's life overnight). In a move typical for dreams, the scope of this institutional world expands to mythic proportions: upgraded to the congress of world writers, this gathering takes place in the vicinity of Mount Parnassus. The dream revises the official hierarchy of the Union of Soviet Writers to accord the place of honor to Akhmatova, who, in actual life, was only marginally allowed to partake of the privilege. Russian poetry personified, Akhmatova, of course, represents the continuity and verity of the poetic tradition as a force that transcends the Soviet in the name of the universal. As a participant in the symposium, she is assigned to "Socrates' house," while the dreamer moves in as her upper-floor neighbor. The image of Akhmatova, who is heartbroken over the fate of her child, found in a desk, lends itself to emblematic reading: recall that her son, Lev, had been in the camps for years and that her poems remained unpublished for years, that is, to use a popular idiom, she was writing "for the desk drawer" (*v stol*). In the end, joining Akhmatova, the dreamer reaches out to a better world—to the future world in which writers may expect to leave an imprint on every article of everyday use.

Let us also follow an intertextual lead supplied by Viacheslav Ivanov: Akhmatova's poems that (she believed) may have served as the dream's source. These are the series "A Page from Classical Antiquity" (*Antichnaia stranichka*, 1961), "The Death of Sophocles" (*Smert' Sofokla*), and "Alexander at Thebe," subtitled "The House of the Poet" (*Aleksandr u Fiv. Dom poeta*). Set in classical Greece, they provide variations on the theme of the poet and the ruler, with the ruler acknowledging the artist's superiority in the face of imminent death. In the finale of the second poem, the "tsar" (Alexander the Great),

---

* Akhmatova read her translations of Chinese poetry in the Ivanovs' dacha in Peredelkino in 1953.

intent on the total destruction of the conquered city, instructs his subordinate to ensure the safety of "the House of the Poet."* Akhmatova once said (to Lidiia Chukovskaia) that these poems contained a lesson on "the *proper relations between the poet and power*."[91] Claimed as a source of Vsevolod Ivanov's dream, these poems give the dream a clear message (at least in the eyes of Viacheslav Ivanov, who put together the whole story of its genesis): the hope for a better world, in which the writer would enjoy the personal protection of the murderous ruler.

This dream and the story about this dream was a product of complex exchange in the writers' circle. To make the trajectory clear: Vsevolod Ivanov's dream about Akhmatova (which was rooted in Akhmatova's poems) was related to Akhmatova by the dreamer's son (Viacheslav Ivanov), noted in Akhmatova's notebook, and described, along with the whole story, in Viacheslav Ivanov's memoirs. Moreover, the knowledge of the dream does not stop with the immediate participants. The poet David Samoilovich Samoilov (1920–1990) wrote in his diary on August 16, 1963:

> Koma [Viacheslav Ivanov's nickname] told us a lot about Vsevolod's last days. He was dying a prolonged and conscious death. He was assessing his life. He had dreams in which he spoke with God. The writer's tragic fate ended with a testimony addressed to God. One of his last dreams was a touching fantasy about a congress of writers in Athens and about Akhmatova. Koma wrote down Vsevolod's dreams and the last conversations he had with him.[92]

Samoilov's diary (published in 2002) shows what this dream story meant for the members of the community: it confirmed their sense of common tragic destiny.

I will make a brief digression to show that Samoilov, too, was a self-conscious dreamer: he also dreamed of pillars of the writers' community, and he too tried to justify his life—the life of his generation—in dreams: "March 11 [1981]. A dream. I had a long conversation with the young Erenburg. He blames our generation for not accomplishing anything. I justify myself: 'We're still recovering from Stalinism.' Freezing March days. Harsh wind. Light." (A reviewer of the memoirs noted that the dream landscape comes from Ehrenburg's famous novel *Thaw*.)[93]

---

* «Ты только присмотри, чтоб цел был Дом Поэта» / "Just watch out that the House of the Poet is safe and sound." I would argue that the wording and the capital letters uncannily suggest (especially to a dreaming mind) the blending of the private house of the Greek poet with a Soviet institution, such as Dom tvorchestva pisatelei, Tsentral'nyi dom literatorov, Dom aktera (the Writers' House, etc.).

Looking at these stories about shared dreams among Soviet writers, one marvels at the collective and mythmaking quality of such an intimate experience as dreaming. To begin with, these writers dreamed common dreams. Akhmatova's vision of herself in the world after the end and Vsevolod Ivanov's dream of Akhmatova at the world congress of writers in Greece belong to the same general genre of eschatological visions. Both dreamers were personally concerned with the end, and with one's life after the end, whether in a catastrophic or utopian key. Moreover, they dreamed their dreams with one another in mind (Vsevolov Ivanov, at least, had Akhmatova in mind). Finally, all of them shared their dreams with other members of the community. These episodes speak both about the making of the writers' community and about the persistence of apocalyptic thinking with historical and political reference. Take the "congress of world writers" dream. Tracing the genesis and transmission of this text, we see the building and sharing of a collective fantasy. A Platonic utopia of sorts, this fantasy, set in the institutional context of the Union of Soviet Writers, pictures a society in which writers are accorded a place of absolute preeminence (a state that honors writers, acutely conscious of their status as world-historical victims of state atrocities). Sharing their dreams (and discovering that they dreamed similar dreams or dreamed of one another), these people gained a sense of connection, intimacy, and significance that served as protection, however precarious, from the social environment that threatened them with annihilation. As professional writers, they drew on literary images, on hermeneutic practices, and on storytelling to reinforce a social network that—as it seemed to them—existed apart from the state and its institutions (if not apart from the real or earthly world itself). Furthermore, exchanging their apocalyptic dreams, they indulged in a mutually reinforced feeling of the exaggerated social, historical, and eschatological significance of their shared lives.

Anna Akhmatova clearly enjoyed a very special status in this community, and that is why she appeared to others in their dreams—not only to those who knew her personally, but also to the members of the younger generation.

The poet Ol'ga Aleksandrovna Sedakova (born in 1949) was regularly visited in her dreams by major Russian writers, especially those marked by martyrdom. She shared her dreams with the literary scholar (verse theorist) Mikhail Leonovich Gasparov, who recorded them in his notebooks, which he published in 2001. One dream concerns Akhmatova:

"How Akhmatova was sick." Akhmatova lay in the middle of the room and was sick. A different, young, Akhmatova, took care of her. Neither of them was real, and they were trying to hide it, that is not to be seen from a certain angle, so they moved in a very strange way. Iu. M. Lotman appeared, the conference began, and it was decided that "everyone should advance into the future, except for N., who is in paper-frail health."[94]

The second dream connects the dreamer to another pillar of the Russian intelligentsia community: Osip Mandelshtam. It is a dream about the terror, death, and immortality, and about the relationship between the poet and power, in which (as in Vsevolod Ivanov's dream of Anna Akhmatova in the House of Socrates) the poet is ultimately acknowledged as the winner:

"How Mandelshtam was killed." We are walking along the Manezhnaia Square—apparently with N. Ia. [Nadezhda Iakovlevna Mandel'shtam]. Three steps ahead of us is O. E. [Osip Emil'evich Mandel'shtam]. It is impossible to come closer to him. At the same time, we know the condition under which he will be arrested, but he doesn't. The condition is if he stops at a booth. There are many booths, with sweets, cigarettes, postcards. He is distracted all the time, and we try to communicate to him from a distance: go, go, go. But in vain. He stopped and is taken away. We come out onto Red Square. There is a parade there. A general directs the troops to move apart. The troops disappear like smoke into all four directions. Then he walks through the empty square up to N. Ia., salutes, and hands her a "Report": 1). I certify that your husband is immortal. 2). He has not invented new words, but he has invented new things. 3). So don't blame me.—The General."[95]

Each of the dreams establishes the dreamer's intimacy, missed in real life (if only by virtue of a time divide), with a cultural hero of considerable symbolic value. Each dream links real and unreal, life and literature, the cultural generation of the "parents" and that of the "children," and it links the past, the present, and the future—all of this under the double sign of history and literature. In the end, with these dreams, the younger poet Ol'ga Sedakova (who shared her dreams with the literary scholar Mikhail Gasparov who published them in his memoir) entered the extended community of the Russian intelligentsia associated with suffering and terror.

A COMMENT ON WRITERS' AND PEASANTS' THEORIES OF DREAMS

A question arises: What did members of this literary community think about the nature of dreams and the validity of interpretation? I will make a digression to discuss some of the operational theories.

During the war, Vsevolod Ivanov recorded significant dreams in his diary (published in 2001):

> [February 11, 1943] In my dream I was fishing with a fishing rod. I was getting good bites. First I pulled out many small fish, then got one huge one. Since I rarely have dreams, particularly such vivid ones, and since in my mind there was empty noise that interfered with my concentration and work, and since misfortunes accustom you to superstition, and since I have no money for my family and don't know where to get it, in short—I got out a book of dream interpretations [*sonnik*], possibly for the first time in my life, and read it. Alas, the book answered me with the ambivalence characteristic of an oracle. To fish is bad. But to catch a big fish is good. I guess that's if you fish with a net, not a rod. And if you fish with a rod, then it's "neither a candle for God, nor a poker for the devil."

A month later:

> [March 19, 1943] A dream: Alexei Tolstoy and I are digging a narrow hole, looking for a treasure. Something white and narrow starts to come into view... [...] When I got up, I looked into a book of dream interpretations, in accordance with our ancestors' custom. I am to expect a great joy, and then an equally great misfortune...[96]

The writer turned to his dreams under the pressure of extreme historical and personal circumstances. From the outcome of war to his immediate prospects for publishing, life was profoundly uncertain. Trying to read his dreams for their predictive value, he resorts (not without embarrassment) to a book of dream interpretation popular among the peasants (*sonnik*). Moreover, he dreamed in images that seemed to come from a peasant dictionary of dreams: fishing (the peasant Arzhilovsky once dreamed of fishing as well) and treasure hunting (with a fellow writer Aleksei Tolstoy, famous for unshakable good luck, or good standing with the authorities). But the age-old wisdom of peasant superstition did not bring relief from uncertainty about the future.

The writer's son, Viacheslav Ivanov, also had prophetic dreams (included in his memoir, written between 1989 and 1994); his view on the nature of clairvoyance in general and dreams in particular was rooted in his infantile experience (not sexual, as Freudians would have it, but political and philological). The memoir contains extensive reflections on this topic: "Since childhood, I have studied the technique of reading between the lines and of juxtaposing pieces from various fragmentary newspaper reports. It is another matter that, as a child, I already knew that it was difficult to convince adults of the validity of logical conclusions. Several days before the war with Hitler began, several people came over to our dacha in Peredelkino..." The memoirist then tells us how, on that day in 1941, at the age of eleven, he shared with his parents' visitors his prophecy that, contrary to the assurances of the state news agency, the war was imminent; but he was not believed. His ability to predict the future was equally strong in the years following Stalin's death: "The years of intense peering into our future, which was not determined by us then, had begun." This time, the knowledge of the future came in dreams: "Over the four years from 1953 to 1957, when I was inwardly focused on the news about the coming changes, I saw three prophetic dreams, each of which was unexpected for me." The first dream pictured the fall of Beria and the explosion of the atomic bomb; the second predicted the fall of Molotov; the third, the fall of Marshal Zhukov. All three were soon proven right (in one case, with a displacement: the Soviet Union exploded a hydrogen, not atomic, bomb, and only on a test basis). The gift of vision served the author well also in later years, especially in the last years of Soviet power, when he became (in his own words) "a politician and a diplomat":

> In the spring of 1977, as I was waking up, I heard: "This regime has to end!" I started to grumble to myself that these intellectuals always want for things to be the way that seems proper to them. Then I suddenly realized: Who am I arguing with? I am alone in the room. Svetlana left for work long ago. In the new epoch, further accurate predictions could be made more reliably not in a state of sleeping or of being half-asleep. I told my friend Robert Kaiser, who at one point worked as a correspondent for the *Washington Post* in Moscow and is now one of the editors of that newspaper, that Gorbachev would come to power and would initiate reform. I told him, and many others, in advance about the possibility of the failure of the August putsch [...] But even more so than when I was a child, I started to encounter a difficulty, and sometimes an impossibility, of convincing others of the obvious.[97]

In his approach to dreams, the author of this memoir—a distinguished scholar—relies on his extensive professional training in philology, cybernetics, and neuroscience, and on his command of the semiotic method. He views the text of his life as inherently, coherently, and profoundly meaningful and highly significant: a coded life. In this case, the modern trust in science blends with the traditional Russian fascination with quasireligious and semimystical knowledge.* Inspired by his unshakable belief in the totality of hidden meaning and

---

* Consider the author's rendition of Karl Popper's theory of "the third world": "Besides the physical world in which we live and the world of cultural objects which we create, there is also a third world of discoveries not yet made, of books not yet written, symphonies not yet performed. They exist in the form of Platonic ideas. The development of culture consists in reading, or decoding, these ideas, gradually reaching them. Two scholars in one field often perform this reading almost simultaneously."

in the limitless interpretive potential of the human intellect, this author sees life as an object for "deciphering," and seeks an explanation of his prophetic power in science.[98] In this world of "semiotic totalitarianism" of sorts, dreams provide a properly inclined mind with an opportunity to read the code in one's sleep, making predictions of future political developments that are fit to be reported to an American journalist. (If Robert Kaiser had printed Ivanov's predictions in the *Washington Post,* Ivanov would have become a prophet in retrospect.) There is only one problem: how to make others accept such visions. Memoirs helped: through his memoirs, this dreamer could share his prophecies with posterity.

A PHILOSOPHER'S DREAMS: YAKOV DRUSKIN

In many ways, Iakov Semenovich Druskin (1902–1980) stands apart from members of the intelligentsia discussed in this book. It is hard to define him. Educated as a philosopher, Druskin made a conscious decision to withdraw from academic institutions and academic circles as early as the mid-1920s. Trained as a pianist, he did not perform. For most of his life, he made a living as a teacher of mathematics in secondary schools. Deep emotional ties linked him to his family (father, mother, sister, and brother—the prominent Soviet musicologist Mikhail Semenovich Druskin) and to his circle of intimate friends—esoteric poets and philosophers who called themselves *chinari*. The circle, quite prominent in the annals of Russian literary culture, included Leonid Lipavsky, Alexander Vvedensky, Daniil Kharms, and Nikolai Oleinikov. Under the conditions of the Soviet regime, Yakov Druskin pursued the classical ideal of the philosopher's life: intensely private, introspective, self-reflective, ascetic, and philosophized through and through. Much of it has been documented in his diary. The diary (kept from 1933 until his death in 1980) is devoted mostly to his thoughts; daily life is almost entirely absent. But not the dreams. One theme dominates Druskin's dreams: death. All of his friends and cohorts, *chinari*, died between 1937 and 1941 in the terror and the war. In his dreams, the dead visited Druskin again and again. When, in 1963, Druskin compiled a book of existential philosophy based on his dreams and diaries, *Dreaming and Waking (Son i iav'),* published only after his death, he devoted a special chapter to dreams of visitations by his slain friends.[99] Such

---

That is what happened with [Roman] Jakobson and me" (*Zvezda,* no. 3, 171). The memoir also mentions the extravagant teaching of the apocalyptic philosopher Nikolai Fedorov, who preached physical resurrection of the dead based on imprints of their personalities left in their bodily remains and handwritten documents. Citing an expert in genetics, the author comments that these ideas seem close to the contemporary genome project, and that the possibility of such resurrections now seems more real than ever (*Zvezda,* no. 2, 203).

dreams started on the day Druskin learned that Daniil Kharms, who was arrested in the besieged Leningrad in August 1941, died in prison:

> 10 February [1942]. D. I. [Daniil Ivanovich Kharms] died on the 3rd or the 4th. That is what I was told yesterday, and if that is true, then a part of life, a part of the world, is gone. At night I dreamed about it several times. Dreams search for the justification of death, and that night D. I.'s death was explained in some way, but I don't remember how. I only remember a bunch of twigs broken in two.[100]

By that time, Druskin was the only member of the circle who was left alive. Oleinikov had been arrested and executed in the fall of 1937. Vvedensky, arrested in September 1941, also died in prison. Lipavsky was killed in the war in the fall of 1941. But in his dreams, until the end of his life, Druskin continued to live in their midst.

As a philosopher, Druskin was intrigued by the comparative ontology of waking and dreaming as two states of consciousness, reflecting on which of them was real. (Known since classical antiquity, this problem had been elaborated by Descartes, Pascal, Schopenhauer, and Sartre, but Druskin, who was certainly familiar with the relevant philosophical sources, did not cite any of them.) The following dream, from 1955, is one of many that develop this theme, inextricably intertwined with the death of his cohorts in the terror:

> I was accused of something, and I was objecting very harshly. Suddenly I saw L. [Leonid Lipavsky] in the doorway. "That surely can't be a dream," I thought. But everyone present started assuring me that that was a dream, too: he has appeared so many times, and each time in a dream. I got angry: "None of you exist. You are all in my dream, except for L." They offered to test whether L. was in my dream. To do that, they put him on the table and started cutting his chest, and he started to heal his wounds through an exertion of his willpower. I helped him, also using my willpower. Blood stopped flowing, the wounds dried up, only scars remained. "But what does that prove?" I thought, and everyone present, including L., started slowly vanishing.[101]

Within this dream, the "I" tries to reverse the ontological status of waking and dreaming, to establish the dream domain—in which the dead are alive and wounds heal by an effort of the will—as true and real.

Again and again, Druskin recorded dreams that tested the reality of death, but in the end, the dreamer always "remembered" that his cohorts were dead:

> [undated] V. [Vvedensky] arrived yesterday, as it turns out. Just now he passed by me, greeted me, but did not even come up to me, and he will leave as early as tomorrow morning.

I went to the Lipavskys. L. [Leonid Lipavsky] was sitting at the table. T. [Tamara Lipavsky] was lying on the table. When I came in, she got off the table and sat down. I said: "V. has changed so much. He has started to resemble a professional Soviet writer. I even mistook him for Sviridov at first." We talked. As I was waking up, I thought: but Vvedensky is gone. But why haven't I seen Kharms in so long? I should call him, and then I remembered: he is gone, too. Then I will call Oleinikov, but he is gone, too. Only Lionya [Leonid Lipavsky] is left. Now completely awake, I remembered: he perished, too. *Wir sind tot. Alles ist tot.*[102]

The "*alles ist tot*" dream is perhaps the saddest of all: the "I" remembers that his friends are dead while still on the border of the dream. But the saddest part is the image of the absurdist poet Vvedensky, who has changed so much as to be mistaken for an official Soviet writer.* This dream is not only a failed attempt to bring the dead to life but also an imaginary extension of interrupted lives. Druskin's dream plays out alternative possibilities. But the final remark (which Druskin might have remembered from literature†) annihilates the subject himself, in two steps. *Wir sind tot:* the "I" may have felt alive, but the "we-self," invested in the intimate group destroyed in the terror and the war, is dead. *Alles is tot:* transcending the dichotomy of subject and object, the dream asserts an all-embracing condition—death. This is not surprising, since even in his waking life, Druskin often felt himself dead. (He made the following diary note: "In November–December of 1941, I crossed a certain boundary—the boundary of life. I saw my strength diminishing, sounds growing fainter, light fading, feelings and sensations dying. I was on the border between this life and the other life. Ghosts appeared—the swollen and dried out faces of the dead. I saw death, including my own death.")[103] As he knew well, it was by pure chance that he, alone in his group, survived the terror and the war.

Another dream touched on a philosophy of history. On January 11, 1943, Druskin recorded the following sequence of dreams:

L. [Lipavsky] came over. I asked him, "Do you think D. I. [D. I. Kharms] is alive?" "He's been executed." "Why?" "There was a teachers' trial." "But he is not a teacher?" "Right, but he did not approve of the Constitution." Then I tried to use hints to find out why he hadn't come over in so long. He answered that he had. "Then why is Tamara so upset?" He produced some cogent argument. I started to think about how to reconcile all of these contradictions and concentrated on that so much

---

* Georgii Vasil'evich Sviridov, mentioned in the dream, is a Soviet composer.
† "*Alles ist tot, und wir sind tot,*" says the German musician Lemm, a character in Ivan Turgenev, *The Nest of the Gentry* (*Dvorianskoe gnezdo*), chapter 44.

that I suddenly woke up, and once again there was no transition between dreaming and waking.

A dream about policemen who taught people how to cross the street, about pink and black smoke.

Three carts were passing by, with Londoners, Poles, and Jews. The Jews, though beaten, were still happy. I pulled up my coat collar a little higher, just in case.

A dream about the end of the world. The end of the world was supposed to take place at some lake. Everything was ready for it there, and there was an empty house. I wondered whether I could save myself in it, but then I realized that it, too, would be destroyed. I started to look for a safe place and found one, but I don't know how to describe it. I remember this lake but do not know how to identify the location of this place; maybe it did not exist in space. But, while staying in this place, I wouldn't have died as the end of the world came about but would have become a rain cloud, or the color of a rain cloud.[104]

In its first part, this dream sequence demonstrates the absurdity of logical cause-and-effect explanations of the events of the Stalinist terror. (Reflecting on the working of the dream in his *Dreaming and Waking,* Druskin wrote that dreams reveal the error of cognition by way of making causal connections, such as "if, then," "that is why" and "because.")[105] In attempting to explain why Kharms was executed, the dream acquires a Kafkaesque quality (and Druskin knew Kafka well).[106] The second dream is not only a philosophical exercise but also a historical panorama in which the dreaming "I" sees himself as a subject of history (the Second World War). This sequence of dreams moves from the Stalinist terror to the war, and, finally, to a vision of the end of the world. In the second (the war dream), the "I" is a bystander, performing a gesture of avoidance and caution as carts with victims of the war (Londoners, Poles, and Jews) move by in a procession. In the third dream, at the site of the end of the world, the "I" is still trying to save himself by manipulating the system of coordinates so as to change the plane of being (recall that the dreamer is a philosopher and mathematician).

(Note that Yakov Druskin dreamed the same dreams as his contemporaries: Akhmatova, whom he did not know and whose poetry he did not like, had an eschatological vision of the world after the end set in a similar landscape of empty waters.)

Shortly after the end of the war, on August 21, 1945 (at six o'clock in the morning), Druskin recorded a long, detailed, and horrifying dream of loss, death, and murder:

Mama took my things [writings] out of the desk drawer and put them on the couch that was on the riverbank, and they slipped into the river.

I said: "What have you done? That is my life!" Then Mama left. Misha [his brother Mikhail] and I are also returning home. Several people, probably assassins, stop us along the road. I keep going—nothing concerns me—but Misha has to face an obstacle: ropes. He skillfully avoids them. The last one has to be cut, and he cuts it. But then for some reason he cuts another rope that is not in his way. I forgot to say that the ropes are connected with knots. The assassins stand in the knots. The head assassin [*glavnyi*] is outside the knots. As soon as M. cut the rope that was not in his way, I thought: he did something excessive, now he will die. And indeed the leader pulls out a gun and shoots at one of the killers, saying "you," then at another, "you," and at Misha "you did something excessive." I want to leave unnoticed. The leader turns to me: nothing concerns you; die. I dodge him, try to justify myself, dash to the river, he shoots at me, and I die.[107]

While Druskin did not comment on this dream, in the context of his diary, the dream invites an allegorical interpretation. The image of murder at the hands of a team of assassins headed by *glavnyi* (roughly translated as "leader") reads as a symbolic model of the mechanism of Stalin's terror (note the interconnection between murderers and victims and the role of the "head assassin"). The situation of the protagonist and his brother also reads as an allegory. In real life, Mikhail Druskin (with whom Yakov shared musical interests) was an active and successful Soviet professional, a member of the academic establishment. (Note the distinction the dream makes between a necessary and an "excessive" action on the part of the active brother, which represents the difference between life and violent death.) By contrast, Yakov Druskin consciously built his life on the avoidance of public exposure: withdrawing from social connections, he gave up the chance for a professional career. The dream seems to challenge his tactics: in the end, the "head assassin" kills him as well.

But let us continue with the rest of the dream. The subject dies four times, thrice he is murdered, and the fourth death is a suicide:

I was told that I killed myself by stabbing myself in the belly four times, in the interval between my first and second death, having seen the leader and being unable to take the vileness. [...] I realized that this death did not count. The leader appeared again and killed others. And I, now experienced, having gone through three deaths, gave advice and helped others save themselves. Then the leader's victim appeared—a woman he killed. She was repulsive and was granted the ability to kill. But I already knew what to do. She, seeing that I am not easy to kill, hands me an axe. I know that if I hit her with the axe, I will not kill her, but instead she will receive a new power to kill me. I plunge the axe into the floor and say: disappear.[108]

In the image of the murdered old woman turned murderer, the vampire myth joins hands with the well-known circumstances of life under the Stalinist terror, in which victims were forced to denounce others, in turn bringing about their destruction. But the dreamer stands firm: nothing can incite him to murder.

Remarkably, another person caught in the terror, the prominent Soviet poet Ol'ga Fedorovna Berggol'ts (1910–1975), also dreamed of murdering an old woman. I will digress to speak about Olga Berggol'ts and her dreams. On July 12, 1942, she recorded in her diary: "I had agonizing, tormenting dreams: the war, the bombings, I killed some horrible old woman (I sometimes kill horrible old women in my dreams)."[109] Berggol'ts survived an arrest and brief incarceration in 1938–39. Returned on release to her public position (even asked to read her poem about Stalin at a public gathering), she was long haunted by traumatic dreams.[110] These two people, Druskin and Berggol'ts, were worlds apart. Berggol'ts, who identified herself with the revolution, was socially and emotionally involved with the Soviet cause and with Stalin, both before and after her arrest. Before her arrest, Berggol'ts had planned a "novel about our generation, about its rise to consciousness, a novel about the subjectivity of the epoch..."[111] After the arrest, she toyed with the idea of writing a letter to Stalin "about the way they feel about him in Soviet prisons. Oh, his name was surrounded with such radiance!" (In the prison cell, to cheer them up, she read to fellow prisoners her poem about Stalin.)[112]

What connected Druskin and Berggol'ts was, of course, the experience of danger and fear. But there was also something else: literature. Indeed, Druskin and Berggol'ts dreamed a "dream of their culture": Raskolnikov's dream.[113] This dream is memorable to every Russian reader: the old woman Raskolnikov has murdered comes to him in a dream. Taking his axe, he strikes her one blow, then another, bends down to peep into her face and turns cold with horror: the old woman is shaking with noiseless laughter. He begins hitting her on the head with all his force, but the old woman, teasing and mocking him, will not die. For Druskin, this episode held special significance: the image of Raskolnikov's old woman was elaborated by his friend Daniil Kharms in his absurdist story "The Old Woman" ("Starukha"), which features the menacing old woman who intrudes into a room in a Soviet communal apartment, just asking to be killed or kicked.[114]

In his dream, Druskin sees himself in the situation of Raskolnikov, who hoped to benefit mankind by murdering one horrible old woman, a pawnbroker, and expropriating her capital. (A common reading is to view Raskolnikov's act as an allegory of socialist revolution.) But while in her dream, Berggol'ts, like Raskolnikov, murders the old woman, Druskin seeks another way out: "She was repulsive and was granted the ability to kill. But I already knew what to do." In fact, as a reader of Dostoevsky and as a subject of a socialist state, even in his dream Druskin knows what *not* to do: violence does not pay. But, taken the specific situation in which he finds himself in the dream, Druskin's dream also says something else: armed resistance to terror does not pay either (it only brings destruction).

It is ironic that Druskin, who had effectively hidden from the social world, shared dreams with his contemporaries, with whom he shared the experiences of the terror, as well as a reading list. His dreams implicate him in the life of the community. The dream of the ropes seems to have told Druskin—in the voice of the "head murderer"—that he too was entangled in the common net. (At least this is how, taking a cue from his diary, I read this dream.)

STALIN'S DREAM

Writing of the dreams of the Nazi terror collected by Charlotte Beradt, Reinhart Koselleck comments: "We don't know the dreams of the enthusiasts, the victors—they dreamed as well, but hardly anyone knows how the content of their dreams related to the visions of those who were crushed by these temporary victors."[115] In the Russian case, we know some of the dreams of enthusiasts.[116] And we happen to know of at least one victor's dream related to the visions of those who were crushed: Stalin's dream. The story can be reconstructed from the diary of Elena Sergeevna Bulgakova (1893–1970), the last wife of the writer Mikhail Afanas'evich Bulgakov (1891–1940). I will relate it from her perspective.

On July 3, 1939, Elena Bulgakova recorded in her diary:

July 3 [1939]. Khmelev called on the phone yesterday morning—he asked to hear the play. His tone of voice was excited and happy: finally, a play by M. A. will once again be performed at the Theater! and so on.

In the evening, Khmelev, Kalish'ian [MKhAT's director], and Ol'ga [Ol'ga Bokshanskaia, E. B.'s sister] came over to our house. Misha read several scenes out loud.

Then we had supper, followed by long conversations. We talked about the play, about MKhAT [the Moscow Art Theater], about the system. Everyone went home when the sun was already rising. Khmelev told us a story. Once, Stalin said to him: you play Aleksei's part quite well. I even have dreams about your small black mustache (Turbin's). I can't forget that.[117]

The new play is Bulgakov's *Batum*, written for the MKhAT: it featured the young Stalin as the main hero. The actor Nikolai Khmelev, well known as Alexei Turbin in Bulgakov's enormously successful *Days of the Turbins* (*Dni Turbinykh*), was supposed to play the role of Stalin. By writing a play about Stalin (set as Christ, thinly disguised), Bulgakov hoped to protect himself from the terror, which had devastated his immediate circle. For several years now, one after another, his friends and enemies in the theater world had been removed from the public domain. Elena Bulgakova regularly noted news and rumors about such arrests in her diary. The Bulgakovs felt themselves under constant threat.

Whatever Bulgakov himself might have felt about his new play, his leading actor was enthralled by the project. After the reading, Khmelev wrote to his wife:

> I visited Bulgakov, heard him read his play about Stalin—great! It may turn everything upside down! I am still under the impression, and under the spell, of this work.
>
> On August 25, Bulgakov is going to submit the play in its finished form to MKhAT. They claim that I should play Stalin. We'll see.
>
> All of this is tempting, incredibly interesting, complicated, devilishly [*d'iavol'ski*] difficult, a huge responsibility, joy, and frightening![118]

Khmelev's list covers the whole range of emotions—from temptation to joy to fear—that Stalin usually evoked in his subjects. And what could offer a more intimate connection to the leader than playing his role in a drama on stage?

In the end, the idea of saving oneself by writing a play about Stalin failed miserably. After initial encouragement, the play was suddenly dismissed at Stalin's personal order when the work was already in full swing. This failure dealt a final blow to Bulgakov: the collapse of this morally questionable enterprise is believed to have precipitated his death on March 10, 1940.

But in July 1939 Elena Bulgakova still looked up to Stalin, hoping that his personal intervention would lead to the improvement of her husband's precarious position in Soviet literature, theater, and society. On March 14, 1937, she confided her daydreams to her diary: "I was constantly thinking about Stalin and wishing that he would take care of Misha and that our fate would change."[119] (This entry does not appear in the version of the diary she prepared for archivization, if not publication, in the 1950s and 1960s.)[120] Her desire was not unreasonable. A patron of the arts, Stalin had intervened in Bulgakov's life on several occasions, and it was his personal liking for Bulgakov's controversial play about the civil war, *Days of the Turbins*, that assured its continued running. Stalin's frequent appearances in the theater audience provoked wild enthusiasm and raised expectations. (In her diary, Elena Bulgakova faithfully noted each of these occasions.) More than once Mikhail Bulgakov addressed Stalin in a letter. On one occasion (in 1930), Stalin responded to Bulgakov's appeal with a phone call (the story became a legend among the artistic intelligentsia).[121]

So, why did Stalin dream of Turbin? He attended performances of Bulgakov's play at least fifteen times.[122] The mustache Nikolai Khmelev wore in the role of the charming and lovable White Guard officer Aleksei Turbin, who submits to the historical necessity of the victory of the Reds, was not unlike Stalin's own famous mustache (his central symbolic attribute, played up in Stalin's cult).[123] Perhaps this is why Stalin dreamed of Khmelev-Turbin? In any case, we know that the Khmelev-Turbin of Bulgakov's play held a strange fascination for Stalin. When Khmelev, who played Stalin's favorite Aleksei Turbin, was chosen to play Stalin in Bulgakov's new play, this made Khmelev-Turbin and Stalin doubles.

Perhaps this is why Elena Bulgakova was so taken by the image she reported in her diary: Stalin dreaming of Turbin's black mustache. This dream reads as an emblem of the fateful relationship between the intelligentsia and power: locked together, they looked at each other as if in a mirror. No wonder they dreamed of each other.

CONCLUDING REMARKS

Like other dreams, the Soviet dream stories articulate basic uncertainties of living: not knowing one's future; not knowing where the dead are; not knowing what one thinks or knows or feels; not knowing what is real and what is not real. But other meanings and functions of these dreams are peculiar and specific to the historical and social situation, which is clearly evident in the way Soviet people recorded and preserved specific dreams, and made them public. We have seen that, while not every dreamer knew how to interpret them, every dreamer wanted to ascribe political reference and historical relevance to his or her dreams, and not only to the dreams of anxiety and fear but also to those of desire.

Whatever else they mean, politicized dreams signify the irresistible penetration of the terror into the most intimate domains of people's lives. For the dreamers themselves, as well as for their readers, such dreams signal the futility of any form of escape. In this way, dreams may have served as instruments of the terror. (In writing about the dreams of the Nazi terror, Beradt described, and emphasized, such an effect.) But dreams also allowed Soviet subjects to see themselves as actors on the social and historical scene, even to confront Stalin personally (recall Arzhilovsky's rape dream). (The dreams from Hitler's Germany collected by Beradt do not display such historical subconsciousness.) Dreams expressed the Soviet people's concern for their future, playing with the possibilities and dangers of participation in the new regime (Arzhilovsky's construction-site dream). Dreams also served as both indicators and instruments of integration into the regime by way of transformation of the self (Prishvin's dream of the flying car). As such, dreams (like some dreams in Beradt's German collection) could predict the future: people dreamed of what they could do to adapt before they actually did it; or, like Druskin, they dreamed of what they could *not* do to adapt.

Note the enduring strength of the prophetic theory of dreams among Soviet people, even highly educated ones, which, modernity notwithstanding, offers a rapprochement of sorts between the intelligentsia and the people. After all, Soviet people lived under conditions of extreme anxiety and they shared a belief in total meaning (recall Meletinskii's dreams, and the Ivanovs, father and son). Note that some dreams did come true because they became social facts (Arzhilovsky's dream of his future arrest used by the NKVD).

Dreams also played out alternative possibilities for self, other, community, and reality. Consider Druskin's dreams in which the dead are alive, and the dream is reality. While some dream stories offered an alternative reality, others questioned the reality of the world of the terror, suggesting that—structured like a dream—it might be just as surreal (Kaverin's dreams).

Dreams of Stalin's subjects were infused with fear, and people faithfully recorded such dreams. As may be expected, dreams, and other symptoms of trauma, served to keep victims in prison long after release. Dreams also maintained fear and guilt in those who escaped prison (Kaverin's dreams). Moreover, long after Stalin's death, dreams could place a person who did not really live in Stalin's time under the rule of terror (Grobman's dream). In this sense dreams work both as indicators of people's reactions to the terror and as instruments of the terror (even extending emotions from the terror into the future, until at least the 1970s).

When Soviet people included dreams about the terror in their personal narratives, they made all of these meanings clear. But this was not all: they also hoped that, as a means of self-expression, telling their dreams would achieve different goals than telling other stories. Within larger narratives of self, dreams marked the experience that remained a mystery and that could not be properly represented in words (this is how Chukovskaia, Prishvin, and Kaverin used their dreams). Indeed, while some were able to convey the terror experience through works of literature, leaving a documentary account did not prove easy, even for professional writers. In this situation, they resorted to reporting their dreams as fictions—dramas for which they acted as authors, directors, players, prompters, spectators, and critics (to echo Jung's definition of dreams). Making their dreams, and their comments on these dreams, a part of their personal narratives, Soviet diarists and memoirists put themselves in the position of onlookers, observing the contradictory emotions and ambivalent judgments that overtook them. Moreover, dreams seemed to offer a mode of representation best suited to deal with the terror. Thus (as the writer Kaverin made clear), the dream experience enacted the subjectivity that rested on the uncertainty of agency and on the modality that fused possibility, impossibility, and necessity—something that the grammatical resources of language, even the Russian language, could barely grasp.

It might not be an exaggeration to say that in totalitarian societies, as in primitive cultures and psychoanalytic communities, dreams carry an additional weight of meaning. Under the Soviet regime dreaming was a social act with specific existential, practical, and political consequences (and not only because the security organs listened to people's dreams). Relating one's dreams to another is an essential part of human intimacy, and people in Stalinist Russia also shared their dreams. Discovering that they had similar dreams, Soviet dreamers received confirmation of the social quality of even their innermost experience, and, moreover, of its historical and mythic (perhaps even cosmic?) quality. (Recall the eschatological dreams of the Akhmatova circle.) In the community of the Soviet intelligentsia, tightly linked by ties of friendship, intermarriage, and sexual exchange—as well as by exchange of literary references—dreams served as a powerful myth-making and community-forging mechanism.

When, at and after the end of the Soviet regime, such dreams appeared in print, they were open to a larger community of readers. For the community torn by the terror, dreaming and sharing those dreams provides connective tissue between insiders and outsiders, friends and foes, the survivors and the dead, and—perhaps most important—between past and present, in their historical quality.

In the first years of the twenty-first century, critical comments about the exaggerated historical consciousness of the Soviet people have started appearing in print in post-Soviet Russia. The strongest of such comments concern dreams—the fact that history has pervaded people's dreams. In 2001 Alexander Piatigorsky (born in 1929), a philosopher and scholar of Buddhism and semiotics who lives in London, published a book of stories based, as he claims, on his and other people's dreams, *Stories and Dreams*.[124] The main theme of Piatigorsky's dream stories is history. To be left out of history (the book claims) was what the Russian people born between the 1910 and the 1930s feared most—more than the interrogations and the camps. This fear surfaced in their dreams. In his spirited review of Piatigorsky's *Stories and Dreams,* the literary scholar Ilya Kalinin (born in 1975) seems to read the book against the grain. These dream stories, the young critic claims, may actually help the people to "wake up from the nightmare of History." The terrible dreams pervaded by historical themes were borne in the consciousness of those "for whom the interrogations, the camps, and the war" meant that they were "active participants or victims of the common and objective historical process." And for these people the loss of historical consciousness has proved to be even more traumatic than the painful historical experiences of the past. Indeed, with the end of the Soviet history, when people's lives moved from the shared "historical" sphere into the individual "biographical" sphere, they seem to have lost their relevance. Conclusion: thinking of history as a "place" in which we all live—this is a posttraumatic nightmare that haunts the Russians even today.[125] The question arises: would today's authors wake up from the "nightmare of History"?

CONCLUSION

Throughout Soviet history, people have felt a need to record what happened to them in their private lives. The demise of the Soviet regime—coinciding with the end of the century—prompted an urge to unveil these personal records. Unpublished (in some cases, privately known) accounts went to press. Those who had not yet written hastened to tell their stories. The living worked on behalf of the dead, collecting, assembling, and publishing extant personal documents. Diverse authors and their publishers have come to construct a converging corpus: the annals of private life, or intimacy, under Soviet power. Different as they are, these accounts describe human lives—families, partnerships, homes, biographies, memories—shaped by violent historical forces, focusing on Stalin's terror and the Second World War (which some experienced vicariously) as defining moments in the Soviet experience.

Whether or not their authors blame the state (most do), diaries and memoirs detail the conditions of state-produced death, separation, and coerced presence (not only in prison cells and trenches, but also in families locked in single rooms of crowded communal apartments), state-produced deformation of the body and mind (achieved by means ranging from starvation, combat, and torture to restricted hygienic and sexual practices to the loaded idiom of Sovietspeak, film, and television). Self-conscious texts written by intellectuals may go so far as to imply that the Soviet regime created an emotional economy of duplicity, deception, and ambiguity (promoted by the need to hide one's thoughts and feelings and to conceal one's parentage, ethnicity, and partnerships, or to form new loyalties, identities, and partnerships without forsaking old ones). Produced from within this economy, most texts (even naive ones) demonstrate how this was achieved.

At least this is how I read these documents: they speak to me about Soviet history as a force that shaped fundamental living forms, such as the triangular structure of the nuclear family and the domestic order of a family home, which—as not only psychoanalysis, but novels too, lead us to believe—give rise to a specific sense of self. What comes through in these documents is a sense of self derived from the experience of danger, fear, deprivation, and pressure (even for those who do not blame the Soviet state); and a self worthy to be submitted as historical material, presented—depending on temperament and literary skill—as a literary monument, a document for the archive, a set of notes, or vignettes.

Concerned with the survival of their established individual and collective identities, today's authors construct on paper both a tangible self and an extended community ("the intelligentsia"), projecting an imaginary continuity of the tradition from imperial to Soviet to post-Soviet Russia. Professional intellectuals make a point of bringing the records of "simple people," even the almost illiterate, into the same space. Some claim exclusion, in full awareness of the dominant presence of others. Whether they have been written or only edited by professional intellectuals, such documents are produced by people who were brought up with acute historicist consciousness (Hegelian, then Marxist), exposed to various forms of apocalypticism (if not firsthand, then through their research or reading in Russian and other intellectual history), at times, infected with the modernist zeal for self-creation or with an internalized drive for self-surveillance, and, in some prominent cases, professionally trained to read the past as a text. Quite a few of the Soviet life stories in this book are underwritten by a peculiar merger of philosophical historicism, secular and religious apocalypticism, the communal ethos of the Russian intelligentsia, and the methodological pathos of literary or cultural scholarship. Some projects are inspired by a desire to redefine the role of intellectuals and the structure of memoirs in the post-Soviet or postmodern world, consciously trying to break free from the general pattern. All of them rely on one another.

And what about those who did *not* write diaries and memoirs? What does their silence signify? We could have learned a lot from those who chose to remain silent. Perhaps they did not share in the idea of History with a capital H? Or they valued privacy above all? Or did they simply know too much?

EPILOGUE

In his memoirs, Mikhail Viktorovich Ardov (the son of Akhmatova's intimate friends, who observed the literary community from early childhood) relates the following episode from the late 1960s, which involves the pillars of the nonconformist literary intelligentsia:

> Meilakh once came from Leningrad to Moscow.[1] I recall how we dropped by to see Nikolai Ivanovich Khardzhiev. Gershtein was there. The host sat at his desk, and Emma Grigor'evna on a chair in front of him. The guest said: "It's a matter of moral obligation that you write memoirs."
> At this point, Khardzhiev, who had so far been entirely immobile, promptly wrapped his fingers in an obscene gesture of denial and threw them into his interlocutor's face.
> To this day, neither Meilakh nor I have been able to forget this "silent scene."[2]

Nikolai Ivanovich Khardzhiev (1903–1996), who could have revealed much, died faithful to his promise to remain silent. But his cohort did not forget this scene. There is irony in the fact that his silent, obscene refusal to write memoirs has now become a public memorialized fact. I will take the liberty to conclude on this note of irony.

APPENDIX: RUSSIAN TEXTS

Listed below are the original Russian texts of quotations found in the book in the English translation. Appendix entries are keyed to the first words of quotations.

PART I: MEMOIRS AND DIARIES PUBLISHED AT THE END OF THE SOVIET EPOCH: AN OVERVIEW

the voices of the people on behalf of whom…
 голос человека, за которого всегда писал интеллектуал. (note 6)

during one's lifetime…
 дневник при жизни нужно хранить в столе. (note 10)

The party solemnly proclaims…
 Партия торжественно провозглашает, что нынешнее поколение людей будет жить при коммунизме»,—сказал Никита Сергеевич. […] Планы выполняются у нас даже раньше срока. (note 13, [p. 176])

life—it is but a collection…
 жизнь, она и есть коллекционирование будущих воспоминаний. (note 19)

resembles a diary rather than a memoir…
 напоминает скорее дневники, чем воспоминания, настоящее и прошедшее тесно переплетаются. (note 28)

To whom is the diary addressed?
 Кому адресован дневник? […] Себе самому. Это разговор с собой, с глазу на глаз […] Повторяю, ведя свои записи, я не думал о читателе,

как, скажем, К. Симонов, который явно готовил дневник на вынос. (note 29)

Many characters are alive and well...
Большинство действующих лиц—благополучно живы и здравствуют в России и за ее пределами; а число упомянутых в книге явно превышает число ее экземпляров. […] Изданная лет через—дцать эта книжка стала бы интересна лишь узкому кругу исследователей...Ныне—встретилась со своими героями, стала фактом их жизни, вступила с ними в диалог. (note 31)

we read memoirs keenly...
Мы читаем мемуары внимательно и с напряжением, но едва ли это означает, что нас так интересует чужая жизнь. Скорее, собственная. (note 33)

This book is gripping...
Книга захватывает, ибо в жизни, во взглядах автора мы узнаем самих себя. Кажется, что и думаем-то и пишем мы сами. (note 35)

you see, you hear […] this apartment...
видишь, слышишь […] и эту квартиру […] Пунина […] и Смирновых за стеной. (note 36)

the reader doesn't read your books, but lives in them...
читатель не читает Ваши книги, а живет в них, он где-то незримо, совсем рядом присутствует, он *видит* все. (note 36)

Inspired by Herzen's words...
Воодушевленный словами Герцена, что мемуары может писать всякий, потому что н и к т о не обязан их читать, я собрал воедино куски воспоминаний, написанных в разное время. (note 43)

We talked about their complex and difficult relationship...
говорили […] о сложных и трудных их отношениях […] как говорят об очень дорогих людях, которым надо помочь. (note 51)

the intelligentsia at a turning point in history.
интеллигенция в переломные моменты истории. (note 52, [p. 291])

not a historical monograph, but the reflection of history...
«Былое и думы» не историческая монография, а отражение истории в человеке, *случайно* попавшемся на ее дороге. (note 55)

The wheels of history rolled across the family hearth...
По семейному очагу прошли колеса истории. Можно ли было в таком случае дать читателю истинное представление о пережитой драме, не рассказав предварительно о колесах истории? (note 56)

Having seen Napoleon, the young Hegel...
Молодой Гегель, увидев Наполеона, говорил, что видел, как в город въехал на белом коне абсолютный дух. Я помню разговоры Бор. Мих. Энгельгарда. Совсем в том же, гегелевском, роде он говорил о всемирно-историческом гении, который в 30-х годах пересек нашу жизнь (он признавал, что это ее не облегчило). (note 58)

Time has now acquired a high-speed automobile...
Время обзавелось теперь быстроходной машиной. [...] Многие из моих сверстников оказались под колесами времени. (note 63)

fix my time...
закрепить свое время, своих друзей, свой дом, а значит свою жизнь. (note 64)

I will start with what we all know...
Начну с самого что ни на есть общеизвестного. В 1956 году произошло знаменательное событие, на какое-то время определившее многие жизненные процессы—XX съезд партии, на котором в открытую заговорили о культе личности Сталина. [...] Что касается меня лично, пятьдесят шестой год—год начала моей судьбы. Весной я заканчивал школу-студию МХАТ, в это же время появилась на экранах моя первая картина...(note 66)

Smirnova lived through the years of Stalin's terror relatively safely...
Годы сталинского террора Смирнова пережила сравнительно благополучно, была советским режимом обласкана и сама от служения ему не уклонялась. [...] И кто бы мог подумать, что за всем этим стоит трудная доля девочки-сироты, дочери погибшего колчаковского офицера, о чем, конечно, приходилось умалчивать и что делало ее, как ни странно, существом полуподпольным. (note 67)

My mother, Zoia Nikolaevna Toporova...
Моя мать, Зоя Николаевна Топорова, умерла во сне ночью с 16 на 17 июня 1997 года после тяжелой ссоры со мной накануне. Через несколько дней–22 июня–ей исполнилось бы 88 лет. [...] родители сошлись в войну–в блокаду–и никогда не жили вместе: у отца была другая семья. [...] [мать] записала в метрику фиктивное отчество

Леонидович [...] Леонидом звали [...] единственного человека, которого она любила по-настоящему,—питерского писателя Леонида Радищева, попавшего в лагерь перед войной и вернувшегося только в 1956 году,—и таким образом мать как бы вовлекла его в процесс моего рождения. [...] Радищев был, разумеется, литературный псевдоним, настоящая фамилия его была Лившиц. (note 68)

Me and my husband lived happily...
Жили мы с мужем очень хорошо, но когда началася война в 1941 году она нас розлучила навсегда. и началися мои страдания. (page 17)

The intimate man is the good man...
Хорош интимный человек. Но существует общественный человек: это трус. Все хорошее—это частный человек, плохое—общественный. (note 72)

simply life that is written into the Soviet period...
просто жизнь, которая вписана в советский период истории. (note 76)

was it worth turning a diary into the *Diary*...
стоило ли превращать дневник в «Дневник», отдавая его в печать? (footnote, page 21n)

Communal apartments, homelessness and vagrancy...
Коммунальные квартиры, бездомность, и бесприютность придавала течению серьезных и несерьезных романов нечистую поспешность. Отсюда немало настоящих трагедий, не говоря уже о все том же страхе. [...] интимная жизнь была тогда более всего «политическим фактом». (note 81)

I remember a shaky streetcar ride...
Помню, как я трясся в тот страшный день в трамвае, и люди подавлено молчали с раскрытыми газетами в руках. (note 84)

fights at the TsDL, drunken debauchery...
драки в ЦДЛ, пьяный разгул, альков [...] филолог обнажается иначе [...] и читатель краснее так, как будто читает описание постельной сцены. (note 86)

I am writing this text with a degree of sincerity...
Я пишу этот текст с шокирующих некоторых искренностью и подробностью, потому что отношусь к первому поколению, родившемуся

без Сталина. И это поколение пока сделало довольно мало попыток рассказать о себе честным языком. Надеюсь, что книга не столько обо мне, сколько о времени; эдакий стриптиз на фоне второй половины двадцатого века, который, слава богу, уже кончился. (note 89)

I simply started calling everyone...
Я стала просто всех обзванивать. Дозвонилась до Светки Ивановой. И говорю:—«Светка, меня вызывают!» Она говорит, чтобы подождала секундочку, и пошла к Коме за советом. (note 94)

I must confess...
Каюсь: я рыдала не только над монументальной исторической трагедией, но прежде всего над собой. Что сделал этот человек со мной, с моей душой, с моими детьми, с моей мамой. [...] Ведь они начисто забыли о том странном факте, что Генералиссимус сотворен из той же самой несовершенной плоти, что и остальные грешные... (note 104)

the god who died...
Мне не было жаль бога, который скончался от инсульта в возрасте семидесяти трех лет, как будто он не бог, а обыкновенный смертный... (note 105)

I did not love Stalin...
Я не любил Сталина, но долго верил в него, и я его боялся. (note 105)

—What did you believe in?...
—Во что ты верила [...] До 1953 года я верила во все, вплоть до «заговора врачей-убийц». Горько оплакивала смерть Сталина. [...] Мною смерть Сталина воспринималась и как горе и как конец. (note 107)

Many of our contemporaries...
Многие наши современники начинают новое летоисчисление с 5-го марта 1953 года—со дня смерти Сталина. (note 109)

How unfree was his thought!
Как несвободна была его мысль! Даже когда он писал в стол, как пишут завещания. (note 118)

It's not up to me or my generation...
Не мне и не моему поколению судить Симонова, но вся его деятельность была настолько точным индикатором взаимодействия власти и литературы, что поневоле о ней приходится вспоминать. (note 119)

If a Soviet man claims...
Но если советский человек утверждает, что не знал о терроре 30-х годов,—не верьте ему! Знали все, и вина за террор, за миллионы погибших людей лежит на нас всех [...] как вел себя народ? Что делала интеллигенция, его духовный авангард? И мы не только не покаялись до сих пор, но даже не ощущаем потребности в покаянии. (note 120)

It's impossible to understand how...
Невозможно понять, что все, о чем она вспоминает, происходило в той самой библиотеке, где в спецхран отправлялись целые пласты литературы, где читателя последовательно и сознательно оставляли в неведении или создавали у него искаженное представление об исторических событиях, науке и культуре. В главной библиотеке Союза, вносившей важный вклад в дело культуры, но в то же время, именно в следствие своей центральной роли, служившей проводником всего того, что проделывала с ней власть. Все мы, работавшие там, в той или иной степени к этому причастны, и признаться в этом больно, но необходимо. (page 32)

Now I think that *then*, we...
Я думаю *теперь*, что *тогда* мы, во всяком случае я, находил в официальном партийном объяснении всего происходившего некую точку опоры, позволявшую не утерять [...] веру. (note 122)

I am still nauseated when I recall...
Мне и сейчас тошно вспоминать, что все следствие мое было построено тщательнейшим образом на «любовных» мотивах, на доносах бывшего мужа моей жены (Моисеенко), давно поклявшегося из мести «снова» засадить меня в тюрьму, а также на показаниях одной дамы, переписка которой со мной через «до востребования» попала в МГБ. В дело была также приплетена Б. Чистова, жена моего друга, которая уже ни в чем не была виновата. Причем пытались шантажировать и ее (безуспешно, так как ей нечего было бояться), и ее мужа. У мужа не только пытались вызвать ревность и мстительность ко мне, но (что было гораздо серьезнее) напоминали ему о том, что он был в плену во время войны, и грозили открыть против него самостоятельное дело. [...] Очные ставки были для свидетелей и для меня взаимно очень неприятны по мотивам психологического свойства. (note 128)

Ira referred to the investigator...
Ира называла следователя не иначе, как Порфирий Петрович. [...] Главным козырем были письма Виктора к другой женщине. Ира прочла—и глядя в неповторимый почерк мужа, твердо сказала, что

письма поддельные. Порфирий Петрович решил переждать. Он был уверен, что чувство оскорбленной гордости сработает (там было несколько обидных строк). (note 131)

But this is what I want to tell you...
Но вот что я хочу вам сказать. Когда его взяли, меня вызвали к следователю и показали мне пачку писем—его писем к другой женщине. Я прочла только одно—больше не надо было. Я думала, что умру. Что было делать? (note 132)

With the end of the Soviet epoch...
С концом советской эпохи и прошедшего в России под ее знаком столетия то, что писалось для себя, потеряло интимность, стало документом. (note 135)

We testify at the trial of history...
Мы даем показания на суде истории—который отнюдь не отодвинут в отдаленное, непредставимое будущее, а идет ежедневно, не прерываясь. (note 137)

[The memoirist] carries on his own self the indelible sign...
[мемуарист] несет на самом себе нестираемый его [времени] знак. (note 137)

The trial of the Communist Party...
Суд над КПСС может состояться не в судебных заседаниях, а на типографских страницах—это самоотчет, самоанализ всех тех, кто жил и действовал в советское время. [...] Да, я уверена: каждый, выступающий нынче в печати, каждый, чувствующий социальную ответственность, должен попробовать написать честную автобиографию, свой очерк пережитого времени. (note 138)

Possibly my testimony...
может быть, и мои показания, если их огласят на процессе, окажутся не вполне бесполезными—порой незначительные детали влияют на прения сторон. (note 140)

mortal like all of us...
смертный, как и все [...] отчет [...] он будет давать бесконечно. (note 143)

to register oneself in history means...
«прописать» себя в истории—значит наделить свою жизнь большим объемом смыслов, чем умещается в сюжете единичной судьбы,

продлить эту жизнь за границы физического существования. (note 148)

The future is more and more densely inhabited...
все плотнее будущее заселяется образами прошлого, все гуще становится этот рукотворный мир. (note 149)

A person from the masses...
массовый человек не только укоренился в текущей жизни, но и рвется в будущее, в это последнее прибежище человека уникального. (note 150)

the return of life to...
возвращении жизни останкам отжившего, в восстановлении умерших, по их произведениям. (note 151)

The Institute must represent...
Институт должен преставлять из себя как бы графическую память человечества из поколения в поколение [...] вместе с тем Институт должен быть международным адресным столом, где будет зафиксирован всякий, так или иначе отметивший свой жизненный путь. (note 155)

"History is always resurrection, and not a trial." N. F. Fedorov.
История—всегда воскрешение, а не суд. Н.Ф. Федоров. (note 157)

Virtual space is practically infinite...
Виртуальное пространство практически безгранично, а новые формы консервации информации позволяют ставить вопрос о долговечном или практически вечном ее хранении. (note 158)

the first to follow this path...
первыми по этому пути двинулись граждане США. Ныне в Интернете свои воспоминания и пожелания потомкам может разместить каждый гражданин этой страны. (note 158)

The next step in the resolution of the problem...
Очередной шаг решения проблемы воскрешения и бессмертия может быть сделан уже сейчас и он может быть начат с тотального сбора всей человеческой информации, созданной на планете Земля. (note 158)

By the laws of nature...
По законам природы жизнь человеческая не может длиться вечно. Если жизнь человека имеет трагический конец, то почему человечество в целом не может иметь трагический конец? (note 160)

I started remembering myself...
 Стал вспоминать о себе, писать книгу о человеке во времени, а получились наброски, зарисовки русских и иных интеллигентов на переломе. (note 162)

Nowadays many grieve...
 Сейчас многие грустят, что интеллигенция уходит. Да не уходит она! Просто становится иной. (note 162)

[Vignettes]—these are reminiscences...
 [Виньетки]—это воспоминания, построенные на каком-то малом, необязательном материале [...] с претензией на изящество и некоторое обобщение [...] в них нет претензии на могучее документирование исторических фактов или хотя бы адекватное отражение моей жизни или профессиональной деятельности [...] В них отделано каждое слово. (note 167)

I was born in the year...
 Я родился в год прихода Гитлера к власти, завершения Беломора и самого страшного голода на Украине. В Москве тоже с едой было плохо. Картошку мама в рот не брала, жила на одной брюкве:
 —Ты у меня брюквенный... (note 169)

This thread was founded in memory of Lidiia Ginzburg...
 Эта лента создана в память о Лидии Гинзбург
 (1902–1990). Человеку «широко известному в узких кругах».
 Умной, беспощадно честной.
 Пережившей многое и многих.
 Содержание ленты—цитаты из книг и записей Лидии Гинзбург. (page 51)

mama's gone...
 Весь день читала Лидию Гинзбург (и—страшно подумать—что целый день моей жизни, а также будущий ее ход (потому что о ЛГ я теперь буду неотступно думать какое-то время, рекомендовать ее своим друзьям....) подвергся такому изменению из-за случайно попавшейся мне на глаза цитате из ЛГ в коммьюнити ru_history). А учебник по Ср. векам ч.2 так и лежит по левую от меня руку. (page 52)

I'm reading Lidiia Ginzburg's diaries.
 Читаю дневники Лидии Гинзбург. (page 52)

I'm sitting at home, ill, reading Lidiia Ginzburg.
Дома сижу, болею, читаю Лидию Гинзбург. (page 53)

I read Lidiia Ginzburg at the dacha...
Читал на даче Лидию Гинзбург, мемуары. там о теме старости интересно...(page 53)

I wouldn't mind getting up early...
меня совершенно не обламывает встать рано утром, прошлепать босиком до кухни и заварить зеленый чай с жасмином, человеку, который мне симпатичен. Меня даже не обламывает сидеть в течении 2-х часов, держа на коленях Его голову, одной рукой перелистывая страницы книги Лидии Гинзбург, а другой—касаться его лица и длинных волос, которые как ручей, разлились по моей кровати. (page 53)

Of all things—I spotted Lidiia Iakovlevna Ginzburg on LJ...
Надо же—в ЖЖ [Живой Журнал] засветилась сама Лидия Яковлевна Гинзбург. Я рада. Но вместо того, чтобы заморачиваться экзистенциальными проблемами, я зачем-то прочитала, что *в доме Лидии Яковлевны не переводились водка, селедка и яйца под майонезом.* (page 53)

☺ And so—I can be just like Ginzburg now...
☺ В общем, буду я сейчас совсем как Гинзбург.
А вообще—мне сложно обсуждать такое, хорошо что можно тихо про это читать. (page 53)

Instead of writing, I read.
Вместо того чтобы писать—я читаю. (note 172)

our Lidiia Ginzburg. That is, now I'll be...
наша Лидия Гинзбург. То есть, я теперь буду такая ученая еврейская старуха. Вчистую освобожденная от давания...(note 172)

April has brought me again...
Апрель опять на несколько дней привел меня в тот же пригород. (page 54)

The shortest night of the year...
Самая короткая ночь в году подходит к концу...

Хорошо и счастливо работается только тогда, когда работа заливает сознание. Я люблю писать по ночам, потому что ночью теряется рассеивающее ощущение движения времени. (page 55)

Two weeks ago Lidia_Ginzburg...
Недели две назад Лидия_Гинзбург писала в ленту, как ценны ночные часы вываливанием вовне хронологии—любимый мой юзер, каждое слово исходит заряженное тяжелым качеством... (page 55)

PART II: TEXTS: CLOSE READINGS
CHAPTER 1: LIDIIA CHUKOVSKAIA'S DIARY OF ANNA AKHMATOVA'S LIFE: "INTIMACY AND TERROR"

To write down our conversations
Записывать наши разговоры? Не значит ли это рисковать ее жизнью? Не писать о ней ничего? Это тоже было бы преступно. (1: 12)

Yesterday I was at Anna Andreevna's on business* (9).
Вчера я была у Анны Андреевны по делу. (1: 17)

The general appearance of the room was one of neglect, ruin...
Общий вид комнаты—запустение, развал. У печки кресло без ноги, ободранное, с торчащими пружинами. Пол не метен. Красивая мебель—резной стул, зеркало в гладкой бронзовой раме, лубки на стенах—не красят, наоборот, еще более подчеркивают убожество. (1: 17)

On 19 September, I left Nikolai Nikolaevich...
19 сентября я ушла от Николая Николаевича. Мы шестнадцать лет прожили вместе. Но я даже не заметила на *этом* фоне. (1: 17)

I can't look at those eyes...
Я не могу видеть этих глаз. Вы заметили? Они как бы отдельно существуют, отдельно от лиц. (1: 22)

My neighbor doesn't love her boy...
Мальчика своего моя соседка не любит. Бьет его. Когда она берет веревку и принимается за него, я ухожу в ванную. Попробовала я один раз с ней говорить—она оттолкнула меня. (1: 22)

What's new? asked Anna Andreevna...
Что у вас?—спросила Анна Андреевна, вскочив с дивана и приблизив к моему лицу расширенные глаза. (1: 22)

This was in Khardzhiev's tiny room...
> Это в крошечной комнате Харджиева, где-то у черта на куличиках, я ехала туда часа два. У Николая Ивановича холодно. Анна Андреевна сидит на диване, накинув пальто на плечи. Пьем из каких-то кружек чай, а потом из них же вино. Николай Иванович небритый, желтый, прислушивается к шагам за стеной—к шагам соседей. (1: 22)

The torture chamber...
> Застенок, поглотивший материально целые кварталы города, а духовно—наши помыслы во сне и наяву, выкрикивавший собственную ремесленно сработанную ложь с каждой газетной полосы, из каждого репродуктора, требовал от нас в то же время, чтобы мы не поминали имени его всуе, даже в четырех стенах, один на один. [...] Окруженный немотой, застенок желал оставаться и всевластным и несуществующим зараз. (1: 12–13)

women stood in line...
> в очередях женщины стояли молча или, шепчась, употребляли лишь неопределенные формы речи: «пришли», «взяли»; Анна Андреевна, навещая меня, читала мне стихи из «Реквиема» тоже шепотом, а у себя в Фонтанном Доме не решалась даже на шепот; внезапно, посреди разговора, она умолкала и, показав мне глазами на потолок и стены, брала клочок бумаги и карандаш; потом громко произносила что-нибудь светское: «хотите чаю?» или «вы очень загорели», потом исписывала клочок быстрым почерком и протягивала мне. Я прочитывала стихи и, запомнив, молча возвращала их ей. «Нынче такая ранняя осень»,—громко говорила Анна Андреевна и, чиркнув спичкой, сжигала бумагу над пепельницей. (1: 13)

It was a ritual...
> Это был обряд: руки, спичка, пепельница,—обряд прекрасный и горестный». (1: 13)

She felt silent. She performed the ritual.
> Умолкла. Совершила обряд. (1: 99)

Day by day, month by month, my fragmentary notes...
> С каждым днем, с каждым месяцем мои обрывочные записи становились все в меньшей степени воспроизведением моей собственной жизни, превращаясь в эпизоды из жизни Анны Ахматовой. [...] В том душевном состоянии, в котором я находилась в те годы,—оглушенном, омертвелом,—я сама все меньше казалась себе взаправду живою, а

моя недожизнь—заслуживающей описания. [...] К 1940 году записей о себе я уже не делала практически никогда, об Анне Андреевне писала все чаще и чаще... Судьба Ахматовой—нечто большее, чем даже ее собственная личность,—лепила тогда у меня на глазах из этой знаменитой и заброшенной, сильной и беспомощной женщины изваяние скорби, сиротства, гордыни, мужества. (1: 13–14)

"Come!"
«Приходите» [...] По телефону мне удалось довольно быстро условиться о шапке, шарфе, свитере. Все, кому я звонила, сразу, без расспросов, понимали все. «Шапка? Шапки нет, но не нужны ли рукавицы?» (1: 42)

everything ached...
Болело все: лицо, ноги, сердце, даже кожа на голове. (1: 63)

I presume I kept up the conversation very badly...
Я наверное очень плохо поддерживала разговор, потому что минут через десять она спросила:
—Вы, кажется, чем-то расстроены?
Я выговорила—не заплакав.
—Боже мой. Боже мой,—повторяла Анна Андреевна,—а я не знала [...] Боже мой!
Мне было пора за Люшей [дочь] к учительнице. Я ушла. (1: 63)

In those years...
В те годы Анна Ахматова жила, завороженная застенком, требующая от себя и от других неотступной памяти о нем, презирающая тех, кто вел себя так, будто его и нету. (1: 12)

The city went on living...
Город жил своей обычной жизнью: работал, учился, влюблялся, читал газеты, отдыхал, слушал радио, ходил в театр, в кино, в гости. Усердно справлял дни рождения друзей и близких. Семьями съезжался на «майские» и «ноябрьские». Весело встречал Новый год... Быть может, это и было самое страшное. (note 8)

The terrible backdrop...
Страшный фон не покидал сознание. Ходили в балет и в гости, играли в покер и отдыхали на даче те именно, кому утро приносило весть о потере близких, кто сами, холодея от каждого вечернего звонка, ждали гостей дорогих... Пока целы, заслонялись, отвлекались: дают—бери.

Отвлечению особенно способствовал летний отдых. [...] Летом 37-го много знакомых ленинградцев поселилось в чудесном лужском Затуленье. Мы там вкушали прелесть лесных озер и Оредежа с его лугами и берегом красной глины. В прогулках, сухопутных и водных, деятельно участвовала и С., у которой тогда сидела сестра в ожидании приговора. Психологически это было возможно в силу типовой ситуации.

Летом 38-го года мы с Жирмунскими и Гуковскими жили в деревне на Полтавщине. Там все еще было полно памятью о голоде, за собой в Ленинграде мы оставили разгром. Время мы проводили самым приятным образом. Совершали экскурсии на челнах, высаживаясь на каком-но необитаемом острове. Ездили на несколько дней в Полтаву с разными смешными дорожными происшествиями. Совесть в это времяпровождение нисколько не вмешивалась. Вероятно, потому, что ведь с каждым могло случиться. Вроде как на войне. (note 9)

The corridor of Punin's apartment...

Коридор пунинской квартиры, где стоит обеденный стол, а в конце за занавеской спит Лева, когда его пускают в этот дом... В коридоре «они», ей предъявляют ордер и спрашивают, где Гумилев. Она знает, что Николай Степанович спрятался у нее в комнате—последняя дверь из коридора налево. Она выводит из-за занавески сонного Леву и толкает его к чекистам: «Вот Гумилев». (note 18)

Strong nerves—

Крепкие нервы—самое отличительное свойство декадентов. Они могли, не сморгнув, выносить ситуации, невозможные для обыкновенного человека.

[Ахматова] могла годами обедать за одним столом с женой своего мужа (Анной Евгеньевной). Причем это отнюдь не был уравновешенный треугольник,—обедая, они не разговаривали друг с другом. (note 22)

I don't have anything against...

Против чужих мужей я не имею ничего—такое случается на каждом шагу, следовательно, это в порядке вещей. Ведь Ахматова отлично сказала про себя: «Чужих мужей вернейшая подруга и многих безутешная вдова». Худо, что они очутились вместе «под крышей Фонтанного Дома». Идиллия была придумана Пуниным, чтобы Ахматовой не пришлось хозяйничать, а ему не надрываться, добывая деньги на два дома. К тому же, жилищный кризис осложнял все разводы и любовные дела. Идиллия не состоялась—разводиться надо до конца. Вероятно, и отношения с Пуниным сложились бы гораздо лучше и проще, если бы не общая квартира. Главное в жизни советского гражданина—кусочек жилплощади. Недаром за жилплощадь совершалось столько преступлений. (note 23)

And you know how it all happened?
—И знаете, как это все было, как я ушла? Я сказала Анне Евгеньевне при нем: «давайте обменяемся комнатами». Ее это очень устраивало, и мы сейчас же начали перетаскивать вещички. Николай Николаевич молчал, потом, когда мы с ним оказались на минуту одни, произнес: «Вы бы еще хоть годик ко мной побыли». (1: 188)

The Punins have taken my kettle…
Пунины взяли мой чайник,—сказала мне Анна Андреевна,—ушли и заперли свои комнаты. Так я чаю и не пила. Ну Бог с ним. (1: 32)

It is noisy at our place…
Шумят у нас. У Пуниных пиршества, патефон до поздней ночи…(1: 26)

—Nikolai Nikolaevich keeps insisting…
—Николай Николаевич очень настаивает, чтобы я выехала.
—Обменяли бы комнату?
—Нет, просто выехала…Знаете, за последние два года я стала дурно думать о мужчинах. Вы заметили, *там* их почти нет…(1: 26)

The renowned poet, Anna Akhmatova, currently lives in Leningrad…
В Ленинграде в исключительно тяжелых материальных и жилищных условиях, живет известная поэтесса Ахматова. Вряд ли нужно говорить Вам о том, как несправедливо это по отношению к самой Ахматовой, которая при всем несоответствии ее поэтического дарования нашему времени, тем не менее была и остается крупнейшим поэтом предреволюционного времени, и какое неблагоприятное впечатление производит это не только на старую поэтическую интеллигенцию, но и на молодежь, немало учившуюся у Ахматовой.
Ахматова до сих пор не имеет ни одного метра собственной жилплощади. Она живет в комнате бывшего своего мужа, с которым она давно разошлась. Не надо доказывать, как это для нее унизительно. (1: 326)

I asked…
Я спросила ее, решилась ли она переехать ко мне.

—Нет. Николай Николаевич сейчас очень определенно напомнил мне мое обещание не передавать комнату людям, ему неизвестным. (1: 216)

I brought up the subject of the apartment…
Я заговорила о квартире. Я так хочу ей человеческого жилья! Без этих шагов и пластинок за стеной, без ежеминутных унижений! Но она, оказывается, совсем по-другому чувствует: она хочет остаться здесь, с тем чтобы Смирновы переехали в новую комнату, а ей отдали бы свою. Хочет жить тут же, но в двух комнатах.
—Право же, известная коммунальная квартира лучше неизвестной. Я тут привыкла. И потом: когда вернется Лева—ему будет комната. Ведь вернется же он когда-нибудь (1: 66).

'T'Anna.'…
«Кани». Понимаете? Направление, куда: «К Ане». (1: 66)

Tanya, who wanted to exchange her room…
Таня, которая собиралась менять свою комнату, остается; Анна Андреевна рада, что не увозят детей. (1: 216)

I arrived about two…
Часа в два я выбралась к ней. Выглядит она очень плохо, глаза усталые, лицо осунувшееся и словно потерявшее четкость очертаний.
—Что с вами? Вы хворали эти дни?
—Нет.
И рассказала мне свою очередную достоевщину, в самом деле и страшную и нудную. Хорошенький клубочек—эти дети, которых она нянчит, и этот Двор Чудес. (1: 134–35)

A. A. suspected that Tanya Smirnova…
А. А. подозревала, что Тане Смирновой, ее соседке, матери Вали и Вовы, поручено за нею следить, и обнаружила какие-то признаки этой слежки. «Всегда выходит так,—сказала она мне,—что я сама оплачиваю собственных стукачей». Деятельность Двора Чудес А.А. называла надзор, который постоянно чувствовала—надзор за собой и своими рукописями. (1: 135n)

Let this apartment be damned!
Будь проклята эта квартира! (1: 192)

First of all, it is vital that…
Прежде всего ей необходимо уехать отсюда, из этой квартиры. Тут травмы идут с обеих сторон, от обоих соседей. (1: 160–61)

I became utterly absorbed in...
я с головой погрузилась в Ташкентские Записные книжки. Они такие страшные! Какой Двор чудес с ними сравнится. (1: 519)

I tried to explain somehow to NN...
Я пыталась как-то объяснить NN, что чувствую какое-то странное освобождение не только от Двора Чудес, но и от себя, своего прошлого. Если бы я нашла что-то новое—тогда такое чувство было бы объяснимым, но ведь ничего нового я не нашла, только последнее прибежище утрачено. (1: 352)

In my presence she got up...
При мне встала, вымыла посуду, сама затопила печь. Меня заставляла сидеть. Сказала фразу очень злую и, в известной мере, увы! правдивую.
—Я ведь в действительности не такая беспомощная. Это больше зловредство с моей стороны. (1: 350)

I went round to Akhmatova's...
Зашла к Ахматовой, она живет у дворника (убитого артснарядом на улице Желябова) в подвале, в темном-темном уголке прихожей, вонючем таком, совершенно достоевщицком, на досках, находящих друг на друга,—матрасишко, на краю—закутанная в платки, с ввалившимися глазами—Анна Ахматова. [...] Сидит в кромешной тьме, даже читать не может, сидит, как в камере смертников. Плакала о Тане Гуревич (Таню все сегодня вспоминают и жалеют) и так хорошо сказала: «Я ненавижу. Я ненавижу Гитлера, я ненавижу Сталина, я ненавижу тех, кто кидает бомбы на Ленинград и на Берлин, кто ведет эту войну, позорную, страшную...». (note 27)

I paid a visit on A. A. Akhmatova...
Заходил к А. А. Ахматовой. Она лежала—болеет. Встретила меня очень приветливо, настроение у нее хорошее, с видимым удовольствием сказала, что приглашена выступить по радио. Она—патриотка, и сознание, что сейчас она душой вместе со всеми, видимо, очень ободряет ее. (note 28)

We keep silent about Leningrad...
Мы о Ленинграде молчим. Или плачем. (1: 416)

The railway station; an evacuation point...
Вокзал; эвакопункт. [...] Проехала Ленинградская Академия художеств. Пунин; Анна Евгеньевна, Ирочка с Малайкой. [...] Страшные лица

ленинградцев. [...] Меня и ее бьют на вокзале дежурные—не пускают на перрон. [...] О Гаршине ничего не знают. NN уверена, что он умер. Умер Женя Смирнов. Таня, Вовочка и Валя при смерти. Умерла Вера Аникиева. В дороге умер Кибрик. Пунин очень плох. (1: 417)

Lev's dead...
Лева умер, Вова умер, Вл. Г. [Гаршин] умер. (1: 440)

The SNK [Council of People's Commissars] sent somebody...
СНК [Совет народных комиссаров] прислал человека, чтобы перевести ее в другую комнату, роскошную и пр. Она была в унынии, смятении, отчаянии, живо напомнившем мне ее состояние духа, когда ей предлагали квартиру в Ленинграде... Мне было немного смешно. Тут, конечно, целая сеть причин сразу: и ее ужас перед бытом, и нелюбовь к переменам, и принципиальное нищенство, и боязнь одиночества. (1: 420)

Why do you think it is...
Как Вы думаете, почему это здесь все без конца ходят друг к другу? (1: 431)

We would talk about people...
мы много говорили о людях. NN была очень резка и откровенна. (1: 431)

Sometimes Ranevskaia...
Иногда входила Раневская, обожающая NN [...] иногда Радзинская. (1: 431)

Enter Elder Basov-Verkhoiantsev...
пришел старец Басов-Верхоянцев, жена которого считалась вождем антиахматовцев, и предложил вынести ведро. [...] Явилась какая-то девица, справилась о здоровье и принесла десять яиц. Затем явился доктор с плоским лицом домработницы. (1: 429)

The room begins to fill...
комната понемногу наполнялась: Браганцева, Мур, Хазин, Дроботова. Пили вино. (1: 444)

These days I only ever see NN...
Все эти дни вижу NN только на людях. «Удар грома; входят все». (1: 417)

Everyone is happy to provide food...
　Все рады накормить, снабдить табаком, вытопить печь, принести воду. Это—настоящее «общественное дело»; настоящее потому, что совершенно добровольное. (1: 419)

Tan'ka would boil...
　Танька варила ей *иногда кое-что*.... (1: 374)

O. R. washed a towel for me...
　О. Р. выстирала мне полотенце, Ная вымыла мне голову и сделала салат оливье, Мария Михайловна сварила яйца...Утром открылась дверь и шофер Толстого принес дрова, яблоки, и варенье. Это мне совсем не понравилось. Я не хочу быть обязанной [Алексею] Толстому. (1: 373)

It turns out that there's a whole gaggle of women...
　Оказывается, что есть целая когорта дам [...] которые возмущены тем, что NN сама не бегает за пирожками, а ей их радостно приносят...Ох, тошно писать обо всем этом. (1: 426–27)

The knowledge that in poverty...
　Сознание, что и в нищете, и в бедствиях, и в горе она—поэзия, она—величие, *она*, а не власть, унижающая ее,—это сознание давало ей силы переносить нищету, унижение, горе. (2: 502)

I am hurt and I disapprove...
　Я обижена и осуждаю. Но я воздержусь сделать оргвыводы: раз Вл. Георг. [Гаршина] нет возле нее, я должна нести свою миссию: NN поручена мне Ленинградцами. (1: 458)

The nighttime rings at the doorbell...
　Ночные звонки «пока вы мирно отдыхали в Сочи, ко мне уже ползли такие ночи и я такие слышала звонки». [...] Ночью в часы любви, я ловила себя на мысли—а вдруг сейчас войдут и прервут? Так и случилось, оставив после себя своеобразный след—смесь двух воспоминаний. (note 41)

Inscribed in [Akhmatova's] book...
　Надпись на книге [Ахматовой]: «Другу Наде, чтобы она еще раз вспомнила, что с нами было». Из того, что с нами было, самое основное и сильное, это страх и его производное—мерзкое чувство позора и полной беспомощности. Этого и вспоминать не надо, «это» всегда с нами. Мы признались друг другу, что «это» оказалось сильнее любви

и ревности, сильнее всех человеческих чувств, доставшихся на нашу долю. С самых первых дней, когда мы были еще храбрыми, до конца пятидесятых годов страх заглушал в нас все, чем обычно живут люди, и за каждую минуту просвета мы платили ночным бредом—наяву и во сне. У страха была физиологическая основа: хорошо вымытые руки с толстыми короткими пальцами шарят по нашим карманам, добродушные лица ночных гостей, их мутные глаза и покрасневшие от бессонницы веки. Ночные звонки–«пока вы мирно отдыхали в Сочи, ко мне уже ползли такие ночи и я такие слышала звонки...». (note 42)

Under my instructions, Tolstaia...
Толстая, проинструктированная мной, добыла ей пропуск в дивный магазин. (1: 418)

I lay dying.
Помирала. (1: 476)

They'd be better off cleaning...
Лучше бы уборную вычистили, клоаку эту. (1: 495)

NN announced that because she was...
NN объявила мне, что так как она помещена в Правительственной палате, то она не считает возможным, чтобы я ее посещала. Не думаете ли Вы, что такая осторожность излишня? Я думаю, Осип на такое способен не был. (1: 499)

Oh, my poor thing...
О, бедная моя. Ведь я не сумею «забыть и простить». (1: 499)

NN takes very good care of AA...
Очень, очень NN бережет АА. И это мне неприятно. (1: 504)

Ranevskaia told me the contents of a telegram...
Раневская сообщила мне текст телеграммы в Ленинград, Лидии Гинзбург: «Больна брюшным тифом подготовьте Гаршина». Очень безжалостно все-таки. Ведь в Ленинград! (1: 501)

singing at power in chorus.
хоровое пение перед властью. (1: 513)

—When you write what Pasternak has written
—Когда пишешь то, что написал Пастернак, не следует претендовать на отдельную палату в больнице ЦК партии.

Это замечание, логически и нравственно будто бы совершенно обоснованное, сильно задело меня. Своей недобротой. Я бы на ее месте обрадовалась. [...]

—Он и не претендует,—сказала я тихим голосом.—[...] Пастернак даже в Союз не велит обращаться, не только выше...Ему больно, он кричит от боли, и все. Но те люди кругом, которые любят его (тут я слегка запнулась), вот они, действительно претендуют. Им хочется, чтобы Пастернак лежал в самой лучшей больнице, какая только есть в Москве. (2: 276)

When she fell ill with typhus in Tashkent...
В Ташкенте, заболев брюшным тифом, Анна Андреевна [...] была очень довольна, когда, усилиями друзей, ее положили в тамошнюю «кремлевку», в отдельную палату...

Помнит ли она об этом? Забыла?

Нет, я радуюсь сейчас за него, как счастлива была тогда за нее, что она в человеческих—т.е. привилегированных—условиях, а не в «демократических», которые у нас, увы! равны бесчеловечным. (2: 277)

My last entry about NN as a person...
Последняя моя запись об NN—о человеке. Как человек она мне больше не интересна. [Несколько строк вырезано—Е. Ч.] Что же осталось? Красота, ум и гений. Немало—но человечески это уже неинтересно мне. Могу читать стихи и любоваться на портреты. (1: 514)

without clarifying their relationship, or acknowledging the reasons.
не выясняя отношений, не узнавая причин. (2: 21)

Anna Andreevna isn't capable...
Анна Андреевна жить одна не в состоянии. (2: 75)

I have become a nomad...
Я потеряла оседлость. [...] Я в Питере не дома и здесь не дома. (2: 362)

I woke up several times...
Ночью я несколько раз просыпалась от счастья. (2: 58)

[we] were bound by *Requiem*...
[нас] связал «Реквием» и другие непечатаемые стихи, доверенные ею моей памяти. (2: 21)

It was hot...
Жара, в горле пересохло. Когда Анна Андреевна предложила мне чаю, я обрадовалась. Ответила строкой:
—«И я прошу как милости...» [...]
—О чем же тут уж так просить?—сказала Анна Андреевна недовольно.
Только в этот миг меня осенило, что она принимает собственные стихи за мою просьбу. (2: 67)

And neither the beginning nor the end...
и ни начала, ни конца. Анна Андревна уверяла меня, что я должна вспомнить все, а я надеялась на нее. (2: 67)

It was, perhaps, precisely because...
Быть может, именно по случаю воскрешения «Подвала памяти» мы многое вспомнили в этот вечер из ленинградских вместе пережитых времен. (2: 68)

And she asked me the question...
И она задала мне тот вопрос, который все сейчас задают друг другу: надеялась ли я дожить до смерти Сталина?
—Нет,—ответила я.—Как-то про это не думалось. Я жила в сознании, что он придан нам навсегда. А вы? Надеялись дожить до его смерти?
Она покачала головой.
Я спросила, как она думает: предполагал ли сам он когда-нибудь умереть?
—Нет,—ответила она.—Наверное, нет. Смерть—это было только для других, и он сам ею ведал. (2: 68)

And I had imagined...
А я-то воображала—это уже позади! (2: 64)

for some reason this joy is poisoned...
почему-то это радость отравленная, как странным образом отравлены все наши теперешние радости. Наверное, интоксикация прошлым. (October 17, 1953; 2: 74)

Because unconsciously...
От того, что бессознательно, того не ведая сами, вы хотите, чтобы этих лет будто и не было, а они *были*. Их нельзя стереть. Время не стоит, оно движется. Арестованных можно из лагерей воротить домой, но ни вас, ни их нельзя воротить в тот день, когда вас разлучили. [...]

вы хотите, чтобы не только люди, но и день вернулся, и чтобы жизнь, насильно прерванная, благополучно началась с того места, где ее прервали. Склеилась там, где ее разрубили топором. Но так не бывает. Нет такого клея. Категория времени вообще гораздо сложнее, чем категория пространства. (2: 199)

Auntie Maria, I am writing about your husband...
Тетя Мария сообщаю Вам про вашего мужа Николая Николаевича. 21 августа 11 часов 45 минут умер неболев ничем. 20 он получиль деньги и приходить комне отдать дольг я нанево посмотрел и говорю Куда вы уежаете. Что вы принесли дольг он мне ответиль я некак немогу тебя отдать всегда ты находиш ответ потом он ушоль. Я утром и шоль наработу он стояль около общежития. Я с ним поздоровалься и говорю почему вы рана так устали он мне ответил чтото неспится думаю что такое обишчали что я дольжен поехать дамой писали мне что уже отдали касьтюм в чистку подготавляют жена комнату и чтото нет посылки наверно ажидают затем говорит я кода браль у тебя денги то купиль у посылочника аднаво украенца яблок 20 штук и вчера взяль банку молока литрову нужно ити позавтракат и ушоль. Через часа два с половиною один приходит и расказовает что сейчас понесли наносилках Неколая Николаевича Пунина у больницу. Я бросиль все и побежал в больницу и как я зашоль к нему он говорит мне вот видеш как утром стояли с тобой а сейчас я убольницы он мне ответель приди комне в 12 часов будет врач я внево спрошу. Что мне можно купиць и так ушол от нево это было ровно 11 часов я пришов 12 часов мне расказывают что Неколай Николаевич умер без петнацатий 12. (note 45)

and we read letters...
читали мы писма что вы неехали отдохнут в деревню ожидали кода приедет Неколай Николаевич. Затем Досвидания привет Ане и маме ее. (note 46)

Lev has returned...
Вернулся Лева.
Застрелился Фадеев. (2: 205)

this rite has become...
этот обряд входит в ритуал реабилитации. Ведь она посмертная; стало быть, сначала надо засвидетельствовать смерть. Все правильно. (2: 247)

most undiarylike of times...
    недневниковое время [...] «слово плохо берет», как сказано у Герцена. (2: 253; 255)

We celebrated thus...
    Праздновали мы так: Анна Андреевна велела смочить полотенце холодной водой, легла и положила его себе на лоб. (2: 189)

"What we went through," spoke Anna Andreevna...
    —Того что мы пережили,—говорила с подушки Анна Андреевна,—да, да, мы все, потому что застенок грозил каждому!—не запечатлела ни одна литература. Шекспировские драмы—все эти эффектные злодейства, страсти, дуэли—мелочь, детские игры по сравнению с жизнью каждого из нас. О том, что пережили казненные и лагерники, я говорить не смею. Это не называемо словом. (2: 189)

I said that lots of people...
    Я сказала, что многие, в особенности из молодых, смущены и ушиблены разоблачением Сталина [...] Пустяки это,—спокойно ответила Анна Андреевна.—«Наркоз отходит», как говорят врачи. (2: 190)

Besides, I don't believe...
    —Да и не верю я, чтобы кто-нибудь чего-нибудь не понимал раньше. Я с ней не согласилась. На своем пути мне довелось встречать людей чистых, искренних, бескорыстных, которые и мысли не допускали, что их обманывают.
    —Неправда!—закричала Анна Андреевна с такой энергией гнева, что я испугалась за ее сердце. [...] Они притворялись. Им выгодно было притворяться перед другими и самими собой. Вы еще тогда понимали все до конца—не давайте же обманывать себя теперь. (2: 190)

Now when the prisoners are returning...
    Теперь арестанты вернутся, и две России глянут друг другу в глаза: та, что сажала, и та, которую посадили. Началась новая эпоха. Мы с вами до нее дожили. (2: 190)

Everyone cried...
    все плакали, кроме нас с Фридой. (2: 196)

the application of physical means of influencing.
    применение физических методов воздействия. (page 103)

Is that really news to you?...
—Для вас это ново? Что он был прям? Для меня нисколько! [...] Кого же ему было стесняться? Мне даже кажется, я эту телеграмму собственными глазами читала. [...] Быть может, читала во сне. Жаль, в те годы мы не записывали своих снов. Это был бы богатейший материал для истории. (2: 198)

What do you think...
—Как вы думаете, он совсем умный?—спросила она.—Понимает здешнюю жизнь? (2: 504)

Hm. It's hard for me to judge foreigners...
Гм. Судить об иностранцах, о степени их ума и интеллигентности мне вообще трудно. Слишком разный у нас с ними жизненный опыт, да и все разное. Да и скольких видела я на своем веку? одного-двух и обчелся. (2: 504)

I talk to him without hiding anything...
Я разговариваю с ним не скрываясь и не осторожничая, но я сама— понимаю ли? По возрасту моему, по опыту уж давненько пора бы понимать, но ведь наша жизнь, при отсутствии честной прессы, так разъединена, что каждый из нас близорук: различает ясно только тех, кто рядом, и только то, что рядом. В стране, лишенной общей памяти, объединяющей людей,—в стране, у которой украдены литература и история, опыт у каждого человека, у каждого круга, у каждого слоя— свой, ограниченный, отдельный. А страна огромна и опыт всей страны не подытожен, не соединен, не собран; хуже—оболган.... (2: 504–5)

I suddenly found myself among things...
Я вдруг оказалась среди давным-давно забытых мною вещей и в другом времени: та же забытая мною гладкая рама туманного зеркала, то же кресло со сломанной ножкой. И тот же маленький столик красного дерева, что стоял двадцать лет назад в комнате Фонтанного дома, куда я так любила приходить. Тогда, до войны; в том, еще моем, Ленинграде. (2: 365)

Things are like sponges—
Вещи, они ведь как губки, впитывают в себя время и вдруг окатывают им человека с головы до ног, если он внезапно встречается с ними после долгой разлуки.
Для Анны Андреевны вещи ее комнаты полны, наверное, 13-м годом; а для меня 37-м... Увидела я их только в 38-м, но они, как и я, свидетели

создания «Реквиема», величайшего памятника той эпохи, эпохи 30-х годов, которая вся вместе именуется «тридцать седьмым».... (2: 365)

All my books, belongings, clothes—
—Все мои книги, вещи, платья,—все утоплено,—сказала Анна Андреевна.—У меня теперь ничего нет. Мне это все равно, это очень идет моей судьбе. Я не огорчаюсь. (2: 462)

Do I write my poems down?...
—Записываю ли я свои стихи? И это спрашиваете вы—вы!
Она подошла к табуретке, на которой стоял чемоданчик, и с яростью принялась выкидывать оттуда на тахту рукописи, книги, тетради, папки, блокноты.
—Как я могу записывать? Как я могу хранить свои стихи? Бритвой взрезают переплеты тетрадей, книг! Вот, вот, поглядите! У папок обрывают тесемки! Я уже в состоянии представить коллекцию оборванных тесемок и выкорчеванных корешков! И здесь *так*, и в Ленинграде *так*! Вот, вот! (2: 419)

How could I answer her?...
Что я могла ей ответить? По-видимому, хранение стихов и в наше новое время возможно только одним-единственным, давно испытанным способом.... (2: 420)

checked the money in the till.
проверила наличность в кассе. (2: 491)

She had long been intending...
Она давно уже собиралась уйти с мною куда-нибудь из-под потолка и проверить, все ли я помню. По ее внезапному вызову я к ней явилась, и мы отправились в ближайший сквер. Почти все скамейки в этот час рабочего дня пусты, мы сели подальше от двух теток, пасущих детей, от пенсионера, читающего газету, подальше от улицы. [...] Она слушала, а я читала вслух стихи, которые столько раз твердила про себя. [...] Я прочитала все до единого. Я спросила, собирается ли она теперь записать их. «Не знаю»,—ответила она, из чего я поняла, что и я пока еще не вправе записывать. «Кроме вас, их должны помнить еще семеро». (2: 491)

And so this miracle text...
Итак, чудо закреплено, «Реквием» не пропадет, даже если враз помрут те семь или одиннадцать человек, которые, как и я, обязаны знать его наизусть. (2: 560)

Mariia Sergeevna recounted this to me...
Мария Сергеевна мне рассказала:
—Наташа [Ильина] принесла мне свои воспоминания об Ахматовой, но она сама не понимает, что написала. Ведь она не подозревает о том, что Анна Андреевна считала ее осведомительницей. Там есть такой эпизод; в тот день, когда разразился скандал с «Доктором Живаго», утром, едва прочтя газеты, Ильина помчалась к Ахматовой спросить, что она по этому поводу думает... Разумеется, Анна Андреевна не могла воспринимать этот визит иначе, как исполнение служебного долга. И тем не менее она сказала: «Поэт всегда прав». То есть Ахматова не побоялась передать такое на Лубянку.... (note 49)

Mikhail Ardov doesn't bother himself with evidence...
Михаил Ардов и не утруждает себя доказательствами, он выступает как свидетель того, что это мнение существовало. Но ведь бытовало и другое мнение, чрезвычайно распространенное—в связях с КГБ многие обвиняли Ардова-старшего. Если мемуарист излагает слухи, касаясь столь щекотливой темы, то почему бы не остановиться прежде всего на слухах, касающихся собственной семьи? (note 51)

Worst of all is the fact that the testimony...
Хуже всего то, что свидетельство авторитетного мемуариста становится тем «источником», на который опираются уже другие (ссылка на свидетельство М. Ардова мне попалась как-то в «Московском комсомольце»).
Проблема разграничения свидетельства и лжесвидетельства—это очень больная проблема. Я не вижу простых способов ее решения. (note 51)

"In 1938," recalled Anna Andreevna
—Мне один человек в 38-м сказал,—припомнила Анна Андреевна.—«Вы бесстрашная. Вы ничего не боитесь». Я ему: «Что вы! Я только и делаю, что боюсь». Правда, разве можно было не бояться? Тебя возьмут и, прежде чем убить, заставят предавать других. (2: 513)

Fear. Fear stays in one's blood...
Страх. В крови остается страх. Чаадаев испугался повторения. Осип [Мандельштам] после первой ссылки воспел Сталина. Потом он сам говорил мне: «это была болезнь». (2: 515)

Everything seemed to me as if...
А мне все казалось, что я опять в Ленинграде, на дворе тридцать седьмой, то же чувство приниженности и несмываемой обиды. (3: 179)

Of course, 1964…
　Конечно, шестьдесят четвертый отнюдь не тридцать седьмой, тут тебе не ОСО [Особое совещание] и не Военное Судилище, осуждающее каждый день на мгновенную смерть или медленное умирание тысячи тысяч людей,—но […] та же непробиваемая стена. (3: 179)

And it's the same old sadistic hate…
　И та же, привычная, вечно насаждаемая сверху, как и антисемитизм, садистская ненависть к интеллигенции. (3: 179)

They might as well spit…
　только бы плюнуть в душу интеллигенции. Большего удовольствия у них нет. Слаще водки. (3: 180)

Frida's account is something unique…
　Фридина запись—это нечто уникальное, Точна, как стенограмма, выразительна как художественное произведение. Жанр? Совершенно новый: документальная драматургия. (3: 182)

Apart from the indignation…
　Кроме возмущения, «дело Бродского» вызывает во мне постылую скуку. Наша обыденность. Словно в поезде едешь по бескрайней степи. Когда не выглядешь в окошко, все одно, одно и одно. Нет, на двадцатые годы не похоже. И на тридцать седьмой не похоже. На «после войны» не похоже. Однако похоже на все. (3: 201)

Just imagine, Joseph said…
　—Вообразите, Иосиф говорит: «Никто для меня пальцем о палец не хочет ударить. Если б они хотели, они освободили бы меня в два дня». («Они»—это мы!) (3: 207)

People are fussing over him…
　За него хлопочут так, как не хлопотали ни за одного человека изо всех восемнадцати миллионов репрессированных! […] А у него типичный лагерный психоз—это мне знакомо—Лева говорил, что я не хочу его возвращения и нарочно держу в лагере…. (3: 207)

Lev spent almost twenty years…
　Лева пробыл в тюрьмах и лагерях лет двадцать без малого, а Иосиф—без малого три недели…. (3: 207)

Who, when, and to what extent understood…
　кто, когда и в какой мере понимал, что творилось вокруг? Я, как всегда, сказала: «Разные люди понимали в разное время».

—Ах, они не понимали?—закричала она.—Ложь. Вздор. Не хотели понимать—дело другое. (3: 103)

Blok's last evening in Petrograd—
Последний вечер Блока в Петрограде—это из моего, из моего подвала памяти—странно, что два подвала, столь разные, могут оказаться бок о бок. В 1921 году мне четырнадцать лет, я—никто, а она уже давно Ахматова, он уже давно—Блок. Он говорит ей свои последние слова. И я тоже где-то тут неподалеку *одновременно*. Сейчас у нас 62-й. Я не я, она не она, его нет. Как это понять? Наше существование? То же время, те же факты—а память разная. Путаюсь. (3: 108)

"I will take a nap," announced Anna Andreevna...
—Я посплю,—объявила Анна Андреевна,—а вы, обе, отойдите туда, к окну, и сядьте возле столика. Аманда! Сейчас Лидия Корнеевна расскажет вам, что такое тридцать седьмой.... (3: 219)

We sat down...
Мы сели. Анна Андреевна повернулась на бок, спиной к нам. Рассказать про тридцать седьмой! [...] Дело не только в том, что Аманда—иностранка. То есть знает одно: в Советском Союзе при Сталине был террор. [...] [террор] или, как нынче принято это называть: «массовые нарушения социалистической законности», «последствия культа личности Сталина». [...] Да ведь террор начался и длится с 1917 года по сей день. Но каждый год у его иная степень массовости, иная направленность. [...] Что знает англичанка о ночах террора, о днях и ночах террора? Кроме самого слова? [...] Да и не англичанка, не иностранка, а любой наш соотечественник младшего поколения? [...] Все разъединены, и у большинства память уворована. [...] Человек деревенский? Человек городской? Интеллигентный? Неинтеллигентный? Все знают и помнят разное. Если вообще помнят. (3: 220)

CHAPTER 2: THE NOTEBOOKS OF THE FORMER PEASANT EVGENIIA KISELEVA: "THE WAR SEPARATED US FOREVER"

Note: original texts of Evgeniia Kiseleva's notebooks are given in the body of Part II.

How These Notebooks Reached the Reader: The Interpreters

E. G. Kiseleva sends her first notebook...
Е. Г. Киселева посылает свою первую тетрадку на «Мосфильм». [...] Женщина высокой культуры, всю жизнь отдающая служению духовности и искусству, тратит свое время на то чтобы сначала

перепечатать рукопись Е. Г. Киселевой, а потом опубликовать ее. […] Мы имеем в виду Е. Н. Ольшанскую, которая опубликовала в 1991 г. в «Новом мире» отрывки из записок. Это была публикация текста в вычищенном от присутствия самого автора, т.е. отредактированном виде, зато с комплиментарным предисловием маститого литератора. […]

Затем эти записки та же Е.Н. Ольшанская передает в центр документации «Народный архив».

Г. И. Попова, хранитель личных фондов, энтузиаст дела, которому она служит, относясь к запискам Е. Г. Киселевой как к ценности—свидетельской и исторической—передала эти записки исследователю, а именно Н. Н. Козловой.

Н. Н. Козлова, которая проработала 20 лет в Институте философии РАН, что по определению казалось бы должно было отвращать ее от предметов такого рода, собственноручно переписала эти записки. Она задыхалась и мерзла в вышеупомянутом Архиве, от руки тщательно переписывая труд пенсионерки. Затем она набрала его на компьютере с сохранением орфографии, прилагая все усилия к тому, чтобы никоим образом не нарушить ход оригинального письма, не поставить, например, по дурной интеллигентской привычку запятую там, где ею пренебрег загадочный автор.

Еще одна женщина-исследователь, лингвист И. И. Сандомирская, вроде бы из чистого любопытства соглашается покопаться в языке пресловутой рукописи, зная за собой большое умение отыскивать тот шурупчик, выкрутив который можно посмотреть, как устроена вся машинка.

Наконец, еще одна женщина, самая молодая из нас—издатель О. Назарова.

[…] Совмещая защиту кандидатской диссертации по философии с работой в нарождающейся рыночной экономике […] сталкивается со всеми вышеперечисленными лицами, а также с упомянутыми тетрадочками. И у нее возникло желание напечатать это.…(note 65)

captivation by the text…
зачарованность текстом; томительное желание понять, непонимание; стремление похвастаться любимым текстом; ревность и страх, что вырвут из рук и уведут. (12)

the interest in 'naive writing'
Интерес к «наивному письму»—симптоматика отхода от советской культуры. (39)

naive texts remain…
наивные тексты пребывают за пределами политического, эстетического и даже морального суждения, потому что жизненны. (note 66)

Our heroine attempts to play...
> наша героиня пытается играть в чужом для нее поле Письма, Литературы. Точно также она играет в поле Социальной жизни, она же просто Жизнь. (note 67)

The Editor (with a capital E)...
> Редактор (с большой буквы) это не Е. Н. Ольшанская. Е. Н. Ольшанская—первый читатель и почитатель. Она лишь открыла этот бесконечный ряд. Затем в него встали и редактор «Нового мира». [...] Персона Редактора имеет множество воплощений—подобно восточному божеству. (note 70)

The "conflict" between...
> «Конфликт» между Е. Г. Киселевой и ее Редактором, продуктом которого и стала публикация в «Новом мире»,—результат столкновения двух взаимно непереводимых идиом. Одна из них наделена нормативной силой, а другая этой силы не имеет. Отсюда—процесс интерпретации наивной идиомы неизбежно сопровождается возникновением отношений господства/подчинения. Правка и редактирование принимают репрессивный характер. Редактор явно выступает как властный субъект, выполняющий дисциплинарные функции. Нет, однако, здесь никакой злонамеренности. Просто публикатор не может себе позволить опубликовать исходный текст в его «естественном состоянии». Рука не поднимается, т.е. в тело Редактора встроена норма, которую нарушить нельзя. (note 72)

E. G. Kiseleva's narrative bears the subtitle...
> Нарратив Е. Г. Киселевой носит подзаголовок «я так хочу назвать кино», публикатор его вычеркивает. Отчего? (41) (page 156)

The names of prewar leaders...
> Имена довоенных вождей практически отсутствуют. [...] 22 июня 1941—единственная историческая дата, которую Е. Г. Киселева упоминает. [...] Большой Истории, с которой постоянно соотносятся записки «культурных», у Е. Г. Киселевой нет. (83)

The manuscript is testament to...
> Рукопись свидетельствует, что Е. Г. Киселева не в состоянии выстроить нарратив в соответствии с линейным временем, в то время, как биография пишется во временной последовательности. (67)

this person is not the historical depravity...
> человек этот—не историческое извращение, не монстр, каким он кажется порой производителю нормы. Но он не действует в истории

как автономный субъект, и это как раз то его свойство, которое так не нравится политикам и интеллектуалам. [...] Не удается обнаружить у пишущих черт активных субъектов, «хозяев» истории, которые бы желали и могли взять на себя ответственность за настоящее, прошлое и будущее. [...] Наивное «ручное» письмо словно подтверждает и иллюстрирует мысль приверженцев постмодернистских методологий о смерти субъекта, об исчезновении автора, о существовании бессубъектных форм культуры. (54)

PART III: DREAMS OF TERROR: INTERPRETATIONS

My entries on the terror...
Мои записи эпохи террора примечательны, между прочим, тем, что в них воспроизводятся полностью одни только сны. Реальность моему описанию не поддавалась; больше того—в дневнике я и не делала попыток ее описывать. Дневником ее было не взять, да мыслимо ли было в ту пору вести настоящий дневник? (note 1)

history entered...
история вошла в быт человека, в его сознание, проникла в самое сердце и стала заполнять даже его сны. (note 2)

This diary was confiscated...
Этот дневник изъят у меня при обыске. В нем сорок листов (40 л.). Аржиловский. 29 августа 1937 г. (note 31)

18 December [1936] You may call it nonsense...
18 XII Назовите чепухой, но тем не менее и сны есть факт. Хочется записать интересный сон. Кто-то сказал мне, что я могу увидеть Сталина. Фигура историческая, увидеть любопытно. И вот... Небольшая комната, простая, мещанская. Сталин пьяный «в дрезину», как говорят. В комнате одни мужчины: из мужиков—я и еще один чернобородый. Не говоря ни слова Виссарионович повалил чернобородого мужика, закрыл простыней и яростно изнасиловал... «И мне то же будет!»—в отчаянии подумал я, припоминая тифлисские обычаи, и хотел бежать; но после сеанса Сталин как будто несколько отрезвел и вступил в разговор:
— Почему вы интересуетесь видеть меня лично?
— Ну, как же: портреты портретами, а живой человек, да еще великий,—совсем другое дело,—сказал я.
В общем, для меня дело кончилось более благополучно и меня даже угощали... Снится мне Сталин второй раз: пред освобождением снился и вот сегодня.... Полагаю, что Сталин снится не зря. [...] Во всяком случае, я не выдумал, а фиксирую факты, хотя и бредовые. (note 32)

28 January [1937]. I wake up at 4.
  28-I. В 4 просыпаюсь. К пяти Лиза уходит на молоканку, я растопляю печь. Сходил за водой на салазках. До ворот ехал благополучно, в воротах высокие салазки повалились, и кадочка—набок. Хорошо, что в руках ведерко с водой: за труды все-таки осталось. Геня ушел в очередь за хлебом: опять волынка с хлебом, огромные очереди, давка. Хлеб дорогих сортов, что и для пролетариата весьма невыгодно. Бок заживает, почти все в порядке; но случилась другая беда: купил себе тесные, твердые валенки, стер палец, который теперь болит. «К худу— худо и вяжется...» Но я сел записать мудреный сон. Еще с вечера приснился, только прилег. Я где-то на новостройках. Почему-то топлю печи и боюсь пожара: как бы не вспыхнули строения. Вдруг слышу шум аэроплана. Появляется низколетящий огромный корабль, нагруженный огромными связками сухих дров, которые, по моему предположению, должны вот-вот вспыхнуть. Думаю: «Как только аэроплан коснется построек, то все вдруг загорит и сам он сгорит». Но столкновения не было: я проснулся в то время, когда корабль пролетал надо мной, почти касаясь хвостом крыш. Это странный сон. Второй немного забыл, но в основном, какая-то газетная статья, в которой последние три строчки ярко говорили о насмешке над русским гражданином. Как будто даже была фраза: «Вот и вытрись!» Сонные мысли, появляющиеся без воли человека... Стоит тихая твердая погода. (note 33)

that same camp newspaper...
  та же лагерная газета, печатавшая мои заметки [...] пошла против меня. [...] Печатная кампания против меня сильно ударила морально, я понял одно: мы прокляты до конца жизни и как бы ты ни перековался—тебе не поверят и при первой возможности заклюют и заплюют. (note 34)

It is so natural...
  Это так же естественно: чуют правду и не прощают нам наших протестов против насилия. (note 35)

I dreamed that I was flying through the air...
  Снилось, что я с кем-то несусь на аэросанях и спрашиваю: «Скорость автомобиля еще сильнее?»—«Немного да»,—отвечает мне неизвестный спутник. Не скатила бы меня Тойба с заводской катушки: не выносит она моего духу. Читал обвинительную речь прокурора по делу троцкисткого центра.... (note 37)

19 April [1937] I had a dream about traveling...
  19–IV. Снились горы, река и движение. Едем. Остановка. Направо прекраснейшая церквовь. Не тюрьма ли? Боюсь я ее. (note 39)

1 May. These dreams...
> 1–V. Эти сны так напугали меня, что всю свою литературу я спрятал и держался до Первого мая. Будто нет ничего особенного, и все оказалось ночной фантазией. (note 40)

In the daytime, I was occupied...
> Днем я был занят делами и с большим увлечением занимался научной работой, а ночью видел травматические сны, видел себя в тюрьме. Хотя я нисколько не суеверен, но при сильно натянутых нервах было неприятно узреть однажды во сне церковь, что по народному поверью предвещает тюрьму. (note 41)

I dreamed: the terrifying Stalin...
> Мне снилось: страшный Сталин приказал мне зажечь костер в комнате, я зажег костер, он разгорелся, но я подбросил сырые дрова, все потухло, и Сталин сейчас прикажет меня казнить. (note 42)

When I was hallucinating...
> Когда у меня были галлюцинации, я видел несколько раз тебя и один раз Надежду Сергеевну. Она подошла ко мне и говорит: «Что же это такое сделали с Вами, Н. И.? Я Иосифу скажу, чтобы он Вас взял на поруки». Это было так реально, что я чуть было не вскочил и не стал писать тебе, чтоб...ты взял меня на поруки! Так у меня реальность была перетасована с бредом. Я знаю, что Н. С. не поверила бы ни за что, что я злоумышлял против тебя, и недаром подсознательное моего несчастного «я» вызвало этот бред. Я с тобой часами разговариваю...Господи, если бы был такой инструмент, чтобы ты видел всю мою расклеванную и истерзанную душу! Если бы ты видел, как я внутренне к тебе привязан, совсем по-другому, чем Стецкие и Тали. Ну, да то «психология»—прости. Теперь нет ангела, который отвел бы меч Аврамов, и роковые судьбы осуществятся! (note 43)

It would be petty to consider my own persona...
> было бы мелочным ставить вопрос о своей собственной персоне *наряду с всемирно-историческими задачами*, лежащими прежде всего на твоих плечах. (note 45)

In an upper corner of my cell...
> в верхнем углу камеры, под потолком, словно на Голгофе, мне виделся распятый на кресте, замученный Бухарин [...] Черный ворон клевал окровавленное, безжизненное тело мученика. (note 46)

You have to write a diary in such a way...
> Надо писать дневник так, чтобы личное являлось на фоне великого исторического события, в этом и есть интерес мемуаров. А события исторические есть всегда, если же нет сейчас видимого, то нужно найти невидимое. (note 49)

18 October [1930]. Yesterday in *Novyi Mir*...
> 18 октября [1930]. Вчера в «Новом мире» был объявлен рекламный список напечатанных в прошлом году авторов, и вот что меня забыли упомянуть или нарочно пропустили,—этот величайший пустяк!—меня расстроило. На ночь я прочитал потрясающий, ужасный рассказ Новикова-Прибоя «Цусима», и всю ночь в кошмарном сне преследовал меня убийца, и я всю ночь держал наготове в кармане револьвер, все время опасаясь, что он сам выстрелит в кармане. (note 53)

Both this disturbed state and this dream...
> И это расстройство, и сон есть индивидуальное проявление господствующей ныне среди интеллигенции мании преследования. У меня доходит до того, что боюсь развертывать новый журнал, все кажется, что меня чем-то заденут и расстроят. Острой формы при общем заболевании бояться.
>
> Спасение, конечно, одно—надо решительно отдаться работе, для чего надо создать хорошие условия. (note 53)

I place value on this cause of remaking geography...
> Я ценю это дело перемены географии тем, что многие бездомные люди, отчаянные, потерявшие всякую радость бытия в процессе творчества новой географии, возродились и, пересоздав географию края, нашли себе в нем новую родину. (note 56)

Motherland is...
> Родина—это участок моего личного труда в общем деле. (note 57)

20 February [1934]. I had not spent the last two summers...
> 20 февраля [1934]. Два последних лета я не жил на Журавлиной родине из-за трудности переезда от меня из Загорска туда, хотя весь переезд сорок верст! [...] да так вот и остался дома сидеть, и прошло два года, я стал тосковать по болотам, как будто действительно, как жураль, заблудился и потерял свою родину. Однажды ночью и даже прямо во сне, мне пришла в голову мысль о том, что выходом в моем положении будет машина: сорок верст для машины какой-нибудь час,—один час—и я на Журавлиной родине. Эта мысль, как бывает во

сне у охотников, растворилась в особенно остро-радостном чувстве природы, где уже не журавли летали и не обыкновенные синицы, а какие-то прелестные птиницы. Утром, сохранив в себе одно лишь чувство приятности сна, я мало-помалу от птиницы до птиницы, как по лестнице, добрался до мысли о машине, и мне показалось, что ведь это возможно: теперь их делают у нас и, если я теперь заявлю, меня запишут в очередь и рано или поздно дадут. (note 59)

Three days later, I had already received a document...
Уже через три дня пришла бумага от Совнаркома с распоряжением дать мне машину; я через несколько дней, обегав издательства, наскреб необходимую сумму для выкупа автомобиля. [...] Одновременно с получением письма от Совнаркома я, вообще по природе своей бесконечно далекий от машин, стал понимать себя в положении земледельца, или кустаря, которому достался по билету лотереи автодора автомобиль: это может быть отличным сюжетом рассказа, в котором можно будет изобразить психологию земледельца и нового для нашей страны человека, водителя машины. Много раз я к этой теме старался подойти и с этой целью осматривал большие заводы. И нет! я не мог найти случая, чтобы не одной головой, а всей личностью, цельно соприкоснуться с машиной. [...] Теперь же так выходило, что машина, как волшебная сила, могущая в любой момент переносить меня к птицам на Журавлиную родину, входила в состав моей творческой личности. (note 60)

28 August [1936]. I had a dream...
28 августа [1936]. Снилось, будто я в телеге вместе с мужиками везу гроб своей матери, и как раз против Хрущевской усадьбы колесо телеги попало в колдобину и гроб полетел на ту сторону. «А тело, скажите, как тело?»—в ужасе повторял я, не смея глянуть в ту сторону. «Тело выехало»,—ответили мне. Я решился посмотреть и увидел, что ноги матери моей задраны вверх и медленно, как будто тело оттаивает, опускаются. Есть ли это безобразное сновидение независимо-случайная игра сонной фантазии, или оно является выражением моей внутренней нескладицы, а может быть, моей сейчас особенно сильной тревоги за существо моей родины-матери? (note 61)

July 12 [1937]. St. Peter's day...
12 июля. Петров день. Начал работу над книгой «Канал» и должен выжать из нее все соки, какие в ней есть. (note 63)

July 21. With this canal...
С этим каналом я как писатель, в сущности, сам попал на канал, и мне надо преодолеть «свою волю».... (note 64)

An apartment in Lavrushivsky...
Квартира в Лаврушинском против Третьяковки начинает казаться безумной мечтой о таком убежище в горле вулкана. И тем не менее расчет совершенно правильный: убежище возможно только в самом горле. (note 65)

August 5. The construction...
5 августа. Строительство моего канала должно в глубине своей быть строительством мира.
11 августа. Врабатывался в «Канал»...
12 августа. Собираемся в Москву принимать квартиру. (note 66)

Here finally...
6 августа. Вот наконец желанная квартира, а жить не с кем. (note 67)

22 September [1938]. Hunting is dear to me...
22 сентября [1938]. Охота мне дорога из-того, что я работаю ногами и не думаю, но все, что пропущено, в голове потом является сразу с такой силой, какой не добьешься в правильной жизни.
Кошмарный сон...Будто бы среди множества людей я, как в лесу, заваленном сучьями в три яруса: люди вплотную везде вокруг и даже подо мной. Я плюнул туда вниз и, взглянув туда, в направлении плевка, увидел, что два доктора режут кому-то толстую ногу. Я вздрогнул и ахнул от ужаса. «Вот барчонок какой,—раздался голос снизу,— неужели еще не привык?»
Я, сконфуженный, поправился очень ловко: «Я не тому ужаснулся, что человека режут, а что я, недоглядев, плюнул туда». И тут я заметил,что всюду по серым, лежащим на земле людям перебегают большие крысы. Одна и по мне поперек прошла по животу, другая ближе, и я даже отпихнул рукой. И вдруг она остановилась и глянула на меня страшно, готовая броситься, и я понял, что она сейчас находится в своих крысиных правах, имеющих силу перед правами человека, и я смертельно обидел ее, и обиженная крыса может сделать со мной что только ей захочется.... (note 69)

February 24. I, as an author...
24 февраля. Мне надо как автору подчинить себя, свое мнение, свое «хочется» единстве мнений, называемому у меня в «Канале» именем «Надо». Словом, я сделаю с собой то самое, что сделают с собой мои герои—строители канала. И вообще «Канал» надо писать так, что мы, находящиеся на свободе, в сравнении с каналоармейцами, только очень относительно свободны, и что мы освещены одним светом этого Надо и что это Надо несет нам ветер истории. (note 71)

August 25. For the whole of the Soviet time...
 25 августа. Моя задача была во все советское время приспособиться к новой среде и остаться самим собой. Эта задача требовала подвига, был подвиг, но сделано все кажется, очень мало: ушло много сил на *освоение* нового. (note 74)

I think that not one person among...
 Думаю, что никто из переламываемых тогда в жерновах ГУЛАГа не вспомнит без омерзения книги, брошюры и статьи, славившие «перековку трудом». И тот же Пришвин, опубликовавший «Государеву дорогу», одной этой лакейской стряпней перечеркнул свою репутацию честного писателя-гуманиста, славившего жизнь! (note 75)

19 February 1937. I don't remember how it starts...
 19 февраля 1937 года. Начала не помню. Я скрываюсь. Приходят люди, которые не знают, что мне нужно скрываться, я свободно говорю с ними. Но один из них как-будто догадывается. Но в комнате полутемно, он плохо видит меня. Я думаю, что один в квартире, и иду из своей комнаты (с дверью прямо на улицу) в другую. Но там кто-то маленький, с большим лицом из милиции. Он спрашивает что-то, как на суде, я, не отвечая, возвращаюсь в свою комнату, открываю дверь прямо на улицу и бегу. Много народу, прямо косяком, десятки автомобилей на повороте. Я бегу во всю мочь, и со мной уже какой-то бедный мальчик. Мы с ним вверх по дороге, за нами гонятся, но вот вся в снегу боковая тропинка в сторону и наверх, в горы. Мы туда. Снег, снег, и какой-то человек, проваливаясь гонит баранов. Я кричу ему: далеко ли до деревни? Не отвечает. Но мы бежим за ним. Небо розовеет все больше, я догадываюсь, что это от света внизу. И вот открывается «устроенная пропасть». Это колония каких-то бегунов, которые здесь живут очень давно. Мы по уступам спускаемся вниз—встречают так себе, не особенно приветливо. Со мной уже Юрий. Его уводят куда-то. Я говорю с этими людьми, вокруг дети—веселые, кричат, играют. Это поселок, построенный в крепости. Мне говорят, где моя койка, но я раньше хочу найти Юрия. По деревянной, с толстыми дубовыми перилами лестнице иду наверх, ищу 42-ой номер, не нахожу. [...] Иду дальше, по другой лестнице, спрашиваю у старой служанки, где 42-ой номер, она говорит: «Да ведь это валютный!» Я говорю, что мне все равно, и меня наконец проводят. Вхожу без стука. За длинным столом—человек восемь, у всех неприятные, квадратные, деревянные лица. Юрий спит, они говорят, что он устал и заснул. Я жду. Они сидят и молчат. Надо заговорить, но лучше молчать. Может быть, они тогда разойдутся. И они расходятся. Юрий просыпается, я спрашиваю его, почему они так переглядывались, когда я вошел. Он

успокаивает: еруднад, обойдется. Потом я записываю все, что видел в «устроенной пропасти», и зачем-то кладу листки на дорогу. Они толстые, как картон. Прибегает мальчишка, другой, не тот, с которым я бежал, и поддает листок ногой. Я бегу и подбираю листки. (note 77)

I was dreaming that I have been summoned...
Мне снилось, что я куда-то вызван, и надо идти туда, где со мной будут разговаривать и требовать, чтобы я все рассказал. На улице провинциального старого города навстречу мне движется колымага—или старинный автомобиль с высокими колесами, напоминающий тяжелую, высокую, неуклюжую колымагу. В ней сидят люди со странными лицами: низкие лбы, бледные, с приплюснутыми носами, громко, уверенно разговаривающие о чем-то, связанном с тем делом, по которому я вызван. Дорогой я спускаюсь в уборную, грязную, в подвале, по скользким ступеням, а когда выхожу, за мной высовывается горбун и кричит с бешенством: «Надо гасить свет!»
Я стою на одном колене у подъезде дома, в который приглашен не только я, но и другие, такие, как Тихонов, начальство. Он кивает мне и поднимается по ступеням, озабоченный, серьезный. Он кидает мне какую-то шутку, и отвечаю полушутя, но думаю, что нас обоих ждут неприятности, но у него обойдется. Наконец вхожу. Это—приемная, но одновременно—парикмахерская. Стригут, бреют. Но столе лежат затрепанные журналы, старые газеты. Сидят молча. Сажусь и я. Можно уйти, но нельзя. Можно вздохнуть, но нельзя. Я уже в кресле, и меня начинают стричь. Пожилой парикмахер, серый, спокойный, аккуратно делает свое дело. В это время из кабинета, куда я должен войти после того, как меня подстригут, появляется один из ехавших в колымаге. Он говорит парикмахеру: «А верно, майор Лыков, этого в Переделкино взяли». Оба смеются. Мне страшно, но я молчу. Я в кресле, и майор с ножницами. Сейчас нагнется и начнет давить на глаза, и ничего нельзя сделать. Сижу и жду. (note 78)

[Anna Akhmatova] recounted the whole of Kafka's novel...
[Анна Ахматова] пересказала нам весь роман Кафки «Процесс» от начала до конца. Отозвалась о романе так:—Когда читаешь, кажется, словно вас кто-то берет за руку и ведет обратно в ваши дурные сны. Рассказала тут же и биографию Кафки. На Западе он гремит, а у нас не издается. (note 80)

August 30 is the day of departure for Budka.
30-ое августа день отъезда в Будку. О[льга] А[лександровна] и Толя [Найман]. Едем небывалой дорогой (парками) через очень странное, очень красивое наводнение. Вода (без ветра) совсем как жидкое

серебро или ртуть. Она тяжело и медленно выливается из берегов, образуя неожиданные островки и грозя бедой. Я в первый раз видела дуб, посаженный Петром Первым. Эсхатологические небеса, почти с грозной надписью. (note 86)

My dream last night exceeded everything…
Мой сон накануне превосходил все, что в этом роде было со мной в жизни. Я видела планету Земля, какой она была через некоторое время (какое?) после ее окончательного уничтожения. Кажется, все бы отдала, чтобы забыть этот сон! (note 86)

The dream on the night of August 30…
Сон на 30 авг[уста] продолжает угнетать меня и с каждым днем все страшнее.
Зато отъезд по таинственному безветряному наводнению все хорошеет. Бесполезно спрашивать о нем моих спутников. (note 86)

I had a dream…
Мне приснился сон: белый, высокий, ленинградский потолок надо мной мгновенно набухает кровью, и алый ее поток обрушивается на меня. Через несколько часов я встретился с Ахматовой: память о сновидении была неотвязчива, я рассказал его.
—Нехудо,—отозвалась она.—Вообще, самое скучное на свете— чужие сны и чужой блуд. Но вы заслужили. Мой сон я видела в ночь на первое октября.
После мировой катастрофы я, одна-одинешенька, стою на земле, на слякоти, на грязи, скольжу, не могу удержаться на ногах, почву размывает. И откуда-то сверху, расширяясь по мере приближенья и поэтому все более мне угрожая, низвергается поток, в который соединились все великие реки мира: Нил, Ганг, Волга, Миссисипи…Только этого не хватало. (note 87)

In […] the letter, I retold Anna Andreevna the dream…
В […] письме я пересказал Анне Андреевне сон—или видение?— моего отца перед смертью. В этом сне переплетались Греция и Китай, но главной героиней сна была Ахматова.
28 июня, когда я пришел к отцу в больницу утром, он был в ясном сознании и рассказал мне сон (сказав сначала: «Последние дни мне много чепухи рассказывают, и сны снятся дикие»): «Я видел во сне всемирный съезд писателей в Греции, на котором, представь себе, была Ахматова. Как раз в это время в Пирее нашли домик Сократа. Ее в нем поселили: там его стол, его кресло. А я поселился в верхнем

этаже. Утром я спускаюсь вниз и вижу: женщина сидит за столом и плачет. Я спрашиваю ее: «Анна Андреевна, что с вами?» Она отвечает, что она видела в этом столе своего ребенка—только он был розовым, а стол черного мрамора. Так было странно ей увидеть свое дитя среди этих клубящихся плит у моря. Я говорю ей: «Ведь даже Гомера—и того не изображают на каждой вещи, а что же нам, простым людям, ждать». И я сказал ей: «Когда-нибудь у нас, как в Китае, поэзия будет на каждом шагу, на каждой вещи». Она ответила: «Может быть».

При встрече Ахматова мне сказала, что видит в этом сне отзвуки двух своих стихотворений на античные темы. А Китай, добавлю от себя,—это и отблеск того чтения переводов, о котором говорилось выше. Так Ахматова нас, ее окружавших, с собой вместе погружала в зазеркалье сновидений и пророческих образов, по сравнению с которыми меркли другие восприятия. (note 90)

Koma told us...
Кома много рассказывал о последних днях Всеволода. Он умирал долго и сознательно. Подводил итоги. Ему снились сны, где он разговаривал с Богом. Трагическая судьба писателя заканчивалась оправданием перед Богом. Один из последних снов—трогательная фантазия о конгрессе писателей в Афинах и об Ахматовой. Сны Всеволода и последние разговоры с ним Кома записал. (note 92)

March 11. A dream...
11 марта. Сон. Я долго разговаривал с молодым Эренбургом. Он упрекает наше поколение за то, что ни из кого ничего не получилось. Я оправдываюсь: «Мы еще отдыхаем от сталинизма». Студеные мартовские дни. Острый ветер. Свет. (note 93)

"How Akhmatova was sick."
«Как болела Ахматова». Ахматова лежала посреди комнаты и болела. Другая Ахматова, молодая, ухаживала за ней. Обе были не настоящие и старались это скрыть, то есть не оказаться в каком-то повороте,—поэтому двигались очень странно. Появился Ю. М. Лотман, началась конференция, и было решено: «Всем плыть в будущее, кроме Н., у которого бумажное здоровье». (note 94)

"How Mandelshtam was killed."
«Как убили Мандельштама». Мы идем по Манежной площади—очевидно, с Н. Як. [Надежда Яковлевна Мандельштам]. Впереди, за три шага О. Э. [Осип Эмильевич Мандельштам]. Подойти к нему нельзя. При этом мы знаем условие, при котором его заберут, а он

нет. Условие—если он остановится у ларька. Ларьков очень много: сладости, сигареты, открытки. Он все время заглядывается, а мы внушаем на расстоянии: иди, иди, иди. Но напрасно. Он остановился и его увели. Мы выходим на Красную площадь. Там парад. Генерал разводит войска. Войска исчезают, как дым, во все четыре стороны. Тогда по пустой площади очень громко он подходит к Н. Я., отдает честь и вручает «Рапорт»: «1) Удостоверяю, что Ваш муж бессмертен. 2) Он не придумал новых слов, но придумал новые вещи. 3) Поэтому не кляните меня.—Генерал». Мы оказываемся в ложе роскошного театра. На сцене—Киев. Лежит мертвый О. Э., а над ним растрепанная женщина кричит: Ой, який ще гарний! (note 95)

[February 11, 1943] In my dream...
[11 февраля 1943] Во сне—рыбачил, на удочку. Клевало хорошо. Сначала натаскал много мелких рыб, а затем поймал огромную. Так как сны, да еще такой резкой отчетливости, вижу редко, и так как в голове пустой шум, мешающий сосредоточению и работе, и так как несчастья приучают к суеверию, и так как нет для семьи денег и не знаю где их достать, словом—достал «сонник», едва ли не в первый раз в жизни, и прочел. Увы, сонник ответил мне с двойственность, обычной для оракула. Рыбу удить плохо. Но поймать большую рыбу—хорошо. Не удочкой, а сетью, очевидно. А, коли удочкой, то, стало быть, ни богу свечка, ни черту кочерга! Статья в «Известиях» не напечатана. Да, и ну их к лешему, устал я от этих статей! (note 96)

[March 19, 1943] A dream: Alexei Tolstoi...
[19 марта 1943] Сон: рыли узкую яму, клад, я и Ал. Н. Толстой. Уже видно что-то белое, узкое...[...] встав, по обычаю предков, взглянул в «Сонник». Предстоит какое-то великое счастье, а затем такое же великое несчастье....(note 96)

In the spring of 1977...
Весной 1977 г. просыпаясь я услышал: «Этот режим должен погибнуть!» Я стал про себя ругаться: эти интеллигенты всегда хотят, чтобы было так, как им бы казалось нужным. Потом я спохватился: а с кем я, собственно, спорю? Я в комнате один, Светлана давно ушла на работу. Дальнейшие верные предсказания уже в новую пору можно было делать более надежно не во сне или в полусне. Своему другу Роберту Кайзеру, когда-то работавшему корреспондентом «Вашингтон пост» в Москве, а теперь одному из редакторов этой газеты, я сказал в 1984 г., что Горбачев придет к власти и начнет реформы. Ему же и многим другим я заранее говорил о вероятности августовского

провалившегося путча. [...] Но в еще большей степени, чем в детстве, я стал видеть трудность, а иногда и невозможность убедить других в очевидном. (note 97)

10 February [1942]. D. I. ...
10 февраля [1942]. 3-го или 4-го умер Д.И. Так мне сказали вчера, и если это правда, то ушла часть жизни, часть мира. Ночью несколько раз снилось. Сны ищут оправдания смерти, и этой ночью смерть Д.И. была как-то объяснена, но я не помню как, помню только переломленный пучок прутьев. (note 100)

I was accused of something...
Меня в чем-то обвинили, я возражал очень резко. Вдруг вижу—в дверях Л. Уж то не сон,—думаю я. Но присутствующие стали уверять меня, что и это сон: сколько раз являлся и все был сон. Я рассердился: «Все вы несуществующие, все вы мой сон, крому Л.». Они предложили испытать, сон ли Л. Для этого положили его на стол и стали резать грудь, а он усилием воли стал заживлять раны. Я ему помогал, тоже усилием воли. Кровь остановилась, раны высохли, остались только шрамы. «Но что это доказывает?»—подумал я, и все присутствующие и Л. стали медленно испаряться. (note 101)

[undated] V. [Vvedensky] arrived yesterday
[без даты] Приехал В., оказывается еще вчера. Сейчас проходил мимо, поклонился, даже не подошел, а завтра утром уезжает.
Я пошел к Липавским, Л. сидел за столом, Т. лежала на столе. Когда я вошел, она сошла со стола, села. Я говорю: «Как В. изменился, он стал похожим на профессионального советского писателя. Вначале я его даже принял за Свиридова». Поговорили. Просыпаясь подумал: но ведь Введенского нет. Но почему я так давно не встречался с Хармсом, позвоню ему, и вспомнил: его тоже нет. Тогда позвоню Олейникову, да ведь и его нет. Остался один Леня, и, окончательно проснувшись, вспомнил: и он погиб. Wir sind tot. Alles ist tot. (note 102)

L. came over...
Пришел Л. Я спросил его: как ты думаешь, Д. И. жив?—Он расстрелян.—Почему?—Было дело преподавателей.—Но он же не преподаватель?—Да, но он неодобрительно относился к конституции. Потом я намеками старался узнать у него, почему он так давно не появлялся. Он ответил, что бывал.—Тогда отчего же Тамара так огорчается?—Он привел какой-то убедительный довод. Я стал думать, как совместить все эти противоречия, и настолько сосредоточился,

что внезапно проснулся, причем снова не было перехода от сна к бодрствованию.

Сон о милиционерах, учивших переходить улицу, о розовом и черном дыме.

Проезжали три повозки: с лондонцами, поляками и евреями. Евреи, хоть и битые, но все же довольны. Я поднял воротник повыше: на всякий случай.

Сон о конце мира. Конец мира должен был произойти на каком-то озере. Там уже все было готово для этого и стоял пустой дом. Я думал, может, в нем можно спастись? Но потом понял: и он погибнет. Я стал искать надежное место и нашел, но как описать его, не знаю. Я помню это озеро, но не знаю, как назвать координаты этого места, может быть, оно не было в пространстве. Но, находясь в этом месте, я не погиб бы при светопреставлении, но стал бы тучей или цветом тучи. (note 104)

Mama took my things [writings] out of the desk drawer...

Мама вынула мои вещи [сочинения] из стола и положила их на диван на берегу реки, и они скатились в реку. Я сказал: «Что ты сделала, ведь это моя жизнь». Потом мама ушла. Мы с Мишей тоже возвращаемся домой. По дороге нас останавливают несколько человек, должно быть, убийцы. Я ухожу дальше: меня ничто не касается, а перед М. препятствие: веревки. Он их умело обходит, последнюю надо разрубить, он разрубает ее. Но затем для чего-то рубит и другую веревку, которая ему уже не мешает. Я забыл сказать, что веревки соединены узлами, в узлах стоят убийцы, главный убийца—вне узлов. Как только М. разрубил веревку, которая ему не мешала, я подумал: он совершил лишнее, он погиб. И действительно, главный выхватывает пистолет и стреляет в одного из убийц, говоря: ты, в другого: ты, в Мишу: ты совершил лишнее. Я хочу незаметно удалиться. Главный оборачивается ко мне: тебя ничто не касается, умри. Я увертываюсь, оправдываюсь, бросаюсь к реке, он стреляет, и я умираю. (note 107)

I was told that I killed myself...

Мне сказали, что я сам себя убил четырьмя ударами ножа в живот, в промежутке между первой и второй смертью, увидя главного и не вынеся мерзости. [...] Я понял, что эта смерть в счет не идет. Снова появился главный и убивал других. Я же, искушенный, пройдя через три смерти, давал советы и помогал спасись другим. Потом появилась жертва главного—убитая им женщина. Она была отвратительна и получила способность убивать. Но я уже знал, что делать. Тогда она, видя, что прямо меня не убить, подает мне топор. Я знаю, ударив ее топором, я не убью ее, но она получит новую силу убить меня. Я вонзаю топор в пол и говорю—исчезни. (note 108)

I had agonizing, tormenting dreams...
снились мучительные, томящие сны: война, бомбежки, я убила какую-то страшную старуху (я иногда убиваю во сне ужасных старух). (note 109)

Before her arrest, Berggol'ts had planned a "novel about...
роман о нашем поколении, о становлении его сознания к моменту его зрелости, роман о субъекте эпохи, о субъекте его сознания. (note 111)

July 3 [1939]. Khmelev called on the phone...
3 июля [1939]. Вчера утром телефонный звонок Хмелева—просит послушать пьесу. Тон повышенный, радостный, наконец опять пьеса М. А. в Театре! и так далее.

Вечером у нас Хмелев, Калишьян, Ольга. Миша читал несколько картин. Потом ужин с долгим сидением после. Разговоры о пьесе, о МХТ, о системе. Разошлись, когда уж совсем солнце вставало. Рассказ Хмелева. Сталин раз сказал ему: хорошо играете Алексея. Мне даже снятся ваши черные усики (турбинские). Забыть не могу. (note 117)

I visited Bulgakov...
Был у Булгакова—слушал пьесу о Сталине—грандиозно! Это может перевернуть все верх дном! Я до сих пор нахожусь под впечатлением и под обаянием этого произведения.

25 августа Булгаков пьесу сдает МХАТу в законченном виде. Утверждают, что Сталина должен играть я. Поживем—увидим.

Заманчиво, необычайно интересно, сложно, дьявольски трудно, очень ответственно, радостно, страшно! (note 118)

NOTES

Footnote. Besides the physical world...
Кроме мира вещей, в котором мы живем, и мира предметов культуры, которые мы создаем, есть еще и третий мир еще несделанных открытий, ненаписанных книг, неисполненных симфоний. Они существуют как платоновские идеи. Развитие культуры состоит в том, что мы их как бы считываем, постепенно до них доходя. Двое ученых в одной области часто осуществляют это считывание почти одновременно. Так было у меня с Якобсоном. (page 196n)

EPILOGUE

Meilakh once came from Leningrad to Moscow...

в Москву приехал Михаил Мейлах. Помнится, мы с ним зашли к Николаю Ивановичу Харджиеву. Там мы застали Герштейн. Хозяин сидел за своим письменным столом, а Эмма Григорьевна на стуле перед ним. В какой-то момент гостья произнесла:

—Вы просто обязаны написать мемуары...

И тут Харджиев, дотоле сидевший в довольно статичной позе, весьма проворно сложил два кукиша и моментально поднес их к самому лицу собеседницы...

Ни Мейлах, ни я не силах забыть эту «немую сцену» до сего дня. (note 2)

NOTES

INTRODUCTION

1 Much has been written about the nascent "memory culture" in late- and post-Soviet Russia, and about its failure. I found the following particularly informing and insightful: Anatoly M. Khazanov, "Whom to Mourn and Whom to Forget? (Re)constructing Collective Memory in Contemporary Russia," in *Reckoning with the Past: Perpetrators, Accomplices and Victims in Twentieth and Twenty-first Century Narratives and Politics,* special issue of *Totalitarian Movements and Political Religions* 9, nos. 2–3 (2008): 293–310.
I thank Anatoly Khazanov for sharing his research before it was published.

2 For obvious reasons, scholarship that treats Soviet diaries and memoirs from a post-Soviet perspective is still young and has not been large in volume. Yet, there have been prominent publications, and they have attracted attention and debate. In his pioneering studies, Jochen Hellbeck used diaries from the 1930s (mostly unpublished archival sources) to generalize about the rise of Soviet subjectivity. See his *Revolution on My Mind: Writing a Diary under Stalin* (Cambridge: Harvard University Press, 2006). For a critique of this approach (based on articles published earlier), see Eric Naiman, "On Soviet Subjects and the Scholars Who Make Them," *The Russian Review* 60, no. 3 (July 2001): 307–15. Distrustful of memoirs and diaries, Orlando Figes has purported to explore the regime's effect on the lives of ordinary people—"what they really think and feel" (his words)—mostly through oral interviews in *The Whisperers: Private Life in Stalin's Russia* (New York: Metropolitan Books, 2007). Not everybody is ready to accept this research as evidence of what Soviet people really feel. See Jochen Hellbeck's critique, "The Ice Forge," *The Nation,* March 3, 2008; and Lewis Siegelbaum, "Witness Protection," *London Review of Books* April 10, 2008. The literary shape of various contemporary Russian memoirs has been explored in essays by Jane Gary Harris, Helena Goscilo, Alexander Prokhorov, Marina Balina, and others that are included in *The Russian Memoir: History and Literature,* ed. and intro. Beth Holmgren (Evanston, Ill.: Northwestern University Press, 2003). Two remarkable articles pose the problems of genre, self, and ethics in late-Soviet and post-Soviet personal documents, Marina Balina's "The Autobiographies of *Glasnost:* The Question of Genre in Russian Autobiographical Memoirs of the 1980s," *a/b: Auto/Biography Studies* 7 (1992): 13–26, and Anne Dwyer's "Runaway Texts: The Many Life Stories of Iurii Trifonov and Christa Wolf," *Russian Review* 64 (October 2005): 605–27.

3 The "end-of-the-epoch" feeling and its narrative expressions have been famously described by Frank Kermode, in *The Sense of an Ending: Studies in the Theory of Fiction with a New Epilogue* (1967; rpr., Oxford: Oxford University Press, 2000).

4 Paul John Eakin, in his influential book on "life stories," describes how a literary scholar pursues a "quasi-anthropological" approach to autobiography, "asking what such texts can teach us about the ways in which individuals in a particular culture experience their sense of being 'I'." *How Our Lives Become Stories: Making Selves* (Ithaca: Cornell University Press, 1999), 4.

5   The obligatory reference to research on autobiography is to Philipe Lejeune, *Le pacte autobiographique* (Paris: Seuil, 1975). A strong statement about memoirs as a historicist genre has been made in Marcus Billson's neglected essay, "The Memoir: New Perspectives on a Forgotten Genre," *Genre* 10 (Summer 1977), 259–83. (Billson also connected memoirs and the "sense of an ending" as defined by Kermode; p. 281). Eakin, in his *How Our Lives Become Stories*, speaks of "memoirs" (distinguished from autobiographies) as a "hitherto neglected class of narratives" (56) and attempts to rehabilitate them by locating a corpus of recent American writings in which "the story of the self, the 'I,' is subordinated to the story of some other" (58). Curiously, his first example is a story of a "feisty Russian emigrant and tireless organizer for the Communist Party" (58). For Russian literary culture, memoirs are not a neglected or forgotten genre: from the mid-nineteenth century to this day, they have remained central. Beth Holmgren makes this clear in her Introduction to *The Russian Memoir* (x).
6   There is no consensus on the definition of the diary. I will take the liberty to refer to my own survey, "What Can Be Done with Diaries?" *Russian Review* 64 (October 2004): 561–73.
7   For such understanding of diary writing, self, and temporality, I am indebted to Stuart Sherman, *Telling Time: Clocks, Diaries, and English Diurnal Form, 1660–1785* (Chicago, 1996); the formula is his (33–34).
8   Peter Fritzsche has suggested that telling autobiographical stories that distinguish between the "I then" and the "I now" recapitulates the philosophical method of historicism. Peter Fritzsche, "The Case of Modern Memory," *Journal of Modern History* 73 (March 2001), 11.
9   Suffice it to name two books that guide readers in this large field of inquiry: Eakin's *How Our Lives Become Stories* (1999), which provides a reassessment of autobiographical writings from a literary and experiential (psychological and anthropological) perspective, and *Telling Stories: The Use of Personal Narratives in the Social Sciences and History* by Mary Jo Maynes, Jennifer L. Pierce, and Barbara Laslett (Ithaca: Cornell University Press, 2008).
10 I have been encouraged by Luisa Passerini's resolve in her *Fascism in Popular Memory* to "[use] concepts which promote analysis without first attempting to resolve all the related theoretical problems" (2). Passerini's classic study of memories of Italian Fascism, based on oral interviews, has also inspired me in other ways. Thus, I share her trust that a picture of the day-to-day reality of living under a dictatorships can be made readable from individual memories, and her belief that, as cultural forms, working-class memories (in her case, oral interviews) can be analyzed with some of the same tools as written texts of high culture. See Luisa Passerini, *Fascism in Popular Memory: The Cultural Experience of the Turin Working Class*, trans. Robert Lumley and Jude Bloomfield (Cambridge: Cambridge University Press, 1987).
11 For a remarkable example of how a phenomenological philosopher theorizes the relationship between "personal narrative," "communal narrative," and "historical time," see David Carr, *Time, Narrative, and History* (Bloomington: Indiana University Press, 1991). Carr also speaks of the "exaggerated historical consciousness" that "overtakes European thought in the eighteenth century and extends to our day" (179). For a psychologist's justification of personal histories, see, for example, Jens Brockmeier, "Autobiography, Narrative, and the Freudian Concept of Life History," *Philosophy, Psychiatry, and Psychology* 4, no. 3 (1997): 175–99. A literary scholar's view, informed psychologically, is elaborated by Peter Brooks in *Psychoanalysis and Storytelling* (Oxford: Blackwell, 1994).
12 The issue of generalizing from personal narratives, in a sociological, ethnographic, and historical key, has been illuminated by Maynes, Pierce and Laslett in *Telling Stories*, 128–31.
13 Hannah Arendt, "On the Nature of Totalitarianism: An Essay in Understanding," *Essays in Understanding, 1930–1954*, ed. Jerome Kohn (New York: Harcourt, Brace and Co., 1994), 338.

PART I

1   I have in mind such paradigm-setting studies as Pierre Nora, "Between Memory and History," intro. to *Les lieux de mémoire* (Paris: Gallimard, 1984), which establishes a contrast between these two concepts, and Cathy Caruth, *Unclaimed Experience: Trauma, Narrative, and History* (Baltimore: John Hopkins University Press, 1996), which treats narratives of traumatic historical

experience from a psychoanalytic perspective. There is an enormous literature that operates with the notions of memory, witnessing, trauma, and "mastering the past" (*Vergangenheitsbewältigung*) based on the experiences of the Holocaust and other major historical atrocities; a few studies deal with Russian and East European material in this perspective. For a sympathetic review of some of this literature, see Peter Fritzsche, "The Case of Modern Memory," *Journal of Modern History* 73 (March 2001): 87–117. For a skeptical view, see Kerwin Lee Klein, "On the Emergence of *Memory* in Historical Discourse," *Representations* 69 (Winter 2000): 127–50.

2 Dnevniki, vospominaniia (Novyi mir); Vospominaniia, dokumenty (Oktiabr'); Memuary. Arkhivy. Svidetel'stva (Znamia); Memuary XX veka (Zvezda); Chastnye vospominaniia o XX veke (Druzhba narodov); Istorik i vremia (Odissei). Moi XX vek (Moscow: Vagrius); XX vek ot pervogo litsa (Moscow: ROSSPEN); XX vek glazami ochevidtsev (Moscow: Olimp/AST); Semeinyi arkhiv XX veka (Moscow: Integraf Servis); Iz rukopisnogo nasledija (Moscow: Knizhnaia palata); Dnevniki i vospominaniia Peterburgskikh uchenykh (St. Petersburg: Evropeiskii dom); Dokumenty zhizni. Interpretatsii (Moscow: Gnozis); Seriia Narodnyi arkhiv (Moscow: Rossiia molodaia/Aero-XX vek); Narodnye memuary (Omsk: Omskii gosudarstvennyi universitet).

3 The guidebook published on the tenth anniversary of the archive's existence claims that by 1998 the archive held more than one hundred thousand files, *Tsentr dokumentatsii "Narodnyi arkhiv": Spravochnik po fondam* (Moscow, 1998). The phrase "people's archive," or "open archive," is used also as a metaphor. A bibliography of documents published in periodicals is entitled "An Open Archive": *Otkrytyi arkhiv: Spravochnik opublikovannykh dokumentov po istorii Rossii XX-go veka iz gosudarstvennykh i semeinykh arkhivov (po otechestvennoi i zhurnal'noi periodike i al'manakham 1985–1996 gg.)*, ed. I. A. Kondakova, 2nd. ed. (Moscow: ROSSPEN, 1999).

4 For documents of "ordinary people," marked as such, see, for example, L. A. Durnov, *Zhizn' vracha: zapiski obykvovennogo cheloveka* [Life of a doctor: Notes of an ordinary man] (Moscow: Vagrius, 2001), or A. G. Man'kov, "Iz dnevnika riadovogo cheloveka (1933–34 gg.) [From the diary of an ordinary man]," *Zvezda*, no. 5 (1994): 134–83, and no. 11 (1995): 167–99. The latter represents the fluidity of the category "ordinary people": published by Man'kov, the well-known Soviet historian, this diary was written by the young Man'kov—worker and student; when the memoir appeared in a book form, the marker "ordinary person" was removed, A. G. Man'kov, *Dnevniki 30-kh godov* (St. Petersburg: Evropeiskii dom, Series: Dnevniki i vospominaniia peterburgskikh uchenykh), 2001).

5 There is a book about the corpus of Soviet camp narratives, Leona Toker's *Return from the Archipelago: Narratives of Gulag Survivors* (Bloomington: Indiana University Press, 2000).

6 Published writings of barely literate peasants and workers include: *Dnevnye zapisi ust'-kulomskogo krest'ianina I. S. Rassykhaeva (1902–1953)* (Moscow: RAN Institut etnologii i antropologii im. Mikhlukho-Maklaia, 1997); *Dnevnik totemskogo krest'ianina A. A. Zamaraeva: 1906–1922 gody* (Moscow: RAN Institut etnologii i antropologii im. Mikhlukho-Maklaia, 1995); *Vospominaniia rabotnitsy M. N. Koltakovoi 'kak ia prozhila zhizn': Publikatsiia i issledovanie teksta*, ed. Boris Osipov (Omsk: Omskii gos. universitet, Series: Narodnye memuary, 1997). The phrase "voices of the people on behalf of whom the intellectuals always spoke" is from N. N. Kozlova, *Gorizonty povsednevnosti Sovetskoi epokhi: Golosa iz khora* (Moscow: IFRAN, 1996), 65. (This edition uses documents from Narodnyi arkhiv.)

7 N. N. Kozlova and I. I. Sandomirskaia, *Ia tak khochu nazvat' kino: "Naivnoe pis'mo." Opyt lingvo-sotsiologicheskogo chteniia* (Moscow: Gnozis, Series: Dokumenty zhizni. Interpretatsii, 1996).

8 David Samoilov, "Iz dnevnika," *Literaturnoe obozrenie*, no. 11 (1990): 93–103; no. 5–6 (1992): 5–56; and no. 7–9 (1992): 52–61; "Podennye zapisi (Iz dnevnikov 1971–1990)," *Znamia*, no. 2 (1992): 148–74; no. 3 (1992): 132–66; "Obshchii dnevnik" [1977–89], *Iskusstvo kino*, no. 5 (1992): 103–19; *Pamiatnye zapiski* (Moscow: Mezhdunarodnoe otnosheniia, 1995). Selections appeared as *Perebiraia nashi daty* (Moscow: Vagrius, 2000). There is also a new edition of these and other documents, entitled *Podennye zapiski* [Daily notes] (Moscow: Vremia, 2002).

9 Iurii Kuvaldin, "Nagibin," *Nevskoe vremia*, March 13, 1996.

10 Iurii Nagibin, *Dnevnik*, ed. Iurii Kuvaldin, 2nd ed. (Moscow: Knizhnyi sad, 1996). The first edition was in 1995. An edition appeared in 2004 from the Moscow publisher Ast.

11 Leonid Zorin, *Avanstsena: Memuarnyi roman* (Moscow: Slovo, 1997) and *Zelenye tetradi* (Moscow: Novoe literaturnoe obozrenie, 1999).
12 Recent editions of Lidiia Chukovskaia's "notes" include: Lidiia Chukovskaia, *Zapiski ob Anne Akhmatovoi* [covering the years 1938–41] (Moscow: Kniga, 1989); *Zapiski ob Anne Akhmatovoi*, vol. 1 [1938–41] and vol. 2 [1952–62] (Khar'kov: Folio, 1996); *Zapiski ob Anne Akhmatovoi*, vol. 1 [1938–41], vol. 2 [1952–62], and vol. 3 [1963–66] (Moscow: Soglasie, 1997). Volume 2 also appeared in the journal *Neva*, no. 4–9 (1993); volume 3 was first published in *Neva*, no. 8–10 (1996). Volumes 1 and 2 were previously published in the West by the YMCA Press (vol. 1 in 1976 and 1984; vol. 2 in 1980).
13 Elvira Filipovich, *Ot sovetskoi pionerki do chelnoka pensionerki (moi dnevnik). Kniga 1 (1944–1972)* (Podol'sk: Saturn, 2000). The appellation "shuttle pensioner" (*chelnok-pensionerka*) is clear to the present-day reader: a stock figure of the first post-Soviet years, this is a retired person who "shuttles" small goods (typically, clothing and household items) between flea markets.
14 Kirill Rogov, ed., *Semidesiatye kak predmet istorii kul'tury* (Moscow and Venice: Rossiia/Russia, 1998). The phrase "history of yesterday," borrowed from Lev Tolstoy, appears in the title of Alexander Zholkovsky's sophisticated essay, "Iz istorii vcherashnego dnia" (135–52).
15 Afer Iuliia Zhukova's review of *An Evening in the Summer Garden* (*Vecher v Letnem sadu. Epizody is istorii "vtoroi kul'tury"* [St. Peterburg: Izdatel'stvo im. N. I. Novikova, 2002]) in *Novaia russkaia kniga*, no. 4–5 (2000): 84.
16 Marietta Chudakova, "Liudskaia molv' i konskii top: Na iskhode sovetskogo vremeni," *Novyi mir*, nos. 1, 3, and 6 (2000).
17 Mariia Arbatova, *Mne 40 let...Avtobiograficheskii roman* (Moscow: Zakharov-Ast, 1999); Mariia Arbatova, *Proshchanie s XX vekom. Avtobiograficheskaia proza*, 2 vols. (Moscow: Eskmo, 2002).
18 In the book-form edition, Andrei Sergeev, *Omnibus: Roman, rasskazy, vospominaniia* (Moscow: NLO, 1997).
19 Aleksei Simonov, *Chastnaia kollektsiia* (Nizhnii Novgorod: Dekom, 1999), 9.
20 Lidiia Ginzburg, *Chelovek za pis'mennym stolom* (Leningrad: Sovetskii pisatel', 1989).
21 Selections of Ginzburg's notes appeared in the journals *Neva* (no. 1, 1987; no. 12, 1988), *Daugava* (no. 1, 1989), *Rodnik* (no. 1, 1989). There are yet other editions.
22 Lidiia Ginzburg, *Zapisnye knizhki: Novoe sobranie* (Moscow: Zakharov, 1999).
23 Evgenii Shvarts, *Zhivu bespokoino...Iz dnevnikov*, ed. Kseniia Kirilenko (Moscow-Leningrad: Sovetskii pisatel', 1990).
24 Evgenii Shvarts, *Proizvedeniia*, 4 vols., ed. M. O. Kryzhanovskaia and I. L. Shershneva (Moscow: Izdatel'stvo Korona Press, 1999).
25 Shvarts, *Telefonnaia knizhka*, ed. Kseniia Kirilenko (Moscow: Iskusstvo, 1997).
26 Aleksandr Shirvindt and Boris Poirovskii, *Byloe bez dum: Popytka dialoga* (Moscow: Tsentrpoligraf, 2001), 263–316.
27 Nagibin, *Dnevnik*, 4.
28 B. G. Tartakovskii, *Vse eto bylo...Vospominaniia ob ischezaiushchem pokolenii* (Moscow: AIRO-XX, 2005), 13.
29 Nagibin, *Dnevnik*, 5, 6.
30 Aleksei Simonov's *Chastnaia kollektsiia*, 47.
31 From Zhukova' review of Severiukhin's memoir in *Novaia russkaia kniga*, 84.
32 I borrowed the language from Michel de Certeau, *The Practice of Everyday Life*, trans. Steven Rendall (Berkeley: University of California Press, 1984), xxi, 167–74.
33 Mikhail Aizenberg, "Chitaia memuary," *Znamia*, no. 1, 2000: 215.
34 Nagibin, *Dnevnik*, 4.
35 Filipovich, *Ot sovetskoi pionerki*, frontispiece.
36 A selection of readers' letters to Chukovskaia, written between 1967 and 1994, was published in *Znamia*, no. 8, 1995. Natalia Il'ina's letter is from September 1969 (letter 13); N. Uritskaia's is from August 30, 1989 (letter 41).
37 The rise of historical consciousness and memoir writing in Russia is discussed by Andrei Tartakovskii, *Russkaia memuaristika XVIII—pervoi poloviny XIX veka* (Moscow: Nauka, 1991), and

Russkaia memuaristika i istoricheskoe soznanie XIX veka (Moscow: Arkheograficheskii tsentr, 1997). Creating a parallel between Russian and European intellectual history, Tartakovskii points to the increase in the number of memoirs and diaries after the invasion of Napoleon. I would argue that "historical consciousness" in the sense discussed above appears much later, in the 1840s, when people who *grew up* during Napoleon's invasion came to maturity in the Hegelian atmosphere of the friendly circles and, later still, in the 1860s, when their autobiographical writings entered the public arena.

38 A whole chain of Russian historians, echoing one another, linked the intimate *kruzhki* of the 1840s, personal documents from that period, Russian psychological prose (culminating in the 1860s and 1870s), and Hegelian historical consciousness. This chain extends from pioneers of the historiography of Russian thought, literature, and the intelligentsia, such as Pavel Annenkov and Alexander Pypin in the 1850s to 1870s, to Pavel Miliukov and Mikhail Gershenzon in the 1900s to 1910s, to Lidiia Ginzburg in the 1950s to 1970s. John Randolph noted the special significance of these intimate roots of the historiography of Russian thought in "'That Historical Family': The Bakunin Archive and the Intimate Theater of History in Imperial Russia, 1780–1925," *Russian Review* 63 (October 2004): 574–93.

39 Lidiia Ginzburg starts her "Notes from the Leningrad Blockade" with this claim. For English translation, see Lidiya Ginzburg, *Blockade Diary*, trans. Alan Myers (London: Harvill, 1995).

40 See Medvedeva-Samoilova's introduction to Samoilov, *Perebiraia nashi daty*, 9, and Samoilov's diary from September 8, 1971 (ibid.).

41 Anatolii Naiman, "A. A. A. cherez tridtsat' tri goda," *Literaturnaia gazeta* no. 34 (5666), August 20, 1997; Iuliia Sycheva, "Liubliu svoi gnev," *Lebed'*, November 16 and 23, 2003 (both cited from http://www.chukfamily.ru/Lidia/Biblio).

42 This theme is developed in great detail in Iuliia Sycheva's "Liubliu svoi gnev."

43 Vasilii Katanian, *Raspechatannaia butylka* (Nizhnii Novgorod: Dekom, 1999), 7 (emphasis in the original).

44 S. V. Zhitomirskaia, *Prosto zhizn'* (Moscow: Rosspen, 2006).

45 Noted in A. I. Dobkin's introduction to N. P. Antsiferov, *Iz dum o bylom. Vospominaniia* (Moscow: Feniks, 1992).

46 Ol'ga Berggol'ts, "Iz dnevnikov," *Neva*, no. 5 (1990): 177.

47 See Faina Ranevskaia, *Dnevnik na klochkakh*, ed. Iurii Danilin (St. Petersburg: Fond russkoi poezii, 1999), 33.

48 Stepan Podlubnyi's diary has been published only in excerpts; Herzen is mentioned in the diary entry for September 9, 1932; TsDNA f. 30 op. 1 ed. khr. 11–18. I thank Jochen Hellbeck for the use of his copy of the archival manuscript.

49 Barbara Walker, "On Reading Soviet Memoirs: A History of the 'Contemporaries' Genre as an Institution of Russian Intelligentsia Culture from the 1790s to the 1970s," *Russian Review* 59 (July 2000): 327–52. Inspired by Walker's remarkably original and far-reaching ideas, I take the liberty to extend and adjust them. While Walker starts in the 1790s (with Radishchev) and traces the genre *vospominaniia sovremennikov* (memoirs of the contemporaries) to the 1970s, I claim Herzen's *My Past and Thoughts* as the central text. Many of the events described by Herzen were revisited in Pavel Annenkov's memoir, *A Remarkable Decade (1838–1848)* (*Zamechatel'noe desiatiletie 1838–1848*). Published in 1880 in Russia, *Zamechatel'noe desiatiletie* told the stories of the same Moscow circles. Echoing Herzen, Annenkov confirmed the validity of the picture drawn in *Byloe i dumy* (published earlier in Europe but known to Russians) and reinforced the idea that the Russian "intelligentsia" (unlike Herzen, Annenkov used this word) was a social formation rooted in the friendly circles. Annenkov's documentary biography of Nikolai Stankevich, the patron of the main Moscow circle, published in 1857, made a move to convert memoir literature into historiography.

50 While the tone of gloom and doom might be specifically Russian, as Karl Löwith showed, Hegel's successors in the West also converted his history of the spirit into "spiritual history" of individual men, who themselves wanted to be "historic." In the twentieth century, Italian Fascism and German Nazism revitalized "the activistic historicism of the [eighteen] forties." See Karl Löwith, *From Hegel to Nietzsche: The Revolution in Nineteenth-Century Thought*, trans. David E. Green (New York: Columbia University Press, 1964), 217–18.

51 Lidiia Libedinskaia, *Zelenaia lampa i mnogoe drugoe* (Moscow: Raduga, 2000), 286–87, 348–49. First published in 1968, the memoir was revised for a second, uncensored, publication in 2000; the last page bears two dates: March 1964 and December 1999.
52 Aleksandr Gertsen, *Byloe i dumy*, ed. and intro. L. Libedinskoi (Moscow: Detskaia literatura, 1960); Lidiia Libedinskaia, *Gertsen v Moskve* (Moscow: Detskaia literatura, 1976).
53 Ludmilla Alexeyeva and Paul Goldberg, *The Thaw Generation: Coming of Age in the Post-Stalin Era* (Boston: Little, Brown and Company, 1990), 10, 13.
54 Lidiia Ginzburg, *"Byloe i dumy" Gertsena* (Leningrad: Goslitizdat, 1957), and *O psikhologicheskoi proze* (Leningrad: Sovetskii pisatel', 1971; 2nd. ed. 1977); Lidiia Chukovskaia, *"Byloe i dumy" Gertsena* (Moscow: Khudozhestvennaia literatura, 1966).
55 Preface to part 5 of Gertsen, *Byloe i dumy* (1866); emphasis in the original. Cited in Lydia Ginzburg, *On Psychological Prose* [1971; 1977], trans. Judson Rosengrant (Princeton: Princeton University Press, 1991), 203.
56 Chukovskaia, *"Byloe i dumy" Gertsena*, 23.
57 Ginzburg, *On Psychological Prose*, 203.
58 Ginzburg, *Chelovek za pis'mennym stolom*, 301. The episode with Hegel and Napoleon (described in Hegel's so-called Jena letter in 1806) has been used as an emblem of personal historicism since the early nineteenth century. See Löwith, *From Hegel to Nietzsche*, 215. Herzen mentioned it in his diary in 1844; Gertsen, *Sobranie sochinenii v tridtsati tomakh*, vol. 2 (Moscow: Izdatel'stvo Akademii Nauk, 1954), 378.
59 Leonid Batkin, "Son razuma: O sotsial'no-kul'turnykh masshtabakh lichnosti Stalina," in *Osmyslit' kul't Stalina* (Moscow: Progress, 1989), 10.
60 R. M. Frumkina, *O nas—naiskosok* (Moscow: Russkie slovari, 1997), 79; see also 53, 113, 117, 189. Frumkina been published an expanded edition with the suggestive title "Inside History," *Vnutri istorii. Esse. Stat'i. Memuarnye ocherki* (Moscow: NLO, 2002).
61 Elsewhere, I have focused on the transmission of the memoir-writing tradition and historical consciousness, positing a chain Hegel-Herzen-Ginzburg: Irina Paperno, "Sovetskii opyt, avtobiograficheskoe pis'mo i istoricheskoe soznanie: Ginzburg, Gertsen, Gegel'," *Novoe literaturnoe obozrenie*, no. 68 (2004): 102–27. Alexander Etkind disagrees; see his "'Odno vremia ia kolebalsia, ne antikhrist li ia," *Novoe literaturnoe obozrenie*, no. 73 (2005): 41–69.
62 I have in mind the work of Igal Halfin and Jochen Hellbeck, including Igal Halfin, *Terror in My Soul: Communist Autobiographies on Trial* (Cambridge: Harvard University Press, 2003); Jochen Hellbeck, *Revolution on My Mind: Diaries from the Stalin Era* (Cambridge: Harvard University Press, 2006). While I would not join the emerging scholarly field of "Soviet subjectivities" that they inaugurated, I have much benefited from Hellbeck's analysis of diaries from the 1930s, especially his treatment of Hegelian historicism. I owe a debt to Igal Halfin for his analysis of Marxist historicism and its eschatological dimension in the 1920s (in *From Darkness to Light: Class Consciousness and Salvation in Revolutionary Russia* [Pittsburgh: University of Pittsburgh Press, 2000].)
63 Ilia Erenburg, *Liudi, gody, zhizn': Vospominaniia v trekh tomakh*, ed. Irina Erenburg and Boris Frezinskii, 3 vols. (Moscow: Sovetskii pisatel', 1990), 1:46, 48.
64 Shirvindt and Poiurovskii, *Byloe bez dum*, 194, 317.
65 Tat'iana Okunevskaia, *Tat'ianin den'* (Moscow: Vagrius, 1998), 7.
66 Mikhail Kozakov, *Akterskaia kniga* (Moscow: Vagrius, 1996), 7.
67 Lidiia Smirnova, *Moia liubov'* (Moscow: Vagrius, 1997), 6.
68 Viktor Toporov, *Dvoinoe dno: Priznaniia skandalista* (Moscow: Zakharov-AST, 1999), 6. The author's mother, Zoia Nikolaevna Toporova, is known in the intelligentsia community as the defense attorney in the case against Iosif Brodsky in 1964. For one reader's strong reaction to Toporov's provocative self-revelations, see Stanislav Shuliak's review, "Paskvil' kak element smekhovoi kul'tury," http://zhurnal.lib.ru/s/shuljak_stanislaw_iwanowich/paskvil.shtml (first published in *Literaturnaia gazeta* in 1999).
69 Filipovich, *Ot sovetskoi pionerki*, 3–4.
70 Rodion Nakhapetov, *Vliublennyi* (Moscow: Vagrius, 1999).
71 Kozlova and Sandomirskaia, *Ia tak khochu*, 210, 89, and 142 respectively.
72 Mikhail Prishvin, "1937 god," *Oktiabr'*, no. 11 (1994): 169; dated June 21, 1937.

73 Veniamin Kaverin, *Epilog: Memuary* (Moscow: Moskovskii rabochii, 1989), 64. Written in the 1970s, this text (one of Kaverin's several memoirs) was published only in 1989.
74 Kozlova and Sandomirskaia, *Ia tak khochu*, 87.
75 Ibid., 99–100.
76 Ibid., 7.
77 Filipovich, *Ot sovetskoi pionerki*, 86, 91, 260–62.
78 For high points, see Nagibin, *Dnevnik*, 35, 37, 73, 81, 160, 541.
79 Iurii Nagibin, *T'ma v kontse tunelia. Moia zolotaia teshcha* (Moscow: PIK, 1994), and *Dafnis i Khloia epokhi kul'ta lichnosti, voliuntarizma i zastoia* (Moscow: PIK, 1995).
80 The dilemmas and paradoxes of Jewish identity in the Soviet Union have been masterfully unfolded in Yuri Slezkine's *The Jewish Century* (Princeton: Princeton University Press, 2004), chap. 4 (see pp. 242 and 340 for key formulations on the shift from the 1920s to the 1940s and beyond).
81 Mikhail German, *Slozhnoe proshedshee (Passé composé)* (St. Petersburg: Iskusstvo-SPB, 2000), 203. A comment on Nagibin's diary appears on p. 526.
82 Iakov Rapoport, *Na rubezhe dvukh vekov: Delo vrachei 1953 goda* (Moscow: Kniga, 1988); all phrases in quotation marks are Rapoport's (207). The memoir first appeared in the journal *Druzhba narodov* in the same year; there are yet other editions. English from Yakov Rapoport, *The Doctor's Plot of 1953* (Cambridge: Harvard University Press, 1991).
83 Ibid., 214
84 Nataliia Iakovlevna Rapoport, "Pamiat'—eto tozhe meditsina," *Iunost'*, no. 4 (1988), intro. Evgenii Evtushenko, 76–81 (the title translates: "Memory is also medicine"). An expanded version of this memoir was published ten years later in the book entitled *To li byl', to li nebyl'* (St. Petersburg: Izdatel'stvo Pushkinskogo fonda, 1998).
85 Mikhail Gasparov, *Zapisi i vypiski* (Moscow: NLO, 2000); the second, enlarged edition appeared in 2008.
86 Igor' Nemirovskii, review of Mikhail Gasparov, *Zapisi i vypiski* in *Novaia russkaia kniga*, no. 6 (2000): 9–10.
87 Paraphrasing Ginzburg, *Chelovek za pis'mennym stolom*, 346.
88 Ginzburg's *Zapisnye knizhki: Novoe sobranie*, frontispiece.
89 Arbatova, *Proshchanie s XX vekom*, 2:9.
90 This phrase, coined by Thomas Lahusen, is from the collection prepared by Veronique Garros, Natalia Korenevskaya, and Thomas Lahusen, eds. *Intimacy and Terror: Soviet Diaries of the 1930s* (New York: New Press, 1995). Here, as elsewhere, I use the word "intimacy" in its common linguistic usage, to refer to both "the personal and inward" and to "shared familiarity."
91 Most obviously, Stalin's terror and war are equated in diaries from the Leningrad blockade. For explicit comparisons, see Berggol'ts, "Blokadnyi dnevnik," *Aprel'*, no. 4 (1991): 133; Shvarts, *Zhivu bespokoino*, 654; and Lidiia Ginzburg, "Vokrug 'Zapisok blokadnogo cheloveka,'" in *Chelovek za pis'mennym stolom*, 590–91.
92 Inna Shikheeva-Gaister, *Semeinaia khronika vremen kul'ta lichnosti 1925–1953* (Moscow: N'iudiamed-AO, 1998).
93 Samoilov, *Perebiraia nashi daty*, 9.
94 Shikheeva-Gaister, *Semeinaia khronika*, 265.
95 Including a joint memoir (in which "Svetka" figures as a character): Raisa Orlova and Lev Kopelev, *My zhili v Moskve* (Moscow: Kniga, 1990; originally published in 1988 in Ann Arbor, Mich.).
96 Petr Dmitriev, *"Soldat Berii": vospominaniia lagernogo okhrannika*, ed. Igor' Kuberskii (Leningrad [sic]: Chas pik, 1991). (The book was written in 1985.)
97 Sergo Lavrent'evich Beria's *Moi otets—Lavrentii Beriia* (Moscow: Sovremennik, Series: Osmyslenie veka: Deti ob ottsakh, 1994); Andrei Georgievich Malenkov, *O moem ottse Georgii Malenkove* (Moscow: NTTS "Tekhnoekos," 1992); Sergei Nikitovich Khrushchev, *Pensioner Soiuznogo znacheniia* (Moscow: Novosti, 1991).
98 On this "children's literature," see Elena Zubkova, "Istoriki i ochevidtsy: Dva vzgliada na poslevoennuiu istoriiu," *Svobodnaia mysl'*, no. 6 (1995): 106–17. (The phrase is hers.)
99 N. S. Khrushchev, *Vremia, liudi, vlast'. Vospominaniia*, 4 vols. (Moscow: Moskovskie novosti, 1999), 2:131.

100 Svetlana Allilueva, *Dvadtsat' pisem k drugu* (Moscow: Zakharov, 2000), 16; Svetlana Alliluyeva, *Twenty Letters to a Friend*, trans. Priscilla Johnson (London 1967), 19. In recent years, this book, first published in the West in 1967, has appeared in Russia in multiple editions.
101 Konstantin Simonov, *Glazami cheloveka moego pokoleniia. Razmyshleniia o I. V. Staline* (Moscow, 1990), 234, 225. First published in the journal *Znamia*, nos. 3, 4, 5 (1988).
102 Kaverin, *Epilog*, 323; 321.
103 G. Ia. Baklanov, *Zhizn', podarennaia dvazhdy* (Moscow: Vagrius, 1999), 117.
104 Evgeniia Ginzburg, *Krutoi marshrut: khronika vremen kul'ta lichnosti* (Moscow: Sovetskii pisatel', 1990), 543, 544–45. English from Eugenia Ginzburg, *Within the Whirlwind*, trans. Ian Boland (New York, 1981), 356.
105 Erenburg, *Liudi, gody, zhizn'*, 3:230.
106 More details on the "death of God" paradigm and eroticized love for Stalin are provided in my "Intimacy with Power: Soviet Memoirists Remember Stalin," in *Personenkulte im Stalinismus / Personality Cults in Stalinism*, ed. Klaus Heller and Jan Plamper (Göttingen: Vandenhoeck and Ruprecht, 2004), 331–61.
107 Raisa Orlova, *Vospominaniia o neproshedshem vremeni* (Moscow: Slovo, 1993), 205 (italics in the original). First published in Ann Arbor, Mich. in 1983.
108 Orlova, *Vospominaniia*, 205.
109 Raisa Orlova, Lev Kopelev, *My zhili v Moskve. 1956–1980* (Moscow: Kniga, 1990), 6. First published in Ann Arbor, Mich. in 1988.
110 Nina Gagen-Torn, *Memoria* (Moscow: Vozvrashchenie, 1994), 370.
111 From Mikhail Polivanov's introduction to the first publication within Russia, in the journal *Iunost'*, no. 8 (1988): 34.
112 Nadezhda Mandelshtam, *Vospominaniia* and *Vtoraia kniga* (Moscow: Soglasie, 1999). Emma Gershtein, *Memuary* (Moscow: Inapress, 1998); English translation: Emma Gerstein, *Moscow Memoirs*, trans. John Crawfoot (London: Harvill, 2003). It was Nikolai Panchenko, in his introduction to the 1999 edition of Nadezhda Mandelshtam, who disparagingly called Emma Gershtein's memoirs "antimemoirs" (*antivospominaniia*) (iii). It should be noted that Nadezhda Mandelshtam's memoirs, especially her *Vtoraia kniga*, had received angry rebuttals already in the 1970s: some spoke in defense of contemporaries (notably, Nikolai Khardzhiev and Anna Akhmatova) whom they felt the memoirist had misrepresented. There is Veniamin Kaverin's letter to N. Ia. Mandelshtam of March 23, 1973, circulated privately. Between 1972 and 1976, Lidiia Chukovskaia worked on a whole book of corrections to Nadezhda Mandelshtam's memoirs (simultaneously with her work on her Akhmatova journals); this unfinished book was published under the title *Dom Poeta* (The House of the Poet), only in 2001 (in Lidiia Chukovskaia, *Sochineniia* [Moscow: Art-fleks, 2001]).
113 From Mikhail Zolotonosov's review of Gershtein's *Memuary* in *Novaia russkaia kniga*, no. 1 (1999): 58.
114 Here I follow Galina Rylkova's sharp analysis of the confrontation between the two memoirs, published (as book review) in *Kritika: Explorations in Russian and Eurasian History* 1, no. 1 (Winter 2000): 224–30. The phrase "authoritarian style of remembering" is hers (22).
115 The wording is Gershtein's, from the memoir essays "Lishniaia liubov'" and "Anna Akhmatova i Lev Gumilev," in her *Memuary*, 206, 345. (Some of the essays in the 1998 book had previously appeared in journals, beginning in 1988.)
116 From a review of Gershtein's memoirs, Galina Bashkirova, "Blagodatnaia pustynia poslednego svidetelia," *Nezavisimaia gazeta*, section *Kulisa*, no. 12 (June 1999). (Rylkova noted this formula.)
117 Gagen-Torn, *Memoria*, 241.
118 Baklanov, *Zhizn', podarennaia dvazhdy*, 123. See also comments on Simonov's confession by Iurii Karabchievskii, "Do byloi slepoty ne unizimsia," *Novyi mir*, no. 1 (1989): 256–61, 257; Leonid Batkin, "Son razuma. O sotsial'no-kul'turnykh masshtabakh lichnosti Stalina," *Znanie-sila*, no. 4 (1989): 72–73; Nataliia Ivanova, "Konstantin Simonov glazami cheloveka moego pokoleniia," *Znamia*, no. 7 (1999): 204.
119 German, *Slozhnoe proshedshee*, 138.
120 Zhitomirskaia, *Prosto zhizn'*, 110. Further references are given in the text.

121 N. I. Tiulina, *Doma i na chuzhbine. Vospominaniia bibliotekaria so schastlivoi sud'boi* (Moscow: Liberiia, 1999; 2nd ed. Moscow: Pashkov Dom, 2006). A detailed response to Zhitomirskaia's memoir from another colleague in the Lenin Library. Valeriia Stel'makh, "V sviazi i po povodu," appeared in *Novoe literaturnoe obozrenie* 81 (2006).

122 B. G. Tartakovskii, *Vse eto bylo...* (2005), 189; emphasis added; further references are given in the text. The memoirs were published posthumously. The wartime diary of Tartakovskii' also appeared in print, B. G. Tartakovskii, *Iz dnevnikov voennykh let* (Moscow: AIRO-XX, 2005).

123 The author of two monographs on memoir writing and historical consciousness in the early nineteenth-century Russia (mentioned above), A. G. Tartakovskii, published a theoretical article "Memoirs as a Cultural Phenomenon" ("Memuaristika kak fenomen kul'tury") in *Voprosy literatury*, no. 1 (1999).

124 Iuliia Eidel'man, *Dnevniki Natana Eidel'mana* (Moscow: Materik, 2003); further references are given in the text. A description of this life arrangement, including a clue to Eidel'man's ciphered marking of sexual encounters with his mistress in his diary, appears on pp. 81–83.

125 G. M. Hamburg, "Writing History and the End of the Soviet Era: The Secret Lives of Natan Eidel'man," *Kritika: Explorations in Russian and Eurasian History* 7, no. 1 (Winter 2006): 91–92. I follow Hamburg's discussion of Eidel'man's family situation (86–87), his fascination with secrecy and concealment (72, 87, 109), and the dilemma of his Jewishness (94–102).

126 Iuliia Eidel'man, *Dnevniki Natana Eidel'mana*, 62. The plan of the "main book" is discussed by Hamburg, "Writing History," 91–92.

127 Iulii Krelin, *Izvivy pamiati: vrachebnoe svidetel'stvo* (Moscow: Zakharov, 2003), 226–58.

128 E. M. Meletinskii, "Vospominaniia. Na voine i v tiur'me," *Izbrannye stat'i. Vospominaniia* (Moscow: RGGU, 1998), 520.

129 Grigorii Pomerants, "V storonu Iry. Iz tekh, kotorykh," *Russkoe bogatvstvo*, no. 2 (6) (1994): 53. Further references are given in the text.

130 The philosophical conversations in the camps have been mentioned both by Pomerants (93) and Meletinskii (551). Pomerants described them in detail in an earlier memoir essay, "Perezhitye abstraktsii" (1953–59) in Pomerants, *Neopublikovannoe* (Frankfurt/Main: Posev, 1972). The name "Viktor" originates from this essay.

131 Pomerants, "V storonu Iry," 53.

132 F. Vigdorova, *Semeinoe schast'e. Liubimaia ulitsa. Povesti* (Moscow: Sovetskii pisatel', 1965), 331.

133 Aleksandra Raskina, "Na pervom meste," www.vavilon/ru/noragal/raskina.html.

134 The workings of the metaphor of the communal apartment, in daily life and in art, have been described by Svetlana Boym in *Common Places: Mythologies of Everyday Life in Russia* (Cambridge: Harvard University Press, 1994), and in *The Future of Nostalgia* (New York: Basic Books, 2001). For ethnographic information, see *Communal Living in Russia: A Virtual Museum of Soviet Everyday Life*, http://kommunalka/colgate.edu.

135 Chudakova, "Liudskaia molv'," *Novyi mir*, no. 6 (2000), 147.

136 Chudakova, "Neskol'ko avtotsitat: Vmesto vvedeniia k razdelu," *Tynianovskie chteniia*, no. 10 (1998): 646.

137 These words first appeared in Chudakova, *Besedy ob arkhivakh* (Moscow: Molodaia gvardiia, 1975), 177, and were echoed in 1998 in "Neskol'ko avtotsitat," 647.

138 Chudakova, "Pod skrip ukliuchin," *Novyi mir*, no. 4 (1993): 136. Further, the author acknowledges the Soviet ring to the word "must."

139 Autobiographical practices of the 1920s and 1930s, in their connection to the state agenda, have been analyzed by Jochen Hellbeck and Igal Halfin (cited above); Sheila Fitzpatrick, "Lives under Fire: Autobiographical Narratives and their Challenges in Stalin's Russia," in *De Russie et d'ailleurs: Feux croisés sur l'histoire*, ed. Marc Ferro (Paris: Institut d'études slaves, 1995); and Chudakova herself: "Sud'ba 'samootcheta-ispovedi' v literature sovetskogo vremeni (1920-e—konets 1930-kh)," in *Literatura sovetskogo proshlogo* (Moscow: Iazyki russkoi kul'tury, 2001).

140 Kaverin, *Epilog*, 36. Zorin, *Avanstsena*, 6.

141 Sergo Beriia, *Moi otets*, 34.

142 Historians traced the phrase "Weltgeschichte ist Weltgericht," which was canonized by Hegel in his *Phenomenology of Spirit*, to the prophetic discourse of the Old Testament. In its secular

meaning, the concept first appears in the *Encyclopédie*. Oswald Spengler concluded his *Decline of the West* with this phrase. See Löwith, *Meaning in History*, 12, and Koselleck, "Historia Magistra Vitae...," in *Future's Past: On the Semantics of Historical Time*, trans. Keith Tribe (Cambridge: MIT Press, 1985), 34.

143 Boris Ilizarov, "V marte, kogda umer Stalin..." *Znanie-sila*, no. 3 (1998): 95.
144 Allilueva, *Kniga dlia vnuchek* (New York: Liberty Publishing House, 1991), 88–91; Russian edition, *Oktiabr'*, no. 6 (1991): 13–86.
145 The apocalyptic thinking in the writings of Evgeniia Kiseleva are discussed in chapter 2 of part 2 of this book.
146 All quotes are from B. S. Ilizarov's introduction to *Tsentr dokumentatsii "Narodnyi arkhiv": Spravochnik po fondam*, v, vii, viii, ix.
147 Most notably, E. Maksimova, "Chastnaia zhizn' sokhranitsia dlia potomkov v narodnom arkhive," *Izvestiia*, June 26, 1993, 10, and Boris Ilizarov, "Kazhdyi imeet pravo na voskreshenie," *Znanie-sila*, no. 3 (1998): 9–15.
148 From the unsigned introduction to "Chelovek v potoke istorii: My nachinaem seriiu publikatsii dokumentov iz 'Narodnogo arkhiva'," *Znanie-sila*, no. 2 (1998): 9.
149 Ilizarov, *Arkhivy zvuka i obraza* (Moscow: AIRO-XX, 1996), 4.
150 Ibid.
151 Nikolai Fedorov, "Muzei, ego smysl i naznachenie," in his *Filosofiia obshchego dela*, vol. 2 (Moscow, 1913), 407. It was probably Fedorov who inspired Ilizarov's project of collecting documents for the People's Archive at a garbage dump. Ilizarov, "Obraz tvoi...Oda pomoike," *Znanie-sila*, no. 6 (1998): 110–17; Fedorov's reflections on the museum value of garbage and its potential for resurrection appear in his "Muzei," 400n1.
152 On Fedorov's ideas in Russian and Soviet literature, see Irene Masing-Delic, *Abolishing Death: A Salvation Myth of Russian Twenteith Century Literature* (Stanford: Stanford University Press, 1992).
153 Ilizarov explicitly mentioned Fedorov in his article "Kazhdyi imeet pravo na voskreshenie," 11. Fedorov's name does not appear in his introduction to the archive's reference guide, but contemporaries recognize the lineage of these ideas. In her tribute to the People's Archive, the writer Valeriia Shubina writes: "The idea [of the People's Archive] can be called a new version of immortality, or more precisely, the next one—there have been so many! [...] Recall N. F. Fedorov and his *Philosophy of the Common Cause*, take Lenin's mausoleum, open up a book by A. Platonov..." Shubina, "Dusha otverzhennykh predmetov," *Znanie-sila*, no. 2 (1998): 12.
154 See Aleksandr Lavrov, "Ot sostavitelia," *Litsa: Biograficheskii al'manakh* (Moscow-St. Petersburg: Feniks-Atheneum), no. 1 (1992): 3.
155 Aleksandr Etkind, "Biograficheskii Institut: Neosushchestvlennyi zamysel N. A. Rybnikova," *Litsa: Biograficheskii al'manakh*, no. 7 (1996).
156 In the seminal publication of Sergei Grechishkin and Aleksandr Lavrov, "Andrei Bely i N. F. Fedorov," *Blokovskii sbornik* 3 (Tartu: Tartuskii gosudarstvennyi universitet, 1979).
157 Aleksandr Gladkov [1912–1976], "'Ia ne priznaiu istoriiu bez podrobnostei ...' (Iz dnevnikovykh zapisei 1945–1973)," in *In Memoriam: Istoricheskii sbornik pamiati A. I. Dobkina* (St. Petersburg: Feniks-Atheneum, 2000).
158 All quotes are from B. S. Ilizarov's introduction to *Tsentr dokumentatsii "Narodnyi arkhiv,"* xii. (The last sentence is printed in bold.)
159 See, for example, Niklas Luhmann, "Describing the Future" [1992], in *Observations on Modernity*, trans. William Whobrey (Stanford: Stanford University Press, 1998), 63–74; and Reinhart Koselleck, "Zeitverkürzung und Beschleunigung: Eine Studie zur Säkularisation," in *Zeitschichten: Studien zur Historik* (Frankfurt/Main: Suhrkamp, 2000). I have benefited from discussing the present-day experience of time with the anthropologist Tobias Rees.
160 Igor' D'iakonov, *Kniga vospominanii* (St. Petersburg: Evropeiskii dom, Series: Dnevniki i vospominaniia peterburgskikh uchenykh, 1995), 254–55, 743–44.
161 A concept traced to Vladimir Vernadskii, "noosphere" is formed from the Greek *noema* (thought) by analogy with "biosphere."
162 All quotations from Andrei Voznesenskii, *Na virtualnom vetru* (Moscow: Vagrius, 1998), 473–75. An analogy can be found in Andrei Malenkov (a scientist), who published an article on

the scientific conception of the apocalypse coauthored with his father. See Malenkov, *O moem ottse*, 108–12.
163 Evgenii Evtushenko, *Volchii pasport* (Moscow: Vagrius, 1998), 503–4.
164 Viktor Rozov, *Udivlenie pered zhizn'iu* (Moscow: Vagrius, 2000), 348–49.
165 In these reflections on postmodernist memoirs, I am closely following Mark Lipovetskii in his *Paralogii: transformatsii (post)modernistskogo diskursa v russkoi kul'ture 1920-kh—2000-kh godov* (Moscow: NLO, 2007), 572–612. The definition of the "new sincerity" is his. I have also borrowed his title: chapter 14 is entitled " 'Ia' v kavychkah."
166 In the book-form edition, Andrei Sergeev, *Omnibus: Roman, rasskazy, vospominaniia* (Moscow: NLO, 1997). Grisha Bruskin, *Proshedshee vremia nesovershennogo vida* (Moscow: NLO, 2001); English translation: *Past Imperfect: Episodes from the Life of a Russian Artist*, trans. Alice Nakhimovsky (Syracuse, N.Y.: Syracuse University Press, 2008).
167 From Aleksandr Zholkovskii, "Avtor—personazh, i iz samykh uiazvimykh," www.e-slovo.ru/255/12pol1.html. There are many different editions of the "vignettes," including A. K. Zholkovskii, *Memuarnye vin'etki i drugie non-fictions* (St. Petersburg,: Zhurnal Zvezda, 2000).
168 Dmitrii Prigov, *Zhivite v Moskve: rukopis' na pravakh romana* (Moscow: NLO, 2000). Page references are given in the text.
169 Sergeev, "Al'bom dlia marok," in *Omnibus*, 99.
170 On July 21, 2007, when I first visited this "community," it had 220 registered members and was watched by 423 users; on my next visit, on October 15, the number of members had grown to 241 and watchers to 455.
171 For analysis of LiveJournal, especially the Russian variety, see Eugene Gorny, "Russian LiveJournal: National Specifics in the Development of a Virtual Community" (version of May 13, 2004), www.ruhr-uni-bochum.de/russ-cyb/library/texts/en/gorny_rlj.pdf. Gorny notes that LiveJournal, conceived by its creator (Stanford University student Brad Fitzpatrick) as a tool for keeping in touch with one's schoolmates, "unexpectedly acquired in Russia the aura of a playground for intellectuals." In other cultures, the Internet diaries can be quite different, as Philippe Lejeune's pioneering study of the subject shows: *Cher Ecran—: Journal personnel ordinateuer internet* (Paris: Seuil, 2000).
172 2006-03-19 poor-ju.livejournal.com/57021.html.
173 From http://community/livejournal.com/lidia_ginsburg for 2006-02-26; 2004-07-02; 2004-10-16; 2004-06-02.
174 The first detailed discussion of Ginzburg's image and legacy (and her archive) can be found in the recent dissertation by Emily Stetson Van Buskirk, "Reality in Search of Literature: Lydia Ginzburg's In-Between Prose" (PhD diss., Harvard University, 2008).

PART II, CHAPTER 1

1 All citations are from: Lidiia Chukovskaia, *Zapiski ob Anne Akhmatovoi*, 3 vols. (Moscow: Soglasie, 1997). For vol. 1, English translations are from Lydia Chukovskaya, *The Akhmatova Journals*, vol. 1, *1938–1941*, trans. Milena Michalski and Sylvia Rubashova (Evanston, Ill.: Northwestern University Press, 2002). Page numbers are indicated in the text: the first number refers to the original; the second, where applicable, to this edition. Throughout the chapter, the translations have been adjusted. Citations from the Tashkent notebooks of volume 1 and from volumes 2 and 3 (which have not appeared in English) and all other translations, unless otherwise indicated, are by Alyson Tapp.
2 I borrowed this formulation from Katerina Clark, "Changing Historical Paradigms in Soviet Culture," in *Late Soviet Culture: From Perestroika to Novostroika*, ed. Thomas Lahusen with Gene Kuperman (Durham, N.C.: Duke University Press, 1993), 300.
3 This ingenious idea has been advanced by the literary scholar Galina Rylkova in *The Archaeology of Anxiety: The Russian Silver Age and Its Legacy* (Pittsburg, Penn.: University of Pittsburgh Press, 2007), 91–92. Rylkova relied on the psychologist Jerome Bruner, who described the psychoanalytic situation in terms of the author's relationship with a "helpful editor," who becomes "complicit in the constructional process." See Bruner, *Acts of Meaning* (Cambridge: Harvard University Press, 1990), 113. Bruner, in turn, relied on Roy Schafer's narrative approach to

psychoanalysis ("Narration in Psychoanalytic Dialogue," in *On Narrative*, ed. W. J. T. Mitchell (Chicago: University of Chicago Press, 1981).

4   This process of creating poetry has been insightfully described in Beth Holmgren's study, *Women's Works in Stalin's Time: On Lidiia Chukovskaia and Nadezhda Mandelshtam* (Bloomington: Indiana University Press, 1993). Holmgren gives a comprehensive analysis of Chukovskaia's life and works and reflects on the historical position of women writers under the terror. The phrases that appear in quotation marks are hers (87).

5   Holmgren read this image differently in her *Women's Works*, 73.

6   Beth Holmgren connects "the documented ritual of hands, match, ashtray" to the mourning rituals of the ancient Greeks as evoked in Mandelshtam's poetry, and describes Chukovskaia as "an ethnographer." Holmgren, *Women Works*, 87–88.

7   Emma Gershtein, *Memuary* (Moscow: Inapress, 1998), 255–56.

8   Lidiia Chukovskaia, "Procherk," in *Sochineniia* (Moscow: Art-Fleks, 2001), 1:144.

9   Lidiia Ginzburg, "I zaodno s pravoporiadkom," in her *Zapisnye knizhki. Vospominaniia. Esse* (St. Petersburg: Iskusstvo, 2002), 286.

10 Rylkova, *The Archaeology of Anxiety*, 67–72. Rylkova uses Chukovskaia's *Notes* extensively and imaginatively to describe Akhmatova's carefully crafted position as a lonely survivor of the prerevolutionary literary culture (the "Silver Age") thrown into Soviet society.

11 The Punin side of this exceptionally well-documented story has been represented in two recent (overlapping, but not identical) editions, N. Punin, *Mir svetel liubov'iu. Dnevniki. Pis'ma*, ed. L. A. Zykov (Moscow: Artist, 2000); *The Diaries of Nikolay Punin 1904–1953*, ed. Sidney Monas and Jennifer Greene Krupala, trans. Jennifer Greene Krupala (Austian: University of Texas Press, 1999).

12 It should be noted that Akhmatova's life in the Marble Palace with Vladimir Shileiko in the 1920s has been documented by another friend who kept a diary (which remained unpublished in his lifetime), Pavel Luknitskii (1902–1972), then, a student who was studying the life and works of Akhmatova's first husband, Nikolai Gumilev. This diary was published in the 1990s: Pavel Luknitskii, *Acumiana. Vstrechi s Annoi Akhmatovoi*, vol. 1 (1924–1925) (Paris: YMCA, 1991); vol. 2 (1926–1927) (Paris-Moscow: YMCA/ Russkii put', 1997). Luknitskii had also made records in an intimate notebook, which was published only in 2005 by his widow: Vera Luknitskaia, *Liubovnik. Rytsar. Letopisets. Tri sensatsii iz Serebrianogo veka* (St. Petersburg: Sudarynia, 2005). Disguised as materials for a novella, this notebook had been written in code. It refers to Akhmatova as A. K. Bakhmutova, to N. N. Punin as P. P. Migailov, to the dog Tap as Norka, and to Nietzsche (whose philosophy Luknitskii discussed with Akhmatova) as Beethoven. Luknitskii changed the years from 1924–1925 to 1921–1922 (but used the exact month and day), and the location from Petrograd to Tashkent. (The intimate notebook reveals that Luknitskii was Akhmatova's lover.) In 1972, shortly before his death, Luknitskii (by that time an established Soviet writer and, in his self-description, a devoted communist) prepared a key for his intimate notebook. Shileiko's side of the story was also published, by his family members: Vladimir Shileiko, *Posledniia liubov'. Perepiska s Annoi Akhmatovoi i Veroi Andreevoi i drugie materialy*, ed. Aleksei i Tamara Shileiko (Moscow: Vagrius, 2003).

13 Letters from the young Nikolai Punin to his father from 1910 to 1914 mention and address "Zhenya" Smirnov fondly among family members (*Mir svetel liubov'iu*, 80; 466.) Years later, in Nikolai Punin's letter to his eleven-year-old daughter Irina (from August 9, 1933), Zhenya also figures as a member of the household (*Mir svetel liubov'iu*, 321; 494).

14 From Irina Punina' oral memoir (October 1994), "Pod krovlei Fontannogo Doma...," in N. I. Popova and O. E. Rubinchik, *Anna Akhmatova i Fontannyi Dom* (St. Petersburg: Nevskii dialekt, 2000), 143–44.

15 From a guide to *Gosudarstvennyi literaturno-memorial'nyi muzei Anny Akhmatovoi v Fontannom dome* (St. Petersburg, 2003).

16 After Popova and Rubinchik, *Anna Akhmatova i Fontannyi Dom*, 68.

17 Irina Punina, "Pod krovlei Fontannogo Doma...," in Popova and Rubinchik, *Anna Akhmatova i Fontannyi Dom*, 145.

18 Nadezhda Mandelshtam, "Iz vospominaiii," in *Vospominaniia ob Anne Akhmatovoi*, ed. V. Ia. Vilenkin et al. (Moscow: Sovetskii pisatel', 1991), 302.

19 Popova and Rubinchik, *Anna Akhmatova i Fontannyi dom*, 68.
20 Vsevolod Petrov, "Fontannyi dom," in *Vospominaniia ob Anne Akhmatovoi*, 224.
21 E. K. Gal'perina-Osmerkina, "Vstrechi s Akhmatovoi," in *Vospominaniia ob Anne Akhmatovoi*, 239–40. Another memoir describes a family dinner that included Akhmatova's son, Lev (and involved a squabble over food): Gershtein, *Memuary*, 241.
22 Lidiia Ginzburg, *Zapisnye knizhki. Vospominaniia. Esse*, 421.
23 Nadezhda Mandelshtam, *Vtoraia kniga* (Moscow: Soglasie, 1999), 369; English from *Hope Abandoned*, trans. Max Hayward (New York: Atheneum, 1974), 361; translation adjusted.
24 Oral communication from a guide in the present-day Anna Akhmatova Apartment Museum (June 2004).
25 Such experimental family relationships have been described in Olga Matich, *Erotic Utopia: The Decadent Imagination in Russia's Fin-de-Siècle* (Madison: Wisconsin University Press, 2005).
26 Family and sexual policies of the early Soviet regime have been described, among others, by Richard Stites, *The Women's Liberation Movement in Russia: Feminism, Nihilism and Bolshevism* (Princeton: Princeton University Press, 1978); Wendy Goldman, *Women, the State, and Revolution* (Cambridge: Cambridge University Press, 1993); and Eric Naiman, *Sex in Public: An Incarnation of Early Soviet Ideology* (Princeton: Princeton University Press, 1997).
27 Olga Berggolts's blockade diary was first published in the almanac *Aprel'* 4 (1991); here 139. Chukovskaia cited it in 1:315.
28 Pavel Luknitskii, *Skvoz' vsiu blokadu* (Leningrad: Lenizdat, 1988), 27. By this time, Luknitskii, Akhmatova's intimate friend, who had documented her life in the 1920s, had become a well-adjusted Soviet writer.
29 Ginzburg, "Zapiski blokadnogo cheloveka" [1942–1962–1983], in her *Zapisnye knizhki. Vospominaniia. Esse*, 611. English from Lidiya Ginzburg, *Blockade Diary*, trans. Alan Myers (London: Harvill, 1995), 3.
30 English from *The Complete Works of Anna Akhmatova*, 2 vols., trans. Judith Hemschemeyer, ed. Roberta Reeder (Somerville, Mass.: Zephyr Press, 1990), 2:187.
31 Information from the commentary to *Mir svetel liubov'iu*, 502.
32 For a historical analysis of the evacuation that makes use of Chukovskaia's notes, see Rebecca Manley, *To the Tashkent Station: Evacuation and Survival in the Soviet Union at War, 1941–1946* (Ithaca: Cornell University Press, 2009).
33 Irina Punina, "Pod krovlei Fontannogo doma...," in Popova and Rubinchik, *Anna Akhmatova i Fontannyi Dom*, 147.
34 Here, I am trying to respond to the most pertinent query voiced by Caryl Emerson, who reviewed the manuscript for Cornell University Press: why Akhmatova could not clean up after herself. As Emerson's question implies, the issue has far-reaching cultural and moral implications.
35 For records of services rendered to Akhmatova, see 1:372–73, 374, 377, 379, 382, 383, 386.
36 Alexander Zholkovsky has pointed out, in several articles, the paradox of Akhmatova's carefully constructed persona ("ostensibly weak, fragile, and victimized but actually strong, manipulative, and powerful"), interpreting these strategies as a resonance of the "power-ridden cultural atmosphere" of Stalinism. In his words, "Akhmatova's amalgam of fear, defensiveness, and domineering is a characteristic instance of siege mentality—so typical of Stalin, his regime, and the entire 'socialist camp.' Akhmatova the 'iron lady' manifested in a grand way the defensive strategies developed by the average *homo Soveticus* under the regime's enormous pressure." From Zholkovsky, "The Obverse of Stalinism": Akhmatova's Self-Serving Charisma of Selflessness," in *Self and Story in Russian History*, ed. Laura Engelstein and Stephanie Sandler (Ithaca: Cornell University Press, 2000), 62–64. Zholkovsky's conception (unveiled in the journal *Zvezda* in 1996) provoked a spirited controversy among Akhmatova scholars and fans.
37 1:362, 378, 381, 385, 397, 401, 404, 409, 436, 449, 458.
38 1:437, 442, 447, 449, 450.
39 Gossip and scandal have long been recognized (by anthropologists and others) as a social force that creates intimacy and binds communities. See Max Gluckman, "Gossip and Scandal," *Current Anthropology* 4, no. 3 (1963): 307–15; and Patricia Meyer Spacks, *Gossip* (New York: Alfred Knopf, 1985), 5.
40 English from *The Complete Works of Anna Akhmatova*, 2:597. Translation adjusted.

41 Roman Timenchik commented on the "love-terror" nexus, introduced this quote from Nadezhda Mandelshtam, and suggested that the two women discussed this subject; see Timenchik, *Anna Akhmatova v 1960-e gody* (Moscow-Toronto: Vodolei Publishers/University of Toronto, 2005), 181.
42 Nadezhda Mandelshtam, "Iz vospominanii," in *Vospominaniia ob Anne Akhmatovoi*, 299.
43 English from *The Complete Works of Anna Akhmatova*, 2:125.
44 The experience of Stalin's death as the "death of God" is discussed in part 1.
45 *Mir svetel liubov'iu*, 432; *The Diaries of Nikolay Punin*, 227. Translation adjusted. Misspellings reflect the substandard spelling of the original.
46 Ibid.
47 Rylkova, *The Anxiety of Influence*, 79. Rylkova interprets the meaning of things in Akhmatova's life differently (78–80).
48 The formula is Hannah Arendt's in *The Human Condition*, 2nd ed. (Chicago: The University of Chicago Press, 1998), 137. I borrow the vocabulary also from a practical study (performed in the 1970s in the Chicago area) by Mihaly Csikszentmihalyi and Eugene Rochberg-Halton, *The Meaning of Things: Domestic Symbols and the Self* (Cambridge: Cambridge University Press, 1981), 15–17.
49 Mikhail Ardov, *Vokrug Ordynki* (St. Petersburg: Inapress, 2000), 67–68. This passage was later included in a larger book of memoirs: Proteirei Mikhail Ardov, *Vse k luchshemu… Vospominaniia. Proza* (Moscow: BSG Press, 2006), 228. Il'ina's short memoir about Akhmatova was published several times. The pre-perestroika editions, for obvious reasons, do not contain the episode with *Doctor Zhivago*. This episode appears in "Anna Akhmatova, kakoi ia ee videla," in Natalia Il'ina, *Dorogi i sud'by* (Moscow: Sovetskaia Rossiia, 1988), 324.
50 All quotes are from Ardov, *Vokrug Ordynki*, 79; *Vse k luchshemu*, 82.
51 Alla Latynina, "Svidetel'stvo i lzhesvidetel'stvo," http://infoart.udm.ru/magazine/arss/ezheg/latynin.
52 The painful conflict between mother and son in the years after his 1949 arrest, when Lev blamed Akhmatova for failing to secure his release, is barely mentioned in Chukovskaia's notes; but the reader may learn of it from other memoir sources, specifically, Emma Gershtein's *Memuary*.
53 In her *Archaeology of Influence* (169–71), Galina Rylkova offers a masterful analysis of what this gesture meant for Akhmatova.

PART II, CHAPTER 2

54 N. N. Kozlova and I. I. Sandomirskaia, *Ia tak khochu nazvat' kino: "Naivnoe pis'mo." Opyt lingvo-sotsiologicheskogo chteniia* (Moscow: Gnozis, 1996), 10–13. In the rest of the chapter, Kiseleva's text is cited from this edition (where it appears in part 2, 89–244) and follows the spelling and punctuation as given; page numbers are in the text. English translations are by Alyson Tapp. The author thanks Johanna Nichols for linguistic consultations. Part 1 of this edition is devoted to the editors' extensive interpretation of Kiseleva's text (7–87).
55 Oral structures (syntax, morphology, etc.) of the type encountered in Kiseleva's text have been described by a group of Soviet linguists who made oral speech into a subfield of linguistics. See comprehensive studies edited by E. A. Zemskaia, *Russkaia razgovornaia rech'. Obshchie voprosy. Slovoobrazovanie. Sintaksis* (Moscow: Nauka, 1981), and *Russkaia razgovornaia rech'. Fonetika. Morfologiia. Leksika. Zhest* (Moscow: Nauka, 1983). Boris Gasparov argued that oral speech of both uneducated and educated people follows the syntactic, semantic, and narrative patterns all its own, and that orality, and not linguistic norm, determines deviation from standard written patterns; see his "Ustnaia rech' kak semioticheskii ob"ekt," in *Semantika nominatsii i semiotika ustnoi rechi* (Tartu: TGU, 1978), 63–112.
56 Noted by Kozlova and Sandomirskaia, *Ia tak khochu*, 10, 20, 27.
57 "Kishmareva, Kiseleva, Tiuricheva" [publication of Elena Ol'shanskaia], *Novyi mir*, no. 2 (1991). Definition from the foreword by the writer Oleg Chukhontsev (27).
58 Kozlova and Sandomirskaia, *Ia tak khochu*, 58–61 (Kozlova's commentary).
59 The primacy of survival has been noted in Kozlova and Sandomirskaia, *Ia tak khochu*, 69; 80–83. Another sociologist, Boris Dubin, though he differs from Kozlova in his understanding of what is

"normative," also treated the story as a source for the "anthropology of the Soviet man" indicative of the "pathological" social structure, and as a story of survival. Boris Dubin, "Granitsy i resursy avtobiograficheskogo pis'ma (po zapiskam Evgenii Kiselevoi)," in *Pravo na imia. Biografiia kak paradigma istoricheskogo protsessa* (St. Petersburg: Memorial, 2005), 19–28.

60 Kozlova and Sandomirskaia misdate the first notebooks as started no earlier than 1977 (10).
61 For a discussion of mnemonic techniques of visualization, I am indebted to the film scholar Oksana Bulgakowa.
62 See, for example, Bessel A. van der Kolk, "Trauma and Memory," in *Traumatic Stress: The Effects of Overwhelming Experience on Mind, Body, and Society*, ed. Bessel A. van der Kolk et al. (New York: Guildorf Press, 1996), 279–302.
63 Kozlova and Sandomirskaia note such occasions (78–80); their interpretation is different (84–85).
64 And not, as her publishers report (7, 11), as a cleaning woman—the work she did later, after the age of sixty.
65 From Kozlova and Sandomirskaia, chapter "Predislovie: Istoriia liubvi," 11–12. (Here and subsequently I indicate the subtitle of the chapter within the editors' extensive interpretation of the text in part 1 of the *Ia tak khochu* edition.)
66 Kozlova and Sandomirskaia, "Naivnoe pis'mo i proizvoditeli normy," 43.
67 Kozlova and Sandomirskaia, "Igry na chuzhom pole," 58.
68 Another edition follows in the footsteps of Kozlova and Sandomirskaia and uses their terms: *"Naivnaia literatura": Issledovaniia i teksty*, ed. S. Iu. Nekliudov (Moscow: Moskovskii obshchestvennyi nauchnyi fond, 2001). It contains a bibliography of other "naive" publications from recent years.
69 "Ours is the first publication of such a text that is faithful to the original, without corrections or editing" (10).
70 Kozlova and Sandomirskaia, "Naivnoe pis'mo i proizvoditeli normy," 42.
71 From the appendix by Sandomirskaia, "Prilozhenie: metod i protsedura pravki," 245–55.
72 From Kozlova and Sandomirskaia, "Naivnoe pis'mo i proizvoditeli normy," 22.
73 Zygmunt Bauman, *Legislators and Interpreters: On Modernity, Post-Modernity and Intellectuals* (Cambridge, UK: Polity Press, 1987); 4–5, 10.
74 Bauman's book *Legislators and Interpreters* is explicitly mentioned on page 24, note 12 of the Kozlova and Sandomirskaia edition. I see traces of the Bauman paradigm also on pp. 27–29.
75 Over the years in which Ol'shanskaia kept trying to get the story published, she was corresponding with Kiseleva and told the author of her efforts. This correspondence, too, has been deposited in the People's Archive.
76 Cited from the frontispiece of the *Naivnoe pis'mo* edition.
77 The author's chosen title (her three names) also does not appear in the text; see the beginning of Notebook 2 on page 129. See also the preface, in which the publishers discuss the title and make a mistake in citing it: «Рукопись 2-й тетради называется: "Киселева. Кишмарева. Тюричева: я хочу чтобы так называлось кино"» (10). The order of names is reversed. The same mistake appears on the table of contents; in this case, there is also a deviation in spelling (the correct spelling is Kiseleva).
78 From A. V. Zakharov, "N. N. Kozlova: Tema zhizni. (Sotsial'naia antropologiia i tvorcheskii put' issledovatelia)," in *Intelligentsiia v obshchestve riska* (Moscow: RGGU, 2003), 508–17.
79 For formulating these conclusions I am indebted to Caryl Emerson, who read the book manuscript for Cornell University Press.

PART III

1 L. K. Chukovskaia's *Zapiski ob Anne Akhmatovoi* (Moscow: Soglasie, 1997), 1:11–12; English from Lydia Chukovskaia, *The Akhmatova Journals*, vol. 1, trans. Milena Michalski and Sylvia Rubashova (New York: Farrar, Strauss and Giroux, 1994), 5.
2 Boris Eikhenbaum, "Tvorchestvo Iu. Tynianova," in *Iurii Tynianov pisatel' i uchenyi. Vospominaniia, razmyshleniia, vstrechi* (Moscow: Molodaia gvardiia, 1966), 73. For this reference, I am indebted to Alyson Tapp.

3   On various uses of dreams in historical scholarship, see Peter Burke's pioneering work, "The Cultural History of Dreams" [1973], in his *Varieties of Cultural History* (Cambridge: Polity Press, 1997), 23–42; and a recent work, Daniel Pick and Lyndal Roper, eds., *Dreams and History: The Interpretation of Dreams from Ancient Greece to Modern Psychoanalysis* (London: Routledge, 2004).
4   Alain Corbin, "Dream Imagery," *A History of Private Life*, ed. Philippe Ariès and Georges Duby, trans. Arthur Goldhammer (Cambridge: Harvard University Press, 1990), 4:514–15.
5   Reinhart Koselleck, "Terror and Dream: Methodological Remarks on the Experience of Time during the Third Reich," *Future's Past: On the Semantics of Historical Time*, trans. Keith Tribe (Cambridge: MIT Press, 1985), 218. I have borrowed the phrase "dreams of terror" from Koselleck.
6   What has been largely abandoned is Freud's dismissal of the manifest content of dreams as a distortion of their "true," latent, meaning; his belief in the impossibility of interpreting dreams unless one has the dreamer's associations; and his insistence that the function of dreams is limited to wish fulfillment. See, for example, Melvin R. Lansky, "The Legacy of *The Interpretation of Dreams,*" in *Essential Papers on Dreams*, ed. Melvin R. Lansky (New York: New York University Press, 1992), 3–31; Erik Homburger Erikson, "The Dream Specimen of Psychoanalysis," ibid., 146; and James L. Fosshage, "The Psychological Function of Dreams: A Revised Psychoanalytic Perspective," *Psychoanalysis and Contemporary Thought* 6, no. 4 (1983): 661.
7   George E. Atwood and Robert D. Stolorow, *Structures of Subjectivity: Explorations in Psychoanalytic Phenomenology* (Hillsdale, NJ: Analytic Press, 1984), 98.
8   Loosely after Ernest Hartmann, "The Psychology and Physiology of Dreaming: A New Synthesis," in *Dreams 1900–2000: Science, Art, and the Unconscious Mind*, ed. Lynn Gamwell (Ithaca: Cornell University Press, 2000), 61–75. This implies not that dreams *are* symbols but that "the dreams can be *turned into* a symbol" and that dreams are experienced as inherently meaningful and symbolic. On this, see Harry T. Hunt, *The Multiplicity of Dreams: Memory, Imagination, and Consciousness* (New Haven: Yale University Press, 1989), 9, 208.
9   Hunt, *The Multiplicity of Dreams*, 214.
10 Both statements from Bert O. States, *Dreaming and Storytelling* (Ithaca: Cornell University Press, 1993), 3 and 76. I was also inspired by his earlier *The Rhetoric of Dreams* (Ithaca: Cornell University Press, 1988).
11 It was Michel Foucault, in his introduction to Ludwig Binswanger's *Dream and Existence*, who insisted that dream is a specific form of experience as well as a form of knowledge. Michel Foucault, "Dream, Imagination and Existence," in Michel Foucault and Ludwig Binswanger, "Dream and Existence," ed. Keith Hoeller, special issue, *Review of Existential Psychology and Psychiatry* 19, no. 1 (1986): 43.
12 Sigmund Freud, *The Interpretation of Dreams, The Standard Edition of the Complete Psychological Works of Sigmund Freud*, trans. and ed. James Strachey (London: Hogarth Press, 1967), 4:112.
13 Jürgen Habermas, *Knowledge and Human Interest*, trans. Jeremy L. Shapiro (Boston: Beacon Press, 1971), 219–20.
14 See, for example, Maurice Blanchot's essay "Sleep, Night," in *The Space of Literature*, trans. Ann Smock (Lincoln: University of Nebraska Press, 1982). This idea was further developed by States, *Dreaming and Storytelling*, 61.
15 Suggested by Foucault, "Dream, Imagination and Existence," 59.
16 This analogy between dream and fiction was developed, in another context, by Sartre in his *L'imaginaire*. See J.-P. Sartre, *The Psychology of Imagination* (New York: Philosophical Library, 1948), 199–206.
17 Carl Gustav Jung, *Dreams*, trans. R. F. C. Hull (Princeton: Princeton University Press, 1967), 52.
18 George Steiner commented on the strength of the belief in the prophetic nature of dreams in modern societies, in spite of the Enlightenment, positivism, and Freud. George Steiner, "Les rêves participents-ils de l'histoire? Deux questions adressées à Freud," *Les débats*, May 25, 1983, 167.
19 According to the psychoanalyst Chrisopher Bollas, the dream constitutes a fictional forerunner of reality, in which, based on prior knowledge, dream thoughts play with the possibilities for the future. Bollas extends Freud's notions that a dreamer creates his future insofar as it is determined

by the past. See Christopher Bollas, *Forces of Destiny: Psychoanalysis and Human Idiom* (Northvale, NJ: Free Association Books, 1989), 47. Heinz Kohut maintains that, in the waking life, reaction to dreams catalyzes change in the self; the dream thus serves as a bridge to the personal future. These psychological approaches were successfully used in a historical study of revolutionary America, Mechal Sobel, *Teach Me Dreams: The Search for Self in the Revolutionary Era* (Princeton: Princeton University Press, 2000).

20 I am extending and reversing Habermas, who speaks of "the unique relation to self that resides in listening to oneself talk": "the intimacy and transparency, the absolute proximity of the expression animated simultaneously by my breath and my meaning-intention." Jürgen Habermas, *The Philosophical Discourse of Modernity: Twelve Lectures*, trans. Frederick G. Lawrence (Cambridge: MIT Press, 1987), 176.

21 The wording is from Paul Ricoeur, *Freud and Philosophy: An Essay in Interpretation*, trans. Denis Savage (New Haven: Yale University Press, 1970), 92–93.

22 A letter to Fliess of December 22, 1897, Freud, *Standard Edition*, 1:273.

23 For information on nightmares, I use John Mack, "Toward a Theory of Nightmares," *Essential Papers on Dreams*, 344.

24 Koselleck, "Terror and Dream, " 218. See also "Afterword to Charlotte Beradt's *The Third Reich of Dreams*" [1981], in Koselleck, *The Practice of Conceptual History: Timing History, Spacing Concepts*, trans. Todd Samuel Presner and others (Stanford, CA: Stanford University Press, 2002), 335.

25 After Koselleck, "Afterword to Charlotte Beradt's *The Third Reich of Dreams*," 333–34.

26 Koselleck, "Terror and Dream," 219.

27 Ibid., 217.

28 Charlotte Beradt, *Das Dritte Reich des Traumes* (Munich: Nymphenburger, 1966); 2nd ed. Frankfurt/Main: Suhrkamp, 1981 (with afterword by Reinhart Koselleck). English: *The Third Reich of Dreams*, trans. Adriane Gottwald, with an essay by Bruno Bettelheim (Chicago: Quadrangle Books, 1968). All citations to this book are taken from the English edition, with page numbers indicated in the text.

29 Biographical information from Martine Leibovici's preface to the French translation of Beradt's book, *Rêves sous le III Reich*, trans. Pierre Saint-Germain, preface Martine Leibovici, afterwords Reinhart Koselleck and Francois Gantheret (Paris: Editions Payot et Rivages, 2002).

30 It should noted that, judging by the photographically reproduced page, Arzhilovsky's diaries are normative in grammar and spelling, and they do not seem to have been edited for publication.

31 Biographical information from A. S. Arzhilovskii, "Dnevnik 36–37-go godov," *Ural*, no. 3 (1992), 138 (published by Konstantin Lagunov), hereafter *Ural*. English: "Diary of Andrei Stepanovich Arzhilovsky," in *Intimacy and Terror: Soviet Diaries of the 1930s*, ed. Veronique Garros, Natalia Korenevskaya, and Thomas Lahusen, trans. Carol A. Flath (New York: New Press, 1995), 111–12, hereafter *Intimacy and Terror*. Selecting diary excerpts for publication, the editors of the *Intimacy and Terror* collection sought to account for, among other "ordinary doings of the Soviet citizens," "their thoughts and dreams," and they included quite a few (xi).

32 Arzhilovsky's diary for 18 December 1936: *Ural*, 148; *Intimacy and Terror*, 132–33 (here and below, the translation has been adjusted).

33 Arzhilovsky's diary for 28 January 1937: *Ural*, 151; *Intimacy and Terror*, 139–40.

34 Arzhilovsky's diary for 31 October 1936: *Ural*, 141; *Intimacy and Terror*, 115). (The translation in *Intimacy and Terror* did not preserve the word "spit.").

35 Arzhilovsky's diary for 31 October 1936: *Ural*, 141; *Intimacy and Terror*, 116.

36 *Ural*, 142; *Intimacy and Terror*, 117.

37 Arzhilovsky's diary for February 3, 1937: *Ural*, 152; *Intimacy and Terror*, 141.

38 Arzhilovsky's diary for January 17, 1937: *Ural*, 150; *Intimacy and Terror*, 138.

39 Arzhilovsky's diary for 19 April 1937: *Ural*, 159; *Intimacy and Terror*, 159.

40 Arzhilovsky's diary for 19 April 1937: *Ural*, 159; *Intimacy and Terror*, 159.

41 E. M. Meletinskii, "Vospominaniia," in his *Izbrannye stat'i. Vospominanniia* (Moscow: RGGU, 1998), 518.

42 Mikhail Grobman, *Leviafan: Dnevniki 1963–1971 godov* (Moscow: Novoe literaturnoe obozrenie, 2002), 469.

43 "'Prosti menia, Koba...': Neizvestnoe pis'mo N. Bukharina," *Istochnik*, no. 0 (1993): 23–24. The letter is dated 10 December 1937.
44 Reported by Bukharin's wife; see A. M. Larina (Bukharina), *Nezabyvaemoe* (Moscow: APN, 1989), 317; English: Anna Larina, *This I Cannot Forget*, trans. Gary Kern, intro. Stephen P. Cohen (New York: W. W. Norton, 1988), 302.
45 "Prosti menia, Koba," 23–24. The Hegelianism of this appeal has been previously noted by Jochen Hellbeck in "With Hegel to Salvation: Bukharin's Other Trial," forthcoming.
46 A. Larina (Bukharina), *Nezabyvaemoe*, 77. English from *This I Cannot Forget*, 103
47 A. Larina (Bukharina), *Nezabyvaemoe*, 44. English from *This I Cannot Forget*, 74.
48 Jacques le Goff uses Misch's notion "oneiric autobiography" in his article "Christianity and Dreams," *The Medieval Imagination*, trans. Arthur Goldhammer (Chicago: The University of Chicago Press, 1988), 200. A classic example is Augustine's *Confessions*, but, according to le Goff, oneiric autobiography is also represented in romanticism and surrealism.
49 M. M. Prishvin, *Dnevniki* (Moscow: Pravda, 1990), 417 (January 29, 1952).
50 M. M. Prishvin, "1930 god," *Oktiabr'*, no. 7 (1989), 146, 161.
51 Ibid., 164 (July 18, 1930).
52 Ibid., 169 (September 5, 1930).
53 Both adjoining quotes from ibid., 172.
54 Thomas Lahusen, *How Life Writes the Book: Real Socialism and Socialist Realism in Stalin's Russia* (Ithaca: Cornell University Press, 1997), 55. In this powerful book, Lahusen has documented the effect of "reforging" on a writer (Vasily Azhaev) who was an inmate of another of such camps.
55 On the Belomor project and it literary counterpart, see Joachim Klein, "Belomorkanal: literatura i propaganda v stalinskoe vremia," *Novoe literaturnoe obozrenie*, no. 71 (2005), 231–62.
56 Prishvin, *Dnevniki*, 204 (August 25, 1933).
57 Prishvin, *Dnevniki*, 204 (September 1, 1933).
58 The circumstances of this trip have been described by Prishvin's recent biographer, Aleksei Varlamov, in his *Prishvin* (Moscow: Molodaia gvardiia, 2003), 335–43. According to Varlamov, this trip produced two essays, but they were not included (as Prishvin initially hoped) in the official 1934 collection that celebrated the project, *Belomorsko-baltiiskii kanal imeni Stalina. Istoriia stroitel'stva*, coedited by the celebrated Russian writer Maxim Gor'ky, the critic Leopold Averbach (one of the leaders of RAPP, soon to die in the terror), and the high-ranking officer of the labor camps administration Semyon Firin.
59 Prishvin, *Dnevniki*, 209–10.
60 Ibid., 210.
61 M. M. Prishvin, "'Zhizn' stala veselei...': Iz dnevnika 1936 goda," *Oktiabr'*, no. 10 (1993), 14.
62 See the entries for 1 and 3 April 1939; M. M. Prishvin, "Dnevnik 1939 goda," *Oktiabr'*, no. 2 (1998), 153–54.
63 Prishvin, "Dnevnik 1937 goda," *Oktiabr'*, no. 9 (1995), 159.
64 Prishvin, "Dnevnik 1937 goda," *Oktiabr'*, no. 9 (1995), 161.
65 Prishvin, "Dnevnik 1937 goda," *Oktiabr'*, no. 11 (1994), 169.
66 All quotes from Prishvin, "Dnevnik 1937 goda," *Oktiabr'*, no. 9 (1995), 162–63.
67 Prishvin, *Dnevniki*, 255 (the comment in omitted in the earlier *Oktiabr'* publication).
68 Prishvin, "Dnevnik 1937 goda," *Oktiabr'*, no. 9 (1995), 165, 169.
69 M. M. Prishvin, "Dnevnik 1938 goda," *Oktiabr'*, no. 1 (1997), 130.
70 M. M. Prishvin, "Dnevnik 1937 goda," *Oktiabr'*, no. 11 (1994), 148.
71 Prishvin, *Dnevniki*, 365.
72 Prishvin, *Dnevniki*, 384 (November 29, 1948).
73 Prishvin, *Dnevniki*, 386 (May 11, 1948).
74 Prishvin, *Dnevniki*, 429.
75 Oleg Volkov, *Pogruzhenie vo t'mu* (Moscow: Molodaia gvardiia, 1989), 175.
76 V. A. Kaverin, *Epilog: Memuary* (Moscow: Moskovskii rabochii, 1989), 224.
77 Ibid., 229–30.
78 Ibid., 191–92.
79 I borrowed the phrase from Sheila Fitzpatrick's *Everyday Stalinism: Ordinary Life in Extraordinary Times. Soviet Russia in the 1930s* (New York: Oxford University Press, 1999); this book describes such Stalinist practices as "purging" and "reforging."

80 Chukovskaia, *Zapiski ob Anne Akhmatovoi* 2:363. *The Trial* was first published in Russian in 1965.
81 I used the work of the psychoanalyst Selma Fraiberg, "Kafka and the Dream," in *Modern Literary Criticism: An Anthology*, ed. Irving Howe (Boston: Beacon Press, 1958), 197.
82 The Akhmatova cult was analyzed by Alexander Zholkovsky, and I use his language. See Zholkovsky, "Anna Akhmatova—piat'desiat let spustia," *Zvezda* 9 (1996), 211–27; "K tekhnologii vlasti v tvorchestve i zhiznetvorchestve Akhmatovoi," *Lebenskunst-Kunstleben*, ed. Schamma Schahadat (Munich: Otto Sagner, 1998), 193–210; and "The Obverse of Stalinism: Akhmatova's Self-Serving Charisma of Selflessness," in *Self and Story in Russian History*, ed. Laura Engelstein and Stephanie Sandler (Ithaca: Cornell University Press, 2000), 46–68.
83 *Zapisnye knizhki Anny Akhmatovoi (1958–1966)* (Moscow-Torino: Einaudi, 1996), 6.
84 Ibid., 660.
85 This dream was recorded in December 1965 in a Moscow hospital. *Zapisnye knizhki Anny Akhmatovoi*, 694–95.
86 The three notes are from *Zapisnye knizhki Akhmatovoi*, 486–87.
87 Anatolii Naiman, *Rasskazy ob Anne Akhmatovoi* (Moscow: Vagrius, 1989), 5.
88 Albrecht Dürer, *Schriftliche Nachlass*, ed. Hans Rupprich (Berlin, 1956), 1:214. Burke, who discussed this, and other, apocalyptic dreams, connected it with the German Peasants' War, as well as with the time of heavy rain. Burke, "The Cultural History of Dreams," 36, 39. For George Steiner, apocalyptic dreams were a sign of the historicity of dreams (which Freud ignored); see his "Les rêves participents-ils de l'histoire?" 161–62.
89 *Zapisnye knizhki Anny Akhmatovoi*, 533.
90 Viacheslav. Vs. [Viacheslav Vsevolodovich] Ivanov, "Besedy s Annoi Akhmatovoi," in *Vospominaniia ob Anne Akhmatovoi* (Moscow: Sovetskii pisatel', 1991), 473–502.
91 Chukovskaia, *Zapiski ob Anne Akhmatovoi* 2:469 (July 2, 1961).
92 David Samoilov, *Podennye zapisi* 1:337.
93 David Samoilov, *Podennye zapiski* (Moscow: Vremia, 2002), 2:154; T. Bek, "David Samoilov, Podennye zapisi," *Voprosy literatury* (January–February 2003): 352.
94 M. L. Gasparov, *Zapisi i vypiski* (Moscow: NLO, 2001), 138.
95 Ibid., 137–38.
96 Vsevolod Ivanov, *Dnevniki* (Moscow: Nasledie, 2001), 260, 292.
97 All quotes are from Viacheslav Vs. Ivanov, "Goluboi zver' (Vospominaniia)," *Zvezda*, no. 3 (1995): 182–83.
98 See Ivanov, "Goluboi zver'," *Zvezda*, no. 3, 182, 196.
99 Ia. S. Druskin's *Son i iav'* has not yet been published in full. Excerpts were prepared for publication by Henry Orlov: Yakov Druskin, *Vblizi vestnikov*, ed. Genrikh Orlov (Washington, DC: H. A. Frager, 1988). The chapter containing dreams about his dead friends appeared in *Sborishche druzei, ostavlennykh sud'boi: A. Vvedenskii, L. Lipavskii, Ia. Druskin, D. Kharms, N. Oleinikov. Chinari v tekstakh, dokumentakh i issledovaniiakh* (n.p., 1998), 1:855–61.
100 Druskin, *Dnevniki* (St. Petersburg: Akademicheskii proekt, 1999), 132; included in Druskin, *Son i iav'*; see *Sborishche druzei*, 857. Kharms died in the prison hospital on February 2, 1942.
101 Druskin, *Dnevniki*, 397; included in his *Son i iav'*; see *Sborishche*, 860.
102 I could not find this dream in the published diary. It is included in Druskin's *Son i iav'*; see *Sborishche*, 861.
103 Druskin, *Son i iav'*, in Druskin, *Vblizi vestnikov*, 65–66.
104 Druskin, *Dnevniki*, 149; included in *Son i iav'*; see *Sborishche druzei*, 859.
105 Druskin, *Vblizi vestnikov*, 35.
106 Yakov Druskin's brother Mikhail wrote that they discovered Kafka in the 1960s. Mikhail Druskin, "Kakim ego znaiu," in Yakov Druskin, *Dnevniki*, 34.
107 Druskin, *Dnevniki*, 249–50.
108 Ibid., 249–50.
109 Ol'ga Berggol'ts, "Iz dnevnikov," *Zvezda*, no. 6 (1990), 168.
110 See records for September 4, 1939: "Iz dnevnikov Ol'gi Berggol'ts," *Neva*, no. 5 (1990): 174.
111 "Iz dnevnikov Ol'gi Berggol'ts," *Neva* no. 5 (1990): 175; December 14, 1939.
112 Ibid., 176.
113 Alain Besançon, in *Histoire et expérience du moi* (Paris: Flammarion, 1971), calls prototypical literary dreams—such as Raskolnikov's dream in Dostoevsky's *Crime and Punishment*—"the

dreams of the culture." Peter Burke echoed the idea of culturally pervasive dreams in his "The Cultural History of Dreams," 29.
114 I thank Anna Muza for suggesting "Starukha" and other comments.
115 Koselleck, "Terror and Dream," 219.
116 Johen Hellbeck discusses two dreams of enthusiasts of the Soviet regime in his dissertation, see Jochen Hellbeck, "Laboratories of the Soviet Self: Diaries from the Stalin Era," (PhD diss., Columbia University, 1998), 152 (the dream of Vladimir Molodtsov), and 191 (the dream of A. I. Zheliaznikov).
117 *Dnevnik Eleny Bulgakovoi*, 270.
118 Cited in the commentaries to *Dnevnik Eleny Bulgakovoi*, 382.
119 Ibid., 368.
120 The published version of Elena Bulgakova's diary follows the edited text that the author prepared for archivization, if not publication, in the 1950s and 1960s. Scholars have established that Bulgakova had amplified and added some anti-Stalinist remarks, while removing some (but not all) remarks that present Stalin and the Stalinist regime in a positive light. See L. Ianovskaia's introduction to the diaires (6–7), and M. Chudakova, "Osvedomiteli v dome Bulgakova v seredine 1930-kh gg," *Tynianovskii sbornik* 9 (1995–96): 391–93. Some (but, according to Chudakova, far from all) revisions were noted in the commentary to the 1990 edition prepared by V. Losev and L. Ianovskaia. I thank Boris Wolfson for attracting my attention to this fact.
121 See Elena Bulgakova's version of the story, *Dnevnik Eleny Bulgakovoi*, 299–300.
122 See V. Petelin, "M. A. Bulgakov i "Dni Turbinykh"," *Ogonek*, no. 10 (March 1969): 27.
123 See photograph in M. A. Bulgakov, *P'esy 1920-kh godov* (Leningrad: Iskusstvo, 1989).
124 Aleksandr Piatigorskii, *Rasskazy i sny* (Moscow: Novoe literaturnoe obozrenie, 2001).
125 Il'ia Kalinin, "Aleksandr Piatigorskii 'Rasskazy i sny,'" *Novaia russkaia kniga*, no. 3/4 (2001), 28.

EPILOGUE

1 The literary scholar Mikhail Borisovich Meilakh (born in 1944) has produced several memoir essays, arranged topically.
2 Proteirei Mikhail Ardov, *Vse k luchshemu... Vospominaniia. Proza* (Moscow: BSG Press, 2006).

INDEX

Listed in bold print are names of the authors whose memoirs and diaries are discussed in this book

actors, as memoir/diary writers, 10, 15–17
Akhmatova, Anna Andreevna (1889–1966), xv, 4, 24–25, 29, 57
  as cultural icon, 59–60
  diary of her life, 4, 60, 63, 79, 270n12
  dreams by and about, 187–194
  See also *Notes about Anna Akhmatova*
Alekseeva, Liudmila Mikhailovna (b. 1927), 12
Allilueva, Nadezhda Sergeevna, 172
Allilueva, Svetlana Iosifovna (b. 1926), 27, 42, 43
ambiguity and ambivalence, 21, 77, 94, 111, 163, 195, 209
Anna Akhmatova Apartment Museum, 67, 68, 69, 70, 106
Annenkov, Pavel, 263n49
Antsiferov, Nikolai Pavlovich (1889–1958), 10
apocalypsis, 14, 42–49, 122, 142–146, 189–190, 193, 200, 210, 268n162
Arbatova, Mariia Ivanovna (b. 1957), 5, 23
archives, 2
  as chronicle of end of the epoch, 43–46
Ardov, Mikhail Viktorovich (b. 1937), 108–110, 211
Ardov, Viktor Efimovich, 108
Arendt, Hannah, xiv, 164
Arens-Punina, Anna Evgen'evna, 67, 70, 71, 81–82
Arzhilovsky, Andrei Stepanovich (1885–1937), 166–170, 275n30
automobile
  in dreams, 169, 176, 183–184, 200

as privilege, 110, 176
as symbol, 14, 169, 176–177

Baklanov, Grigorii Iakovlevich (b. 1923), 27, 30
Batkin, Leonid Mikhailovich (b. 1932), 13
Batum (Bulgakov), 204
Bauman, Zygmunt, 153–154
Belomor Canal, 13n, 51, 61, 166, 175, 178–179, 181–182, 276n55, 276n58
Beradt, Charlotte, 164–165, 203, 205
Berggol'ts, Ol'ga Fedorovna (1910–1975), 10, 79, 202
Beria, Lavrentii, 26
Beria, Sergo Lavrent'evich (b. 1924), 26, 42
Berlin, Isaiah, 188n
betrayal, 30, 37–39, 78, 88, 91–93, 110, 114, 127
Brezhnev, Leonid
  death of, 142–143
Brodsky, Iosif, 112–114
Bronshtein, Matvei Petrovich, 60, 64, 101
Bruskin, Grisha (b. 1945), 49–50, 51
Bukharin, Nikolai Ivanovich (1888–1938), 171–172
Bulgakov, Mikhail Afanas'evich, 34, 184, 203, 204
Bulgakova, Elena Sergeevna (1893–1970), 203–205, 278n120

camp inmates, as memoir/diary writers, 2, 15, 26, 28–30, 35, 36, 166, 182
Chaadaev, Pyotr, 112

children
  of divorced parents, 31, 37, 39, 67, 68, 82
  of former servants, 67–68, 76–77, 270n13
  illegitimate, 11, 16, 19, 20, 23, 124, 127
  multiple husbands/wives and, 18–20, 32, 67–68, 70, 82, 122–125, 127
  of Stalin, 27, 42–43
  of Stalin's right-hand men, 2, 26, 41
chinari (literary group), 197
Chudakov, Aleksandr Pavlovich (1938–2005), 5
Chudakova, Marietta Omarovna (b. 1937), 5, 41–42
Chukovskaia, Elena Tsezarevna, 64, 77–78, 84
Chukovskaia, Lidiia Korneevna (1907–1996), xv, 4, 5, 8, 10, 12–13, 57, 182, 186, 266n112
  dreams, recording of, 161
  on historicism, 12–13
  See also *Notes about Anna Akhmatova*
communal apartment, 15, 17–18, 21, 31, 50, 59, 61, 66–69, 78, 82–83, 91, 95
  as cultural institution, 67, 69, 75–77
  in dreams, 69–70, 185, 187
  family/marriage and, 67, 70–74
  instrument of state control, 76–77
  in literature, 69–70, 81, 202
  Soviet society, metaphor for, xiv, 8, 20, 41, 44
  the terror and, 62, 69, 73, 74
  See also living conditions
community building, xii, 24–41, 210
  collectively disclosed stories, 35–40
  disagreements and controversies, 29–33
  dreams as instruments of, 187–194, 207
  family memoirs and, 33–35
  joining the ranks of victims, 25–27
  Stalin, remembering, 27–29
  texts, connecting through, 24–25

Days of the Turbins / (Dni Turbinykh) (Bulgakov), 204
"death of God" (metaphor), 28, 97–98, 266n106
D'iakonov, Igor Mikhailovich (1915–1999), 47–48
diaries
  definition of, xiii
  family production of, 33–35
  makeshift form of, 5–7
  memoirs, fusion with, 7
  multiple publications of, 2–4, 6–7, 262n12
  written on behalf of another, 4, 63
  See also notes
dissidents, as memoir/diary writers, 2, 12, 13, 16, 25, 28, 36, 50

Dmitriev, Petr, 26
doctors, as memoir/diary writers, 22, 35
Doctor Zhivago scandal, 108–109, 111
Dostoevsky, Fyodor, 37, 39, 61, 202–203, 277n113
dreams, xiii
  Akhmatova and, 69–70, 103, 187–189
  apocalypsis and, 188–192, 200
  approach to, xiii, 165–166
  community building and, 187–194, 207
  death and, 80, 197–203
  definitions of, 162–163
  functions of, 205–206
  literature and, 40–41, 162, 186–187, 200, 202
  Nazi Germany and, 164–165, 205
  oneiric autobiography and, 173, 182
  peasants and, 120n, 166–170, 195
  as prophecy, 163, 170, 195–197, 206
  as records/testimonies of the terror, 161–162, 163–165, 182, 206–207
  as representations of the terror, 178, 180, 183–186, 199–200
  sexuality and, 167, 178
  Stalin and, 166–167, 171, 203–205
Druskin, Iakov Semenovich (1902–1980), 190, 197–203
Druskin, Mikhail, 197, 201

Eidel'man, Natan Iakovlevich (1930–1989), 32, 33–35
Eidel'man (née Madora), Iuliia Moiseevna, 33–34
Eikhenbaum, Boris, 161
end of the epoch, xi–xii, 7, 23, 41–42, 46–49, 55–56, 209–210
  archives as chronicle of, 43–46
Engel'gard, Boris, 13n
Engel'gard, Nataliia, 13n
Erenburg, Ilya Grigor'evich (1891–1967), 14, 28
erlebte Rede (narrative device), 119, 145
ethnography, memoir writing as, xii, 19, 57, 60, 63, 85, 101, 119
Evtushenko, Evgenii (b. 1933), 22, 25–26, 48–49

Fadeev, Aleksandr, 72–73, 100
family
  former peasants and, 118, 120, 122–129, 147
  intelligentsia and, 29, 41
  living space and, 66–77, 82, 146–149
  multiple/parallel families, 16, 18–23, 32–35, 67–72, 75–77, 81–82, 124–128
  Soviet state and, 75–77, 132, 143, 146–149, 160, 209–210

the terror and, 20–22, 24–25, 28, 35–39,
  76–77, 81–82, 98–100
 war and, 81–82, 122–124, 138–139, 145
 See also marriage
fear
 dreams and, 162, 164–165, 171, 174, 202,
  184–185, 204, 210
 historical continuity and and, 145–146, 160
 the terror and, 18, 21, 22, 24, 28 90
 the war and, 62, 95, 212, 141–142
Fedorov, Nikolai, 44–45, 197n
Filipovich, Elvira Grigor'evna (b. 1934), 4,
  8, 16, 19
film
 dream and, 169
 life as, 3, 19, 118, 120, 131, 133–134, 156
 watching films, 139–141
film makers, as memoir/diary writers, 6, 10,
  15–17, 19
food
 scarce, 51, 74, 168
 shared, 79, 99
 See also hunger; meals
Freud, Sigmund, 162, 164, 274n6
Frumkina, Rebbeka Markovna (b. 1931), 13

Gagen-Torn, Nina Ivanovna (1900–1986),
  29, 30
Garshin, Vladimir, 65, 75, 79, 81, 82, 84
Gasparov, Mikhail Leonovich (1935–2005),
  22–23, 193
German, Iurii, 31
German, Mikhail Iur'evich (b. 1933), 31
Gershtein, Emma Grigor'evna (1903–2002),
  29–30, 64
Ginzburg, Evgeniia Semenovna (1906–1977),
  2, 24, 28, 30
Ginzburg, Lidiia Iakovlevna (1902–1990), 6,
  12–14, 55, 80, 92
 on Akhmatova, 70, 75–76
 on historicism, 12–13
 LiveJournal community, 51–55
 on the terror, 65–66
**Gladkov, Aleksandr Konstantinovich
  (1912–1976)**, 45
glasnost policy, xi, 1
Golubeva, Marta, 81, 98
Gorbachev, Mikhail, 142–144
Gorbatenko, Ivan Prokof'evich, 98–100
Grobman, Mikhail (b. 1939), 171
Gumilev, Lev Nikolevich, 30, 64, 68, 81, 82
 arrest of, 60, 61, 63–64, 68, 74
 dream about, 69
 mother, relationship with, 30, 82, 272n52
 release of, 100

Gumilev, Nikolai Stepanovich, 67n, 69, 72
Gurevich, Tatiana, 79

Habermas, Jürgen, 162
Haight, Amanda, 115–116
Hegelianism, 36
 Fedorov and, 45–46
 historicism and, 11, 13–15, 172, 210, 263n50,
  264n58, 264n61
 Marxism and, 14
 metaphors of, 42–43
 shunned, 49
Herzen, Alexander, 103, 112
 influence on Soviet memoirists, 10–15, 17,
  25, 34, 42, 62, 101
historians, as memoir/diary writers, 2, 5, 7, 10,
  12–13, 15, 21, 29, 31–35, 41, 43, 45, 55,
  261n4
historical consciousness/historicism, xii, 9–15,
  27, 42–45, 55, 157, 160, 167n, 172,
  209–210
 rejection of, 207–208

Il'ina, Natalia Iosifovna (1914–1994), 8,
  108–110
Ilizarov, Boris Semenovich, 43
intelligentsia, xi–xii, 2–3
 as community, 24–25, 41, 50–51, 190, 194,
  207, 210
 end of, 46–49
 family and, 29, 41
 historical thinking and, 9–15, 60, 160
 identity of, xii, 60, 112
 Jewishness and, 21, 34
 moral values of, 38, 47n, 60, 78, 83–84,
  86–87, 94, 106
 the "people" and, 2–3, 31–32, 116–117, 145,
  150–158, 167, 206
 post-Soviet era, 46–51, 151–154, 158
 privileges of, 60, 94
 standing apart from, 15, 50, 197
 state/power and, 11, 47n, 48–49, 60, 78–79,
  86–87, 112, 174, 205
 traditional/old Russian, 9–15, 73, 84, 160, 173
Internet, 45–47, 51–55
intimacy
 communal apartments and, 75–77
 dreams and, 163, 173, 190, 193–194, 205, 207
 history and xii, 2, 11, 17, 21, 23, 42, 57, 62,
  106, 117, 159–160, 173, 193
 intelligentsia and, 9, 11–12, 25, 41
 memoir/diary writing and, xii, 19, 59, 62–63,
  92, 95, 209
 between memoirist/diarist and reader, 8, 20,
  26, 41, 53, 194

intimacy *(continued)*
  postmodern authors and, 49, 51
  revelation of, xii, 3-4, 8, 19-24, 30, 33-35,
     50, 95, 209-210
  Stalin and, 171-172, 204
  state/power and, 18, 20-22, 24, 26, 35-41,
     57, 75-77, 117, 146, 160, 173, 209-210
  television and, 140, 146
  the terror and, 19, 24, 37, 56, 59-62, 88, 99,
     110, 117
  war and, 82, 85, 88, 92-94
Ivanov, Viacheslav Vsevolodovich (b. 1929),
     25, 190-192
  prophetic dreams, 195-197
Ivanov, Vsevold Viacheslavovich (1895-1963),
     190, 195

jealousy, 124, 151
  the terror and, 35-37, 90, 92
Jews, 20-22, 25, 27, 31, 34, 36-37, 54, 96, 169,
     171, 178, 265n80
Jung, Carl Gustav, 163

Kafka, Franz, 186-187, 200
Kaganovich, Lazar' Moiseevich (1893-1991),
     26
Kaganovich, Maia, 26n
Kalinin, Ilya, 207-208
Kaminskaia, Anna "Malaika," 71, 82
Kaminskii, Genrikh, 71, 82
Katanian, Vasilii Abgarovich (1934-1999), 10
Kaverin, Veniamin Aleksandrovich (1902-
     1989), 18, 42
  dreams, 182-187
  Stalin's death, reaction to, 27
Khardzhiev, Nikolai Ivanovich (1903-1996),
     62, 211
Kharms, Daniil, 197, 198, 202
Khmelev, Nikolai, 204-205
Khrushchev, Nikita Sergeevich (1894-1971), 4
  memoirs, 26-27
  secret speech, 101, 102-103
  Stalin's death, reaction to, 27
Khrushchev, Sergei Nikitovich (b. 1935), 26
Kiseleva, Evgeniia Grigor'evna (1916-1990),
     xv, 3, 19, 24, 43, 118
  See also Notebooks of Evgeniia Kiseleva
Kopelev, Lev Zinov'evich (1912-1997), 28
Koselleck, Reinhart, 162, 164, 203
Kozakov, Mikhail Mikhailovich (b. 1934),
     15
Kozlova, Natalia Nikitichna, 118, 150, 152
Krelin, Iulii Zusmanovich (1929-2006), 35
Kuniaev, Stanislav, 21n
Kuvaldin, Iurii, 21n

Landmarks / *(Vekhi),* 84
Larina (Bukharina), Anna Mikhailovna
     (1914-1996), 172
Latynina, Alla, 110-111
Lavrov, Aleksandr Vasil'evich, 45
Leningrad blockade, 13n, 16, 23, 28, 48, 79-81,
     92
  the terror and, 24, 80, 265n91
Libedinskaia, Lidiia Borisovna (1921-2006),
     11-12
Lipavsky, Leonid, 197, 198
literary scholars, as memoir/diary writers, xv,
     5-6, 10, 12-23, 29, 50, 55, 65, 66, 87,
     161, 193-194, 207, 278n1
LiveJournal website, 51-55
living conditions/space
  formative pressure of, 62, 147
  shortage, 72-73, 146-147
  state and, 67-69, 72, 75-77, 82-83, 95,
     146-148, 179
  the terror and, 66, 71, 73
  See also communal apartment; family;
     marriage
love
  the terror and, 16, 35-39, 65, 88-90,
     272n41
  war and, 92, 138-139
love affairs
  housing and, 21, 71
  state and, 21
  the terror and, 30, 35-36
  war and, 12, 37
Luknitskii, Pavel, 79-80, 270n12, 271n28

Malenkov, Andrei Georgievich (b. 1937), 26,
     268n162
Malenkov, Georgii, 26
Malia, Martin, 103-104
Mandelshtam, Nadezhda Iakovlevna
     (1899-1980), 1-2, 25, 29, 69-71, 73,
     76, 89-90, 91-93, 95, 194
Mandelshtam, Osip, 29, 92, 100n, 112, 194
Man'kov, Arkadii Georgievich (1913-2006),
     261n4
marriage
  categories of, 70, 75-77, 125, 127-128
  See also family
Marxism, 14
The Master and Margarita (Bulgakov), 184
meals, 66
  dreams and, 167
  family and, 70, 123, 126, 271n121
  as form of sociability, 35, 53, 62, 75, 83,
     85-86, 119n, 126-127, 203
  See also food

Meilakh, Mikhail, 211, 278n1
Meletinskii, Eleazar Moiseevich (1918–2005), 35–36, 36n, 170
memoirs
  antimemoirs, 29
  as corpus, xi–xii, 8–9
  definition of, xii
  diaries, fusion with, 7
  family production of, 17, 22, 24, 28
  flexible text form, 5–7
  historical consciousness and, 9–10, 12–15
  historical narratives, framing as, 15–17
  makeshift form of, 5–7
  multiple publication of, 2, 3, 5, 100n, 264n51, 264n60, 265n82, 272n49
  readership, 7–8
  of recent past, 3–5, 8
  as response to other memoirs, 29–30
  time span covered in, 4–5
  See also community building
"memoirs of contemporaries" genre, 11, 263n49
metaphors, 175
  dreams and, 162, 165
  in memoirs/diaries, xiv, 14–15, 17, 41–43, 56, 102, 153, 160, 261n3
  religious belief and, 43, 47
  See also "privatization of history"; "trial of history"; "wheel of history"
Misch, Georg, 173
Moiseenko, Iurii Illarionovich, 100n
Morozov, Alexander, 100n
Murav'eva, Irina Ignat'evna, 36–37
My Past and Thoughts / (Byloe i dumy) (Herzen), 10–15, 25, 34, 62, 263n49

Nagibin, Iurii Markovich (1920–1994), 3, 7, 19–21, 31, 134
Naiman, Anatoly, 188n, 189
"naive writing," 151–152
Naive Writing / (Naivnoe pis'mo), 151–152
  See also Notebooks of Evgeniia Kiseleva
Nakhapetov, Rodion Rafailovich (b. 1944), 17
names
  authorship and, 3, 52, 54, 155–156
  disclosure of in memoirs, 36–37, 39–40, 47–48, 91
  uncertainty of, 16, 20–21, 23, 31n
neighbors
  children of, 61, 74
  in communal apartment, 61, 67–68, 73–77
  family and, 75–76
  fear of, 62
  gossip and, 88
  helping, 141
  hygiene and, 74, 91

  peasants as, 119n, 128
  as readers, 26
  and surveillance, 74, 76–77
  writers as, 15, 88, 111, 179
NKVD (People's Commisariat of Internal Affairs), 73, 76, 166, 171
Notebooks of Evgeniia Kiseleva, xv, 3, 17, 19, 57, 118–158
  idiosyncratic language of, 118–119
  notebook 1, 120–134
    beginning, 120–122
    domestic violence, 126–127, 128
    first marriage, 120, 122–124
    second marriage, 124–128
    Soviet policy, approval of, 130–132
    Soviet society, participation in, 129–130
    visual-spatial quality of narrative, 120–123, 126–127, 133–134
  notebooks 2 and 3, 134–150
    family conflicts in, 136
    housing shortage in, 146–147, 147–149
    memory, 136–139
    structure of, 135–136
    television and apocalypsis, 141–145
    television as emotional trigger, 139–141
  Notes about Anna Akhmatova, comparison to, 159–160
  publication of, 118, 150–158
    competition between publishers, 152–155, 156
    disappearance of author, 155–156
    naive writing, 151–152
    person without subjecthood, 156–158
notes
  as genre, 3–4, 6, 9, 10–13, 22–23, 33, 51–55
  multiple publications of, 6, 23, 85, 265
Notes about Anna Akhmatova (Chukovskaia), xv, 4, 5, 10, 18–19, 25, 57, 59–117
  communal apartment in, 66–75
  foreword to first publication of, 161
  interruption in, 95
  Notebooks of Evgeniia Kiseleva, comparison to, 159–160
  opening pages, 60–62
  post-Stalin, 95–115
    Akhmatova's manuscripts, 106–108
    camp prisoners, return of, 98–101
    fear, historical continuity of, 111–114
    foreigners, interactions with, 103–104, 115–116
    historical experience, commonality *vs.* difference, 114–117
    historical meaning of domestic things, 104–106
    Khrushchev's secret speech, 101–103

Notes about Anna Akhmatova (Chukovskaia), (continued)
   memoirs as historical evidence, 108–111
   memory, 96–97
   reactions to Stalin's death, 96, 97–98
   publication of, 59, 262n12
   readers' responses to, 8
   the terror in, 60–66
   wartime diaries, 77–95
     gossip, 87–90
     hardships and privileges, 91–95
     helplessness, power of, 85–87
     poverty, love of, 82–85
     publication of, 77–78
novels, memoirs/diaries and, 3, 5, 9, 20–21, 23, 38–40
Novyi mir (literary journal), 118, 119, 152

obmen (exchanges of living space), 72
Odissei (journal), 2
Okunevskaia, Tatiana Kirillovna (1914–2002), 15
Oleinikov, Nikolai, 197, 198
Ol'shanskaia, Elena, 118, 150, 152, 156, 273n75
Ol'shevskaia, Nina Antonovna, 108
One Day in the Life of Ivan Denisovich (Solzhenitsyn), 112, 119
oneiric autobiography, 173, 182
"ordinary people," as memoir/diary writers, 2–4, 8, 43, 44, 70, 261n4
Orlova, Raisa Davydovna (1918–1989), 28
Ostrovskii, Efim, 5n

Pasternak, Boris, 93, 111
   See also *Doctor Zhivago* scandal
peasants, as memoir/diary writers, 2–3, 11, 17, 19, 43, 118, 166–170, 261n6
People's Archive (*Narodnyi arkhiv*), 2, 43–44, 45–46, 46n, 118, 150–151
perekovka (reforging), 166, 175, 178, 182, 276n54, 276n79
Petrovykh, Mariia Sergeevna, 108–109
philosophers, as memoir/diary writers, 197–203, 207
"Philosophical Letter" (Chaadaev), 112
Piatigorsky, Alexander (b. 1929), 207–208
Podlubnyi, Stepan (1914–1998), 11
Poem without a Hero / (Poema bez geroia) (Akhmatova), 24–25, 60
politicians, as memoir/diary writers, 2, 5n, 26–27
Pomerants, Grigorii Solomonovich (b. 1918), 36–37, 40, 90n
postmodernist authors, as memoir/diary writers, 5–6, 49–51

Prigov, Dmitrii Aleksandrovich (1940–2007), 49, 50–51
"privatization of history" (metaphor), 9
privileges, 72, 79, 83, 110, 175–177, 179, 191
   intelligentsia values and, 60, 93, 110, 175–177
   intimacy and, 93
   survival and, 79, 91–95
Privshin, Mikhail Mikhailovich (1873–1954), 18
   dreams, 173–181
Prokopenko, Galina (b. 1922), 17
propiska (mandatory registration of residence), 44
Punin, Nikolai Nikolaevich, 18, 61n, 67, 67n, 68, 81, 82
   death of, 98–100
Punina, Irina, 67, 68–69, 71, 82, 83, 95
Punins, 80, 81
"purging," 185

Ranevskaia, Faina Georgievna (1896–1984), 10–11, 87, 88, 91, 92
Rapoport, Iakov L'vovich (1898–1996), 22
Rapoport, Natalia Iakovlevna, 22, 25
RAPP (Russian Association of Proletarian Writers), 173, 174
Raskolnikov's dream, 202–203
readers, of memoirs and diaries, xii, 7–8, 39–40, 60, 119, 150–152, 207
   addressed, 7, 8, 133–134, 136, 139
   emotions of, 20, 22, 110
   future/foreign, 63
   invited to participate, 29, 50, 51
   responses of, 21, 29, 30, 51–55
Reagan, Ronald, 144–145
reforging (*perekovka*), 166, 175, 178, 182, 276n54, 276n79
religious beliefs, 43–45, 46–48, 121–122, 143–146, 177n, 210
Requiem (Akhmatova), 69, 107–108, 112
Rozov, Viktor Sergeevich (b. 1913), 49

salvation, 46–49, 56, 142–145
Samoilov, David Samoilovich (1920–1990), 3, 5–6, 10, 26
   dreams, 192
Sandormirskaia, Irina Il'inichna, 118, 151, 152
scholars, as memoir/diary writers, 2–4, 10–13, 35–36, 118–119, 150–158, 170, 190–192, 195–197
   See also historians; literary scholars
Sedakova, Ol'ga Aleksandrovna (b. 1949), 193–194
Sergeev, Andrei Iakovlevich (1933–1998), 6, 49, 50, 51

INDEX | 285

Severiukhin, Dmitrii Iakovlevich (b. 1954), 4–5, 7–8
sexual life
 as political/historical fact, 19–22, 35–39, 76, 88–90, 178, 195, 209
 revealed in memoirs/diaries, 19–21, 23, 30, 120n, 267n124
Shikheeva-Gaister, Inna Aronovna (b. 1925), 24–25
Shileiko, Vladimir Kazimirovich, 67, 270n12
Shirvindt, Aleksandr Anatol'evich (b. 1934), 15
Shubina, Valeriia, 268n153
Shvartz, Evgenii L'vovich (1896–1958), 6–7
Simonov, Aleksei Kirillovich (b. 1939), 6, 7, 27, 30–31, 31n
Simonov, Konstantin (1915–1979), 7, 27, 30–31
Smirnova, Lidiia Nikolaevna (1915–2007), 16
social participation
 avoidance of, 197, 201
 desire for, 6, 80, 129–130, 160, 166–170, 175, 177, 203, 206
Solzhenitsyn, Alexander, 112, 119
"Soviet experience," xiv
Stalin, Iosif, 34
 death of, 27–29, 43, 50, 97, 101, 266n106
 dream of, 203–205
 love for, 12, 27–28, 30, 97, 172
 as patron of the arts, 204–205
 reactions to death of, 27–29, 96, 97–98
 surveillance, 18–19, 40, 65, 74–75, 77, 106–110
 dreams and, 165
 self-surveillance, 42, 44, 210

Tartakovskii, Andrei Grigor'evich, 33, 263n37
Tartakovskii, Boris Grigor'evich (1911–2002), 7, 32–33
"Tashkent notebooks." See *Notes about Anna Akhmatova*, wartime diaries
television, as mechanism of state control, 146
things (domestic objects), 61, 66–67, 104–106, 120n
The Third Reich of Dreams / (*Das Dritte Reich des Traumes*) (Beradt), 164–165, 203, 205–206
Tikhonov, Nikolai Semenovich, 185
Tiulina, Nataliia Ivanovna, 32
Tolstoy, Aleksei, 86, 91, 195

Tolstoy, Leo, 10, 12, 80, 100
Toporov, Viktor Leonidovich (b. 1946), 16, 21n
Toporova, Zoia Nikolaevna, 16, 264n68
The Trial (Kafka), 186–187
"trial of history" (metaphor), 42–43, 45, 267n142
Tynianov, Yury Nikolaevich, 184

Union of Soviet Writers, 22, 72, 79, 82, 88, 95, 111, 174, 185
 country cottages, allotment by, 191
 dreams and, 185, 191–193
 luxury cooperative, building of, 179
 membership privileges, 72–73, 79, 82, 93, 95, 100, 102, 179, 188, 191
Uritskaia, N., 8

Varlamov, Aleksei, 276n58
Vigdorova, Frida Abramovna, 38–40, 102, 113
Voinovich, Vladimir, 16
Volkov, Oleg Vasil'evich (1900–1992), 180
Voznesenskii, Andrei Andreevich (b. 1933), 48
Vvedensky, Alexander, 197, 198
Vyshinskii, Andrei, 72, 73

War and Peace (*Voina i mir*) (Tolstoy), 10, 12, 80, 100, 152
"wheel of history" (metaphor), 13–14, 42
workers, as memoir/diary writers, 26, 261n4, 261n6
writers
 community of, 25, 29–30, 84–88, 91–94, 108–109, 111, 190–194
 dreams of, 188–195, 199, 202
 as memoir/diary writers, 2–3, 5–6, 10–12, 18–21, 25, 100, 173, 182, 270n112, 276n54
 See also Union of Soviet Writers
writers, children of
 as memoir/diary writers, 31, 108–111, 190–192, 195–197, 211

Zakharov (publisher), 6, 23
Zelenaia, Rina, 87
Zhitomirskaia, Sarra Vladimirovna (1916–2002), 10, 31–33
Zholkovsky, Alexander (b. 1937), 50, 87, 271n36
Zorin, Leonid Genrikhovich (b. 1924), 3, 5, 42

www.ingramcontent.com/pod-product-compliance
Lightning Source LLC
Chambersburg PA
CBHW051210300426
44116CB00006B/513